The Letters Of Charles Dickens

THE LETTERS OF

Charles Dickens

THE LETTERS

OF

·CHARLES DICKENS

EDITED BY

HIS SISTER-IN-LAW AND HIS ELDEST DAUGHTER

IN TWO VOLUMES

VOL. II.

1857 to 1870

NEW YORK
CHARLES SCRIBNER'S SONS
743 AND 745 BROADWAY
1879

NEW YORK: J. J. LITTLE & CO., PRINTERS,
10 TO 20 ASTOR PLACE.

BOOK II.—*Continued.*

NEW YORK: J. J. LITTLE & CO., PRINTERS,
10 TO 20 ASTOR PLACE.

BOOK II.—*Continued.*

THE LETTERS

CHARLES DICKENS.

1857.

THIS was a very full year in many ways. In February, Charles Dickens obtained possession of Gad's Hill, and was able to turn workmen into it. In April he stayed, with his wife and sister-in-law, for a week or two at Wate's Hotel, Gravesend, to be at hand to superintend the beginning of his alterations of the house, and from thence we give a letter to Lord Carlisle. He removed his family, for a summer residence in the house, in June; and he finished " Little Dorrit " there early in the summer. One of his first visitors at Gad's Hill was the famous writer, Hans Christian Andersen. In January "The Frozen Deep" had been played at the Tavistock House theatre with such great success, that it was necessary to repeat it several times, and the theatre was finally demolished at the end of that month. In June Charles Dickens heard, with great grief,

3

of the death of his dear friend Douglas Jerrold ; and as a testimony of admiration for his genius and affectionate regard for himself, it was decided to organise, under the management of Charles Dickens, a series of entertainments, " in memory of the late Douglas Jerrold," the fund produced by them (a considerable sum) to be presented to Mr. Jerrold's family. The amateur company, including many of Mr. Jerrold's colleagues on " Punch," gave subscription performances of "The Frozen Deep ; " the Gallery of Illustration, in Regent Street, being engaged for the purpose. Charles Dickens gave two readings at St. Martin's Hall of " The Christmas Carol " (to such immense audiences and with such success, that the idea of giving public readings for his *own* benefit first occurred to him at this time). The professional actors, among them the famous veteran actor, Mr. T. P. Cooke, gave a performance of Mr. Jerrold's plays of " The Rent Day " and " Black-eyed Susan," in which Mr. T. P. Cooke sustained the character in which he had originally made such great success when the play was written. A lecture was given by Mr. Thackeray, and another by Mr. W. H. Russell. Finally, the Queen having expressed a desire to see the play, which had been much talked of during that season, there was another performance before her Majesty and the Prince Consort at the Gallery of Illustration in July, and at the end of that month Charles Dickens read his " Carol " in the Free Trade Hall, at Manchester. And to wind up the " Memorial Fund " entertainments, " The Frozen Deep " was played again at Manchester, also in the great Free Trade Hall, at the end of August. For the business of these entertainments he secured the assistance of. Mr. Arthur Smith, of whom he writes to Mr. Forster, at this time : " I have got hold of Arthur Smith, as the best man of business I know, and go to work with him to-morrow morning." And when he began his own public readings, both in town and country, he felt himself most fortunate in having the co-operation of this invaluable man of business, and also of his zealous friendship and pleasant companionship.

In July, his second son, Walter Landor, went to India as a cadet in the "Company's service," from which he was afterwards transferred to the 42nd Royal Highlanders. His father and his elder brother went to see him off, to Southampton. From this place Charles Dickens writes to Mr. Edmund Yates, a young man in whom he had been interested from his boyhood, both for the sake of his parents and for his own sake, and for whom he had always an affectionate regard.

In September he made a short tour in the North of England, with Mr. Wilkie Collins, out of which arose the "Lazy Tour of Two Idle Apprentices," written by them jointly, and published in "Household Words." Some letters to his sister-in-law during this expedition are given here, parts of which (as is the case with many letters to his eldest daughter and his sister-in-law) have been published in Mr. Forster's book.

The letters which follow are almost all on the various subjects mentioned in our notes, and need little explanation.

His letter to Mr. Procter makes allusion to a legacy lately left to that friend.

The letters to Mr. Dilke, the original and much-respected editor of "The Athenæum," and to Mr. Forster, on the subject of the "Literary Fund," refer, as the letters indicate, to a battle which they were carrying on together with that institution.

A letter to Mr. Frank Stone is an instance of his kind, patient, and judicious criticism of a young writer, and the letter which follows it shows how thoroughly it was under-stood and how perfectly appreciated by the authoress of the "Notes" referred to. Another instance of the same kind criticism is given in a second letter this year to Mr. Edmund Yates.

[*To Mr. B. W. Procter.*]

TAVISTOCK HOUSE, *January 2nd*, 1857.

MY DEAR PROCTER,

I have to thank you for a delightful book, which has given me unusual pleasure. My delight in it has been a little dashed by certain farewell verses, but I have made up my mind (and you have no idea of the obstinacy of my character) not to believe them.

Perhaps it is not taking a liberty—perhaps it is—to con-gratulate you on Kenyon's remembrance. Either way I can't help doing it with all my heart, for I know no man in the world (myself excepted) to whom I would rather the money went.   Affectionately yours ever.

[*To Sir James Emerson Tennent.*]

TAVISTOCK HOUSE, *January 9th*, 1857.

MY DEAR TENNENT,

I must thank you for your earnest and affectionate let-ter. It has given me the greatest pleasure, mixing the play in my mind confusedly and delightfully with Pisa, the Valetta, Naples, Herculanæum—God knows what not.

As to the play itself; when it is made as good as my care can make it, I derive a strange feeling out of it, like writing a book in company; a satisfaction of a most singular kind, which has no exact parallel in my life; a something that I suppose to belong to the life of a labourer in art alone, and which has to me a conviction of its being actual truth without its pain, that I never could adequately state if I were to try never so hard.

You touch so kindly and feelingly on the pleasure such little pains give, that I feel quite sorry you have never seen this drama in progress during the last ten weeks here. Every Monday and Friday evening during that time we have been at work upon it. I assure you it has been a remarkable lesson to my young people in patience, perseverance, punctuality, and order; and, best of all, in that kind of humility which is got from the earned knowledge that whatever the right hand finds to do must be done with the heart in it, and in a desperate earnest.

When I changed my dress last night (though I did it very quickly), I was vexed to find you gone. I wanted to have secured you for our green-room supper, which was very pleasant. If by any accident you should be free next Wednesday night (our last), pray come to that green-room supper. It would give me cordial pleasure to have you there.

Ever, my dear Tennent, very heartily yours.

[*To M. de Cerjat.*]

TAVISTOCK HOUSE, *Monday Night, Jan. 17th,* 1857.

MY DEAR CERJAT,

So wonderfully do good (epistolary) intentions become confounded with bad execution, that I assure you I la-

boured under a perfect and most comfortable conviction
that I had answered your Christmas Eve letter of 1855.
More than that, in spite of your assertions to the contrary,
I still strenuously believe that I did so! I have more than
half a mind ("Little Dorrit" and my other occupations
notwithstanding) to charge you with having forgotten my
reply!! I have even a wild idea that Townshend reproached me, when the last old year was new, with writing
to you instead of to him!!! We will argue it out, as well
as we can argue anything without poor dear Haldimand,
when I come back to Elysée. In any case, however, don't
discontinue your annual letter, because it has become an
expected and a delightful part of the season to me.

With one of the prettiest houses in London, and every
conceivable (and inconceivable) luxury in it, Townshend
is voluntarily undergoing his own sentence of transporta-
tion in Nervi, a beastly little place near Genoa, where you
would as soon find a herd of wild elephants in any villa as
comfort. He has a notion that he *must* be out of England
in the winter, but I believe him to be altogether wrong (as
I have just told him in a letter), unless he could just take
his society with him.

Workmen are now battering and smashing down my
theatre here, where we have just been acting a new play
of great merit, done in what I may call (modestly speaking
of the getting-up, and not of the acting) an unprecedented
way. I believe that anything so complete has never been
seen. We had an act at the North Pole, where the slightest
and greatest thing the eye beheld were equally taken from

the books of the Polar voyagers. Out of thirty people, there were certainly not two who might not have gone straight to the North Pole itself, completely furnished for the winter! It has been the talk of all London for these three weeks. And now it is a mere chaos of scaffolding, ladders, beams, canvases, paint-pots, sawdust, artificial snow, gas-pipes, and ghastliness. I have taken such pains with it for these ten weeks in all my leisure hours, that I feel now shipwrecked—as if I had never been without a play on my hands before. A third topic comes up as this ceases.

Down at Gad's Hill, near Rochester, in Kent—Shakespeare's Gad's Hill, where Falstaff engaged in the robbery —is a quaint little country-house of Queen Anne's time. I happened to be walking past, a year and a half or so ago, with my sub-editor of "Household Words," when I said to him: "You see that house? It has always a curious interest for me, because when I was a small boy down in these parts I thought it the most beautiful house (I suppose because of its famous old cedar-trees) ever seen. And my poor father used to bring me to look at it, and used to say that if ever I grew up to be a clever man perhaps I might own that house, or such another house. In remembrance of which, I have always in passing looked to see if it was to be sold or let, and it has never been to me like any other house, and it has never changed at all." We came back to town, and my friend went out to dinner. Next morning he came to me in great excitement, and said: "It is written that you were to have that house at Gad's

Hill. The lady I had allotted to me to take down to dinner yesterday began to speak of that neighbourhood. 'You know it?' I said; 'I have been there to-day.' 'O yes,' said she, 'I know it very well. I was a child there, in the house they call Gad's Hill Place. My father was the rector, and lived there many years. He has just died, has left it to me, and I want to sell it.' 'So,' says the sub-editor, 'you must buy it. Now or never!'" I did, and hope to pass next summer there, though I may, perhaps, let it afterwards, furnished, from time to time.

All about myself I find, and the little sheet nearly full! But I know, my dear Cerjat, the subject will have its interest for you, so I give it its swing. Mrs. Watson was to have been at the play, but most unfortunately had three children sick of gastric fever, and could not leave them. She was here some three weeks before, looking extremely well in the face, but rather thin. I have not heard of your friend Mr. Percival Skelton, but I much misdoubt an amateur artist's success in this vast place. I hope you detected a remembrance of our happy visit to the Great St. Bernard in a certain number of "Little Dorrit"? Tell Mrs. Cerjat, with my love, that the opinions I have expressed to her on the subject of cows have become matured in my mind by experience and venerable age; and that I denounce the race as humbugs, who have been getting into poetry and all sort of places without the smallest reason. Haldimand's housekeeper is an awful woman to consider. Pray give him our kindest regards and remembrances, if you ever find him in a mood to take it. "Our" means Mrs. Dickens's, Georgie's, and mine. We often, often talk of our old days at Lausanne, and send loving regards to Mrs. Cerjat and all your house.

Adieu, my dear fellow ; ever cordially yours.

[*To Mr. W. C. Macready.*]

Tavistock House, *January* 28*th*, 1857.

MY DEAREST MACREADY,

Your friend and servant is as calm as Pecksniff, saving for his knitted brows now turning into cordage over Little Dorrit. The theatre has disappeared, the house is restored to its usual conditions of order, the family are tranquil and domestic, dove-eyed peace is enthroned in this study, fire-eyed radicalism in its master's breast.

I am glad to hear that our poetess is at work again, and shall be very much pleased to have some more contributions from her.

Love from all to your dear sister, and to Katie, and to all the house.

We dined yesterday at Frederick Pollock's. I begged an amazing photograph of you, and brought it away. It strikes me as one of the most ludicrous things I ever saw in my life. I think of taking a public-house, and having it copied larger, for the size. You may remember it ? Very square and big—the Saracen's Head with its hair cut, and in modern gear ? Staring very hard ? As your particular friend, I would not part with it on any consideration. I will never get such a wooden head again.

Ever affectionately.

[*To Miss Mary Boyle.*]

TAVISTOCK HOUSE, *February 7th*, 1857.

MY DEAR MARY,

Half-a-dozen words on this, my birthday, to thank you for your kind and welcome remembrance, and to assure you that your Joseph is proud of it.

For about ten minutes after his death, on each occasion of that event occurring, Richard Wardour was in a floored condition. And one night, to the great terror of Devonshire, the Arctic Regions, and Newfoundland (all of which localities were afraid to speak to him, as his ghost sat by the kitchen fire in its rags), he very nearly did what he never did, went and fainted off, dead, again. But he always plucked up, on the turn of ten minutes, and became facetious.

Likewise he chipped great pieces out of all his limbs (solely, as I imagine, from moral earnestness and concussion of passion, for I never knew him to hit himself in any way) and terrified Aldersley * to that degree, by lunging at him to carry him into the cave, that the said Aldersley always shook like a mould of jelly, and muttered, " By G——, this is an awful thing ! "

Ever affectionately.

P.S.—I shall never cease to regret Mrs. Watson's not having been there.

---

* The part played in " The Frozen Deep " by its author, Mr. Wilkie Collins.

[*To Rev. James White.*]

TAVISTOCK HOUSE, *Sunday, Feb. 8th,* 1857.

MY DEAR WHITE,

I send these lines by Mary and Katey, to report my love to all.

Your note about the *Golden Mary* gave me great pleasure ; though I don't believe in one part of it ; for I honestly believe that your story, as really belonging to the rest of the narrative, had been generally separated from the other stories, and greatly liked. I had not that particular shipwreck that you mentioned in my mind (indeed I doubt if I know it), and John Steadiman merely came into my head as a staunch sort of name that suited the character. The number has done " Household Words " great service, and has decidedly told upon its circulation.

You should have come to the play. I much doubt if anything so complete will ever be seen again. An incredible amount of pains and ingenuity was expended on it, and the result was most remarkable even to me.

When are you going to send something more to H. W. ? Are you lazy ? ? Low-spirited ? ? ? Pining for Paris ? ? ? ?

Ever affectionately.

[*To Mr. C. W. Dilke.*]

OFFICE OF '' HOUSEHOLD WORDS,''

Thursday, March 19th, 1857.

MY DEAR MR. DILKE,

Forster has another notion about the Literary Fund. Will you name a day next week—that day being neither

Thursday nor Saturday—when we shall hold solemn council there at half-past four?

For myself, I beg to report that I have my war-paint on, that I have buried the pipe of peace, and am whooping for committee scalps.

.Ever faithfully yours.

[To The Earl of Carlisle.]

GRAVESEND, KENT, *Wednesday, April 15th*, 1857.

MY DEAR LORD CARLISLE,

I am writing by the river-side for a few days, and at the end of last week —— appeared here with your note of introduction. I was not in the way; but as —— had come express from London with it, Mrs. Dickens opened it, and gave her (in the limited sense which was of no use to her) an audience. She did not quite seem to know what she wanted of me. But she said she had understood at Stafford House that I had a theatre in which she could read; with a good deal of modesty and diffidence she at last got so far. Now, my little theatre turns my house out of window, costs fifty pounds to put up, and is only two months taken down; therefore, is quite out of the question. This Mrs. Dickens explained, and also my profound inability to do anything for —— readings which they could not do for themselves. She appeared fully to understand the explanation, and indeed to have anticipated for herself how powerless I must be in such a case.

She described herself as being consumptive, and as being subject to an effusion of blood from the lungs;

about the last condition, one would think, poor woman, for the exercise of public elocution as an art.

Between ourselves, I think the whole idea a mistake, and have thought so from its first announcement. It has a fatal appearance of trading upon Uncle Tom, and am I not a man and a brother? which you may be by all means, and still not have the smallest claim to my attention as a public reader. The town is over-read from all the white squares on the draught-board; it has been considerably harried from all the black squares—now with the aid of old banjoes, and now with the aid of Exeter Hall; and I have a very strong impression that it is by no means to be laid hold of from this point of address. I myself, for example, am the meekest of men, and in abhorrence of slavery yield to no human creature, and yet I don't admit the sequence that I want Uncle Tom (or Aunt Tomasina) to expound "King Lear" to me. And I believe my case to be the case of thousands.

I trouble you with this much about it, because I am naturally desirous you should understand that if I could possibly have been of any service, or have suggested anything to this poor lady, I would not have lost the opportunity. But I cannot help her, and I assure you that I cannot honestly encourage her to hope. I fear her enterprise has no hope in it.

In your absence I have always followed you through the papers, and felt a personal interest and pleasure in the public affection in which you are held over there.* At the

---

* The Earl of Carlisle was at this time Viceroy of Ireland.

same time I must confess that I should prefer to have you here, where good public men seem to me to be dismally wanted. I have no sympathy with demagogues, but am a grievous Radical, and think the political signs of the times to be just about as bad as the spirit of the people will admit of their being. In all other respects I am as healthy, sound, and happy as your kindness can wish. So you will set down my political despondency as my only disease.

On the tip-top of Gad's Hill, between this and Rochester, on the very spot were Falstaff ran away, I have a pretty little old-fashioned house, which I shall live in the hope of showing you one day. Also I have a little story respecting the manner in which it became mine, which I hope (on the same occasion in the clouds) to tell you. Until then and always, I am, dear Lord Carlisle,

Yours very faithfully and obliged.

[*To Mr. John Forster.*]

TAVISTOCK HOUSE, *May 13th,* 1857.

MY DEAR FORSTER,

I have gone over Dilke's memoranda, and I think it quite right and necessary that those points should be stated. Nor do I see the least difficulty in the way of their introduction into the pamphlet. But I do not deem it possible to get the pamphlet written and published before the dinner. I have so many matters pressing on my attention, that I cannot turn to it immediately on my release from my book just finished. It shall be done and distributed early next month.

As to anything being lost by its not being in the hands of the people who dine (as you seem to think), I have not the least misgiving on that score. They would say, if it were issued, just what they will say without it.

Lord Granville is committed to taking the chair, and will make the best speech he can in it. The pious —— will cram him with as many distortions of the truth as his stomach may be strong enough to receive. ——, with Bardolphian eloquence, will cool his nose in the modest merits of the institution. —— will make a neat and appropriate speech on both sides, round the corner and over the way. And all this would be done exactly to the same purpose and in just the same strain, if twenty thousand copies of the pamphlet had been circulated.

Ever affectionately.

[*To Rev. James White.*]

TAVISTOCK HOUSE, *Friday, May 22nd,* 1857.

MY DEAR WHITE,

My emancipation having been effected on Saturday, the ninth of this month, I take some shame to myself for not having sooner answered your note. But the host of things to be done as soon as I was free, and the tremendous number of ingenuities to be wrought out at Gad's Hill, have kept me in a whirl of their own ever since.

We purpose going to Gad's Hill for the summer on the 1st of June ; as, apart from the master's eye being a necessary ornament to the spot, I clearly see that the workmen yet lingering in the yard must be squeezed out by bodily pressure, or they will never go. How will this suit you and yours ? If you will come down, we can take you all in, on your way north ; that is to say, we shall have that ample verge and room enough, until about the eighth ; when Hans Christian Andersen (who has been " coming " for about three years) will come for a fortnight's stay in England. I shall like you to see the little old-fashioned place. It strikes me as being comfortable.

So let me know your little game. And with love to Mrs. White, Lotty, and Clara,

Believe me, ever affectionately yours.

[*To Mr. Frank Stone, A.R.A.*]

OFFICE OF " HOUSEHOLD WORDS," *Monday, June 1st,* 1857.

MY DEAR STONE,

I know that what I am going to say will not be agreeable ; but I rely on the authoress's good sense ; and say it, knowing it to be the truth.

These " Notes " are destroyed by too much smartness. It gives the appearance of perpetual effort, stabs to the heart the nature that is in them, and wearies by the manner and not by the matter. It is the commonest fault in the world (as I have constant occasion to observe here), but it is a very great one. Just as you couldn't bear to have an épergne or a candlestick on your table, supported by a light figure always on tiptoe and evidently in an impossible attitude for the sustainment of its weight, so all readers would be more or less oppressed and worried by this presentation of everything in one smart point of view, when they know it must have other, and weightier, and more solid properties. Airiness and good spirits are always delightful, and are inseparable from notes of a cheerful trip ; but they should sympathise with many things as well as see them in a lively way. It is but a word or a touch that expresses this humanity, but without that little embellishment of good nature there is no such thing as humour. In this little MS. everything is too much patronised and condescended to, whereas the slightest touch of feeling for the rustic who is of the earth earthy, or of sisterhood with the homely servant who has made her face shine in her desire to please, would make a difference that the writer can scarcely imagine without trying it. The only relief in the twenty-one slips is the little bit about the chimes. It *is* a relief, simply because it is an indication of some kind of sentiment. You don't want any sentiment laboriously made out in such a thing. You don't want any maudlin show of it. But you do want a pervading suggestion that it is there. It makes all the difference between being playful and being cruel. Again I must say, above all things—especially to young people writing : For the love of God, don't condescend! Don't assume the attitude of saying, " See how clever I am, and what fun everybody else is ! " Take any shape but that.

I observe an excellent quality of observation throughout, and think the boy at the shop, and all about him, particularly good. I have no doubt whatever that the rest of the journal will be much better if the writer chooses to make it so. If she considers for a moment within herself, she will know that she derived pleasure from everything she saw, because she saw it with innumerable lights and shades upon it, and bound to humanity by innumerable fine links ; she cannot possibly communicate anything of that pleasure to another by showing it from one little limited point only, and that point, observe, the one from which it is impossible to detach the exponent as the patroness of a whole universe of inferior souls. This is what everybody would mean in objecting to these notes (supposing them to be published), that they are too smart and too flippant.

As I understand this matter to be altogether between us three, and as I think your confidence, and her's, imposes a duty of friendship on me, I discharge it to the best of my ability. Perhaps I make more of it than you may have meant or expected ; if so, it is because I am interested and wish to express it. If there had been anything in my objection not perfectly easy of removal, I might, after all, have hesitated to state it ; but that is not the case. A very little indeed would make all this gaiety as sound and wholesome and good-natured in the reader's mind as it is in the writer's.

Affectionately always.

[*To Miss Ellen Stone.*]

GAD'S HILL PLACE, HIGHAM, *Thursday, June 4th,* 1857.
MY DEAR MISS STONE,

Coming home here last night, from a day's business in London, I found your most excellent note awaiting me, in which I have had a pleasure to be derived from none but good and natural things. I can now honestly assure you that I believe you will write *well*, and that I have a lively hope that I may be the means of showing you yourself in print one day. Your powers of graceful and light-hearted observation need nothing but the little touches on which we are both agreed. And I am perfectly sure that they will be as pleasant to you as to anyone, for nobody can see so well as you do, without feeling kindly too.

To confess the truth to you, I was half sorry, yesterday, that I had been so unreserved ; but not half as sorry, yesterday, as I am glad to-day. You must not mind my adding that there is a noble candour and modesty in your note, which I shall never be able to separate from you henceforth.

Affectionately yours always.

[To Mr. Henry Austin.]

GAD'S HILL, *Saturday, June 6th*, 1857.
MY DEAR HENRY,

Here is a very serious business on the great estate respecting the water supply. Last night, they had pumped the well dry merely in raising the family supply for the day ; and this morning (very little water having been got into the cisterns) it is dry again ! It is pretty clear to me that we must look the thing in the face, and at once bore deeper, dig, or do some beastly thing or other, to secure this necessary in abundance. Meanwhile I am in a most plaintive and forlorn condition without your presence and counsel. I raise my voice in the wilderness and implore the same ! ! !

Wild legends are in circulation among the servants how that Captain Goldsmith on the knoll above—the skipper .in that crow's-nest of a house—has millions of gallons of water always flowing for him. Can he have damaged my well ? Can we imitate him, and have our millions of gallons ? Goldsmith or I must fall, so I conceive.

If you get this, send me a telegraph message informing me when I may expect comfort. I am held by four of the family while I write this, in case I should do myself a mischief—it certainly won't be taking to drinking water.

Ever affectionately (most despairingly).

[To Mr. W. C. Macready.]

TAVISTOCK HOUSE, Monday, July 13th, 1857.

MY DEAREST MACREADY,

Many thanks for your Indian information. I shall act upon it in the most exact manner. Walter sails next Monday. Charley and I go down with him to Southampton next Sunday. We are all delighted with the prospect of seeing you at Gad's Hill. These are my Jerrold engagements : On Friday, the 24th, I have to repeat my reading at St. Martin's Hall ; on Saturday, the 25th, to repeat " The Frozen Deep " at the Gallery of Illustration for the last time. On Thursday, the 30th, or Friday, the 31st, I shall probably read at Manchester. Deane, the general manager of the Exhibition, is going down to-night, and will arrange all preliminaries for me. If you and I went down to Manchester together, and were there on a Sunday, he would give us the whole Exhibition to ourselves. It is probable, I think (as he estimates the receipts of a night about seven hundred pounds), that we may, in about a fortnight or so after the reading, play "The Frozen Deep" at Manchester. But of this contingent engagement I at present know no more than you do.

Now, will you, upon this exposition of affairs, choose you own time for coming to us, and, when you have made your choice, write to me at Gad's Hill? I am going down this afternoon for rest (which means violent cricket with the boys) after last Saturday night; which was a teaser, but triumphant. The St. Martin's Hall audience was, I must confess, a very extraordinary thing. The two thousand and odd people were like one, and their enthusiasm was something awful.

Yet I have seen that before, too. Your young remembrance cannot recall the man; but he flourished in my day—a great actor, sir—a noble actor—thorough artist! I have seen him do wonders in that way. He retired from the stage early in life (having a monomaniacal delusion that he was old), and is said to be still living in your county.

All join in kindest love to your dear sister and all the rest.

Ever, my dearest Macready,

Most affectionately yours.

[*To Mr. Edmund Yates.*]

TAVISTOCK HOUSE, *Sunday, July 19th,* 1857.

MY DEAR YATES,

Although I date this ashore, I really write it from Southampton (don't notice this fact in your reply, for I shall be in town on Wednesday). I have come here on an errand which will grow familiar to you before you know that Time has flapped his wings over your head. Like me, you will find those babies grow to be young men before you are quite sure they are born. Like me, you will have great teeth drawn with a wrench, and will only then know that you ever cut them. I am here to send Walter away over what they call, in Green Bush melodramas, "the Big Drink," and I don't at all know this day how he comes to be mine, or I his.

I don't write to say this—or to say how seeing Charley, and he going aboard the ship before me just now, I suddenly came into possession of a photograph of my own back at sixteen and twenty, and also into a suspicion that I had doubled the last age. I merely write to mention that Telbin and his wife are going down to Gad's Hill with us, about mid-day next Sunday, and that if you and Mrs. Yates will come too, we shall be delighted to have you. We can give you a bed, and you can be in town (if you have such a savage necessity) by twenty minutes before ten on Monday morning.

I was very much pleased (as I had reason to be) with your account of the reading in *The Daily News.* I thank you heartily.

[*To Mr. T. P. Cooke.*]

IN REMEMBRANCE OF THE LATE MR. DOUGLAS JERROLD.

COMMITTEE'S OFFICE, GALLERY OF ILLUSTRATION,
REGENT STREET, *Thursday, July 30th,* 1857.

MY DEAR MR. COOKE,

I cannot rest satisfied this morning without writing to congratulate you on your admirable performance of last night. It was so fresh and vigorous, so manly and gallant, that I felt as if it splashed against my theatre-heated face, along with the spray of the breezy sea. What I felt everybody felt ; I should feel it quite an impertinence to take myself out of the crowd, therefore, if I could by any means help doing so. But I can't ; so I hope you will feel that you bring me on yourself, and have only yourself to blame.

Always faithfully yours.

[*To Mrs. Compton.*]

GAD'S HILL PLACE, HIGHAM BY ROCHESTER,
Sunday Night, Aug. 2nd, 1857.

MY DEAR MRS. COMPTON,

We are going to play " The Frozen Deep " (pursuant to requisition from town magnates, etc.) at Manchester, at the New Free Trade Hall on the nights of Friday and Saturday, the 21st and 22nd August.

The place is out of the question for my girls. Their action could not be seen, and their voices could not be heard. You and I have played, there and elsewhere, so

VOL. II.—2

sociably and happily, that I am emboldened to ask you whether you would play my sister-in-law Georgina's part (Compton and babies permitting).

We shall go down in the old pleasant way, and shall have the Art Treasures Exhibition to ourselves on the Sunday ; when even " he " (as Rogers always called every pretty woman's husband) might come and join us.

What do you say ? What does he say ? and what does baby say ? When I use the term "baby," I use it in two tenses—present and future.

Answer me at this address, like the Juliet I saw at Drury Lane—when was it ?—yesterday.   And whatever your answer is, if you will say that you and Compton will meet us at the North Kent Station, London Bridge, next Sunday at a quarter before one, and will come down here for a breath of sweet air and stay all night, you will give your old friends great pleasure.   Not least among them,

Yours faithfully.

[To Mr. W. C. Macready.]

GAD'S HILL PLACE, HIGHAM BY ROCHESTER,
Monday, Aug. 3rd, 1857.

MY DEAREST MACREADY,

I write to you in reference to your last note, as soon as I positively know our final movements in the Jerrold matter.

We are going to wind up by acting at Manchester (on solemn requisition), on the evenings of Friday and Saturday, the 21st and 22nd (actresses substituted for the girls, of course). We shall have to leave here on the morning of the 20th. You thought of coming on the 16th; can't you make it a day or two earlier, so as to be with us a whole week? Decide and pronounce. Again, cannot you bring Katey with you? Decide and pronounce thereupon, also.

I read at Manchester last Friday. As many thousand people were there as you like to name. The collection of pictures in the Exhibition is wonderful. And the power with which the modern English school asserts itself is a very gratifying and delightful thing to behold. The care for the common people, in the provision made for their comfort and refreshment, is also admirable and worthy of all commendation. But they want more amusement, and particularly (as it strikes me) *something in motion*, though it were only a twisting-fountain. The thing is too still after their lives of machinery, and art flies over their heads in consequence.

I hope you have seen my tussle with the "Edinburgh." I saw the chance last Friday week, as I was going down to read the "Carol" in St. Martin's Hall. Instantly turned to, then and there, and wrote half the article. Flew out of bed early next morning, and finished it by noon. Went down to Gallery of Illustration (we acted that night), did the day's business, corrected the poofs in Polar costume in dressing-room, broke up two numbers of "Household Words" to get it out directly, played in "Frozen Deep" and "Uncle John," presided at supper of company, made no end of speeches, went home and gave in completely for four hours, then got sound asleep, and next day was as fresh as you used to be in the far-off days of your lusty youth.

All here send kindest love to your dear good sister and all the house.

Ever and ever affectionately.

[*To Mr. Frank Stone, A.R.A.*]

TAVISTOCK HOUSE, *Sunday Afternoon, Aug. 9th,* 1857.

MY DEAR STONE,

Now here, without any preface, is a good, confounding, stunning question for you—would you like to play "Uncle John" on the two nights at Manchester?

It is not a long part. You could have a full rehearsal on the Friday, and I could sit in the wing at night and pull you through all the business. Perhaps you might not object to being in the thing in your own native place, and the relief to me would be enormous.

This is what has come into my head lying in bed to-day (I have been in bed all day), and this is just my plain reason for writing to you.

It's a capital part, and you are a capital old man. You know the play as we play it, and the Manchester people don't. Say the word, and I'll send you my own book by return of post.

The agitation and exertion of Richard Wardour are so great to me, that I cannot rally my spirits in the short space of time I get. The strain is so great to make a show of doing it, that I want to be helped out of "Uncle

John " if I can. Think of yourself far more than me ; but if you half think you are up to the joke, and half doubt your being so, then give me the benefit of the doubt and play the part.

Answer me at Gad's Hill.

Ever affectionately.

P.S.—If you play, I shall immediately announce it to all concerned. If you don't, I shall go on as if nothing had happened, and shall say nothing to anyone.

[*To Mr. Henry Austin.*]

GAD'S HILL PLACE, *Saturday, Aug.* 15*th,* 1857.

MY DEAR HENRY,

At last, I am happy to inform you, we have got at a famous spring ! ! It rushed in this morning, ten foot deep. And our friends talk of its supplying " a ton a minute for yourself and your family, sir, for nevermore."

They ask leave to bore ten feet lower, to prevent the possibility of what they call " a choking with sullage." Likewise, they are going to insert " a rose-headed pipe ; " at the mention of which implement, I am (secretly) well-nigh distracted, having no idea of what it means. But I have said " Yes," besides instantly standing a bottle of gin. Can you come back, and can you get down on Monday morning, to advise and endeavour to decide on the mechanical force we shall use for raising the water ? I would return with you, as I shall have to be in town until

Thursday, and then to go to Manchester until the following Tuesday.

I send this by hand to John, to bring to you.

Ever affectionately.

[*To Mr. Frank Stone, A.R.A.*]

GAD'S HILL PLACE, *Monday, Aug. 17th,* 1857.

MY DEAR STONE,

I received your kind note this morning, and write this reply here to take to London with me and post in town, being bound for that village and three days' drill of the professional ladies who are to succeed the Tavistock girls.

My book I enclose. There is a slight alteration (which does not affect you) at the end of the first act, in order that the piece may be played through without having the drop curtain down. You will not find the situations or business difficult, with me on the spot to put you right. .

Now, as to the dress. You will want a pair of pumps, and a pair of white silk socks ; these you can get at Manchester. The extravagantly and anciently-frilled shirts that I have had got up for the part, I will bring you down ; large white waistcoat, I will bring you down ; large white hat, I will bring you down ; dressing-gown, I will bring you down ; white gloves and ditto choker you can get at Manchester. There then remain only a pair of common nankeen tights, to button below the calf, and blue wedding-coat. The nankeen tights you had best get made at once ; my " Uncle John " coat I will send you down in a parcel by to-morrow's train, to have altered in Manchester to your shape and figure. You will then be quite independent of Christian chance and Jewish Nathan, which latter poten-tate is now at Canterbury with the cricket amateurs, and might fail.

A Thursday's rehearsal is (unfortunately) now imprac-ticable, the passes for the railway being all made out, and the company's sailing orders issued. But, as I have already suggested, with a careful rehearsal on Friday morning, and with me at the wing at night to put you right, you will find yourself sliding through it easily. There is nothing in the least complicated in the business. As to the dance, you have only to knock yourself up for a twelve-month and it will go nobly.

After all, too, if you *should,* through any unlucky break-down, come to be afraid of it, I am no worse off than I was before, if I have to do it at last. Keep your pecker up with that.

I am heartily obliged to you, my dear old boy, for your affectionate and considerate note, and I wouldn't have you do it, really and sincerely—immense as the relief will be to me—unless you are quite comfortable in it, and able to enjoy it. Ever affectionately.

[*To Mr. Frank Stone, A.R.A.*]

Office of " Household Words," *Tuesday, Aug. 18th,* 1857.
My dear Stone,

I sent you a telegraph message last night, in total con-tradiction of the letter you received from me this morning.

The reason was simply this : Arthur Smith and the other business men, both in Manchester and here, urged upon me, in the strongest manner, that they were afraid of the change ; that it was well known in Manchester that I had done the part in London ; that there was a danger of its being considered disrespectful in me to give it up ; also that there was a danger that it might be thought that I did so at the last minute, after an immense let, whereas I might have done it at first, etc. etc. etc. Having no desire but for the success of our object, and a becoming recognition on my part of the kind Manchester public's cordiality, I gave way, and thought it best to go on.

I do so against the grain, and against every inclination, and against the strongest feeling of gratitude to you. My people at home will be miserable too when they hear I am going to do it. If I could have heard from you sooner, and got the bill out sooner, I should have been firmer in considering my own necessity of relief. As it is, I sneak under ; and I hope you will feel the reasons, and approve.

Ever affectionately.

[To Mr. Henry Austin.]

GAD'S HILL PLACE, *Wednesday, Sept. 2nd,* 1857.
MY DEAR HENRY,

The second conspirator has been here this morning to ask whether you wish the windlass to be left in the yard, and whether you will want him and his mate any more, and, if so, when ? Of course he says (rolling something in the form of a fillet in at one broken tooth all the while, and rolling it out at another) that they could wish fur to have the windlass if it warn't any ways a hill conwenience fur to fetch her away. I have told him that if he will come back on Friday he shall have your reply. Will you, therefore, send it me by return of post? He says he'll "look up" (as if he was an astronomer) "a Friday arter-dinner."

On Monday I am going away with Collins for ten days or a fortnight, on a "tour in search of an article" for "Household Words." We have not the least idea where we are going; but *he* says, "Let's look at the Norfolk coast," and *I* say, "Let's look at the back of the Atlantic." I don't quite know what I mean by that ; but have a general impression that I mean something knowing.

I am horribly used up after the Jerrold business. Low spirits, low pulse, low voice, intense reaction. If I were not like Mr. Micawber, "falling back for a spring," on Monday, I think I should slink into a corner and cry.

Ever affectionately.

[*To Miss Hogarth.*]

ALLONBY, CUMBERLAND, *Wednesday Night, Sept. 9th,* 1857.
MY DEAR GEORGY,

*   *   *   *   *

Think of Collins's usual luck with me ! We went up a Cumberland mountain yesterday—a huge black hill, fifteen hundred feet high. We took for a guide a capital innkeeper hard by. It rained in torrents—as it only does rain in a hill country—the whole time. At the top, there were black mists and the darkness of night. It then came out that the innkeeper had not been up for twenty years, and he lost his head and himself altogether ; and we couldn't get down again ! What wonders the Inimitable performed with his compass until it broke with the heat and wet of his pocket no matter ; it did break, and then we wandered about, until it was clear to the Inimitable that the night must be passed there, and the enterprising travellers probably die of cold. We took our own way about coming down, struck, and declared that the guide might wander where he would, but we would follow a watercourse we lighted upon, and which must come at last to the river. This necessitated amazing gymnastics ; in the course of which performances, Collins fell into the said watercourse with his ankle sprained, and the great ligament of the foot and leg swollen I don't know how big.

How I enacted Wardour over again in carrying him down, and what a business it was to get him down ; I may say in Gibb's words : " Vi lascio a giudicare ! " But he was got down somehow, and we got off the mountain somehow ; and now I carry him to bed, and into and out of carriages, exactly like Wardour in private life. I don't believe he will stand for a month to come. He has had a doctor, and can wear neither shoe nor stocking, and has his foot wrapped up in a flannel waistcoat, and has a breakfast saucer of liniment, and a horrible dabbling of lotion incessantly in progress. We laugh at it all, but I doubt very much whether he can go on to Doncaster. It will be a miserable blow to our H. W. scheme, and I say nothing about it as yet; but he is really so crippled that I doubt the getting him there. We have resolved to fall to work to-morrow morning and begin our writing; and there, for the present, that point rests.

This is a little place with fifty houses, five bathing-machines, five girls in straw hats, five men in straw hats, and no other company. The little houses are all in half-mourning—yellow stone on white stone, and black; and it reminds me of what Broadstairs might have been if it had not inherited a cliff, and had been an Irishman. But this is a capital little homely inn, looking out upon the sea; and we are really very comfortably lodged. I can just stand upright in my bedroom. Otherwise, it is a good deal like one of Ballard's top-rooms. We have a very obliging and comfortable landlady; and it is a clean nice place in a rough wild country. We came here haphazard, but could not have done better.

We lay last night at a place called Wigton—also in half-mourning—with the wonderful peculiarity that it had no population, no business, no streets to speak of; but five linendrapers within range of our small windows, one linendraper's next door, and five more linendrapers round the corner. I ordered a night-light in my bedroom. A queer little old woman brought me one of the common Child's night-lights, and seeming to think that I looked at it with interest, said: "It's joost a vara keeyourious thing, sir, and joost new coom oop. It'll burn awt hoors a' end, an no gootther, nor no waste, nor ony sike a thing, if you can creedit what I say, seein' the airticle."

Of course *I* shall go to Doncaster, whether or no (please God), and my postage directions to you remain unchanged. Love to Mamey, Katey, Charley, Harry, and the darling Plorn.

Ever affectionately.

[*To Miss Hogarth.*]

LANCASTER, *Saturday Night, Sept.* 12th, 1857.

MY DEAR GEORGY,

I received your letter at Allonby yesterday, and was delighted to get it. We came back to Carlisle last night (to a capital inn, kept by Breach's brother), and came on here to-day. We are on our way to Doncaster; but Sabbath observance throws all the trains out; and although it is not a hundred miles from here, we shall have, as well as I can make out the complicated lists of trains, to sleep at Leeds—which I particularly detest as an odious place— to-morrow night.

Accustomed as you are to the homage which men delight to render to the Inimitable, you would be scarcely prepared for the proportions it assumes in this northern country. Station-masters assist him to alight from carriages, deputations await him in hotel entries, innkeepers bow down before him and put him into regal rooms, the town goes down to the platform to see him off, and Collins's ankle goes into the newspapers ! ! !

It is a great deal better than it was, and he can get into new hotels and up the stairs with two thick sticks, like an admiral in a farce. His spirits have improved in a corresponding degree, and he contemplates cheerfully the keeping house at Doncaster. I thought (as I told you) he would never have gone there, but he seems quite up to the mark now. Of course he can never walk out, or see anything of any place. We have done our first paper for H. W., and sent it up to the printer's.

The landlady of the little inn at Allonby lived at Greta Bridge, in Yorkshire, when I went down there before "Nickelby," and was smuggled into the room to see me, when I was secretly found out. She is an immensely fat woman now. "But I could tuck my arm around her waist then, Mr. Dickens," the landlord said when she told me the story as I was going to bed the night before last. "And can't you do it now," I said, "you insensible dog? Look at me! Here's a picture!" Accordingly, I got round as much of her as I could; and this gallant action was the most successful I have ever performed, on the whole. I think it was the dullest little place I ever entered; and what with the monotony of an idle sea, and what with the monotony of another sea in the room (occasioned by Collins's perpetually holding his ankle over a pail of salt water, and laving it with a milk jug), I struck yesterday, and came away.

We are in a very remarkable old house here, with genuine old rooms and an uncommonly quaint staircase. I have a state bedroom, with two enormous red four-posters in it, each as big as Charley's room at Gad's Hill. Bellew is to preach here to-morrow. "And we know he is a friend of yours, sir," said the landlord, when he presided over the serving of the dinner (two little salmon trout; a sirloin steak; a brace of partridges; seven dishes of sweets; five dishes of dessert, led off by a bowl of peaches; and in the centre an enormous bride-cake—"We always have it here, sir," said the landlord, "custom of the house." (Collins turned pale, and estimated the dinner at half a guinea each.)

This is the stupidest of letters, but all description is gone, or going, into "The Lazy Tour of Two Idle Apprentices."

Kiss the darling Plorn, who is often in my thoughts. Best love to Charley, Mamey, and Katie. I will write to you again from Doncaster, where I shall be rejoiced to find another letter from you.

Ever affectionately, my dearest Georgy.

[*To Miss Hogarth.*]

ANGEL HOTEL, DONCASTER, *Tuesday, Sept. 15th*, 1857.

MY DEAR GEORGY,

I found your letter here on my arrival yesterday. I had hoped that the wall would have been almost finished by this time, and the additions to the house almost finished too—but patience, patience!

We have very good, clean, and quiet apartments here, on the second floor, looking down into the main street, which is full of horse jockeys, bettors, drunkards, and other blackguards, from morning to night—and all night. The races begin to-day and last till Friday, which is the Cup Day. I am not going to the course this morning, but have engaged a carriage (open, and pair) for to-morrow and Friday.

"The Frozen Deep's" author gets on as well as could be expected. He can hobble up and down stairs when absolutely necessary, and limps to his bedroom on the same floor. He talks of going to the theatre to-night in a cab, which will be the first occasion of his going out, except to travel, since the accident. He sends his kind regards and thanks for enquiries and condolence. I am perpetually tidying the rooms after him, and carrying all sorts of untidy things which belong to him into his bedroom, which is a picture of disorder. You will please to imagine mine, airy and clean, little dressing-room attached, eight water jugs (I never saw such a supply), capital sponge-bath, perfect arrangement, and exquisite neatness. We breakfast at half-past eight, and fall to work for H. W. afterwards. Then I go out, and—hem! look for subjects.

The mayor called this morning to do the honours of the town, whom it pleased the Inimitable to receive with great courtesy and affability. He propounded invitation to public *déjeûner*, which it did *not* please the Inimitable to receive, and which he graciously rejected.

That's all the news. Everything I can describe by hook or by crook, I describe for H. W. So there is nothing of that sort left for letters.

Best love to dear Mamey and Katey, and to Charley, and to Harry. Any number of kisses to the noble Plorn.

Ever affectionately.

[*To Mr. Arthur Ryland.*]

GAD'S HILL PLACE, *Saturday Evening, Oct. 3rd,* 1857.

MY DEAR SIR,

I have had the honour and pleasure of receiving your letter of the 28th of last month, informing me of the distinction that has been conferred upon me by the Council of the Birmingham and Midland Institute.

Allow me to assure you with much sincerity, that I am highly gratified by having been elected one of the first honorary members of that establishment. Nothing could have enhanced my interest in so important an undertaking ; but the compliment is all the more welcome to me on that account.

I accept it with a due sense of its worth, with many acknowledgments and with all good wishes.

I am ever, dear Sir, very faithfully yours.

[*To Mr. Edmund Yates.*]

TAVISTOCK HOUSE, *Monday Night, Nov. 16th,* 1857.

MY DEAR YATES,

I retain the story with pleasure ; and I need not tell you that you are not mistaken in the last lines of your note.

Excuse me, on that ground, if I say a word or two as to what I think (I mention it with a view to the future) might be better in the paper. The opening is excellent. But it passes too completely into the Irishman's narrative, does not light it up with the life about it, or the circumstances under which it is delivered, and does not carry through it, as I think it should with a certain indefinable subtleness, the thread with which you begin your weaving. I will tell Wills to send me the proof, and will try to show you what I mean when I shall have gone over it carefully.

Faithfully yours always.

[*To Mr. Frank Stone, A.R.A.*]

Tavistock House, *Wednesday, Dec. 13th,* 1857.

MY DEAR STONE,

I find on enquiry that the "General Theatrical Fund" has relieved non-members in one or two instances ; but that it is exceedingly unwilling to do so, and would certainly not do so again, saving on some very strong and exceptional case. As its trustee, I could not represent to it that I think it ought to sail into those open waters, for I very much doubt the justice of such cruising, with a reference to the interests of the patient people who support it out of their small earnings.

Affectionately ever.

BOOK III.

1858 TO 1870.

1858.

ALL through this year, Charles Dickens was constantly moving about from place to place. After much and careful consideration, he had come to the determination of, for the future, giving readings for his own benefit. And although in the spring of this year he gave one reading of his " Christmas Carol " for a charity, all the other readings, beginning from the 29th April, and ever after, were for himself. In the autumn of this year he made reading tours in England, Scotland, and Ireland, always accompanied by his friend and secretary, Mr. Arthur Smith. At Newcastle, Charles Dickens was joined by his daughters, who accompanied him in his Scotch tour. The letters to his sister-in-law, and to his eldest daughter, are all given here, and will be given in all future reading tours, as they form a complete diary of his life and movements at these times. To avoid the constant repetition of the two names, the beginning of the letters will be dispensed with in all cases where they follow each other in unbroken succession. The Mr. Frederick Lehmann mentioned in the letter written from Sheffield, had married a daughter of Mr. Robert Chambers, and niece of Mrs. Wills. Coming to settle in London a short time after this date, Mr. and Mrs. Lehmann became intimately known to Charles Dickens and his family—more especially to his eldest daughter, to whom they have been, and are, the kindest and truest of friends. The " pretty little boy " mentioned as being under Mrs. Wills's care, was their eldest son.

We give the letter to Mr. Thackeray, not because it is one of very great interest, but because, being the only one

45

we have, we are glad to have the two names associated together in this work.

The "little speech" alluded to in this first letter to Mr.
Macready was one made by Charles Dickens at a public
dinner, which was given in aid of the Hospital for Sick
Children, in Great Ormond Street.   He afterwards (early
in April) gave a reading from his "Christmas Carol" for
this same charity.

The Christmas number of "Household Words," men-
tioned in a letter to Mr. Wilkie Collins, was called "A
House to Let," and contained stories written by Charles
Dickens, Mr. Wilkie Collins, and other contributors to
"Household Words."

[*To Mr. W. Wilkie Collins.*]

TAVISTOCK HOUSE, *Sunday, Jan. 17th,* 1858.

MY DEAR WILKIE,

I am very sorry to receive so bad an account of the foot.
But I hope it is all in the past tense now.

I met with an incident the other day, which I think is a
good deal in your way, for introduction either into a long
or short story.   Dr. Sutherland and Dr. Monro went over
St. Luke's with me (only last Friday), to show me some
distinctly and remarkably developed types of insanity.
Among other patients, we passed a deaf and dumb man,
now afflicted with incurable madness too, of whom they
said that it was only when his madness began to develop
itself in strongly-marked mad actions, that it began to be
suspected.   "Though it had been there, no doubt, some
time."   This led me to consider, suspiciously, what employ-

ment he had been in, and so to ask the question. "Aye," says Dr. Sutherland, "that is the most remarkable thing of all, Mr. Dickens. He was employed in the transmission of electric-telegraph messages ; and it is impossible to conceive what delirious despatches that man may have been sending about all over the world!"

Rejoiced to hear such good report of the play.

Ever faithfully.

[*To Mr. Edmund Yates.*]

TAVISTOCK HOUSE, *Tuesday, Feb. 2nd,* 1858.

MY DEAR YATES,

Your quotation is, as I supposed, all wrong. The text is *not* "which his 'owls was organs." When Mr. Harris went into an empty dog-kennel, to spare his sensitive nature the anguish of overhearing Mrs. Harris's exclamations on the occasion of the birth of her first child (the Princess Royal of the Harris family), "he never took his hands away from his ears, or came out once, till he was showed the baby." On encountering that spectacle, he was (being of a weakly constitution) "took with fits." For this distressing complaint he was medically treated ; the doctor "collared him, and laid him on his back upon the airy stones"—please to observe what follows—"and she was told, to ease her mind, his 'owls was organs."

That is to say, Mrs. Harris, lying exhausted on her bed, in the first sweet relief of freedom from pain, merely covered with the counterpane, and not yet "put comfortable," hears a noise apparently proceeding from the back-yard, and says, in a flushed and hysterical manner : "What 'owls are those ?   Who is a-'owling ?   Not my ugebond ?" Upon which the doctor, looking round one of the bottom posts of the bed, and taking Mrs. Harris's pulse in a re-assuring manner, says, with much admirable presence of mind : "Howls, my dear madam ?—no, no, no !   What are we thinking of ?   Howls, my dear Mrs. Harris ?   Ha, ha, ha !   Organs, ma'am, organs.   Organs in the streets, Mrs. Harris ; no howls."

Yours faithfully.

[To Mr. W. M. Thackeray.]

TAVISTOCK HOUSE, Tuesday, Feb. 2nd, 1858.

MY DEAR THACKERAY,

The wisdom of Parliament, in that expensive act of its greatness which constitutes the Guild, prohibits that cor-poration *from doing anything* until it shall have existed in a perfectly useless condition for seven years.   This clause (introduced by some private-bill magnate of official might) seemed so ridiculous, that nobody could believe it to have this meaning ; but as I felt clear about it when we were on the very verge of granting an excellent literary annuity, I referred the point to counsel, and my construction was confirmed without a doubt.

It is therefore needless to enquire whether an associa-tion in the nature of a provident society could address it-self to such a case as you confide to me.   The prohibition has still two or three years of life in it.

But, assuming the gentleman's title to be considered as an " author " as established, there is no question that it comes within the scope of the Literary Fund.   They would habitually "lend" money if they did what I consider to be their duty ; as it is they only give money, but they give it in such instances.

I have forwarded the envelope to the Society of Arts, with a request that they will present it to Prince Albert, approaching H.R.H. in the Siamese manner.

Ever faithfully.

[*To Mr. John Forster.*]

TAVISTOCK HOUSE, *Wednesday Night, Feb. 3rd*, 1858.

MY DEAR FORSTER,

I beg to report two phenomena :

1. An excellent little play in one act, by Marston, at the Lyceum ; title, " A Hard Struggle ; " as good as " La Joie fait Peur," though not at all like it.

2. Capital acting in the same play, by Mr. Dillon.   Real good acting, in imitation of nobody, and honestly made out by himself ! !

I went (at Marston's request) last night, and cried till I sobbed again.   I have not seen a word about it from Oxenford.   But it is as wholesome and manly a thing altogether as I have seen for many a day.   (I would have given a hundred pounds to have played Mr. Dillon's part).

Love to Mrs. Forster.

Ever affectionately.

VOL. II.—3

[*To Dr. Westland Marston.*]

TAVISTOCK HOUSE, *Wednesday, Feb. 3rd,* 1858.

MY DEAR MARSTON,

I most heartily and honestly congratulate you on your charming little piece. It moved me more than I could easily tell you, if I were to try. Except " La Joie fait Peur," I have seen nothing nearly so good, and there is a subtlety in the comfortable presentation of the child who is to become a devoted woman for Reuben's sake, which goes a long way beyond Madame de Girardin. I am at a loss to let you know how much I admired it last night, or how heartily I cried over it. A touching idea, most delicately conceived and wrought out by a true artist and poet, in a spirit of noble, manly generosity, that no one should be able to study without great emotion.

It is extremely well acted by all concerned ; but Mr. Dillon's performance is really admirable, and deserving of the highest commendation. It is good in these days to see an actor taking such pains, and expressing such natural and vigorous sentiment. There is only one thing I should have liked him to change. I am much mistaken if any man—least of all any such man—would crush a letter written by the hand of the woman he loved. Hold it to his heart unconsciously and look about for it the while, he might ; or he might do any other thing with it that expressed a habit of tenderness and affection in association with the idea of her ; but he would never crush it under any circumstances. He would as soon crush her heart.

You will see how closely I went with him, by my minding so slight an incident in so fine a performance. There is no one who could approach him in it; and I am bound to add that he surprised me as much as he pleased me.

I think it might be worth while to try the people at the Français with the piece. They are very good in one-act plays; such plays take well there, and this seems to me well suited to them. If you would like Samson or Regnier to read the play (in English), I know them well, and would be very glad indeed to tell them that I sent it with your sanction because I had been so much struck by it.

Faithfully yours always.

[*To Monsieur Regnier.*]

TAVISTOCK HOUSE, LONDON, W.C., *Thursday, Feb. 11th*, 1858.

MY DEAR REGNIER,

I want you to read the enclosed little play. You will see that it is in one act—about the length of "La Joie fait Peur." It is now acting at the Lyceum Theatre here, with very great success. The author is Mr. Westland Marston, a dramatic writer of reputation, who wrote a very well-known tragedy called "The Patrician's Daughter," in which Macready and Miss Faucit acted (under Macready's management at Drury Lane) some years ago.

This little piece is so very powerful on the stage, its interest is so simple and natural, and the part of Reuben is such a very fine one, that I cannot help thinking you might make one grand *coup* with it, if with your skilful hand you arranged it for the Français. I have communicated this idea of mine to the author, "*et là-dessus je vous écris.*" I am anxious to know your opinion, and shall expect with much interest to receive a little letter from you at your convenience.

Mrs. Dickens, Miss Hogarth, and all the house send a thousand kind loves and regards to Madame Regnier and the dear little boys. You will bring them to London when you come, with all the force of the Français—will you not?

Ever, my dear Regnier, faithfully your Friend.

[*To Monsieur Regnier.*]

TAVISTOCK HOUSE, *Saturday, Feb. 20th,* 1858.

MY DEAR REGNIER,

Let me thank you with all my heart for your most patient and kind letter. I made its contents known to Mr. Marston, and I enclose you his reply. You will see that he cheerfully leaves the matter in your hands, and abides by your opinion and discretion.

You need not return his letter, my friend. There is great excitement here this morning, in consequence of the failure of the Ministry last night to carry the bill they brought in to please your Emperor and his troops. I, for one, am extremely glad of their defeat.

"Le vieux P——," I have no doubt, will go staggering down the Rue de la Paix to-day, with his stick in his hand and his hat on one side, predicting the downfall of everything, in consequence of this event. His handwriting shakes more and more every quarter, and I think he mixes a great deal of cognac with his ink. He always gives me some astonishing piece of news (which is never true), or some suspicious public prophecy (which is never verified), and he always tells me he is dying (which he never is).

Adieu, my dear Regnier, accept a thousand thanks from me, and believe me, now and always,

Your affectionate and faithful Friend.

[*To Mr. W. C. Macready.*]

TAVISTOCK HOUSE, *March 15th,* 1858.

MY DEAREST MACREADY,

I have safely received your cheque this morning, and will hand it over forthwith to the honorary secretary of the hospital. I hope you have read the little speech in the hospital's publication of it. They had it taken by their own shorthand-writer, and it is done verbatim.

You may be sure that it is a good and kind charity. It is amazing to me that it is not at this day ten times as large and rich as it is. But I hope and trust that I have happily been able to give it a good thrust onward into a great course. We all send our most affectionate love to all the house. I am devising all sorts of things in my mind, and am in a state of energetic restlessness incomprehensible to the calm philosophers of Dorsetshire. What a dream it is, this work and strife, and how little we do in the dream after all ! Only last night, in my sleep, I was bent upon getting over a perspective of barriers, with my hands and feet bound.   Pretty much what we are all about, waking, I think ?

But, Lord ! (as I said before) you smile pityingly, not bitterly, at this hubbub, and moralise upon it, in the calm evenings when there is no school at Sherborne.

Ever affectionately and truly.

[*To Mrs. Hogge.*]*

TAVISTOCK HOUSE, TAVISTOCK SQUARE, LONDON, W.C.,

Wednesday, April 14th, 1858.

MY DEAR MRS. HOGGE,

After the profoundest cogitation, I come reluctantly to the conclusion that I do not know that orphan. If you were the lady in want of him, I should certainly offer *myself*. But as you are not, I will not hear of the situation.

It is wonderful to think how many charming little people there must be, to whom this proposal would be like a revelation from Heaven. Why don't I know one, and come to Kensington, boy in hand, as if I had walked (I wish to God I had) out of a fairy tale ! But no, I do *not* know that orphan. He is crying somewhere, by himself, at this moment. I can't dry his eyes. He is being neglected by some ogress of a nurse. I can't rescue him.

I will make a point of going to the Athenæum on Monday night ; and if I had five hundred votes to give, Mr. Macdonald should have them all, for your sake.

---

* Niece to the Rev. W. Harness.

I grieve to hear that you have been ill, but I hope that the spring, when it comes, will find you blooming with the rest of the flowers.

Very faithfully yours.

[*To Mr. Edmund Yates.*]

TAVISTOCK HOUSE, TAVISTOCK SQUARE, LONDON, W.C.,
Wednesday, April 28th, 1858.

MY DEAR YATES,

For a good many years I have suffered a great deal from charities, but never anything like what I suffer now. The amount of correspondence they inflict upon me is really incredible. But this is nothing. Benevolent men get behind the piers of the gates, lying in wait for my going out ; and when I peep shrinkingly from my study-windows, I see their pot-bellied shadows projected on the gravel. Benevolent bullies drive up in hansom cabs (with engraved portraits of their benevolent institutions hanging over the aprons, like banners on their outward walls), and stay long at the door. Benevolent area-sneaks get lost in the kitchens and are found to impede the circulation of the knife-cleaning machine. My man has been heard to say (at The Burton Arms) "that if it was a wicious place, well and good—*that* an't door work ; but that wen all the Christian wirtues is always a-shoulderin' and a-helberin' on you in the 'all, a-tryin' to git past you and cut upstairs into master's room, why no wages as you couldn't name wouldn't make it up to you."

Persecuted ever.

[*To Mrs. Yates.*]

(THE CHARMING ACTRESS, THE MOTHER OF MR. EDMUND
YATES.)

TAVISTOCK HOUSE, TAVISTOCK SQUARE, W.C.,
Saturday Evening, May 15*th*, 1858.

MY DEAR MRS. YATES,

Pray believe that I was sorry with all my heart to miss you last Thursday, and to learn the occasion of your absence ; also that, whenever you can come, your presence will give me a new interest in that evening. No one alive can have more delightful associations with the lightest sound of your voice than I have ; and to give you a minute's interest and pleasure, in acknowledgment of the uncountable hours of happiness you gave me when you were a mysterious angel to me, would honestly gratify my heart.

Very faithfully and gratefully yours.

[*To M. de Cerjat.*]

GAD'S HILL, *Wednesday, July* 7*th*, 1858.

MY DEAR CERJAT,

I should vainly try to tell you—so I *won't* try—how affected I have been by your warm-hearted letter, or how thoroughly well convinced I always am of the truth and earnestness of your friendship. I thank you, my dear, dear fellow, with my whole soul. I fervently return that friendship and I highly cherish it.

You want to know all about me ? I am still reading in

London every Thursday, and the audiences are very great, and the success immense. On the 2nd of August I am going away on a tour of some four months in England, Ireland, and Scotland. I shall read, during that time, not fewer than four or five times a week. It will be sharp work; but probably a certain musical clinking will come of it, which will mitigate the hardship.

At this present moment I am on my little Kentish freehold (*not* in top-boots, and not particularly prejudiced that I know of), looking on as pretty a view out of my study window as you will find in a long day's English ride. My little place is a grave red brick house (time of George the First, I suppose), which I have added to and stuck bits upon in all manner of ways, so that it is as pleasantly irregular, and as violently opposed to all architectural ideas, as the most hopeful man could possibly desire. It is on the summit of Gad's Hill. The robbery was committed before the door, on the man with the treasure, and Falstaff ran away from the identical spot of ground now covered by the room in which I write. A little rustic alehouse, called The Sir John Falstaff, is over the way—has been over the way, ever since, in honour of the event. Cobham Woods and Park are behind the house; the distant Thames in front; the Medway, with Rochester, and its old castle and cathedral, on one side. The whole stupendous property is on the old Dover Road, so when you come, come by the North Kent Railway (not the South-Eastern) to Strood or Higham, and I'll drive over to fetch you.

The blessed woods and fields have done me a world of good, and I am quite myself again.   The children are all as happy as children can be.   My eldest daughter, Mary, keeps house, with a state and gravity becoming that high position ; wherein she is assisted by her sister Katie, and by her aunt Georgina, who is, and always has been, like another sister.   Two big dogs, a bloodhound and a St. Bernard, direct from a convent of that name, where I think you once were, are their principal attendants in the green lanes.   These latter instantly untie the neckerchiefs of all tramps and prowlers who approach their presence, so that they wander about without any escort, and drive big horses in basket-phaetons through murderous bye-ways, and never come to grief.   They are very curious about your daughters, and send all kinds of loves to them and to Mrs. Cerjat, in which I heartily join.

You will have read in the papers that the Thames in London is most horrible.   I have to cross Waterloo or London Bridge to get to the railroad when I come down here, and I can certify that the offensive smells, even in that short whiff, have been of a most head-and-stomach-distending nature.   Nobody knows what is to be done ; at least everybody knows a plan, and everybody else knows it won't do ; in the meantime cartloads of chloride of lime are shot into the filthy stream, and do something I hope. You will know, before you get this, that the American telegraph line has parted again, at which most men are sorry, but very few surprised.   This is all the news, ex-cept that there is an Italian Opera at Drury Lane, price eighteen-pence to the pit, where Viardot, by far the greatest artist of them all, sings, and which is full when the dear opera can't let a box ; and except that the weather has been exceptionally hot, but is now quite cool. On the top of this hill it has been cold, actually cold at night, for more than a week past.

I am going over to Rochester to post this letter, and must write another to Townshend before I go. My dear Cerjat, I have written lightly enough, because I want you to know that I am becoming cheerful and hearty. God bless you ! I love you, and I know that you love me.

Ever your attached and affectionate.

[To Miss Hogarth.]

WEST HOE, PLYMOUTH, Thursday, Aug. 5th, 1858.

MY DEAREST GEORGY,

I received your letter this morning with the greatest pleasure, and read it with the utmost interest in all its domestic details.

We had a most wonderful night at Exeter. It is to be regretted that we cannot take the place again on our way back. It was a prodigious cram, and we turned away no end of people. But not only that, I think they were the finest audience I have ever read to. I don't think I ever read, in some respects, so well ; and I never beheld anything like the personal affection which they poured out upon me at the end. It was really a very remarkable sight, and I shall always look back upon it with pleasure.

Last night here was not so bright. There are quarrels of the strangest kind between the Plymouth people and the Stonehouse people. The room is at Stonehouse (Tracy says the wrong room ; there being a Plymouth room in this hotel, and he being a Plymouthite). We had a fair house, but not at all a great one. All the notabilities come this morning to "Little Dombey," for which we. have let one hundred and thirty stalls, which local admiration of local greatness considers very large. For "Mrs. Gamp and the Boots," to-night, we have also a very promising let. But the races are on, and there are two public balls to-night, and the yacht squadron are all at Cherbourg to boot. Arthur is of opinion that "Two Sixties" will do very well for us. I doubt the "Two Sixties" myself. *Mais nous verrons.*

The room is a very handsome one, but it is on the top of a windy and muddy hill, leading (literally) to nowhere ; and it looks (except that it is new and *mortary*) as if the subsidence of the waters after the Deluge might have left it where it is. I have to go right through the company to get to the platform. Big doors slam and resound when anybody comes in ; and all the company seem afraid of one another. Nevertheless they were a sensible audience last night, and much impressed and pleased.

Tracy is in the room (wandering about, and never finishing a sentence), and sends all manner of sea-loves to you and the dear girls. I send all manner of land-loves to you from myself, out of my heart of hearts, and also to my dear Plorn and the boys.

Arthur sends his kindest love. He knows only two characters. He is either always corresponding, like a Secretary of State, or he is transformed into a rout-furniture dealer of Rathbone Place, and drags forms about with the greatest violence, without his coat.

I have no time to add another word.

Ever, dearest Georgy, your most affectionate.

[*To Miss Dickens.*]

LONDON, *Saturday, Aug. 7th,* 1858.

MY DEAREST MAMEY,

The closing night at Plymouth was a very great scene, and the morning there was exceedingly good too. You will be glad to hear that at Clifton last night, a torrent of five hundred shillings bore Arthur away, pounded him against the wall, flowed on to the seats over his body, scratched him, and damaged his best dress suit. All to his unspeakable joy.

This is a very short letter, but I am going to the Burlington Arcade, desperately resolved to have all those wonderful instruments put into operation on my head, with a view to refreshing it.

Kindest love to Georgy and to all.

Ever your affectionate.

[*To Miss Dickens.*]

SHREWSBURY, *Thursday, Aug. 12th,* 1858.

A wonderful audience last night at Wolverhampton. If such a thing can be, they were even quicker and more intelligent than the audience I had in Edinburgh. They were so wonderfully good and were so much on the alert this morning by nine o'clock for another reading, that we are going back there at about our Bradford time. I never saw such people. And the local agent would take no money, and charge no expenses of his own.

This place looks what Plorn would call "ortily" dull. Local agent predicts, however, "great satisfaction to Mr. Dickens, and excellent attendance." I have just been to look at the hall, where everything was wrong, and where I have left Arthur making a platform for me out of dining-tables.

If he comes back in time, I am not quite sure but that he is himself going to write to Gad's Hill. We talk of coming up from Chester *in the night to-morrow, after the reading ;* and of showing our precious selves at an apparently impossibly early hour in the Gad's Hill breakfast-room on Saturday morning.

I have not felt the fatigue to any extent worth mentioning ; though I get, every night, into the most violent heats. We are going to dine at three o'clock (it wants a quarter now) and have not been here two hours, so I have seen nothing of Clement.

Tell Georgy with my love, that I read in the same room in which we acted, but at the end opposite to that where our stage was. We are not at the inn where the amateur company put up, but at The Lion, where the fair Miss Mitchell was lodged alone. We have the strangest little rooms (sitting-room and two bed-rooms all together), the ceilings of which I can touch with my hand. The windows bulge out over the street, as if they were little stern-windows in a ship. And a door opens out of the sitting-room on to a little open gallery with plants in it, where one leans over a queer old rail, and looks all downhill and slantwise at the crookedest black and yellow old houses, all manner of shapes except straight shapes. To get into this room we come through a china closet; and the man in laying the cloth has actually knocked down, in that repository, two geraniums and Napoleon Bonaparte.

I think that's all I have to say, except that at the Wolverhampton theatre they played " Oliver Twist " last night (Mr. Toole the Artful Dodger), " in consequence of the illustrious author honouring the town with his presence." We heard that the device succeeded very well, and that they got a good many people.

John's spirits have been equable and good since we rejoined him. Berry has always got something the matter with his digestion—seems to me the male gender of Maria Jolly, and ought to take nothing but Revalenta Arabica. Bottled ale is not to be got in these parts, and Arthur is thrown upon draught.

My dearest love to Georgy and to Katey, also to Marguerite. Also to all the boys and the noble Plorn.

Ever your affectionate Father.

[*To Miss Hogarth.*]

TAVISTOCK HOUSE, TAVISTOCK SQUARE, LONDON, W.C.,
Wednesday Morning, Aug. 18*th*, 1858.

I write this hurried line before starting, to report that

my cold is decidedly better, thank God (though still bad), and that I hope to be able to stagger through to-night. After dinner yesterday I began to recover my voice, and I think I sang half the Irish Melodies to myself, as I walked about to test it. I got home at half-past ten, and mustard-poulticed and barley-watered myself tremendously.

Love to the dear girls, and to all.

Ever affectionately.

[*To Miss Hogarth.*]

ADELPHI HOTEL, LIVERPOOL, *Friday Night, Aug. 20th,* 1858.

I received your welcome and interesting letter to-day, and I write you a very hurried and bad reply; but it is *after the reading*, and you will take the will for the deed under these trying circumstances, I know.

We have had a tremendous night; the largest house I have ever had since I first began—two thousand three hundred people. To-morrow afternoon, at three, I read again.

My cold has been oppressive, and is not yet gone. I have been very hard to sleep too, and last night I was all but sleepless. This morning I was very dull and seedy; but I got a good walk, and picked up again. It has been blowing all day, and I fear we shall have a sick passage over to Dublin to-morrow night.

Tell Mamie (with my dear love to her and Katie) that I

will write to her from Dublin—probably on Sunday. Tell her too that the stories she told me in her letter were not only capital in themselves, but *excellently told* too.

What Arthur's state has been to-night—he, John, Berry, and Boylett, all taking money and going mad together—you *cannot* imagine. They turned away hundreds, sold all the books, rolled on the ground of my room knee-deep in checks, and made a perfect pantomime of the whole thing. He has kept quite well, I am happy to say, and sends a hundred loves.

In great haste and fatigue.

Ever affectionately.

[*To Miss Dickens.*]

MORRISON'S HOTEL, DUBLIN, *Monday, Aug. 23rd*, 1858.

We had a nasty crossing here. We left Holyhead at one in the morning, and got here at six. Arthur was incessantly sick the whole way. I was not sick at all, but was in as healthy a condition otherwise as humanity need be. We are in a beautiful hotel. Our sitting-room is exactly like the drawing-room at the Peschiere in all its dimensions. I never saw two rooms so exactly resembling one another in their proportions. Our bedrooms too are excellent, and there are baths and all sorts of comforts.

The Lord Lieutenant is away, and the place looks to me as if its professional life were away too. Nevertheless, there are numbers of people in the streets. Somehow, I

hardly seem to think we are going to do enormously here ;
but I have scarcely any reason for supposing so (except
that a good many houses are shut up) ; and I *know* nothing about it, for Arthur is now gone to the agent and to
the room. The men came by boat direct from Liverpool.
They had a rough passage, were all ill, and did not get
here till noon yesterday. Donnybrook Fair, or what remains of it, is going on, within two or three miles of Dublin. They went out there yesterday in a jaunting-car, and
John described it to us at dinner-time (with his eyebrows
lifted up, and his legs well asunder), as " Johnny Brooks's
Fair ; " at which Arthur, who was drinking bitter ale,
nearly laughed himself to death. Berry is always unfortunate, and when I asked what had happened to Berry on
board the steamboat, it appeared that " an Irish gentleman
which was drunk, and fancied himself the captain, wanted
to knock Berry down."

I am surprised by finding this place very much larger
than I had supposed it to be. Its bye-parts are bad enough,
but cleaner, too, than I had supposed them to be, and certainly very much cleaner than the old town of Edinburgh.
The man who drove our jaunting-car yesterday hadn't a
piece in his coat as big as a penny roll, and had had his
hat on (apparently without brushing it) ever since he was
grown up. But he was remarkably intelligent and agreeable, with something to say about everything. For instance, when I asked him what a certain building was, he
didn't say " courts of law " and nothing else, but : " Av you
plase, sir, it's the foor coorts o' looyers, where Misther

O'Connell stood his trial wunst, ye'll remimber, sir, afore I tell ye of it." When we got into the Phœnix Park, he looked round him as if it were his own, and said: "THAT'S a park, sir, av yer plase." I complimented it, and he said : "Gintlemen tills me as they'r bin, sir, over Europe, and never see a park aqualling ov it. 'Tis eight mile roond, sir, ten mile and a half long, and in the month of May the hawthorn trees are as beautiful as brides with their white jewels on. Yonder's the vice-regal lodge, sir ; in them two corners lives the two sicretirries, wishing I was them, sir. There's air here, sir, av yer plase ! There's scenery here, sir ! There's mountains—thim, sir ! Yer coonsider it a park, sir ? It is that, sir ! "

You should have heard John in my bedroom this morning endeavouring to imitate a bath-man, who had resented his interference, and had said as to the shower-bath : " Yer'll not be touching *that*, young man. Divil a touch yer'll touch o' that insthrument, young man ! " It was more ridiculously unlike the reality than I can express to you, yet he was so delighted with his powers that he went off in the absurdest little gingerbeery giggle, backing into my portmanteau all the time.

My dear love to Katie and to Georgy, also to the noble Plorn and all the boys. I shall write to Katie next, and then to Aunty. My cold, I am happy to report, is very much better. I lay in the wet all night on deck, on board the boat, but am not as yet any the worse for it. Arthur was quite insensible when we got to Dublin, and stared at our luggage without in the least offering to claim it. He

left his kindest love for all before he went out. I will keep
the envelope open until he comes in.

Ever, my dearest Mamie,

Your most affectionate Father.

[*To Miss Hogarth.*]

MORRISON'S HOTEL, DUBLIN, *Wednesday, Aug. 25th*, 1858.

I begin my letter to you to-day, though I don't know
when I may send it off. We had a very good house last
night, after all, that is to say, a great rush of shillings and
good half-crowns, though the stalls were comparatively
few. For "Little Dombey," this morning, we have an
immense stall let—already more than two hundred—and
people are now fighting in the agent's shop to take more.
Through some mistake of our printer's, the evening reading
for this present Wednesday was dropped, in a great part of
the announcements, and the agent opened no plan for it.
I have therefore resolved not to have it at all. Arthur
Smith has waylaid me in all manner of ways, but I remain
obdurate. I am frightfully tired, and really relieved by
the prospect of an evening—overjoyed.

They were a highly excitable audience last night, but
they certainly did not comprehend—internally and intel-
lectually comprehend—"The Chimes" as a London audience do. I am quite sure of it. I very much doubt the
Irish capacity of receiving the pathetic ; but of their quickness as to the humorous there can be no doubt. I shall

see how they go along with Little Paul, in his death, presently.

While I was at breakfast this morning, a general officer was announced with great state—having a staff at the door—and came in, booted and plumed, and covered with Crimean decorations. It was Cunninghame, whom we knew in Genoa—then a captain. He was very hearty indeed, and came to ask me to dinner. Of course I couldn't go. Olliffe has a brother at Cork, who has just now (noon) written to me, proposing dinners and excursions in that neighbourhood which would fill about a week; I being there a day and a half, and reading three times. The work will be very severe here, and I begin to feel depressed by it. (By "here," I mean Ireland generally, please to observe.)

We meant, as I said in a letter to Katie, to go to Queenstown yesterday and bask on the seashore. But there is always so much to do that we couldn't manage it after all. We expect a tremendous house to-morrow night as well as to-day; and Arthur is at the present instant up to his eyes in business (and seats), and, between his regret at losing to-night, and his desire to make the room hold twice as many as it *will* hold, is half distracted. I have become a wonderful Irishman—must play an Irish part some day—and his only relaxation is when I enact "John and the Boots," which I consequently do enact all day long. The papers are full of remarks upon my white tie, and describe it as being of enormous size, which is a wonderful delusion, because, as you very well know, it is a small tie. Gener-

ally, I am happy to report, the Emerald press is in favour
of my appearance, and likes my eyes. But one gentleman
comes out with a letter at Cork, wherein he says that
although only forty-six I look like an old man. *He* is a
rum customer, I think.

The Rutherfords are living here, and wanted me to dine
with them, which, I needn't say, could not be done; all
manner of people have called, but I have seen only two.
John has given it up altogether as to rivalry with the Boots,
and did not come into my room this morning at all. Boots
appeared triumphant and alone. He was waiting for me
at the hotel-door last night. " Whaa't sart of a hoose,
sur ? " he asked me. " Capital." " The Lard be praised
fur the 'onor o' Dooblin ! "

Arthur buys bad apples in the streets and brings them
home and doesn't eat them, and then I am obliged to put
them in the balcony because they make the room smell
faint. Also he meets countrymen with honeycomb on their
heads, and leads them (by the buttonhole when they have
one) to this gorgeous establishment and requests the bar
to buy honeycomb for his breakfast ; then it stands upon
the sideboard uncovered and the flies fall into it. He buys
owls, too, and castles, and other horrible objects, made in
bog-oak (that material which is not appreciated at Gad's
Hill) ; and he is perpetually snipping pieces out of newspapers and sending them all over the world. While I am
reading he conducts the correspondence, and his great
delight is to show me seventeen or eighteen letters when I
come, exhausted, into the retiring-place. Berry has not

got into any particular trouble for forty-eight hours, except that he is all over boils. I have prescribed yeast, but ineffectually. It is indeed a sight to see him and John sitting in pay-boxes, and surveying Ireland out of pigeon-holes.

Same Evening before Bed-time.

Everybody was at "Little Dombey" to-day, and although I had some little difficulty to work them up in consequence of the excessive crowding of the place, and the difficulty of shaking the people into their seats, the effect was unmistakable and profound. The crying was universal, and they were extraordinarily affected. There is no doubt we could stay here a week with that one reading, and fill the place every night. Hundreds of people have been there to-night, under the impression that it would come off again. It was a most decided and complete success.

Arthur has been imploring me to stop here on the Friday after Limerick, and read "Little Dombey" again. But I have positively said " No." The work is too hard. It is not like doing it in one easy room, and always the same room. With a different place every night, and a different audience with its own peculiarity every night, it is a tremendous strain. I was sick of it to-day before I began, then got myself into wonderful train.

Here follows a dialogue (but it requires imitation), which I had yesterday morning with a little boy of the house—

landlord's son, I suppose—about Plorn's age. I am sitting on the sofa writing, and find him sitting beside me.

INIMITABLE.   Holloa, old chap.

YOUNG IRELAND.   Hal-loo!

INIMITABLE (*in his delightful way*).   What a nice old fellow you are.   I am very fond of little boys.

YOUNG IRELAND.   Air ye?   Ye'r right.

INIMITABLE.   What do you learn, old fellow?

YOUNG IRELAND (*very intent on Inimitable, and always childish, except in his brogue*).   I lairn wureds of three sillibils, and wureds of two sillibils, and wureds of one sillibil.

INIMITABLE (*gaily*).   Get out, you humbug!   You learn only words of one syllable.

YOUNG IRELAND (*laughs heartily*).   You may say that it is mostly wureds of one sillibil.

INIMITABLE.   Can you write?

YOUNG IRELAND.   Not yet.   Things comes by deegrays.

INIMITABLE.   Can you cipher?

YOUNG IRELAND (*very quickly*).   Wha'at's that?

INIMITABLE.   Can you make figures?

YOUNG IRELAND.   I can make a nought, which is not asy, being roond.

INIMITABLE.   I say, old boy, wasn't it you I saw on Sunday morning in the hall, in a soldier's cap?   You know—in a soldier's cap?

YOUNG IRELAND (*cogitating deeply*).   Was it a very good cap?

INIMITABLE.   Yes.

YOUNG IRELAND.   Did it fit unkommon?

INIMITABLE.   Yes.

YOUNG IRELAND.   Dat was me!

There are two stupid old louts at the room, to show people into their places, whom John calls "them two old Paddies," and of whom he says, that he "never see nothing like them (snigger) hold idiots" (snigger).   They bow and walk backwards before the grandees, and our men hustle them while they are doing it.

We walked out last night, with the intention of going to the theatre ; but the Piccolomini establishment (they were doing the "Lucia ") looked so horribly like a very bad jail, and the Queen's looked so blackguardly, that we came back again, and went to bed. I seem to be always either in a railway carriage, or reading, or going to bed. I get so knocked up, whenever I have a minute to remember it, that then I go to bed as a matter of course.

I send my love to the noble Plorn, and to all the boys. To dear Mamie and Katie, and to yourself of course, in the first degree. I am looking forward to the last Irish reading on Thursday, with great impatience. But when we shall have turned this week, once knocked off Belfast, I shall see land, and shall (like poor Timber in the days of old) "keep up a good heart." I get so wonderfully hot every night in my dress clothes, that they positively won't dry in the short interval they get, and I have been obliged to write to Doudney's to make me another suit, that I may have a constant change.

Ever, my dearest Georgy, most affectionately.

[*To Miss Dickens.*]

BELFAST, *Saturday, Aug.* 28*th*, 1858.

When I went down to the Rotunda at Dublin on Thursday night, I said to Arthur, who came rushing at me : "You needn't tell me. I know all about it." The moment I had come out of the door of the hotel (a mile off), I had come against the stream of people turned away. I had struggled against it to the room. There, the crowd in all the lobbies and passages was so great, that I had a difficulty in getting in. They had broken all the glass in the pay-boxes. They had offered frantic prices for stalls. Eleven bank-notes were thrust into that pay-box (Arthur saw them) at one time, for eleven stalls. Our men were flattened against walls, and squeezed against beams. Ladies stood all night with their chins against my· platform. Other ladies sat all night upon my steps. You never saw such a sight. And the reading went tremendously ! It is much to be regretted that we troubled ourselves to go anywhere else in Ireland. We turned away people enough to make immense houses for a week.

We arrived here yesterday at two. The room will not hold more than from eighty to ninety pounds. The same scene was repeated with the additional feature, that the people are much rougher here than in Dublin, and that there was a very great uproar at the opening of the doors, which, the police in attendance being quite inefficient and only looking on, it was impossible to check. Arthur was in the deepest misery because shillings got into stalls, and half-crowns got into shillings, and stalls got nowhere, and there was immense confusion. It ceased, however, the moment I showed myself ; and all went most brilliantly, in spite of a great piece of the cornice of the ceiling falling with a great crash within four or five inches of the head of a young lady on my platform (I was obliged to have people there), and in spite of my gas suddenly going out at the time of the game of forfeits at Scrooge's nephew's, through some Belfastian gentleman accidentally treading on the flexible pipe, and needing to be relighted.

We shall not get to Cork before mid-day on Monday ; it being difficult to get from here on a Sunday. We hope to be able to start away to-morrow morning to see the Giant's Causeway (some sixteen miles off), and in that case we shall sleep at Dublin to-morrow night, leaving here by the train at half-past three in the afternoon. Dublin, you must understand, is on the way to Cork. This is a fine place, surrounded by lofty hills. The streets are very wide, and the place is very prosperous. The whole ride from Dublin here is through a very picturesque and various country ; and the amazing thing is, that it is all particularly neat and orderly, and that the houses (outside at all events) are all brightly whitewashed and remarkably clean. I want to climb one of the neighbouring hills before this morning's "Dombey." I am now waiting for Arthur, who has gone to the bank to remit his last accumulation of treasure to London.

Our men are rather indignant with the Irish crowds, because in the struggle they don't sell books, and because, in the pressure, they can't force a way into the room afterwards to sell them. They are deeply interested in the success, however, and are as zealous and ardent as possible. I shall write to Katie next. Give her my best love, and kiss the darling Plorn for me, and give my love to all the boys.

Ever, my dearest Mamie,

Your most affectionate Father.

[*To Miss Hogarth.*]

MORRISON'S HOTEL, DUBLIN, *Sunday Night, Aug. 29th,* 1858.

I am so delighted to find your letter here to-night (eleven o'clock), and so afraid that, in the wear and tear of this strange life, I have written to Gad's Hill in the wrong order, and have not written to you, as I should, that I resolve to write this before going to bed. You will find it a wretchedly stupid letter ; but you may imagine, my dearest girl, that I am tired.

The success at Belfast has been equal to the success here. Enormous ! We turned away half the town. I think them a better audience, on the whole, than Dublin ; and the personal affection there was something overwhelming. I wish you and the dear girls could have seen the people look at me in the street ; or heard them ask me, as I hurried to the hotel after reading last night, to "do me the honour to shake hands, Misther Dickens, and God bless you, sir ; not ounly for the light you've been to me this night, but for the light you've been in mee house, sir (and God love your face), this many a year." Every night, by-the-bye, since I have been in Ireland, the ladies have beguiled John out of the bouquet from my coat. And yesterday morning, as I had showered the leaves from my geranium in reading "Little Dombey," they mounted the platform, after I was gone, and picked them all up as keepsakes !

I have never seen *men* go in to cry so undisguisedly as they did at that reading yesterday afternooh. They made no attempt whatever to hide it, and certainly cried more than the women. As to the " Boots" at night, and " Mrs. Gamp " too, it was just one roar with me and them ; for they made me laugh so that sometimes I *could not* compose my face to go on.

You must not let the new idea of poor dear Landor efface the former image of the fine old man. I wouldn't blot him out, in his tender gallantry, as he sat upon that bed at Forster's that night, for a million of wild mistakes at eighty years of age.

I hope to be at Tavistock House before five o'clock next Saturday morning, and to lie in bed half the day, and come home by the 10.50 on Sunday.

Tell the girls that Arthur and I have each ordered at Belfast a trim, sparkling, slap-up *Irish jaunting-car ! ! !* I flatter myself we shall astonish the Kentish people. It is the oddest carriage in the world, and you are always falling off. But it is gay and bright in the highest degree. Wonderfully Neapolitan.

What with a sixteen mile ride before we left Belfast, and a sea-beach walk, and a two o'clock dinner, and a seven hours' railway ride since, I am—as we say here— " a thrifle weary." But I really am in wonderful force, considering the work. For which I am, as I ought to be, very thankful.

Arthur was exceedingly unwell last night—could not cheer up at all. He was so very unwell that he left the hall (!) and became invisible after my five minutes' rest. I found him at the hotel in a jacket and slippers, and with a hot bath just ready. He was in the last stage of prostration. The local agent was with me, and proposed that he (the wretched Arthur) should go to his office and balance the accounts then and there. He went, in the jacket and slippers, and came back in twenty minutes, *perfectly well*, in consequence of the admirable balance. He is now sitting opposite to me ON THE BAG OF SILVER, forty pounds (it must be dreadfully hard), writing to Boulogne.

I suppose it is clear that the next letter I write is Katie's. Either from Cork or from Limerick, it shall report further. At Limerick I read in the theatre, there being no other place.

Best love to Mamie and Katie, and dear Plorn, and all the boys left when this comes to Gad's Hill; also to my dear good Anne, and her little woman.

Ever affectionately.

[To Mr. W. Wilkie Collins.]

GAD'S HILL PLACE, HIGHAM BY ROCHESTER, KENT,
Monday, Sept. 6th, 1858.

MY DEAR WILKIE,

First, let me report myself here for something less than eight-and-forty hours. I come last (and direct—a pretty hard journey) from Limerick. The success in Ireland has been immense.

The work is very hard, sometimes overpowering; but I am none the worse for it, and arrived here quite fresh.

Secondly, will you let me recommend the enclosed letter from Wigan, as the groundwork of a capital article, in your way, for H. W. ? There is not the least objection to a plain reference to him, or to Phelps, to whom the same thing happened a year or two ago, near Islington, in the case of a clever and capital little daughter of his. I think it a capital opportunity for a discourse on gentility, with a glance at those other schools which advertise that the " sons of gentlemen only " are admitted, and a just recognition of the greater liberality of our public schools. There are tradesmen's sons at Eton, and Charles Kean was at Eton, and Macready (also an actor's son) was at Rugby. Some such title as " Scholastic Flunkeydom," or anything infinitely contemptuous, would help out the meaning. Surely such a schoolmaster must swallow all the silver forks that the pupils are expected to take when they come, and are not expected to take away with them when they go. And of course he could not exist, unless he had flunkey customers by the dozen.

Secondly—no, this is thirdly now—about the Christmas number. I have arranged so to stop my readings, as to be available for it on *the 15th of November*, which will leave me time to write a good article, if I clear my way to one. Do you see your way to our making a Christmas number of this idea that I am going very briefly to hint? Some disappointed person, man or woman, prematurely disgusted with the world, for some reason or no reason (the person should be young, I think) retires to an old lonely house, or an old lonely mill, or anything you like, with one attendant, resolved to shut out the world, and hold no

communion with it. The one attendant sees the absurdity of the idea, pretends to humour it, but really thus to
slaughter it. Everything that happens, everybody that
comes near, every breath of human interest that floats into
the old place from the village, or the heath, or the four
cross-roads near which it stands, and from which belated
travellers stray into it, shows beyond mistake that you
can't shut out the world ; that you are in it, to be of it ;
that you get into a false position the moment you try to
sever yourself from it ; and that you must mingle with it,
and make the best of it, and make the best of yourself into
the bargain.

If we could plot out a way of doing this together, I
would not be afraid to take my part. If we could not,
could we plot out a way of doing it, and taking in stories
by other hands ? If we could not do either (but I think
we could), shall we fall back upon a round of stories
again ? That I would rather not do, if possible. Will
you think about it ?

And can you come and dine at Tavistock House *on
Monday, the 20th September, at half-past five?* I purpose
being at home there with the girls that day.

Answer this, according to my printed list for the week.
I am off to Huddersfield on Wednesday morning.

I think I will now leave off ; merely adding that I have
got a splendid brogue (it really is exactly like the people),
and that I think of coming out as the only legitimate successor of poor Power.

Ever, my dear Wilkie, affectionately yours.

[*To Miss Mary Boyle.*]

STATION HOTEL, YORK, *Friday, Sept. 10th*, 1858.

DEAREST MEERY,

First let me tell you that all the magicians and spirits in your employ have fulfilled the instructions of their wondrous mistress to admiration. Flowers have fallen in my path wherever I have trod ; and when they rained upon me at Cork I was more amazed than you ever saw me.

Secondly, receive my hearty and loving thanks for that same. (Excuse a little Irish in the turn of that sentence, but I can't help it).

Thirdly, I have written direct to Mr. Boddington, explaining that I am bound to be in Edinburgh on the day when he courteously proposes to do me honour.

I really cannot tell you how truly and tenderly I feel your letter, and how gratified I am by its contents. Your truth and attachment are always so precious to me that I can*not* get my heart out on my sleeve to show it you. It is like a child, and, at the sound of some familiar voices, " goes and hides."

You know what an affection I have for Mrs. Watson, and how happy it made me to see her again—younger, much, than when I first knew her in Switzerland.

God bless you always !

Ever affectionately yours.

VOL. II.—4*

[*To Miss Hogarth.*]

Royal Hotel, Scarborough, *Sunday, Sept.* 11*th*, 1858.
My dearest Georgy,

We had a very fine house indeed at York. All kinds of applications have been made for another reading there, and no doubt it would be exceedingly productive ; but it cannot be done. At Harrogate yesterday ; the queerest place, with the strangest people in it, leading the oddest lives of dancing, newspaper reading, and tables d'hôte. The piety of York obliging us to leave that place for this at six this morning, and there being no night train from Harrogate, we had to engage a special engine. We got to bed at one, and were up again before five ; which, after yesterday's fatigues, leaves me a little worn out at this present.

I have no accounts of this place as yet, nor have I received any letter here. But the post of this morning is not yet delivered, I believe. We have a charming room, overlooking the sea. Leech is here (living within a few doors), with the partner of his bosom, and his young family. I write at ten in the morning, having been here two hours ; and you will readily suppose that I have not seen him.

Of news, I have not the faintest breath. I seem to have been doing nothing all my life but riding in railway-carriages and reading. The railway of the morning brought us through Castle Howard, and under the woods of Easthorpe, and then just below Malton Abbey, where I went to poor Smithson's funeral. It was a most lovely morning, and, tired as I was, I couldn't sleep for looking out of window.

Yesterday, at Harrogate, two circumstances occurred which gave Arthur great delight. Firstly, he chafed his legs sore with his black bag of silver. Secondly, the landlord asked him as a favour, " If he could oblige him with a little silver." He obliged him directly with some forty pounds' worth ; and I suspect the landlord to have repented of having approached the subject. After the reading last night we walked over the moor to the railway, three miles, leaving our men to follow with the luggage in a light cart. They passed us just short of the railway, and John was making the night hideous and terrifying the sleeping country, by *playing the horn* in prodigiously horrible and unmusical blasts.

My dearest love, of course, to the dear girls, and to the noble Plorn. Apropos of children, there was one gentleman at the " Little Dombey " yesterday morning, who exhibited, or rather concealed, the profoundest grief. After crying a good deal without hiding it, he covered his face with both his hands, and laid it down on the back of the seat before him, and really shook with emotion. He was not in mourning, but I supposed him to have lost some child in old time. There was a remarkably good fellow of thirty or so, too, who found something so very ludicrous in " Toots," that he *could not* compose himself at all, but laughed until he sat wiping his eyes with his handkerchief. And whenever he felt " Toots " coming again he began to laugh and wipe his eyes afresh, and when he came he gave a kind of cry, as if it were too much for him. It was uncommonly droll, and made me laugh heartily.

Ever, dear Georgy, your most affectionate.

[*To Miss Dickens.*]

SCARBOROUGH ARMS, LEEDS, *Wednesday, Sept. 15th,* 1858.

MY DEAREST MAMIE,

I have added a pound to the cheque. I would recommend your seeing the poor railway man again and giving him ten shillings, and telling him to let you see him again in about a week. If he be then still unable to lift weights and handle heavy things, I would then give him another ten shillings, and so on.

Since I wrote to Georgy from Scarborough, we have had, thank God, nothing but success. The Hull people (not generally considered excitable, even on their own showing) were so enthusiastic, that we were obliged to promise to go back there for two readings. I have positively resolved not to lengthen out the time of my tour, so we are now arranging to drop some small places, and substitute Hull again and York again. But you will perhaps have heard this in the main from Arthur. I know he wrote to you after the reading last night. This place I have always doubted, knowing that we should come here when it was recovering from the double excitement of the festival and the Queen. But there is a very large hall let indeed, and the prospect of to-night consequently looks bright.

Arthur told you, I suppose, that he had his shirt-front and waistcoat torn off last night ? He was perfectly enraptured in consequence. Our men got so knocked about that he gave them five shillings apiece on the spot. John passed several minutes upside down against the wall, with his head amongst the people's boots. He came out of the difficulty in an exceedingly touzled condition, and with his face much flushed. For all this, and their being packed as you may conceive they would be packed, they settled down the instant I went in, and never wavered in the closest attention for an instant. It was a very high room, and required a great effort.

Oddly enough, I slept in this house three days last year with Wilkie. Arthur has the bedroom I occupied then, and I have one two doors from it, and Gordon has the one between. Not only is he still with us, but he *has* talked of going on to Manchester, going on to London, and coming back with us to Darlington next Tuesday ! ! !

These streets look like a great circus with the season just finished. All sorts of garish triumphal arches were put up for the Queen, and they have got smoky, and have been looked out of countenance by the sun, and are blistered and patchy, and half up and half down, and are hideous to behold. Spiritless men (evidently drunk for some time in the royal honour) are slowly removing them, and on the whole it is more like the clearing away of " The Frozen Deep " at Tavistock House than anything within your knowledge—with the exception that we are not in the least sorry, as we were then. Vague ideas are in Arthur's head that when we come back to Hull, we are to come here, and are to have the Town Hall (a beautiful building), and read to the million. I can't say yet. That depends. I remember that when I was here before (I came from Rockingham to make a speech), I thought them a dull and slow audience. I hope I may have been mistaken. I never saw better audiences than the Yorkshire audiences generally.

I am so perpetually at work or asleep, that I have not a scrap of news. I saw the Leech family at Scarboro', both in my own house (that is to say, hotel) and in theirs. They were not at either reading. Scarboro' is gay and pretty, and I think Gordon had an idea that we were always at some such place.

Kiss the darling Plorn for me, and give him my love; dear Katie too, giving her the same. I feel sorry that I cannot get down to Gad's Hill this next time, but I shall look forward to our being there with Georgy, after Scotland. Tell the servants that I remember them, and hope they will live with us many years.

                Ever, my dearest Mamie,
                        Your most affectionate Father.

[*To Miss Hogarth.*]

KING'S HEAD, SHEFFIELD, *Friday, Sept. 17th,* 1858.

I write you a few lines to Tavistock House, thinking you may not be sorry to find a note from me there on your arrival from Gad's Hill.

Halifax was too small for us. I never saw such **an au-**dience though. They were really worth reading to for nothing, though I didn't do exactly that. It is as horrible a place as I ever saw, I think.

The run upon the tickets here is so immense that Arthur is obliged to get great bills out, signifying that no more can be sold. It will be by no means easy to get into the place the numbers who have already paid. It is the hall we acted in. Crammed to the roof and the passages. We must come back here towards the end of October, and are again altering the list and striking out small places.

The trains are so strange and unintelligible in this part of the country that we were obliged to leave Halifax at eight this morning, and breakfast on the road—at Huddersfield again, where we had an hour's wait. Wills was in attendance on the platform, and took me (here at Sheffield, I mean) out to Frederick Lehmann's house to see Mrs. Wills. She looked pretty much the same as ever, I thought, and was taking care of a very pretty little boy. The house and grounds are as nice as anything *can* be in this smoke. A heavy thunderstorm is passing over the town, and it is raining hard too.

This is a stupid letter, my dearest Georgy, but I write in a hurry, and in the thunder and lightning, and with the crowd of to-night before me.

Ever most affectionately.

[*To Miss Hogarth.*]

STATION HOTEL, NEWCASTLE-ON-TYNE,
Sunday, Sept. 26th, 1858.

EXTRACT.

The girls (as I have no doubt they have already told you for themselves) arrived here in good time yesterday, and in very fresh condition.   They persisted in going to the room last night, though I had arranged for their remaining quiet.

We have done a vast deal here.   I suppose you know that we are going to Berwick, and that we mean to sleep there and go on to Edinburgh on Monday morning, arriving there before noon ?   If it be as fine to-morrow as it is to-day, the girls will see the coast piece of railway between Berwick and Edinburgh to great advantage.   I was anxious that they should, because that kind of pleasure is really almost the only one they are likely to have in their present trip.

Stanfield and Roberts are in Edinburgh, and the Scottish Royal Academy gave them a dinner on Wednesday, to which I was very pressingly invited.   But, of course, my going was impossible.   I read twice that day.

Remembering what you do of Sunderland, you will be surprised that our profit there was very considerable.   I read in a beautiful new theatre, and (I thought to myself) quite wonderfully.   Such an audience I never beheld for rapidity and enthusiasm.   The room in which we acted (converted into a theatre afterwards) was burnt to the ground a year or two ago. We found the hotel, so bad in our time, really good. I walked from Durham to Sunderland, and from Sunderland to Newcastle.

Don't you think, as we shall be at home at eleven in the forenoon this day fortnight, that it will be best for you and Plornish to come to Tavistock House for that Sunday, and for us all to go down to Gad's Hill next day? My best love to the noble Plornish. If he is quite reconciled to the postponement of his trousers, I should like to behold his first appearance in them. But, if not, as he is such a good fellow, I think it would be a pity to disappoint and try him.

And now, my dearest Georgy, I think I have said all I have to say before I go out for a little air. I had a very hard day yesterday, and am tired.

Ever your most affectionate.

[To Mr. John Forster.]

TAVISTOCK HOUSE, TAVISTOCK SQUARE, LONDON,
Sunday, Oct. 10th, 1858.

MY DEAR FORSTER,

As to the truth of the readings, I cannot tell you what the demonstrations of personal regard and respect are. How the densest and most uncomfortably-packed crowd will be hushed in an instant when I show my face. How the youth of colleges, and the old men of business in the town, seem equally unable to get near enough to me when they cheer me away at night. How common people and gentlefolks will stop me in the streets and say : " Mr.

Dickens, will you let me touch the hand that has filled my home with so many friends?" And if you saw the mothers, and fathers, and sisters, and brothers in mourning, who invariably come to "Little Dombey," and if you studied the wonderful expression of comfort and reliance with which they hang about me, as if I had been with them, all kindness and delicacy, at their own little death-bed, you would think it one of the strangest things in the world.

As to the mere effect, of course I don't go on doing the thing so often without carefully observing myself and the people too in every little thing, and without (in consequence) greatly improving in it.

At Aberdeen, we were crammed to the street twice in one day. At Perth (where I thought when I arrived there literally could be nobody to come), the nobility came posting in from thirty miles round, and the whole town came and filled an immense hall. As to the effect, if you had seen them after Lilian died, in "The Chimes," or when Scrooge woke and talked to the boy outside the window, I doubt if you would ever have forgotten it. And at the end of "Dombey," yesterday afternoon, in the cold light of day, they all got up, after a short pause, gentle and simple, and thundered and waved their hats with that astonishing heartiness and fondness for me, that for the first time in all my public career they took me completely off my legs, and I saw the whole eighteen hundred of them reel on one side as if a shock from without had shaken the hall.

The dear girls have enjoyed themselves immensely, and their trip has been a great success. I hope I told you (but I forget whether I did or no) how splendidly Newcastle* came out. I am reminded of Newcastle at the moment because they joined me there.

I am anxious to get to the end of my readings, and to be at home again, and able to sit down and think in my own study. But the fatigue, though sometimes very great indeed, hardly tells upon me at all. And although all our people, from Smith downwards, have given in, more or less, at times, I have never been in the least unequal to the work, though sometimes sufficiently disinclined for it. My kindest and best love to Mrs. Forster.

Ever affectionately.

[*To Miss Dickens.*]

ROYAL HOTEL, DERBY, *Friday, Oct. 22nd*, 1858.

MY DEAREST MAMIE,

I am writing in a very poor condition ; I have a bad cold all over me, pains in my back and limbs, and a very sensitive and uncomfortable throat. There was a great draught up some stone steps near me last night, and I daresay that caused it.

The weather on my first two nights at Birmingham was so intolerably bad—it blew hard, and never left off raining for one single moment—that the houses were not what

---

* The birthplace of Mr. Forster.

they otherwise would have been. On the last night the weather cleared, and we had a grand house.

Last night at Nottingham was almost, if not quite, the most amazing we have had. It is not a very large place, and the room is by no means a very large one, but three hundred and twenty stalls were let, and all the other tickets were sold.

Here we have two hundred and twenty stalls let for to-night, and the other tickets are gone in proportion. It is a pretty room, but not large.

I have just been saying to Arthur that if there is not a large let for York, I would rather give it up, and get Monday at Gad's Hill. We have telegraphed to know. If the answer comes (as I suppose it will) before post time, I will tell you in a postscript what we decide to do. Coming to London in the night of to-morrow (Saturday), and having to see Mr. Ouvry on Sunday, and having to start for York early on Monday, I fear I should not be able to get to Gad's Hill at all. You won't expect me till you see me.

Arthur and I have considered Plornish's joke in all the immense number of aspects in which it presents itself to reflective minds. We have come to the conclusion that it is the best joke ever made. Give the dear boy my love, and the same to Georgy, and the same to Katey, and take the same yourself. Arthur (excessively low and inarticulate) mutters that he " unites."

[We knocked up Boylett, Berry, and John so frightfully yesterday, by tearing the room to pieces and altogether reversing it, as late as four o'clock, that we gave them a supper last night.   They shine all over to-day, as if it had been entirely composed of grease.]

Ever, my dearest Mamie,   .

Your most affectionate Father.

[*To Miss Hogarth.*]

WOLVERHAMPTON, *Wednesday, Nov. 3rd*, 1858.

Little Leamington came out in the most amazing manner yesterday—turned away hundreds upon hundreds of people.   They are represented as the dullest and worst of audiences.   I found them very good indeed, even in the morning.

There awaited me at the hotel, a letter from the Rev. Mr. Young, Wentworth Watson's tutor, saying that Mrs. Watson wished her boy to shake hands with me, and that he would bring him in the evening.   I expected him at the hotel before the readings.   But he did not come.   He spoke to John about it in the room at night. The crowd and confusion, however, were very great, and I saw nothing of him.   In his letter he said that Mrs. Watson was at Paris on her way home, and would be at Brighton at the end of this week.   I suppose I shall see her there at the end of next week.

We find a let of two hundred stalls here, which is very large for this place.   The evening being fine too, and blue being to be seen in the sky beyond the smoke, we expect to have a very full hall.   Tell Mamey and Katey that if they had been with us on the railway to-day between Leamington and this place, they would have seen (though it is only an hour and ten minutes by the express) fires and smoke indeed. We came through a part of the Black Country that you know, and it looked at its blackest. All the furnaces seemed in full blast, and all the coal-pits to be working.

It is market-day here, and the ironmasters are standing out in the street (where they always hold high change), making such an iron hum and buzz, that they confuse me horribly. In addition, there is a bellman announcing something—not the readings, I beg to say—and there is an excavation being made in the centre of the open place, for a statue, or a pump, or a lamp-post, or something or other, round which all the Wolverhampton boys are yelling and struggling.

And here is Arthur, begging to have dinner at half-past three instead of four, because he foresees "a wiry evening" in store for him. Under which complication of distractions, to which a waitress with a tray at this moment adds herself, I sink, and leave off.

My best love to the dear girls, and to the noble Plorn, and to you. Marguerite and Ellen Stone not forgotten. All yesterday and to-day I have been doing everything to the tune of :

> And the day is dark and dreary.

Ever, dearest Georgy,
Your most affectionate and faithful.

P.S.—I hope the brazier is intolerably hot, and half stifles all the family. Then, and not otherwise, I shall think it in satisfactory work.

[*To Rev. James White.*]

TAVISTOCK HOUSE, TAVISTOCK SQUARE, LONDON, W.C.,
Friday, Nov. 5th, 1858.

MY DEAR WHITE,

May I entreat you to thank Mr. Carter very earnestly and kindly in my name, for his proffered hospitality ; and, further, to explain to him that since my readings began, I have known them to be incompatible with all social enjoyments, and have neither set foot in a friend's house nor sat down to a friend's table in any one of all the many places I have been to, but have rigidly kept myself to my hotels. To this resolution I must hold until the last. There is not the least virtue in it. It is a matter of stern necessity, and I submit with the worst grace possible.

Will you let me know, either at Southampton or Portsmouth, whether any of you, and how many of you, if any, are coming over, so that Arthur Smith may reserve good seats ? Tell Lotty I hope she does not contemplate coming to the morning reading ; I always hate it so myself.

Mary and Katey are down at Gad's Hill with Georgy and Plornish, and they have Marguerite Power and Ellen Stone staying there. I am sorry to say that even my benevolence descries no prospect of their being able to come to my native place.

On Saturday week, the 13th, my tour, please God, ends. My best love to Mrs. White, and to Lotty, and to Clara.

Ever, my dear White, affectionately yours.

[*To Mr. Frank Stone, A.R.A.*]

Tavistock House, Tavistock Square, London, W.C.,
Monday, Dec. 13th, 1858.

MY DEAR STONE,

Many thanks for these discourses. They are very good, I think, as expressing what many men have felt and thought ; otherwise not specially remarkable. They have one fatal mistake, which is a canker at the foot of their ever being widely useful. Half the misery and hypocrisy of the Christian world arises (as I take it) from a stubborn determination to refuse the New Testament as a sufficient guide in itself, and to force the Old Testament into alliance with it—whereof comes all manner of camel-swallowing and of gnat-straining. But so to resent this miserable error, or to (by any implication) depreciate the divine goodness and beauty of the New Testament, is to commit even a worse error. And to class Jesus Christ with Mahomet is simply audacity and folly. I might as well hoist myself on to a high platform, to inform my disciples that the lives of King George the Fourth and of King Alfred the Great belonged to one and the same category.

Ever affectionately.

[*To Mr. B. W. Procter.*]

TAVISTOCK HOUSE, *Sunday, Dec. 18th,* 1858.

MY DEAR PROCTER,

A thousand thanks for the little song. I am charmed with it, and shall be delighted to brighten "Household Words" with such a wise and genial light. I no more believe that your poetical faculty has gone by, than I believe that you have yourself passed to the better land. You and it will travel thither in company, rely upon it. So I still hope to hear more of the trade-songs, and to learn that the blacksmith has hammered out no end of iron into good fashion of verse, like a cunning workman, as I know him of old to be.

Very faithfully yours, my dear Procter.

1859.

NARRATIVE.

DURING the winter, Charles Dickens was living at Tavistock House, removing to Gad's Hill for the summer early in June, and returning to London in November. At this time a change was made in his weekly journal. "Household Words" became absolutely his own—Mr. Wills being his partner and editor, as before—and was "incorporated with 'All the Year Round,'" under which title it was known thenceforth. The office was still in Wellington Street, but in a different house. The first number with the new name appeared on the 30th April, and it contained the opening of "A Tale of Two Cities."

The first letter which follows shows that a proposal for

VOL. II.—5

a series of readings in America had already been made to him. It was carefully considered and abandoned for the time. But the proposal was constantly renewed, and the idea never wholly relinquished for many years before he actually decided on making so distant a " reading tour."

Mr. Procter contributed to the early numbers of " All the Year Round " some very spirited "Songs of the Trades." We give notes from Charles Dickens to the veteran poet, both in the last year, and in this year, expressing his strong approval of them.

The letter and two notes to Mr. (afterwards Sir Antonio) Panizzi, for which we are indebted to Mr. Louis Fagan, one of Sir A. Panizzi's executors, show the warm sympathy and interest which he always felt for the cause of Italian liberty, and for the sufferings of the State prisoners who at this time took refuge in England.

We give a little note to the dear friend and companion of Charles Dickens's daughters, " Lotty " White, because it is a pretty specimen of his writing, and because the young girl, who is playfully " commanded " to get well and strong, died early in July of this year. She was, at the time this note was written, first attacked with the illness which was fatal to all her sisters. Mamie and Kate Dickens went from Gad's Hill to Bonchurch to pay a last visit to their friend, and he writes to his eldest daughter there. Also we give notes of loving sympathy and condolence to the bereaved father and mother.

In the course of this summer Charles Dickens was not well, and went for a week to his old favourite, Broadstairs —where Mr. Wilkie Collins and his brother, Mr. Charles Allston Collins, were staying—for sea-air and change, preparatory to another reading tour, in England only. His letter from Peterborough to Mr. Frank Stone, giving him an account of a reading at Manchester (Mr. Stone's native town), was one of the last ever addressed to that affectionate friend, who died very suddenly, to the great grief of Charles Dickens, in November. The letter to Mr. Thomas Longman, which closes this year, was one of introduction to that gentleman of young Marcus Stone, then just beginning his career as an artist, and to whom the premature death of his father made it doubly desirable that he should have powerful helping hands.

Charles Dickens refers, in a letter to Mrs. Watson, to his portrait by Mr. Frith, which was finished at the end of 1858. It was painted for Mr. Forster, and is now in the "Forster Collection" at South Kensington Museum.

The Christmas number of this year, again written by several hands as well as his own, was "The Haunted House." In November, his story of "A Tale of Two Cities" was finished in "All the Year Round," and in December was published, complete, with dedication to Lord John Russell.

[*To Mr. Arthur Smith.*]

TAVISTOCK HOUSE, TAVISTOCK SQUARE, LONDON, W.C.,
Wednesday, Jan. 26th, 1859.

MY DEAR ARTHUR,

Will you first read the enclosed letters, having previously welcomed, with all possible cordiality, the bearer, Mr. Thomas C. Evans, from New York?

You having read them, let me explain that Mr. Fields is a highly respectable and influential man, one of the heads of the most classical and most respected publishing house in America; that Mr. Richard Grant White is a man of high reputation; and that Felton is the Greek

Professor in their Cambridge University, perhaps the most distinguished scholar in the States.

The address to myself, referred to in one of the letters, being on its way, it is quite clear that I must give some decided and definite answer to the American proposal. Now, will you carefully discuss it with Mr. Evans before I enter on it at all? Then, will you dine here with him on Sunday—which I will propose to him—and arrange to meet at half-past four for an hour's discussion?

The points are these:

First. I have a very grave question within myself whether I could go to America at all.

Secondly. If I did go, I could not possibly go before the autumn.

Thirdly. If I did go, how long must I stay?

Fourthly. If the stay were a short one, could *you* go?

Fifthly. What is his project? What could I make? What occurs to you upon his proposal?

I have told him that the business· arrangements of the readings have been from the first so entirely in your hands, that I enter upon nothing connected with them without previous reference to you.

Ever faithfully.

[*To M. de Cerjat.*]

Tavistock House, *Tuesday, Feb. 1st,* 1859.

MY DEAR CERJAT,

I received your always welcome annual with even more interest than usual this year, being (in common with my two girls and their aunt) much excited and pleased by your account of your daughter's engagement. Apart from the high sense I have of the affectionate confidence with which you tell me what lies so tenderly on your own heart, I have followed the little history with a lively sympathy and regard for her. I hope, with you, that it is full of promise, and that you will all be happy in it. The separation, even in the present condition of travel (and no man can say how much the discovery of a day may advance it), is nothing. And so God bless her and all of you, and may the rosy summer bring her all the fulness of joy that we all wish her.

To pass from the altar to Townshend (which is a long way), let me report him severely treated by Bully, who rules him with a paw of iron ; and complaining, moreover, of indigestion. He drives here every Sunday, but at all other times is mostly shut up in his beautiful house, where I occasionally go and dine with him *tête-à-tête*, and where we always talk of you and drink to you. That is a rule with us from which we never depart. He is " seeing a volume of poems through the press ; " rather an expensive amusement. He has not been out at night (except to this house) save last Friday, when he went to hear me read " The Poor Traveller," " Mrs. Gamp," and " The Trial " from " Pickwick." He came into my room at St. Martin's Hall, and I fortified him with weak brandy-and-water. You will be glad to hear that the said readings are a greater *furore* than they ever have been, and that every night on which they now take place—once a week—hundreds go away, unable to get in, though the hall holds thirteen hundred people. I dine with —— to-day, by-the-bye, along with his agent ; concerning whom I observe him to be always divided between an unbounded confidence and a little latent suspicion. He always tells me that he is a gem of the first water ; oh yes, the best of business men ! and then says that he did not quite like his conduct respecting that farm-tenant and those hayricks.

There is a general impression here, among the best-informed, that war in Italy, to begin with, is inevitable, and will break out before April. I know a gentleman at Genoa (Swiss by birth), deeply in with the authorities at Turin, who is already sending children home.

In England we are quiet enough. There is a world of talk, as you know, about Reform bills ; but I don't believe there is any general strong feeling on the subject. According to my perceptions, it is undeniable that the public has fallen into a state of indifference about public affairs, mainly referable, as I think, to the people who administer them—and there I mean the people of all parties—which is a very bad sign of the times. The general mind seems weary of debates and honourable members, and to have taken *laissez-aller* for its motto.

My affairs domestic (which I know are not without their interest for you) flow peacefully. My eldest daughter is a capital housekeeper, heads the table gracefully, delegates certain appropriate duties to her sister and her aunt, and they are all three devotedly attached. Charley, my eldest boy, remains in Barings' house. Your present correspondent is more popular than he ever has been. I rather think that the readings in the country have opened up a new public who were outside before; but however that may be, his books have a wider range than they ever had, and his public welcomes are prodigious. Said correspondent is at present overwhelmed with proposals to go and read in America. Will never go, unless a small fortune be first paid down in money on this side of the Atlantic. Stated the figure of such payment, between ourselves, only yesterday. Expects to hear no more of it, and assuredly will never go for less. You don't say, my dear Cerjat, when you are coming to England! Somehow I feel that this marriage ought to bring you over, though I don't know why. You shall have a bed here and a bed at Gad's Hill, and we will go and see strange sights together. When I was in Ireland, I ordered the brightest jaunting-car that ever was seen. It has just this minute arrived per steamer from Belfast. Say you are coming, and you shall be the first man turned over by it; somebody must be (for my daughter Mary drives anything that can be harnessed, and I know of no English horse that would understand a jaunting-car coming down a Kentish hill), and you shall be that somebody if you will. They turned the basket-phaeton over, last summer, in a bye-road—Mary and the other two—and had to get it up again; which they did, and came home as if nothing had happened. They send their loves to Mrs. Cerjat, and to you, and to all, and particularly to the dear *fiancée*. So do I, with all my heart, and am ever your attached and affectionate friend.

[To Mr. Antonio Panizzi.]

TAVISTOCK HOUSE, *Monday Night, March 14th,* 1859.
MY DEAR PANIZZI,

If you should feel no delicacy in mentioning, or should see no objection to mentioning, to Signor Poerio, or any of the wronged Neapolitan gentlemen to whom it is your happiness and honour to be a friend on their arrival in this country, an idea that has occurred to me, I should regard it as a great kindness in you if you would be my exponent. I think you will have no difficulty in believing that I would not, on any consideration, obtrude my name or projects upon any one of those noble souls, if there were any reason of the slightest kind against it. And if you see any such reason, I pray you instantly to banish my letter from your thoughts.

It seems to me probable that some narrative of their ten years' suffering will, somehow or other, sooner or later, be by some of them laid before the English people. The just interest and indignation alive here, will (I suppose) elicit it. False narratives and garbled stories will, in any case, of a certainty get about. If the true history of the matter is to be told, I have that sympathy with them and respect for them which would, all other considerations apart, render it unspeakably gratifying to me to be the means of its diffusion. What I desire to lay before them is simply this: If for my new successor to "Household Words" a narrative of their ten years' trial could be written, I would take any conceivable pains to have it rendered into English, and presented in the sincerest and best way to a very large and comprehensive audience. It should be published exactly as you might think best for them, and remunerated in any way that you might think generous and right. They want no mouthpiece and no introducer, but perhaps they might have no objection to be associated with an English writer, who is possibly not unknown to them by some general reputation, and who certainly would be animated by a strong public and private respect for their honour, spirit, and unmerited misfortunes. This is the whole matter ; assuming that such a thing is to be done, I long for the privilege of helping to do it. These gentlemen might consider it an independent means of. making money, and I should be delighted to pay the money.

In my absence from town, my friend and sub-editor, Mr. Wills (to whom I had expressed my feeling on the subject), has seen, I think, three of the gentlemen together. But as I hear, returning home to-night, that they are in your good hands, and as nobody can be a better judge than you of anything that concerns them, I at once decide to write to you and to take no other step whatever. Forgive me for the trouble I have occasioned you in the reading of this letter, and never think of it again if you think that by pursuing it you would cause them an instant's uneasiness.

Believe me, very faithfully yours.

[*To Mr. Antonio Panizzi.*]

TAVISTOCK HOUSE, *Tuesday, March* 15*th*, 1859.

MY DEAR PANIZZI,

Let me thank you heartily for your kind and prompt letter. I am really and truly sensible of your friendliness.

I have not heard from Higgins, but of course I am ready to serve on the Committee.

Always faithfully yours.

[*To Mr. W. B. Procter.*]

TAVISTOCK HOUSE, *Saturday, March* 19*th*, 1859.

MY DEAR PROCTER,

I think the songs are simply ADMIRABLE ! and I have no doubt of this being a popular feature in " All the Year Round." I would not omit the sexton, and I would not omit the spinners and weavers ; and I would omit the hack-writers, and (I think) the alderman ; but I am not so clear about the chorister. The pastoral I a little doubt finding audience for ; but I am not at all sure yet that my doubt is well founded.

Had I not better send them all to the printer, and let you have proofs kept by you for publishing? I shall not have to make up the first number of " All the Year Round " until early in April. I don't like to send the manuscript back, and I never do like to do so when I get anything that I know to be thoroughly, soundly, and unquestionably good. I am hard at work upon my story, and expect a magnificent start. With hearty thanks,

                          Ever yours affectionately.

[*To Mr. Edmund Yates.*]

TAVISTOCK HOUSE, TAVISTOCK SQUARE. LONDON, W.C.,
                          Tuesday, March 29th, 1859.

MY DEAR EDMUND,

1. I think that no one seeing the place can well doubt that my house at Gad's Hill is the place for the letter-box. The wall is accessible by all sorts and conditions of men, on the bold high road, and the house altogether is the great landmark of the whole neighbourhood. Captain Goldsmith's *house* is up a lane considerably off the high road ; but he has a garden *wall* abutting on the road itself.

2. "The Pic-Nic Papers" were originally sold to Colburn, for the benefit of the widow of Mr. Macrone, of St. James's Square, publisher, deceased. Two volumes were contributed—of course gratuitously—by writers who had had transactions with Macrone. Mr. Colburn, wanting three volumes in all for trade purposes, added a third, consisting of an American reprint. Of that volume I didn't know, and don't know, anything. The other two I edited, gratuitously as aforesaid, and wrote the Lamplighter's story in. It was all done many years ago. There was a preface originally, delicately setting forth how the book came to be.

3. I suppose —— to be, as Mr. Samuel Weller expresses it somewhere in "Pickwick," "ravin' mad with the con-

sciousness o' willany." Under their advertisement in *The Times* to-day, you will see, without a word of comment, the shorthand writer's verbatim report of the judgment.

Ever faithfully.

[*To Mr. Antonio Panizzi.*]

"ALL THE YEAR ROUND" OFFICE, *Thursday, April 7th*, 1859.
MY DEAR PANIZZI,

If you don't know, I think you should know that a number of letters are passing through the post-office, purporting to be addressed to the charitable by "Italian Exiles in London," asking for aid to raise a fund for a tribute to "London's Lord Mayor," in grateful recognition of the reception of the Neapolitan exiles. I know this to be the case, and have no doubt in my own mind that the whole thing is an imposture and a "do." The letters are signed "Gratitudine Italiana."

Ever faithfully yours.

[*To Miss White.*]

TAVISTOCK HOUSE, TAVISTOCK SQUARE, LONDON, W.C.,
Monday, April 18th, 1859.

MY DEAR LOTTY,

This is merely a notice to you that I must positively insist on your getting well, strong, and into good spirits, with the least possible delay. Also, that I look forward to seeing you at Gad's Hill sometime in the summer, staying with the girls, and heartlessly putting down the Plorn. You know that there is no appeal from the Plorn's inimit-

able father. What *he* says must be done. Therefore I
send you my love (which please take care of), and my
commands (which please obey).

Ever your affectionate.

[*To the Hon. Mrs. Watson.*]

TAVISTOCK HOUSE, TAVISTOCK SQUARE, LONDON, W.C.,
Tuesday, May 31st, 1859.
MY DEAR MRS. WATSON,

You surprise me by supposing that there is ever latent
a defiant and roused expression in the undersigned lamb !
Apart from this singular delusion of yours, and wholly
unaccountable departure from your usual accuracy in all
things, your satisfaction with the portrait is a great pleasure to me. It has received every conceivable pains at
Frith's hands, and ought on his account to be good. It
is a little too much (to my thinking) as if my next-door
neighbour were my deadly foe, uninsured, and I had just
received tidings of his house being afire ; otherwise very
good.

I cannot tell you how delighted we shall be if you would
come to Gad's Hill. You should see some charming
woods and a rare old castle, and you should have such a
snug room looking over a Kentish prospect, with every
facility in it for pondering on the beauties of its master's
beard ! *Do* come, but you positively *must not* come and
go on the same day.

We retreat there on Monday, and shall be there all the
summer.

My small boy is perfectly happy at Southsea, and likes the school very much. I had the finest letter two or three days ago, from another of my boys—Frank Jeffrey—at Hamburg. In this wonderful epistle he says : "Dear papa, I write to tell you that I have given up all thoughts of being a doctor. My conviction that I shall never get over my stammering is the cause; all professions are barred against me. The only thing I should like to be is a gentleman farmer, either at the Cape, in Canada, or Australia. With my passage paid, fifteen pounds, a horse, and a rifle, I could go two or three hundred miles up country, sow grain, buy cattle, and in time be very comfortable."

Considering the consequences of executing the little commission by the next steamer, I perceived that the first consequence of the fifteen pounds would be that he would be robbed of it—of the horse, that it would throw him—and of the rifle, that it would blow his head off; which probabilities I took the liberty of mentioning, as being against the scheme. With best love from all,

Ever believe me, my dear Mrs. Watson,

Your faithful and affectionate.

·

[*To Mrs. White.*]

TAVISTOCK HOUSE, *Sunday, June 5th,* 1859.

MY DEAR MRS. WHITE,

I do not write to you this morning because I have anything to say—I well know where your consolation is set,

and to what beneficent figure your thoughts are raised—
but simply because you are so much in my mind that it is
a relief to send you and dear White my love.   You are
always in our hearts and on our lips.   May the great God
comfort you ! You know that Mary and Katie are coming
on Thursday.   They will bring dear Lotty what she little
needs with you by her side—love; and I hope their company will interest and please her.   There is nothing that
they, or any of us, would not do for her.   She is a part of
us all, and has belonged to us, as well as to you, these
many years.

Ever your affectionate and faithful.

[To Miss Dickens.]

GAD'S HILL, HIGHAM BY ROCHESTER, KENT,
Monday, June 11th, 1859.

MY DEAREST MAMIE,

On Saturday night I found, very much to my surprise
and pleasure, the photograph on my table at Tavistock
House.   It is not a very pleasant or cheerful presentation
of my daughters ; but it is wonderfully like for all that,
and in some details remarkably good.   When I came home
here yesterday I tried it in the large Townshend stereoscope, in which it shows to great advantage.   It is in the
little stereoscope at present on the drawing-room table.
One of the balustrades of the destroyed old Rochester
bridge has been (very nicely) presented to me by the contractor for the works, and has been duly stonemasoned and
set up on the lawn behind the house.   I have ordered a

sun-dial for the top of it, and it will be a very good object indeed. The Plorn is highly excited to-day by reason of an institution which he tells me (after questioning George) is called the "Cobb, or Bodderin," holding a festival at The Falstaff. He is possessed of some vague information that they go to Higham Church, in pursuance of some old usage, and attend service there, and afterwards march round the village. It so far looks probable that they certainly started off at eleven very spare in numbers, and came back considerably recruited, which looks to me like the difference between going to church and coming to dinner. They bore no end of bright banners and broad sashes, and had a band with a terrific drum, and are now (at half-past two) dining at The Falstaff, partly in the side room on the ground-floor, and partly in a tent improvised this morning. The drum is hung up to a tree in The Falstaff garden, and looks like a tropical sort of gourd. I have presented the band with five shillings, which munificence has been highly appreciated. Ices don't seem to be provided for the ladies in the gallery—I mean the garden ; they are prowling about there, endeavouring to peep in at the beef and mutton through the holes in the tent, on the whole, in a debased and degraded manner.

Turk somehow cut his foot in Cobham Lanes yesterday, and Linda hers. They are both lame, and looking at each other. Fancy Mr. Townshend not intending to go for another three weeks, and designing to come down here for a few days—with Henri and Bully—on Wednesday ! I wish you could have seen him alone with me on Saturday ; he was so extraordinarily earnest and affectionate on my belongings and affairs in general, and not least of all on you and Katie, that he cried in a most pathetic manner, and was so affected that I was obliged to leave him among the flower-pots in the long passage at the end of the dining-room. It was a very good piece of truthfulness and sincerity, especially in one of his years, able to take life so easily.

Mr. and Mrs. Wills are here now (but I daresay you know it from your aunt), and return to town with me to-morrow morning. We are now going on to the castle. Mrs. Wills was very droll last night, and told me some good stories. My dear, I wish particularly to impress upon you and dear Katie (to whom I send my other best love) that I hope your stay will not be very long. I don't think it very good for either of you, though of course I know that Lotty will be, and must be, and should be the first consideration with you both. I am very anxious to know how you found her and how you are yourself.

Best love to dear Lotty and Mrs. White. The same to Mr. White and Clara. We are always talking about you all.

Ever, dearest Mamie, your affectionate Father.

[*To Rev. James White.*]

GAD'S HILL PLACE, HIGHAM BY ROCHESTER, KENT,
Thursday, July 7th, 1859.

MY DEAR WHITE,

I send my heartiest and most affectionate love to Mrs. White and you, and to Clara. You know all that I could add ; you have felt it all ; let it be unspoken and unwritten —it is expressed within us.

Do you not think that you could all three come here, and stay with us ? You and Mrs. White should have your own large room and your own ways, and should be among us when you felt disposed, and never otherwise. I do hope you would find peace here. Can it not be done ?

We have talked very much about it among ourselves, and the girls are strong upon it. Think of it—do !

Ever your affectionate.

[*To Mr. John Forster.*]

GAD'S HILL, *Thursday Night, Aug. 25th,* 1859.

MY DEAR FORSTER,

. Heartily glad to get your letter this morning.

I cannot easily tell you how much interested I am by what you tell me of our brave and excellent friend the Chief Baron, in connection with that ruffian. I followed the case with so much interest, and have followed the miserable knaves and asses who have perverted it since, with so much indignation, that I have often had more than half a mind to write and thank the upright judge who tried him. I declare to God that I believe such a service one of the greatest that a man of intellect and courage can render to society. Of course I saw the beast of a prisoner (with my mind's eye) delivering his cut-and-dried speech, and read in every word of it that no one but the murderer could have delivered or conceived it. Of course I have been driving the girls out of their wits here, by incessantly proclaiming that there needed no medical evidence either way, and that the case was plain without it. Lastly, of course (though a merciful man—because a merciful man I mean), I would hang any Home Secretary (Whig, Tory, Radical, or otherwise) who should step in between that black scoundrel and the gallows. I can*not* believe—and my belief in all wrong as to public matters is enormous—that such a thing will be done.

I am reminded of Tennyson, by thinking that King Arthur would have made short work of the amiable Smethurst, whom the newspapers strangely delight to call "Doctor," by-the-bye, and to make a sort of gentleman of. How fine the "Idylls" are! Lord! what a blessed thing it is to read a man who can write! I thought nothing could be grander than the first poem till I came to the third; but when I had read the last, it seemed to be absolutely unapproached and unapproachable.

To come to myself. I have written and begged the "All the Year Round" publisher to send you directly four weeks' proofs beyond the current number, that are in type. I hope you will like them. Nothing but the interest of the subject, and the pleasure of striving with the difficulty of the forms of treatment, nothing in the mere way of money, I mean, could also repay the time and trouble of the incessant condensation. But I set myself the little task of making a *picturesque* story, rising in every chapter with characters true to nature, but whom the story itself should express, more than they should express themselves, by dialogue. I mean, in other words, that I fancied a story of incident might be written, in place of the bestiality that *is* written under that pretence, pounding the characters out in its own mortar, and beating their own interests out of them. If you could have read the story all at once, I hope you wouldn't have stopped halfway.

As to coming to your retreat, my dear Forster, think how helpless I am. I am not well yet. I have an instinctive feeling that nothing but the sea will restore me, and I am planning to go and work at Ballard's, at Broadstairs, from next Wednesday to Monday. I generally go to town on Monday afternoon. All Tuesday I am at the office, on Wednesday I come back here, and go to work again. I don't leave off till Monday comes round once more. I am fighting to get my story done by the first week in October. On the 10th of October I am going away to read for a fortnight at Ipswich, Norwich, Oxford, Cambridge, and a few other places. Judge what my spare time is just now !

I am very much surprised and very sorry to find from the enclosed that Elliotson has been ill. I never heard a word of it.

Georgy sends best love to you and to Mrs. Forster, so do I, so does Plorn, so does Frank. The girls are, for five days, with the Whites at Ramsgate. It is raining, intensely hot, and stormy. Eighteen creatures, like little tortoises, have dashed in at the window and fallen on the paper since I began this paragraph ● (that was one !). I am a wretched sort of a creature in my way, but it is a way that gets on somehow. And all ways have the same finger-post at the head of them, and at every turning in them.

Ever affectionately.

[*To Miss Dickens and Miss Katie Dickens.*]

ALBION, BROADSTAIRS, *Friday, Sept. 2nd,* 1859.

MY DEAREST MAMIE AND KATIE,

I have been "moved" here, and am now (Ballard having added to the hotel a house we lived in three years) in our old dining-room and sitting-room, and our old drawing-room as a bedroom. My cold is so bad, both in my throat and in my chest, that I can't bathe in the sea; Tom Collin dissuaded me—thought it "bad"—but I get a heavy shower-bath at Mrs. Crampton's every morning. The baths are still hers and her husband's, but they have retired and live in "Nuckells"—are going to give a stained-glass window, value three hundred pounds, to St. Peter's Church. Tom Collin is of opinion that the Miss Dickenses has growed two fine young women—leastwise, asking pardon, ladies. An evangelical family of most disagreeable girls prowl about here and trip people up with tracts, which they put in the paths with stones upon them to keep them from blowing away. Charles Collins and I having seen a bill yesterday—about a mesmeric young lady who did feats, one of which was set forth in the bill, in a line by itself, as

THE RIGID LEGS,

—were overpowered with curiosity, and resolved to go. It came off in the Assembly Room, now more exquisitely desolate than words can describe. Eighteen shillings was the "take." Behind the screen among the company, we heard mysterious gurglings of water before the entertainment began, and then a slippery sound which occasioned me to whisper C. C. (who laughed in the most ridiculous manner), "Soap." It proved to be the young lady washing herself. She must have been wonderfully dirty, for she took a world of trouble, and didn't come out clean after all—in a wretched dirty muslin frock, with blue ribbons. She was the alleged mesmeriser, and a boy who distributed bills the alleged mesmerised. It was a most preposterous imposition, but more ludicrous than any poor sight I ever saw. The boy is clearly out of pantomime, and when he pretended to be in the mesmeric state, made the company back by going in among them head over heels, backwards, half-a-dozen times, in a most insupportable way. The pianist had struck ; and the manner in which the lecturer implored "some lady" to play a "polker," and the manner in which no lady would ; and in which the few ladies who were there sat with their hats on, and the elastic under their chins, as if it were going to blow, is never to be forgotten. I have been writing all the morning, and am going for a walk to Ramsgate. This is a beast of a letter, but I am not well, and have been addling my head.

Ever, dear Girls, your affectionate Father.

[*To Mr. W. Wilkie Collins.*]

GAD'S HILL PLACE, HIGHAM BY ROCHESTER, KENT,

Friday Night, Sept. 16th, 1859.

MY DEAR WILKIE,

Just a word to say that I have received yours, and that I look forward to the reunion on Thursday, when I hope to have the satisfaction of recounting to you the plot of a play that has been laid before me for commending advice.

Ditto to what you say respecting the *Great Eastern*. I went right up to London Bridge by the boat that day, on purpose that I might pass her. I thought her the ugliest and most unshiplike thing these eyes ever beheld. I wouldn't go to sea in her, shiver my ould timbers and rouse me up with a monkey's tail (man-of-war metaphor), not to chuck a biscuit into Davy Jones's weather eye, and see double with my own old toplights.

Turk has been so good as to produce from his mouth, for the wholesome consternation of the family, eighteen feet of worm. When he had brought it up, he seemed to think it might be turned to account in the housekeeping and was proud. Pony has kicked a shaft off the cart, and is to be sold. Why don't you buy her? she'd never kick with you.

Barber's opinion is, that them fruit-trees, one and all, is touchwood, and not fit for burning at any gentleman's fire ; also that the stocking of this here garden is worth less than nothing, because you wouldn't have to grub up nothing, and something takes a man to do it at three-and-sixpence a day. Was "left desponding" by your reporter.

I have had immense difficulty to find a man for the stable-yard here.   Barber having at last engaged one this morning, I enquired if he had a decent hat for driving in, to which Barber returned this answer :

" Why, sir, not to deceive you, that man flatly say that he never have wore that article since man he was ! "

I am consequently fortified into my room, and am afraid to go out to look at him   Love from all.

Ever affectionately.

[*To Monsieur Regnier.*]

GAD'S HILL PLACE, HIGHAM BY ROCHESTER, KENT,

Saturday, Oct. 15*th,* 1859.

MY DEAR REGNIER,

You will receive by railway parcel the proof-sheets of a story of mine, that has been for some time in progress in my weekly journal, and that will be published in a complete volume about the middle of November.   Nobody but Forster has yet seen the latter portions of it, or will see them until they are published.   I want you to read it for two reasons.   Firstly, because I hope it is the best story I have written.   Secondly, because it treats of a very remarkable time in France; and I should very much like to know what you think of its being dramatised for a French theatre.   If you should think it likely to be done, I should be glad to take some steps towards having it well done.   The story is an extraordinary success here, and I think the end of it is certain to make a still greater sensation.

Don't trouble yourself to write to me, *mon ami*, until you shall have had time to read the proofs. Remember, they are *proofs*, and *private;* the latter chapters will not be before the public for five or six weeks to come.

With kind regards to Madame Regnier, in which my daughters and their aunt unite,

Believe me, ever faithfully yours.

P.S.—The story (I daresay you have not seen any of it yet) is called " A Tale of Two Cities."

[*To Mr. Frank Stone, A.R.A.*]

PETERBOROUGH, *Wednesday Evening, Oct.* 19*th,* 1859.

MY DEAR STONE,

We had a splendid rush last night—exactly as we supposed, with the pressure on the two shillings, of whom we turned a crowd away. They were a far finer audience than on the previous night ; I think the finest I have ever read to. They took every word of the " Dombey " in quite an amazing manner, and after the child's death, paused a little, and then set up a shout that it did one good to hear. Mrs. Gamp then set in with a roar, which lasted until I had done. I think everybody for the time forgot everything but the matter in hand. It was as fine an instance of thorough absorption in a fiction as any of us are likely to see ever again.

—— (in an exquisite red mantle), accompanied by her sister (in another exquisite red mantle) and by the deaf

VOL. II.—6

lady, (who leaned a black head-dress, exactly like an old-fashioned tea-urn without the top, against the wall), was charming. HE couldn't get at her on account of the pressure. HE tried to peep at her from the side door, but she (ha, ha, ha !) was unconscious of his presence. I read to her, and goaded him to madness. He is just sane enough to send his kindest regards.

This is a place which—except the cathedral, with the loveliest front I ever saw—is like the back door to some other place. It is, I should hope, the deadest and most utterly inert little town in the British dominions. The magnates have taken places, and the bookseller is of opinion that "such is the determination to do honour to Mr. Dickens, that the doors *must* be opened half an hour before the appointed time." You will picture to yourself Arthur's quiet indignation at this, and the manner in which he remarked to me at dinner, " that he turned away twice Peterborough last night."

A very pretty room—though a Corn Exchange—and a room we should have been glad of at Cambridge, as it is large, bright, and cheerful, and wonderfully well lighted.

The difficulty of getting to Bradford from here to-morrow, at any time convenient to us, turned out to be so great, that we are all going in for Leeds (only three-quarters of an hour from Bradford) to-night after the reading, at a quarter past eleven. We are due at Leeds a quarter before three.

So no more at present from,

Yours affectionately.

[*To Mr. W. R. Sculthorpe.*]

TAVISTOCK HOUSE, TAVISTOCK SQUARE, LONDON, W.C.,
Thursday, Nov. 10*th,* 1859.

DEAR SIR,

Judgment must go by default. I have not a word to plead against Dodson and Fogg. I am without any defence to the action; and therefore, as law goes, ought to win it.

Seriously, the date of your hospitable note disturbs my soul. But I have been incessantly writing in Kent and reading in all sorts of places, and have done nothing in my own personal character these many months; and now I come to town and our friend* is away! Let me take that defaulting miscreant into council when he comes back.

Faithfully yours.

[*To Monsieur Regnier.*]

TAVISTOCK HOUSE, TAVISTOCK SQUARE, LONDON, W.C.,
Wednesday, Nov. 16*th,* 1859.

MY DEAR REGNIER,

I send you ten thousand thanks for your kind and explicit letter. What I particularly wished to ascertain from you was, whether it is likely the Censor would allow such a piece to be played in Paris. In the case of its being likely, then I wished to have the piece as well done as possible, and would even have proposed to come to Paris to see it rehearsed. But I very much doubted whether the

---

* Mr. Edmund Yates.

general subject would not be objectionable to the Government, and what you write with so much sagacity and with such care convinces me at once that its representation would be prohibited. Therefore I altogether abandon and relinquish the idea. But I am just as heartily and cordially obliged to you for your interest and friendship, as if the book had been turned into a play five hundred times. I again thank you ten thousand times, and am quite sure that you are right. I only hope you will forgive my causing you so much trouble, after your hard work.

My girls and Georgina send their kindest regards to Madame Regnier and to you. My Gad's Hill house (I think I omitted to tell you, in reply to your enquiry) is on the very scene of Falstaff's robbery. There is a little *cabaret* at the roadside, still called The Sir John Falstaff. And the country, in all its general features, is, at this time, what it was in Shakespeare's. I hope you will see the house before long. It is really a pretty place, and a good residence for an English writer, is it not?

Macready, we are all happy to hear from himself, is going to leave the dreary tomb in which he lives, at Sherborne, and to remove to Cheltenham, a large and handsome place, about four or five hours' railway journey from London, where his poor girls will at least see and hear some life. Madame Céleste was with me yesterday, wishing to dramatise " A Tale of Two Cities " for the Lyceum, after bringing out the Christmas pantomime. I gave her my permission and the book ; but I fear that her company (troupe) is a very poor one.

This is all the news I have, except (which is no news at all) that I feel as if I had not seen you for fifty years, and that

I am ever your attached and faithful Friend.

[*To Mr. T. Longman.*]

TAVISTOCK HOUSE, *Monday, Nov. 28th,* 1859.

MY DEAR LONGMAN,

I am very anxious to present to you, with the earnest hope that you will hold him in your remembrance, young Mr. Marcus Stone, son of poor Frank Stone, who died suddenly but a little week ago. You know, I daresay, what a start this young man made in the last exhibition, and what a favourable notice his picture attracted. He wishes to make an additional opening for himself in the illustration of books. He is an admirable draughtsman, has a most dexterous hand, a charming sense of grace and beauty, and a capital power of observation. These qualities in him I know well of my own knowledge. He is in all things modest, punctual, and right ; and I would answer for him, if it were needful, with my head.

If you will put anything in his way, you will do it a second time, I am certain.

Faithfully yours always.

1860.

NARRATIVE.

THIS winter was the last spent at Tavistock House. Charles Dickens had for some time been inclining to the idea of making his home altogether at Gad's Hill, giving up his London house, and taking a furnished house for the sake of his daughters for a few months of the London season. And, as his daughter Kate was to be married this summer to Mr. Charles Collins, this intention was confirmed and carried out. He made arrangements for the sale of Tavistock House to Mr. Davis, a Jewish gentleman, and he gave up possession of it in September. Up to this time Gad's Hill had been furnished merely as a temporary summer residence—pictures, library, and all best furniture being left in the London house. He now set about beautifying and making Gad's Hill thoroughly comfortable and homelike. And there was not a year afterwards, up to the year of his death, that he did not make some addition or improvement to it. He also furnished, as a private residence, a sitting-room and some bedrooms at his office in Wellington Street, to be used, when there was no house in London, as occasional town quarters by himself, his daughter, and sister-in-law.

He began in this summer his occasional papers for "All the Year Round," which he called "The Uncommercial Traveller," and which were continued at intervals in his journal until 1869.

In the autumn of this year he began another story, to be published weekly in "All the Year Round." The letter to Mr. Forster, which we give, tells him of this beginning and gives him the name of the book. The first number of "Great Expectations" appeared on the 1st December. The Christmas number, this time, was written jointly by himself and Mr. Wilkie Collins. The scene was laid at Clovelly, and they made a journey together into Devonshire and Cornwall, for the purpose of this story, in November.

The letter to Sir Edward Bulwer Lytton is, unfortunately, the only one we have as yet been able to procure. The present Lord Lytton, the Viceroy of India, has kindly endeavoured to help us even during his absence from England. But it was found to be impossible without his own assistance to make the necessary search among his father's papers. And he has promised us that, on his return, he will find and lend to us, many letters from Charles Dickens, which are certainly in existence, to his distinguished fellow-writer and great friend. We hope, therefore, it may be possible for us at some future time to be able to publish these letters, as well as those addressed to the present Lord Lytton (when he was Mr. Robert Lytton, otherwise "Owen Meredith," and frequent contributor to "Household Words" and "All the Year Round)." We have the same hope with regard to letters addressed to Sir Henry Layard, at present Ambassador at Constantinople, which, of course, for the same reason, cannot be lent to us at the present time.

We give a letter to Mr. Forster on one of his books on the Commonwealth, the "Impeachment of the Five Members;" which, as with other letters which we are glad to publish on the subject of Mr. Forster's own works, was not used by himself for obvious reasons.

A letter to his daughter Mamie (who, after her sister's marriage, paid a visit with her dear friends the White family to Scotland, where she had a serious illness) introduces a recent addition to the family, who became an important member of it, and one to whom Charles Dickens was very tenderly attached—her little white Pomeranian dog "Mrs. Bouncer" (so called after the celebrated lady of that name in "Box and Cox"). It is quite necessary to make this formal introduction of the little pet animal (who lived to be a very old dog and died in 1874), because future letters to his daughter contain constant references

and messages to "Mrs. Bouncer," which would be quite
unintelligible without this explanation. "Boy," also referred to in this letter, was his daughter's horse. The little dog and the horse were gifts to Mamie Dickens from
her friends Mr. and Mrs. Arthur Smith, and the sister of
the latter Miss Craufurd.

[*To Mr. W. C. Macready.*]

TAVISTOCK HOUSE, *Monday, Jan. 2nd*, 1860.

MY DEAREST MACREADY,

A happy New Year to you, and many happy years! I
cannot tell you how delighted I was to receive your Christmas letter, or with what pleasure I have received Forster's
emphatic accounts of your health and spirits. But when
was I ever wrong? And when did I not tell you that you
were an impostor in pretending to grow older as the rest
of us do, and that you had a secret of your own for reversing the usual process! It happened that I read at
Cheltenham a couple of months ago, and that I have
rarely seen a place that so attracted my fancy. I had
never seen it before. Also I believe the character of its
people to have greatly changed for the better. All sorts
of long-visaged prophets had told me that they were dull,
stolid, slow, and I don't know what more that is disagreeable. I found them exactly the reverse in all respects;
and I saw an amount of beauty there—well—that is not
to be more specifically mentioned to you young fellows.

Katie dined with us yesterday, looking wonderfully well, and singing "Excelsior" with a certain dramatic fire in her, whereof I seem to remember having seen sparks afore now. Etc. etc. etc.

With kindest love from all at home to all with you,

Ever, my dear Macready, your most affectionate.

[*To Mr. W. Wilkie Collins.*]

TAVISTOCK HOUSE, TAVISTOCK SQUARE, LONDON, W.C.,
Saturday Night, Jan. 7th, 1860.

MY DEAR WILKIE,

I have read this book with great care and attention. There cannot be a doubt that it is a very great advance on all your former writing, and most especially in respect of tenderness. In character it is excellent. Mr. Fairlie as good as the lawyer, and the lawyer as good as he. Mr. Vesey and Miss Halcombe, in their different ways, equally meritorious. Sir Percival, also, is most skilfully shown, though I doubt (you see what small points I come to) whether any man ever showed uneasiness by hand or foot without being forced by nature to show it in his face too. The story is very interesting, and the writing of it admirable.

I seem to have noticed, here and there, that the great pains you take express themselves a trifle too much, and you know that I always contest your disposition to give an audience credit for nothing, which necessarily involves the forcing of points on their attention, and which I have

VOL. II.—6*

always observed them to resent when they find it out—as they always will and do. But on turning to the book again, I find it difficult to take out an instance of this. It rather belongs to your habit of thought and manner of going about the work. Perhaps I express my meaning best when I say that the three people who write the narratives in these proofs have a DISSECTIVE property in common, which is essentially not theirs but yours; and that my own effort would be to strike more of what is got *that way* out of them by collision with one another, and by the working of the story.

You know what an interest I have felt in your powers from the beginning of our friendship, and how very high I rate them? *I* know that this is an admirable book, and that it grips the difficulties of the weekly portion and throws them in masterly style. No one else could do it half so well. I have stopped in every chapter to notice some instance of ingenuity, or some happy turn of writing; and I am absolutely certain that you never did half so well yourself.

So go on and prosper, and let me see some more, when you have enough (for your own satisfaction) to show me. I think of coming in to back you up if I can get an idea for my series of gossiping papers. One of these days, please God, we may do a story together; I have very odd half-formed notions, in a mist, of something that might be done that way.

Ever affectionately.

[*To Mr. John Forster.*]

11, WELLINGTON STREET, NORTH STRAND, LONDON, W.C.,

Wednesday, May 2nd, 1860.

MY DEAR FORSTER,

It did not occur to me in reading your most excellent, interesting, and remarkable book, that it could with any reason be called one-sided. If Clarendon had never written his " History of the Rebellion," then I can understand that it might be. But just as it would be impossible to answer an advocate who had misstated the merits of a case for his own purpose, without, in the interests of truth, and not of the other side merely, re-stating the merits and showing them in their real form, so I cannot see the practicability of telling what you had to tell without in some sort championing the misrepresented side, and I think that you don't do that as an advocate, but as a judge.

The evidence has been suppressed and coloured, and the judge goes through it and puts it straight. It is not *his* fault if it all goes one way and tends to one plain conclusion. Nor is it his fault that it goes the further when it is laid out straight, or seems to do so, because it was so knotted and twisted up before.

I can understand any man's, and particularly Carlyle's, having a lingering respect that does not like to be disturbed for those (in the best sense of the word) loyal gentlemen of the country who went with the king and were so true to him. But I don't think Carlyle sufficiently considers that the great mass of those gentlemen *didn't know the truth*, that it was a part of their loyalty to believe what they were told on the king's behalf, and that it is reasonable to suppose that the king was too artful to make known to *them* (especially after failure) what were very acceptable designs to the desperate soldiers of fortune about White-hall. And it was to me a curious point of adventitious interest arising out of your book, to reflect on the probability of their having been as ignorant of the real scheme in Charles's head, as their descendants and followers down to this time, and to think with pity and admiration that they believed the cause to be so much better than it was. This is a notion I was anxious to have expressed in our account of the book in these pages. For I don't suppose Clarendon, or any other such man to sit down and tell posterity something that he has not "tried on" in his own time. Do you?

In the whole narrative I saw nothing anywhere to which I demurred. I admired it all, went with it all, and was proud of my friend's having written it all. I felt it to be all square and sound and right, and to be of enormous importance in these times. Firstly, to the people who (like myself) are so sick of the shortcomings of representative government as to have no interest in it. Secondly, to the humbugs at Westminster who have come down—a long, long way—from those men, as you know. When the great remonstrance came out, I was in the thick of my story, and was always busy with it; but I am very glad I didn't read it then, as I shall read it now to much better purpose. All the time I was at work on the " Two Cities," I read no books but such as had the air of the time in them.

To return for a final word to the Five Members. I thought the marginal references overdone. Here and there, they had a comical look to me for that reason, and reminded me of shows and plays where everything is in the bill.

Lastly, I should have written to you—as I had a strong inclination to do, and ought to have done, immediately after reading the book—but for a weak reason ; of all things in the world I have lost heart in one—I hope no other—I cannot, times out of calculation, make up my mind to write a letter.

Ever, my dear Forster, affectionately yours.

[*To M. de Cerjat.*]

TAVISTOCK HOUSE, *Thursday, May 3rd*, 1860.

MY DEAR CERJAT,

The date of this letter would make me horribly ashamed of myself, if I didn't know that *you* know how difficult letter-writing is to one whose trade it is to write.

You asked me on Christmas Eve about my children. My second daughter is going to be married in the course of the summer to Charles Collins, the brother of Wilkie Collins, the novelist. The father was one of the most famous painters of English green lanes and coast pieces. He was bred an artist ; is a writer, too, and does "The Eye Witness," in "All the Year Round." He is a gentleman, accomplished, and amiable. My eldest daughter has not yet started any conveyance on the road to matrimony (that I know of) ; but it is likely enough that she will, as she is very agreeable and intelligent. They are both very pretty. My eldest boy, Charley, has been in Barings' house for three or four years, and is now going to Hong Kong, strongly backed up by Barings, to buy tea on his own account, as a means of forming a connection and seeing more of the practical part of a merchant's calling, before starting in London for himself. His brother Frank (Jeffrey's godson) I have just recalled from France and Germany, to come and learn business, and qualify himself to join his brother on his return from the Celestial Empire. The next boy, Sydney Smith, is designed for the navy, and is in training at Portsmouth, awaiting his nomination. He is about three foot high, with the biggest eyes ever seen, and is known in the Portsmouth parts as "Young Dickens, who can do everything."

Another boy is at school in France ; the youngest of all has a private tutor at home. I have forgotten the second in order, who is in India. He went out as ensign of a non-existent native regiment, got attached to the 42nd Highlanders, one of the finest regiments in the Queen's service ; has remained with them ever since, and got made a lieutenant by the chances of the rebellious campaign, before he was eighteen. Miss Hogarth, always Miss Hogarth, is the guide, philosopher, and friend of all the party, and a very close affection exists between her and the girls. I doubt if she will ever marry. I don't know whether to be glad of it or sorry for it.

I have laid down my pen and taken a long breath

after writing this family history. I have also considered whether there are any more children, and I don't think there are. If I should remember two or three others presently, I will mention them in a postscript.

We think Townshend looking a little the worse for the winter, and we perceive Bully to be decidedly old upon his legs, and of a most diabolical turn of mind. When they first arrived the weather was very dark and cold, and kept them indoors. It has since turned very warm and bright, but with a dusty and sharp east wind. They are still kept indoors by this change, and I begin to wonder what change will let them out. Townshend dines with us every Sunday. You may be sure that we always talk of you and yours, and drink to you heartily.

Public matters here are thought to be rather improving ; the deep mistrust of the gentleman in Paris being counteracted by the vigorous state of preparation into which the nation is getting. You will have observed, of course, that we establish a new defaulter in respect of some great trust, about once a quarter. The last one, the cashier of a City bank, is considered to have distinguished himself greatly, a quarter of a million of money being high game.

No, my friend, I have not shouldered my rifle yet, but I should do so on more pressing occasion. Every other man in the row of men I know—if they were all put in a row—is a volunteer though. There is a tendency rather to overdo the wearing of the uniform, but that is natural enough in the case of the youngest men. The turn-out is generally very creditable indeed. At the ball they had (in a perfectly unventilated building), their new leather belts and pouches smelt so fearfully that it was, as my eldest daughter said, like shoemaking in a great prison. She, consequently, distinguished herself by fainting away in the most inaccessible place in the whole structure, and being brought out (horizontally) by a file of volunteers, like some slain daughter of Albion whom they were carrying into the street to rouse the indignant valour of the populace.

Lord, my dear Cerjat, when I turn to that page of your letter where you write like an ancient sage in whom the fire has paled into a meek-eyed state of coolness and virtue, I half laugh and half cry ! *You* old ! *You* a sort of hermit ? Boh ! Get out.

With this comes my love and all our loves, to you and Mrs. Cerjat, and your daughter. I add my special and particular to the sweet "singing cousin." When shall you and I meet, and where ? Must I come to see Townshend ? I begin to think so.

Ever, my dear Cerjat, your affectionate and faithful.

[*To Sir Edward Bulwer Lytton.*]

GAD'S HILL, *Tuesday, June 5th,* 1860.

MY DEAR BULWER LYTTON,

I am very much interested and gratified by your letter concerning "A Tale of Two Cities." I do not quite agree with you on two points, but that is no deduction from my pleasure.

In the first place, although the surrender of the feudal privileges (on a motion seconded by a nobleman of great rank) was the occasion of a sentimental scene, I see no reason to doubt, but on the contrary, many reasons to believe, that some of these privileges had been used to the frightful oppression of the peasant, quite as near to the time of the Revolution as the doctor's narrative, which, you will remember, dates long before the Terror. And surely when the new philosophy was the talk of the salons and the slang of the hour, it is not unreasonable or unallowable to suppose a nobleman wedded to the old cruel ideas, and representing the time going out, as his nephew represents the time coming in ; as to the condition of the peasant in France generally at that day, I take it that if anything be certain on earth it is certain that it was intolerable. No *ex post facto* enquiries and provings by figures will hold water, surely, against the tremendous testimony of men living at the time.

There is a curious book printed at Amsterdam, written to make out no case whatever, and tiresome enough in its literal dictionary-like minuteness, scattered up and down the pages of which is full authority for my marquis. This is "Mercier's Tableau de Paris." Rousseau is the authority for the peasant's shutting up his house when he had a bit of meat. The tax-taker was the authority for the wretched creature's impoverishment.

I am not clear, and I never have been clear, respecting that canon of fiction which forbids the interposition of accident in such acase as Madame Defarge's death. Where the accident is inseparable from the passion and emotion of the character, where it is strictly consistent with the whole design, and arises out of some culminating proceeding on the part of the character which the whole story has led up to, it seems to me to become, as it were, an act of divine justice. And when I use Miss Pross (though this is quite another question) to bring about that catastrophe, I have the positive intention of making that half-comic intervention a part of the desperate woman's failure, and of opposing that mean death—instead of a desperate one in the streets, which she wouldn't have minded—to the dignity of Carton's wrong or right ; this *was* the design, and seemed to be in the fitness of things.

Now, as to the reading. I am sorry to say that it is out of the question this season. I have had an attack of rheumatism—quite a stranger to me—which remains hovering about my left side, after having doubled me up in the back, and which would disable me from standing for two hours. I have given up all dinners and town engagements, and come to my little Falstaff House here, sensible of the necessity of country training all through the summer. Smith would have proposed any appointment to see you on the subject, but he has been dreadfully ill with tic. Whenever I read in London, I will gladly put a night aside for your purpose, and we will plot to connect your name with it, and give it some speciality. But this could not be before Christmas time, as I should not be able to read sooner, for in the hot weather it would be useless. Let me hear from you about this when you have considered it. It would greatly diminish the expenses, remember.

Ever affectionately and faithfully.

[*To the Lord John Russell.*]

GAD'S HILL PLACE, HIGHAM BY ROCHESTER, KENT,
Sunday, June 17th, 1860.

MY DEAR LORD JOHN RUSSELL,

I cannot thank you enough for your kind note and its most welcome enclosure. My sailor-boy comes home from Portsmouth to-morrow, and will be overjoyed. His masters have been as anxious for getting his nomination as though it were some distinction for themselves.

Ever your faithful and obliged.

[*To the Earl of Carlisle.*]

GAD'S HILL PLACE, HIGHAM BY ROCHESTER, KENT,
Wednesday, Aug. 8th, 1860.

MY DEAR LORD CARLISLE,

Coming back here after an absence of three days in town, I find your kind and cordial letter lying on my table. I heartily thank you for it, and highly esteem it. I understand that the article on the spirits to which you refer was written by —— (he played an Irish porter in one scene of Bulwer's comedy at Devonshire House). Between ourselves, I think it must be taken with a few grains of salt, imperial measure. The experiences referred to "came off " at ——, where the spirit of —— (among an extensive and miscellaneous bodiless circle) *dines* sometimes ! Mr.

——, the high priest of the mysteries, I have some considerable reason—derived from two honourable men—for mistrusting. And that some of the disciples are very easy of belief I know.

This is Falstaff's own Gad's Hill, and I live on the top of it. All goes well with me, thank God! I should be thoroughly delighted to see you again, and to show you where the robbery was done. My eldest daughter keeps my house, and it is one I was extraordinarily fond of when a child.

My dear Lord Carlisle, ever affectionately yours.

P.S.—I am prowling about, meditating a new book.

[*To Mr. W. H. Wills.*]

OFFICE OF "ALL THE YEAR ROUND,"
Tuesday, Sept. 4th, 1860.

MY DEAR WILLS,

Your description of your sea-castle makes your room here look uncommonly dusty. Likewise the costermongers in the street outside, and the one customer (drunk, with his head on the table) in the Crown Coffeé House over the way, in York Street, have an earthy, and, as I may say, a land-lubberly aspect. Cape Horn, to the best of *my* belief, is a tremendous way off, and there are more bricks and cabbage-leaves between this office and that dismal point of land than *you* can possibly imagine.

Coming here from the station this morning, I met, coming from the execution of the Wentworth murderer, such a tide of ruffians as never could have flowed from any point but the gallows. Without any figure of speech it turned one white and sick to behold them.

Tavistock House is cleared to-day, and possession delivered up. I must say that in all things the purchaser has behaved thoroughly well, and that I cannot call to mind any occasion when I have had money dealings with a Christian that have been so satisfactory, considerate, and trusting.

I am ornamented at present with one of my most intensely preposterous and utterly indescribable colds. If you were to make a voyage from Cape Horn to Wellington Street, you would scarcely recognise in the bowed form, weeping eyes, rasped nose, and snivelling wretch whom you would encounter here, the once gay and sparkling, etc. etc.

Everything else here is as quiet as possible. Business reports you receive from Holsworth. Wilkie looked in to-day, going to Gloucestershire for a week. The office is full of discarded curtains and coverings from Tavistock House, which Georgina is coming up this evening to select from and banish. Mary is in raptures with the beauties of Dunkeld, but is not very well in health. The Admiral (Sydney) goes up for his examination to-morrow. If he fails to pass with credit, I will never believe in anybody again, so in that case look out for your own reputation with me.

This is really all the news I have, except that I am lazy, and that Wilkie dines here next Tuesday, in order that we may have a talk about the Christmas number.

I beg to send my kind regard to Mrs. Wills, and to enquire how she likes wearing a hat, which of course she does.   I also want to know from her in confidence whether *Crwllm festidiniog llymthll y wodd?*

Yesterday I burnt, in the field at Gad's Hill, the accumulated letters and papers of twenty years.   They sent up a smoke like the genie when he got out of the casket on the seashore ; and as it was an exquisite day when I began, and rained very heavily when I finished, I suspect my correspondence of having overcast the face of the heavens.

Ever faithfully.

P.S.—Kind regard to Mr. and Mrs. Novelli.*

I have just sent out for *The Globe.*   No news.

Hullah's daughter (an artist) tells me that certain female students have addressed the Royal Academy, entreating them to find a place for their education.   I think it a capital move, for which I can do something popular and telling in *The Register.*   Adelaide Procter is active in the business, and has a copy of their letter.   Will you write to her for that, and anything else she may have about it, telling her that I strongly approve, and want to help them myself ?

[To the Hon. Mrs. Watson.]

GAD'S HILL PLACE, HIGHAM BY ROCHESTER, KENT,
Friday Night, Sept. 14th, 1860.
MY DEAR MRS. WATSON,

I lose no time in answering your letter ; and first as to

---

* With whom Mr. and Mrs. Wills were staying at Aberystwith.

business, the school in the High Town at Boulogne was excellent. The boys all English, the two proprietors an old Eton master and one of the Protestant clergymen of the town. The teaching unusually sound and good. The manner and conduct developed in the boys quite admirable. But I have never seen a gentleman so perfectly acquainted with boy-nature as the Eton master. There was a perfect understanding between him and his charges; nothing pedantic on his part, nothing slavish on their parts. The result was, that either with him or away from him, the boys combined an ease and frankness with a modesty and sense of responsibility that was really above all praise. Alfred went from there to a great school at Wimbledon, where they train for India and the artillery and engineers. Sydney went from there to Mr. Barrow, at Southsea. In both instances the new masters wrote to me of their own accord, bearing quite unsolicited testimony to the merits of the old, and expressing their high recognition of what they had done. These things speak for themselves.

Sydney has just passed his examination as a naval cadet and come home, all eyes and gold buttons. He has twelve days' leave before going on board the training-ship. Katie and her husband are in France, and seem likely to remain there for an indefinite period. Mary is on a month's visit in Scotland ; Georgina, Frank, and Plorn are at home here ; and we all want Mary and her little dog back again. I have sold Tavistock House, am making this rather complete in its way, and am on the restless eve of beginning a new big book ; but mean to have a furnished house in town (in some accessible quarter) from February or so to June. May we meet there.

Your handwriting is always so full of pleasant memories to me, that when I took it out of the post-office at Rochester this afternoon it quite stirred my heart. But we must not think of old times as sad times, or regard them as anything but the fathers and mothers of the present. We must all climb steadily up the mountain after the talking bird, the singing tree, and the yellow water, and must all bear in mind that the previous climbers who were scared into looking back got turned into black stone.

Mary Boyle was here a little while ago, as affectionate at heart as ever, as young, and as pleasant. Of course we talked often of you. So let me know when you are established in Halfmoon Street, and I shall be truly delighted to come and see you.

For my attachments are strong attachments and never weaken. In right of bygones, I feel as if "all Northamptonshire" belonged to me, as all Northumberland did to Lord Bateman in the ballad. In memory of your warming your feet at the fire in that waste of a waiting-room when I read at Brighton, I have ever since taken that watering-place to my bosom as I never did before. And you and Switzerland are always one to me, and always inseparable.

Charley was heard of yesterday, from Shanghai, going to Japan, intending to meet his brother Walter at Calcutta, and having an idea of beguiling the time between whiles by asking to be taken as an amateur with the English

Chinese forces. Everybody caressed him and asked him everywhere, and he seemed to go. With kind regards, my dear Mrs. Watson,

Ever affectionately yours.

[*To Mr. Edmund Yates.*]

GAD'S HILL PLACE, HIGHAM BY ROCHESTER. KENT,
Sunday, Sept. 23rd, 1860.

ON THE DEATH OF HIS MOTHER.

MY DEAR E. Y.,

I did not write to you in your bereavement, because I knew that the girls had written to you, and because I instinctively shrunk from making a form of what was so real. *You* knew what a loving and faithful remembrance I always had of your mother as a part of my youth—no more capable of restoration than my youth itself. All the womanly goodness, grace, and beauty of my drama went out with her. To the last I never could hear her voice without emotion. I think of her as of a beautiful part of my own youth, and this dream that we are all dreaming seems to darken.

But it is not to say this that I write now. It comes to the point of my pen in spite of me.

"Holding up the Mirror" is in the next week's number. I have taken out all this funeral part of it. Not because I disliked it (for, indeed, I thought it the best part of the paper), but because it rather grated on me, going over the proof at that time, as a remembrance that would be better

VOL. II.—7

reserved a little while. Also because it made rather a mixture of yourself as an individual, with something that does not belong or attach to you as an individual. You can have the MS.; and as a part of a paper describing your own juvenile remembrances of a theatre, there it is, needing no change or adaption.

Ever faithfully.

[*To Miss Dickens.*]

GAD'S HILL PLACE, HIGHAM BY ROCHESTER, KENT,
Sunday, Sept. 23rd, 1860.

MY DEAREST MAMIE,

If you had been away from us and ill with anybody in the world but our dear Mrs. White, I should have been in a state of the greatest anxiety and uneasiness about you. But as I know it to be impossible that you could be in kinder or better hands, I was not in the least restless about you, otherwise than as it grieved me to hear of my poor dear girl's suffering such pain. I hope it is over now for many a long day, and that you will come back to us a thousand times better in health than you left us.

Don't come back too soon. Take time and get well restored. There is no hurry, the house is not near to-rights yet, and though we all want you, and though Boy wants you, we all (including Boy), deprecate a fatiguing journey being taken too soon.

As to the carpenters, they are absolutely maddening. They are always at work, yet never seem to do anything. Lillie was down on Friday, and said (his eye fixed on

Maidstone, and rubbing his hand to conciliate his moody employer) that " he didn't think there would be very much left to do after Saturday, the 29th."

I didn't throw him out of the window. Your aunt tells you all the news, and leaves me no chance of distinguishing myself, I know. You have been told about my brackets in the drawing-room, all about the glass rescued from the famous stage-wreck of Tavistock House, all about everything here and at the office. The office is really a success. As comfortable, cheerful, and private as anything of the kind can possibly be.

I took the Admiral (but this you know too, no doubt) to Dollond's, the mathematical instrument maker's, last Monday, to buy that part of his outfit. His sextant (which is about the size and shape of a cocked hat) on being applied to his eye, entirely concealed him. Not the faintest vestige of the distinguished officer behind it was perceptible to the human vision. All through the City, people turned round and stared at him with the sort of pleasure people take in a little model. We went on to Chatham this day week, in search of some big man-of-war's-man, who should be under obligation to salute him—unfortunately found none. But this no doubt you know too, and all my news falls flat.

I am driven out of my room by paint, and am writing in the best spare room. The whole prospect is excessively wet ; it does not rain now, but yesterday it did tremendously, and it rained very heavily in the night. We are even muddy ; and that is saying a great deal in this dry country of chalk and sand. Everywhere the corn is lying out and saturated with wet. The hops (nearly everywhere) look as if they had been burnt.

In my mind's eye I behold Mrs. Bouncer, still with some traces of her late anxiety on her faithful countenance, balancing herself a little unequally on her bow fore-legs, pricking up her ears, with her head on one side, and slightly opening her intellectual nostrils. I send my loving and respectful duty to her.

To dear Mrs. White, and to White, and to Clara, say anything from me that is loving and grateful.

My dearest Mamie,

Ever and ever your most affectionate Father.

[*To Miss Hogarth.*]

OFFICE OF "ALL THE YEAR ROUND,"

Monday Night, Sept. 24th, 1860.

MY DEAREST GEORGY,

At the Waterloo station we were saluted with "Hallo ! here's Dickens ! " from divers naval cadets, and Sir Richard Bromley introduced himself to me, who had his cadet son with him, a friend of Sydney's. We went down together, and the boys were in the closest alliance. Bromley being Accountant-General of the Navy, and having influence on board, got their hammocks changed so that they would be serving side by side, at which they were greatly pleased. The moment we stepped on board, the "Hul-lo ! here's Dickens ! " was repeated on all sides, and the Admiral (evidently highly popular) shook hands with about fifty of his messmates. Taking Bromley for my model (with whom I fraternised in the most pathetic manner), I gave Sydney a sovereign before stepping over the side. He was as little overcome as it was possible for a boy to be, and stood waving the gold-banded cap as we came ashore in a boat.

There is no denying that he looks very small aboard a great ship, and that a boy must have a strong and decided speciality for the sea to take to such a life. Captain Harris was not on board, but the other chief officers were, and were highly obliging. We went over the ship. I should say that there can be little or no individuality of address to any particular boy, but that they all tumble through their education in a crowded way. The Admiral's servant (I mean our Admiral's) had an idiotic appearance, but perhaps it did him injustice (a mahogany-faced marine by station). The Admiral's washing apparatus is about the size of a muffin-plate, and he could easily live in his chest. The meeting with Bromley was a piece of great good fortune, and the dear old chap could not have been left more happily.

Ever, my dearest Georgy, your most affectionate.

[*To Miss Power.*]

Office of "All the Year Round,"
Tuesday, Sept. 25th, 1860.

My dear Marguerite,

I like the article exceedingly, and think the translations *admirable*—spirited, fresh, bold, and evidently faithful. I will get the paper into the next number I make up, No. 78.   I will send a proof to you for your correction, either next Monday or this day week.   Or would you like to come here next Monday and dine with us at five, and go over to Madame Céleste's opening?   Then you could correct your paper on the premises, as they drink their beer at the beer-shops.

Some of the introductory remarks on French literature I propose to strike out, as a little too essayical for this purpose, and likely to throw out a large portion of the large audience at starting, as suggesting some very different kind of article.   My daring pen shall have imbued its murderous heart with ink before you see the proof.

With kind regards,

Ever affectionately.

[*To Mr. John Forster.*]

GAD'S HILL PLACE, HIGHAM BY ROCHESTER, KENT,
Thursday, Oct. 4th, 1860.

MY DEAR FORSTER,

It would be a great pleasure to me to come to you, an immense pleasure, and to sniff the sea I love (from the shore); but I fear I must come down one morning and come back at night.   I will tell you why.

Last week, I got to work on a new story.   I called a council of war at the office on Tuesday.   It was perfectly clear that the one thing to be done was, for me to strike in.   I have therefore decided to begin a story, the length of the "Tale of Two Cities," on the 1st of December—

begin publishing, that is. I must make the most I can out óf the book. When I come down, I will bring you the fir'st two or three weekly parts. The name is, "GREAT EXPECTATIONS." I think a good name?

Now the preparations to get ahead, combined with the absolute necessity of my giving a good deal of time to the Christmas number, will tie me to the grindstone pretty tightly. It will be just as much as I can hope to do. Therefore, what I had hoped would be a few days at Eastbourne diminish to a few hours.

I took the Admiral down to Portsmouth. Every maritime person in the town knew him. He seemed to know every boy on board the *Britannia*, and was a tremendous favourite evidently. It was very characteristic of him that they good-naturedly helped him, he being so very small, into his hammock at night. But he couldn't rest in it on these terms, and got out again to learn the right way of getting in independently. Official report stated that " after a few spills, he succeeded perfectly, and went to sleep." He is perfectly happy on board, takes tea with the captain, leads choruses on Saturday nights, and has an immense marine for a servant.

I saw Edmund Yates at the office, and he told me that during all his mother's wanderings of mind, which were almost incessant at last, she never once went back to the old Adelphi days until she was just dying, when he heard her say, in great perplexity : " I can *not* get the words."

Best love to Mrs. Forster.

Ever, my dear Forster, affectionately.

OFFICE OF "ALL THE YEAR ROUND,"

Wednesday, Oct. 24th, 1860.

MY DEAR WILKIE,

I have been down to Brighton to see Forster, and found your letter there on arriving by express this morning. I also found a letter from Georgina, describing that Mary's horse went down suddenly on a stone, and how Mary was thrown, and had her riding-habit torn to pieces, and has a deep cut just above the knee—fortunately not in the knee itself, which is doing exceedingly well, but which will probably incapacitate her from walking for days and days to come. It is well it was no worse. The accident occurred at Milton, near Gravesend, and they found Mary in a public-house there, wonderfully taken care of and looked after.

I propose that we start on Thursday morning, the 1st of November. The train for Penzance leaves the Great Western terminus at a quarter-past nine in the morning. It is a twelve hours' journey. Shall we meet at the terminus at nine? I shall be here all the previous day, and shall dine here.

Your account of your passage goes to my heart through my stomach. What a pity I was not there on board to present that green-visaged, but sweet-tempered and un-complaining spectacle of imbecility, at which I am so expert under stormy circumstances, in the poet's phrase :

As I sweep
Through the deep,
When the stormy winds do blow.

What a pity I am not there, at Meurice's, to sleep the sleep of infancy through the long plays where the gentlemen stand with their backs to the mantelpieces. What a pity I am not with you to make a third at the Trois Frères, and drink no end of bottles of Bordeaux, without ever getting a touch of redness in my (poet's phrase again) "innocent nose." But I must go down to Gad's to-night, and get to work again. Four weekly numbers have been ground off the wheel, and at least another must be turned before we meet. They shall be yours in the slumberous railway-carriage.

I don't think Forster is at all in good health. He was tremendously hospitable and hearty. I walked six hours and a half on the downs yesterday, and never stopped or sat. Early in the morning, before breakfast, I went to the nearest baths to get a shower-bath. They kept me waiting longer than I thought reasonable, and seeing a man in a cap in the passage, I went to him and said : " I really must request that you'll be good enough to see about this shower-bath ; " and it was Hullah ! waiting for another bath.

Rumours were brought into the house on Saturday night, that there was a " ghost " up at Larkins's monument. Plorn was frightened to death, and I was apprehensive of the ghost's spreading and coming there, and causing " warning " and desertion among the servants.

VOL. II.—7*

Frank was at home, and Andrew Gordon was with us. Time, nine o'clock. Village talk and credulity amazing. I armed the two boys with a short stick apiece, and shouldered my double-barrelled gun, well loaded with shot. " Now observe," says I to the domestics, " if anybody is playing tricks and has got a head, I'll blow it off." Immense impression. New groom evidently convinced that he has entered the service of a bloodthirsty demon. We ascend to the monument. Stop at the gate. Moon is rising. Heavy shadows. " Now, look out !" (from the bloodthirsty demon, in a loud, distinct voice). " If the ghost is here and I see him, so help me God I'll fire at him !" Suddenly, as we enter the field, a most extraordinary noise responds—terrific noise—human noise—and yet superhuman noise. B. T. D. brings piece to shoulder. "Did you hear that, pa?" says Frank. "I did," says I. Noise repeated—portentous, derisive, dull, dismal, damnable. We advance towards the sound. Something white comes lumbering through the darkness. An asthmatic sheep ! Dead, as I judge, by this time. Leaving Frank to guard him, I took Andrew with me, and went all round the monument, and down into the ditch, and examined the field well, thinking it likely that somebody might be taking advantage of the sheep to frighten the village. Drama ends with discovery of no one, and triumphant return to rum-and-water.

Ever affectionately.

[*To Miss Hogarth.*]

Bideford, North Devon, *Thursday Night, Nov. 1st,* 1860.

My dearest Georgy,

I write (with the most impracticable iron pen on earth) to report our safe arrival here, in a beastly hotel. We start to-morrow morning at nine on a two days' posting between this and Liskeard in Cornwall. We are due in Liskeard (but nobody seems to know anything about the roads) on Saturday afternoon, and we purpose making an excursion in that neighbourhood on Sunday, and coming up from Liskeard on Monday by Great Western fast train, which will get us to London, please God, in good time on Monday evening. There I shall hear from you, and know whether dear Mamie will move to London too.

We had a pleasant journey down here, and a beautiful day. No adventures whatever. Nothing has happened to Wilkie, and he sends love.

We had stinking fish for dinner, and have been able to drink nothing, though we have ordered wine, beer, and brandy-and-water. There is nothing in the house but two tarts and a pair of snuffers. The landlady is playing cribbage with the landlord in the next room (behind a thin partition), and they seem quite comfortable.

Ever, my dearest Georgy, your most affectionate.

· [*To Miss Mary Boyle.*]

OFFICE OF " ALL THE YEAR ROUND,"
Friday, Dec. 28*th,* 1860.

MY DEAR MARY,

I cannot tell you how much I thank you for the beautiful cigar-case, and how seasonable, and friendly, and good, and warm-hearted it looked when I opened it at Gad's Hill. Besides which, it is a cigar-case, and will hold cigars ; two crowning merits that I never yet knew to be possessed by any article claiming the same name. For all of these reasons, but more than all because it comes from you, I love it, and send you eighteen hundred and sixty kisses, with one in for the new year.

Both excellent stories and perfectly new. Your Joe swears that he never heard either—never a word or syllable of either—after he laughed at 'em this blessed day.

I have no news, except that I am not quite well, and am being doctored. Pray read " Great Expectations." I think it is very droll. It is a very great success, and seems universally liked. I suppose because it opens funnily, and with an interest too.

I pass my time here (I am staying here alone) in working, taking physic, and taking a stall at a theatre every night. On Boxing Night I was at Covent Garden. A dull pantomime was " worked " (as we say) better than I ever saw a heavy piece worked on a first night, until suddenly and without a moment's warning, every scene on that immense stage fell over on its face, and disclosed chaos by gaslight behind! There never was such a business; about sixty people who were on the stage being extinguished in the most remarkable manner. Not a soul was hurt. In the uproar, some moon-calf rescued a porter pot, six feet high (out of which the clown had been drinking when the accident happened), and stood it on the cushion of the lowest proscenium box, P.S., beside a lady and gentleman, who were dreadfully ashamed of it. The moment the house knew that nobody was injured, they directed their whole attention to this gigantic porter pot in its genteel position (the lady and gentleman trying to hide behind it), and roared with laughter. When a modest footman came from behind the curtain to clear it, and took it up in his arms like a Brobdingnagian baby, we all laughed more than ever we had laughed in our lives. I don't know why.

We have had a fire here, but our people put it out before the parish-engine arrived, like a drivelling perambulator, with *the beadle in it*, like an imbecile baby. Popular opinion, disappointed in the fire having been put out, snowballed the beadle. God bless it!

Over the way at the Lyceum, there is a very fair Christmas piece, with one or two uncommonly well-done nigger songs—one remarkably gay and mad, done in the finale to a scene. Also a very nice transformation, though I don't know what it means.

The poor actors waylay me in Bow Street, to represent their necessities; and I often see one cut down a court when he beholds me coming, cut round Drury Lane to face me, and come up towards me near this door in the freshest and most accidental way, as if I was the last person he expected to see on the surface of this globe. The other day, there thus appeared before me (simultaneously with a scent of rum in the air) one aged and greasy man, with a pair of pumps under his arm. He said he thought if he could get down to somewhere (I think it was Newcastle), he would get "taken on" as Pantaloon, the existing Pantaloon being "a stick, sir—a mere muff." I observed that I was sorry times were so bad with him. "Mr. Dickens, you know our profession, sir—no one knows it better, sir—there is no right feeling in it. I was Harlequin on your own circuit, sir, for five-and-thirty years, and was displaced by a boy, sir!—a boy!"

So no more at present, except love to Mrs. Watson and Bedgey Prig and all, from my dear Mary.

Your ever affectionate

JOE.

P.S.—DON'T I pine neither?

P.P.S.—I did my best to arouse Forster's worst feelings ; but he had got into a Christmas habit of mind, and wouldn't respond.

NARRATIVE.

1861.

THIS, as far as his movements were concerned, was again a very unsettled year with Charles Dickens. He hired a furnished house in the Regent's Park, which he, with his household, occupied for some months. During the season he gave several readings at St. James's Hall. After a short summer holiday at Gad's Hill, he started, in the autumn, on a reading tour in the English provinces. Mr. Arthur Smith, being seriously ill, could not accompany him in this tour ; and Mr. Headland, who was formerly in office at the St. Martin's Hall, was engaged as business-manager of these readings. Mr. Arthur Smith died in October, and Charles Dickens's distress at the loss of this loved friend and companion is touchingly expressed in many of his letters of this year.

There are also sorrowful allusions to the death of his brother-in-law, Mr. Henry Austin, which sad event like-wise happened in October. And the letter we give to Mrs. Austin (" Letitia ") has reference to her sad affliction.

In June of this year he paid a short visit to Sir E. B. Lytton at Knebworth, accompanied by his daughter and sister-in-law, who also during his autumn tour joined him in Edinburgh. But this course of readings was brought rather suddenly to an end on account of the death of the Prince Consort.

Besides being constantly occupied with the business of these readings, Charles Dickens was still at work on his story of "Great Expectations," which was appearing weekly in "All the Year Round." The story closed on the 3rd of August, when it was published as a whole in three volumes, and inscribed to Mr. Chauncey Hare Towns-hend. The Christmas number of "All the Year Round" was called "Tom Tiddler's Ground," to which Charles Dickens contributed three stories.

Our second letter in this year is given more as a speci-men of the claims which were constantly being made upon Charles Dickens's time and patience, than because we consider the letter itself to contain much public interest ; excepting, indeed, as showing his always considerate and courteous replies to such constant applications.

"The fire" mentioned in the letter to Mr. Forster was the great fire in Tooley Street. The "Morgan" was an American sea-captain, well known in those days, and greatly liked and respected. It may interest our readers to know that the character of Captain Jorgan, in the Christmas number of the previous year, was suggested by this pleasant sailor, for whom Charles Dickens had a hearty liking. Young Mr. Morgan was, during the years he passed in England, a constant visitor at Gad's Hill. The "Elwin" mentioned in the letter written from Bury St. Edmunds, was the Rev. Whitwell Elwin, a Norfolk gentleman, well known in the literary world, and who was for many years editor of "The Quarterly Review."

The explanation of the letter to Mr. John Agate, of Dover, we give in that gentleman's own words :

"There are few public men with the strain upon their time and energies which he had particularly (and which I know better now that I have read his life), who would have spared the time to have written such a long courteous letter.

"I wrote to him rather in anger, and left the letter myself at The Lord Warden, as I and my family were very much disappointed, after having purchased our tickets so long before, to find we could not get into the room, as money was being received, but this kind letter explained all."

[*To Miss Hogarth.*]

OFFICE OF "ALL THE YEAR ROUND,"
Wednesday, Jan. 9th, 1861.

MY DEAREST GEORGY,

"We" are in the full swing of stopping managers from playing "A Message from the Sea." I privately doubt the strength of our position in the Court of Chancery, if we try it; but it is worth trying.

I am aware that Mr. Lane of the Britannia sent an emissary to Gad's Hill yesterday. It unfortunately happens that the first man " we " have to assert the principle against is a very good man, whom I really respect.

I have no news except that I really hope and believe I am gradually getting well. If I have no check, I hope to be soon discharged by the medico.   Ever affectionately.

P.S.—Best love to Mamie, also to the boys and Miss Craufurd.

OFFICE OF " ALL THE YEAR ROUND,"
26, WELLINGTON STREET, W.C.,
Tuesday Evening, Jan. 9th, 1861.

DEAR SIR,

I feel it quite hopeless to endeavour to present my position before you, in reference to such a letter as yours, in its plain and true light. When you suppose it would have cost Mr. Thackeray " but a word " to use his influence to obtain you some curatorship or the like, you fill me with the sense of impossibility of leading you to a more charitable judgment of Mr. Dickens.

Nevertheless, I will put the truth before you. Scarcely a day of my life passes, or has passed for many years, without bringing me some letters similar to yours. Often they will come by dozens—scores—hundreds. My time and attention would be pretty well occupied without them, and the claims upon me (some very near home), for all the influence and means of help that I do and do not possess, are not commonly heavy. I have no power to aid you towards the attainment of your object. It is the simple exact truth, and nothing can alter it. So great is the disquietude I constantly undergo from having to write to some new correspondent in this strain, that, God knows, I would resort to another relief if I could.

Your studies from nature appear to me to express an excellent observation of nature, in a loving and healthy spirit. But what then ? The dealers and dealers' prices of which you complain will not be influenced by that honest opinion. Nor will it nave the least effect upon the President of the Royal Academy, or the Directors of the School of Design. Assuming your supposition to be correct that these authorities are adverse to you, I have no more power than you have to render them favou.able. And assuming them to be quite disinterested and dispassionate towards you, I have no voice or weight in any appointment that any of them make.

I will retain your packet over to-morrow, and will then cause it to be sent to your house. I write under the pressure of occupation and business, and therefore write briefly.

Faithfully yours.

[*To M. de Cerjat.*]

OFFICE OF " ALL THE YEAR ROUND,"
Friday, Feb. 1st, 1861.

MY DEAR CERJAT,

You have read in the papers of our heavy English frost. At Gad's Hill it was so intensely cold, that in our warm dining-room on Christmas Day we could hardly sit at the table. In my study on that morning, long after a great fire of coal and wood had been lighted, the thermometer was I don't know where below freezing. The bath froze, and all the pipes froze, and remained in a stony state for five or six weeks. The water in the bedroom-jugs froze, and blew up the crockery. The snow on the top of the house froze, and was imperfectly removed with axes. My beard froze as I walked about, and I couldn't detach my cravat and coat from it until I was thawed at the fire. My boys and half the officers stationed at Chatham skated away without a check to Gravesend—five miles off—and repeated the performance for three or four weeks. At last the thaw came, and then everything split, blew up, dripped, poured, perspired, and got spoilt. Since then we have had a small visitation of the plague of servants ; the cook (in a riding-habit) and the groom (in a dress-coat and jewels) having mounted Mary's horse and mine, in our absence, and scoured the neighbouring country at a rattling pace. And when I went home last Saturday, I innocently wondered how the horses came to be out of condition, and gravely consulted the said groom on the subject, who gave it as his opinion " which they wanted reg'lar work." We are now coming to town until midsummer. Having sold my own house, to be more free and independent, I have taken a very pretty furnished house, No. 3, Hanover Terrace, Regent's Park. This, of course, on my daughter's account. For I have very good and cheerful bachelor rooms here, with an old servant in charge, who is the cleverest man of his kind in the world, and can do anything, from excellent carpentery to excellent cookery, and has been with me three-and-twenty years.   •

The American business is the greatest English sensation at present. I venture to predict that the struggle of violence will be a very short one, and will be soon succeeded by some new compact between the Northern and Southern States. Meantime the Lancashire mill-owners are getting very uneasy.

The Italian state of things is not regarded as looking very cheerful. What from one's natural sympathies with a people so oppressed as the Italians, and one's natural antagonism to a pope and a Bourbon (both of which superstitions I do suppose the world to have had more than enough of), I agree with you concerning Victor Emmanuel, and greatly fear that the Southern Italians are much degraded. Still, an united Italy would be of vast importance to the peace of the world, and would be a rock in Louis Napoleon's way, as he very well knows. Therefore the idea must be championed, however much against hope.

My eldest boy, just home from China, was descried by Townshend's Henri the moment he landed at Marseilles, and was by him borne in triumph to Townshend's rooms. The weather was snowy, slushy, beastly ; and Marseilles was, as it usually is to my thinking, well-nigh intolerable. My boy could not stay with Townshend, as he was coming on by express train ; but he says : " I sat with him and saw him dine. He had a leg of lamb, and a tremendous cold." That is the whole description I have been able to extract from him.

This journal is doing gloriously, and "Great Expectations" is a great success. I have taken my third boy, Frank (Jeffrey's godson), into this office. If I am not mistaken, he has a natural literary taste and capacity, and may do very well with a chance so congenial to his mind, and being also entered at the Bar.

Dear me, when I have to show you about London, and we dine *en garçon* at odd places, I shall scarcely know where to begin. Only yesterday I walked out from here in the afternoon, and thought I would go down by the Houses of Parliament. When I got there, the day was so beautifully bright and warm, that I thought I would walk on by Millbank, to see the river. I walked straight on *for three miles* on a splendid broad esplanade overhanging the Thames, with immense factories, railway works, and whatnot erected on it, and with the strangest beginnings and ends of wealthy streets pushing themselves into the very Thames. When I was a rower on that river, it was all broken ground and ditch, with here and there a public-house or two, an old mill, and a tall chimney. I had never seen it in any state of transition, though I suppose myself to know this rather large city as well as anyone in it.

*   *   *   *   *   *

[*To Mr. E. M. Ward, R.A.*]

3, HANOVER TERRACE, REGENT'S PARK,
Saturday Night, March 9th, 1861.

MY DEAR WARD,

I cannot tell you how gratified I have been by your letter, and what a splendid recompense it is for any pleasure

I am giving you. Such generous and earnest sympathy from such a brother-artist gives me true delight. I am proud of it, believe me, and moved by it to do all the better.

Ever faithfully yours.

[*To Mr. W. C. Macready.*]

"ALL THE YEAR ROUND" OFFICE, *Tuesday, June 11th,* 1861.
MY DEAREST MACREADY,

There is little doubt, I think, of my reading at Cheltenham somewhere about November. I submit myself so entirely to Arthur Smith's arrangements for me, that I express my sentiments on this head with modesty. But I think there is scarcely a doubt of my seeing you then.

I have just finished my book of " Great Expectations," and am the worse for wear. Neuralgic pains in the face have troubled me a good deal, and the work has been pretty close. But I hope that the book is a good book, and I have no doubt of very soon throwing off the little damage it has done me.

What with Blondin at the Crystal Palace and Leotard at Leicester Square, we seem to be going back to barbaric excitements. I have not seen, and don't intend to see, the Hero of Niagara (as the posters call him), but I have been beguiled into seeing Leotard, and it is at once the most fearful and most graceful thing I have ever seen done.

Clara White (grown pretty) has been staying with us.

I am sore afraid that *The Times,* by playing fast and loose with the American question, has very seriously compromised this country. The Americans northward are perfectly furious on the subject; and Motley the historian (a very sensible man, strongly English in his sympathies) assured me the other day that he thought the harm done very serious indeed, and the dangerous nature of the daily widening breach scarcely calculable.

Kindest and best love to all. Wilkie Collins has just come in, and sends best regard.

Ever most affectionately, my dearest Macready.

[*To Mr. John Forster.*]

GAD'S HILL, *Monday, July 1st*, 1861.

MY DEAR FORSTER,

* * * * * *

You will be surprised to hear that I have changed the end of " Great Expectations " from and after Pip's return to Joe's, and finding his little likeness there.

Bulwer (who has been, as I think I told you, extraordinarily taken by the book), so strongly urged it upon me, after reading the proofs, and supported his views with such good reasons, that I resolved to make the change. You shall have it when you come back to town. I have put in a very pretty piece of writing, and I have no doubt the story will be more acceptable through the alteration.

I have not seen Bulwer's changed story. I brought back the first month with me, and I know the nature of his changes throughout; but I have not yet had the revised proofs. He was in a better state at Knebworth than I have ever seen him in all these years, a little weird occasionally regarding magic and spirits, but perfectly fair and frank under opposition. He was talkative, anecdotical, and droll ; looked young and well, laughed heartily, and enjoyed some games we played with great zest. In his artist character and talk he was full of interest and matter, but that he always is. Socially, he seemed to me almost a new man. I thoroughly enjoyed myself, and so did Georgina and Mary.

The fire I did not see until the Monday morning, but it was blazing fiercely then, and was blazing hardly less furiously when I came down here again last Friday. I was here on the night of its breaking out. If I had been in London I should have been on the scene, pretty surely.

You will be perhaps surprised to hear that it is Morgan's conviction (his son was here yesterday), that the North will put down the South, and that speedily. In his management of his large business, he is proceeding steadily on that conviction. He says that the South has no money and no credit, and that it is impossible for it to make a successful stand. He may be all wrong, but he is certainly a very shrewd man, and he has never been, as to the United States, an enthusiast of any class.

Poor Lord Campbell's seems to me as easy and good a death as one could desire. There must be a sweep of these men very soon, and one feels as if it must fall out like the breaking of an arch—one stone goes from a prominent place, and then the rest begin to drop. So one looks towards Brougham, and Lyndhurst, and Pollock.

I will add no more to this, or I know I shall not send it ; for I am in the first desperate laziness of having done my book, and think of offering myself to the village school as a live example of that vice for the edification of youth.

Ever, my dear Forster, affectionately.

[*To the Hon. Mrs. Watson.*]

GAD'S HILL PLACE, HIGHAM BY ROCHESTER, KENT,
Monday, July 8th, 1861.

MY DEAR MRS. WATSON,

I have owed you a letter for so long a time that I fear you may sometimes have misconstrued my silence. But I hope that the sight of the handwriting of your old friend will undeceive you, if you have, and will put that right.

During the progress of my last story, I have been working so hard that very, very little correspondence—except enforced correspondence on business—has passed this pen. And now that I am free again, I devote a few of my first leisure moments to this note.

You seemed in your last to think that I had forgotten you in respect of the Christmas number. Not so at all. I discussed with them here where you were, how you were to be addressed, and the like ; finally left the number in a blank envelope, and did not add the address to it until it would have been absurd to send you such stale bread. This was my fault, but this was all. And I should be so pained at heart if you supposed me capable of failing in my truth and cordiality, or in the warm remembrance of the time we have passed together, that perhaps I make more of it than you meant to do.

VOL. II.—8

My sailor-boy is at home—I was going to write, for the holidays, but I suppose I must substitute "on leave." Under the new regulations, he must not pass out of the *Britannia* before December. The younger boys are all at school, and coming home this week for the holidays. Mary keeps house, of course, and Katie and her husband sur-· prised us yesterday, and are here now. Charley is holiday-making at Guernsey and Jersey. He has been for some time seeking a partnership in business, and has not yet found one. The matter is in the hands of Mr. Bates, the managing partner in Barings' house, and seems as slow a matter to adjust itself as ever I looked on at. Georgina is, as usual, the general friend and confidante and factotum of the whole party.

Your present correspondent read at St. James's Hall in the beginning of the season, to perfectly astounding audiences ; but finding that fatigue and excitement very difficult to manage in conjunction with a story, deemed it prudent to leave off reading in high tide and mid-career, the rather by reason of something like neuralgia in the face. At the end of October I begin again ; and if you are at Brighton in November, I shall try to see you there. I deliver myself up to Mr. Arthur Smith, and I know it is one of the places for which he has put me down.

This is all about me and mine, and next I want to know why you never come to Gad's Hill, and whether you are never coming. The stress I lay on these questions you will infer from the size of the following note of interrogation **?**

I am in the constant receipt of news from Lausanne. Of Mary Boyle, I daresay you have seen and heard more than I have lately. Rumours occasionally reach me of her acting in every English shire incessantly, and getting in a harvest of laurels all the year round. Cavendish I have not seen for a long time, but when I did see him last, it was at Tavistock House, and we dined together jovially. Mention of that locality reminds me that when you DO come here, you will see. the pictures looking wonderfully better, and more precious than they ever did in town. Brought together in country light and air, they really are quite a baby collection.and very pretty.

I direct this to Rockingham, supposing you to be there in this summer time. If you are as leafy in Northamptonshire as we are in Kent, you are greener than you have been for some years. I hope you may have seen a large-headed photograph with little legs, representing the undersigned, pen in hand, tapping his forehead to knock an idea out. It has just sprung up so abundantly in all the shops, that I am ashamed to go about town looking in at the picture-windows, which is my delight. It seems to me extraordinarily ludicrous, and much more like than the grave portrait done in earnest. It made me laugh when I first came upon it, until I shook again, in open sunlighted Piccadilly.

Pray be a good Christian to me, and don't be retributive in measuring out the time that shall pass before you write to me. And believe me ever,

Your affectionate and faithful.

[*To Mr. W. Wilkie Collins.*]

OFFICE OF "ALL THE YEAR ROUND,"
Wednesday, Aug. 28th, 1861.

MY DEAR WILKIE,

I have been going to write to you ever since I received your letter from Whitby, and now I hear from Charley that you are coming home, and must be addressed in the Rue Harley. Let me know whether you will dine here this day week at the usual five. I am at present so addle-headed (having hard Wednesday work in Wills's absence) that I can't write much.

I have got the "Copperfield" reading ready for delivery, and am now going to blaze away at "Nickleby," which I don't like half as well. Every morning I "go in" at these marks for two or three hours, and then collapse and do nothing whatever (counting as nothing much cricket and rounders).

In my time that curious railroad by the Whitby Moor was so much the more curious, that you were balanced against a counter-weight of water, and that you did it like Blondin. But in these remote days the one inn of Whitby was up a back-yard, and oyster-shell grottoes were the only view from the best private room. Likewise, sir, I have posted to Whitby. "Pity the sorrows of a poor old man."

The sun is glaring in at these windows with an amount of ferocity insupportable by one of the landed interest, who lies upon his back with an imbecile hold on grass, from lunch to dinner. Feebleness of mind and head are the result.

Ever affectionately.

P.S.—The boys have multiplied themselves by fifty daily, and have seemed to appear in hosts (especially in the hottest days) round all the corners at Gad's Hill. I call them the prowlers, and each has a distinguishing name attached, derived from his style of prowling.

[To Mr. Arthur Smith.]

GAD'S HILL PLACE, HIGHAM BY ROCHESTER, KENT,
Tuesday, Sept. 3rd, 1861.

MY DEAR ARTHUR,

I cannot tell you how sorry I am to receive your bad account of your health, or how anxious I shall be to receive a better one as soon as you can possibly give it.

If you go away, don't you think in the main you would be better here than anywhere ? You know how well you would be nursed, what care we should take of you, and how perfectly quiet and at home you would be, until you become strong enough to take to the Medway. Moreover, I think you would be less anxious about the tour, here, than away from such association. I would come to Worthing to fetch you, I needn't say, and would take the most careful charge of you. I will write no more about this, because I wish to avoid giving you more to read than can be helped; but I do sincerely believe it would be at once your wisest and least anxious course. As to a long journey into Wales, or any long journey, it would never do. Nice is not to be thought of. Its dust, and its sharp winds (I know it well), towards October are very bad indeed.

I send you the enclosed letters, firstly, because I have no circular to answer them with, and, secondly, because I fear I might confuse your arrangements by interfering with the correspondence. I shall hope to have a word from you very soon. I am at work for the tour every day, except my town Wednesdays.

Ever faithfully.

P.S.—Kindest regards from all.

[*To Mr. John Watkins.*]

GAD'S HILL PLACE, HIGHAM BY ROCHESTER, KENT,
Saturday Night, Sept. 28th, 1861.

DEAR MR. WATKINS,

In reply to your kind letter I must explain that I have not yet brought down any of your large photographs of myself, and therefore cannot report upon their effect here. I think the " cartes " are all liked.

A general howl of horror greeted the appearance of No. 18, and a riotous attempt was made to throw it out of window. I calmed the popular fury by promising that it should never again be beheld within these walls. I think I mentioned to you when you showed it to me, that I felt persuaded it would not be liked. It has a grim and wasted aspect, and perhaps might be made useful as a portrait of the Ancient Mariner.

I feel that I owe you an apology for being (innocently) a difficult subject. When I once excused myself to Ary Scheffer while sitting to him, he received the apology as strictly his due, and said with a vexed air: " At this moment, *mon cher* Dickens, you look more like an energetic Dutch admiral than anything else ; " for which I apologised again.

In the hope that the pains you have bestowed upon me will not be thrown away, but that your success will prove of some use to you, believe me,

Faithfully yours.

[*To Mr. Edmund Yates.*]

· GAD'S HILL PLACE, HIGHAM BY ROCHESTER, KENT,
Sunday, Oct. 6th, 1861.

AFTER THE DEATH OF MR. ARTHUR SMITH.

MY DEAR EDMUND,

Coming back here to-day, I find your letter.

I was so very much distressed last night in thinking of it all, and I find it so very difficult to preserve my composure when I dwell in my mind on the many times fast approaching when I shall sorely miss the familiar face, that I am hardly steady enough yet to refer to the readings like a man. But your kind reference to them makes me desirous to tell you that I took Headland (formerly of St. Martin's Hall, who has always been with us in London) to conduct the business, when I knew that our poor dear fellow could never do it, even if he had recovered strength to go ; and that I consulted with himself about it when I saw him for the last time on earth, and that it seemed to please him, and he said : " We couldn't do better."

Write to me before you come ; and remember that I go to town Wednesday mornings.

Ever faithfully.

[*To Miss Dickens.*]

Office of "All the Year Round,"
Thursday, Oct. 10*th*, 1861.

My dearest Mamie,

I received your affectionate little letter here this morning, and was very glad to get it.   Poor dear Arthur is a sad loss to me, and indeed I was very fond of him.   But the readings must be fought out, like all the rest of life.

Ever your affectionate.

[*To Mr. W. C. Macready.*]

Gad's Hill Place, Higham by Rochester, Kent,
Sunday, Oct. 13*th*, 1861.

My dearest Macready,

This is a short note.   But the moment I know for certain what is designed for me at Cheltenham, I write to you in order that you may know it from me and not by chance from anyone else.

I am to read there on the evening of Friday, the 3rd of January, and on the morning of Saturday, the 4th ; as I have nothing to do on Thursday, the 2nd, but come from

Leamington, I shall come to you, please God, for a quiet dinner that day.

The death of Arthur Smith has caused me great distress and anxiety. I had a great regard for him, and he made the reading part of my life as light and pleasant as it *could* be made. I had hoped to bring him to see you, and had pictured to myself how amused and interested you would have been with his wonderful tact and consummate mastery of arrangement. But it's all over.

I begin at Norwich on the 28th, and am going north in the middle of November. I am going to do "Copperfield," and shall be curious to test its effect on the Edinburgh people. It has been quite a job so to piece portions of the long book together as to make something continuous out of it; but I hope I have got something varied and dramatic. I am also (not to slight *your* book) going to do "Nickleby at Mr. Squeers's." It is clear that both must be trotted out at Cheltenham.

With kindest love and regard to all your house,

Ever, my dearest Macready, your most affectionate.

P.S.—Fourth edition of "Great Expectations" almost gone !

[*To Miss Hogarth.*]

ANGEL HOTEL, BURY ST. EDMUNDS,
Wednesday, Oct. 13th, 1861.

MY DEAREST GEORGY,

I have just now received your welcome letter, and I hasten to report (having very little time) that we had a

VOL. II.—8*

splendid hall last night, and that I think " Nickleby " tops
all the readings.   Somehow it seems to have got in it, by
accident, exactly the qualities best suited to the purpose,
and it went last night not only with roars, but with a general hilarity and pleasure that I have never seen surpassed.

We are full here for to-night.

Fancy this : last night at about six, who should walk in
but Elwin !   He was exactly in his usual state, only more
demonstrative than ever, and had been driven in by some
neighbours who were coming to the reading.   I had tea
up for him, and he went down at seven with me to the
dismal den where I dressed, and sat by the fire while I
dressed, and was childishly happy in that great privilege !
During the reading he sat on a corner of the platform and
roared incessantly.   He brought in a lady and gentleman
to introduce while I was undressing, and went away in a
perfect and absolute rapture.

[*To Miss Hogarth.*]

ROYAL HOTEL, NORWICH, *Tuesday, Oct. 29th,* 1861.

I cannot say that we began well last night.   We had
not a good hall, and they were a very lumpish audience
indeed.   This did not tend to cheer the strangeness I felt
in being without Arthur, and I was not at all myself.   We
have a large let for to-night, I think two hundred and fifty
stalls, which is very large, and I hope that both they and
I will go better.   I could have done perfectly last night, if
the audience had been bright, but they were an intent and

staring audience. They laughed though very well, and the storm made them shake themselves again. But they were not magnetic, and the great big place was out of sorts somehow.

To-morrow I will write you another short note, however short. It is " Nickleby " and the " Trial " to-night ; "Copperfield " again to-morrow. A wet day here, with glimpses of blue. I shall not forget Katey's health at dinner. A pleasant journey down.

Ever, my dearest Georgy, your most affectionate.

[*To Miss Hogarth.*]

THE GREAT WHITE HORSE, IPSWICH, *Friday, Nov. 1st,* 1861.

I cannot quite remember in the whirl of travelling and reading, whether or no I wrote you a line from Bury St. Edmunds. But I think (and hope) I did. We had a fine room there, and " Copperfield " made a great impression. At mid-day we go on to Colchester, where I shall expect the young Morgans. I sent a telegram on yesterday, after receiving your note, to secure places for them. The answer returned by telegraph was : " No box-seats left but on the fourth row." If they prefer to sit on the stage (for I read in the theatre, there being no other large public room), they shall. Meantime I have told John, who went forward this morning with the other men, to let the people at the inn know that if three travellers answering that description appear before my dinner-time, they are to dine with me.

Plorn's admission that he likes the school very much indeed, is the great social triumph of modern times.

I am looking forward to Sunday's rest at Gad's, and shall be down by the ten o'clock train from town. I miss poor Arthur dreadfully. It is scarcely possible to imagine how much. It is not only that his loss to me socially is quite irreparable, but that the sense I used to have of compactness and comfort about me while I was reading is quite gone. And when I come out for the ten minutes, when I used to find him always ready for me with something cheerful to say, it is forlorn. I cannot but fancy, too, that the audience must miss the old speciality of a pervading gentleman.

Nobody I know has turned up yet except Elwin. I have had many invitations to all sorts of houses in all sorts of places, and have of course accepted them every one.

Love to Mamie, if she has come home, and to Bouncer, if *she* has come ; also Marguerite, who I hope is by this time much better.

Ever, my dear Georgy, your most affectionate.

[*To Mrs. Henry Austin.*]

GAD'S HILL, *Sunday, Nov. 3rd,* 1861.

EXTRACT.

I am heartily glad to hear that you have been out in the air, and I hope you will go again very soon and make a point of continuing to go. There is a soothing influence in the sight of the earth and sky, which God put into them for our relief when He made the world in which we are all to suffer, and strive, and die.

I will not fail to write to you from many points of my tour, and if you ever want to write to me you may be sure of a quick response, and may be certain that I am sympathetic and true.

Ever affectionately.

[*To Miss Dickens.*]

FOUNTAIN HOTEL, CANTERBURY, *Windy Night, Nov. 4th,* 1861.
MY DEAREST MAMIE,

A word of report before I go to bed. An excellent house to-night, and an audience positively perfect. The greatest part of it stalls, and an intelligent and delightful response in them, like the touch of a beautiful instrument. "Copperfield" wound up in a real burst of feeling and delight.

Ever affectionately.

[*To Mr. John Agate.*]

LORD WARDEN HOTEL, DOVER, *Wednesday, Nov. 6th,* 1861.
SIR,

I am exceedingly sorry to find, from the letter you have addressed to me, that you had just cause of complaint in being excluded from my reading here last night. It will now and then unfortunately happen when the place of reading is small (as in this case), that some confusion and inconvenience arise from the local agents over-estimating, in perfect good faith and sincerity, the capacity of the room. Such a mistake, I am assured, was made last night ; and thus all the available space ˏwasˊ filled before the people in charge were at all prepared for that circumstance.

You may readily suppose that I can have no personal knowledge of the proceedings of the people in my employment at such a time. But I wish to assure you very earnestly, that they are all old servants, well acquainted with my principles and wishes, and that they are under the strongest injunction to avoid any approach to mercenary dealing ; and to behave to all comers equally with as much consideration and politeness as they know I should myself display. The recent death of a much-regretted friend of mine, who managed this business for me, and on whom these men were accustomed to rely in any little difficulty, caused them (I have no doubt) to feel rather at a loss in your case. Do me the favour to understand that under any other circumstances you would, as a matter of course, have been provided with any places whatever that could be found, without the smallest reference to what you had originally paid. This is scanty satisfaction to you, but it is so strictly the truth, that yours is the first complaint of the kind I have ever received.

I hope to read in Dover again, but it is quite impossible that I can make any present arrangement for that purpose. Whenever I may return here, you may be sure I shall not fail to remember that I owe you a recompense for a disappointment. In the meanwhile I very sincerely regret it.

Faithfully yours.

[*To Miss Hogarth.*]

BEDFORD HOTEL, BRIGHTON, *Thursday, Nov. 7th,* 1861.

MY DEAR GEORGY,

*　　*　　*　　*　　*

The Duchess of Cambridge comes to-night to " Copper-field." The bad weather has not in the least touched us, and beyond all doubt a great deal of money has been left untaken at each place.

The storm was most magnificent at Dover. All the great side of The Lord Warden next the sea had to be emptied, the break of the sea was so prodigious, and the noise was so utterly confounding. The sea came in like a great sky of immense clouds, for ever breaking suddenly into furious rain. All kinds of wreck were washed in. Miss Birmingham and I saw, among other things, a very pretty brass-bound chest being thrown about like a feather. On Tuesday night, the unhappy Ostend packet could not get in, neither could she go back, and she beat about the Channel until noon yesterday. I saw her come in then, *with five men at the wheel;* such a picture of misery, as to the crew (of passengers there were no signs), as you can scarcely imagine.

The effect at Hastings and at Dover really seems to have outdone the best usual impression, and at Dover they wouldn't go, but sat applauding like mad. The most deli-cate audience I have seen in any provincial place is Can-terbury. The audience with the greatest sense of humour certainly is Dover. The people in the stalls set the example of laughing, in the most curiously unreserved way; and they really laughed when Squeers read the boys' letters, with such cordial enjoyment, that the contagion extended to me, for one couldn't hear them without laughing too.

So, thank God, all goes well, and the recompense for the trouble is in every way great. There is rather an alarming breakdown at Newcastle, in respect of all the bills having been, in some inscrutable way, lost on the road. I have resolved to send Berry there, with full powers to do all manner of things, early next week.

The amended route-list is not printed yet, because I am trying to get off Manchester and Liverpool; both of which I strongly doubt, in the present state of American affairs. Therefore I can't send it for Marguerite; but I can, and do, send her my love and God-speed. This is addressed to the office because I suppose you will be there to-morrow.

Ever affectionately.

[*To the Earl of Carlisle.*]

GAD'S HILL PLACE, HIGHAM BY ROCHESTER, KENT,
November 15*th*, 1861.

MY DEAR LORD CARLISLE,

You knew poor Austin, and what his work was, and how he did it. If you have no private objection to signing the enclosed memorial (which will receive the right signatures before being presented), I think you will have no public objection. I shall be heartily glad if you can put your name to it, and shall esteem your doing so as a very kind service. Will you return the memorial under cover to Mr. Tom Taylor, at the Local Government Act Office, Whitehall? He is generously exerting himself in further-ance of it, and so delay will be avoided.

My dear Lord Carlisle, faithfully yours always.

[*To Miss Mary Boyle.*]

GAD'S HILL PLACE, HIGHAM BY ROCHESTER, KENT,
Sunday, Nov. 17th, 1861.

MY DEAR MARY,

I am perfectly enraptured with the quilt. It is one of the most tasteful, lively, elegant things I have ever seen; and I need not tell you that while it is valuable to me for its own ornamental sake, it is precious to me as a rainbow-hint of your friendship and affectionate remem-brance.

Please God you shall see it next summer occupying its allotted place of state in my brand-new bedroom here. You shall behold it then, with all cheerful surroundings, the envy of mankind.

My readings have been doing absolute wonders. Your Duchess and Princess came to hear first " Nickleby " and the " Pickwick Trial," then "Copperfield," at Brighton. I think they were pleased with me, and I am sure I was with them; for they are the very best audience one could possibly desire. I shall always have a pleasant remem-brance of them.

On Wednesday I am away again for the longest part of my trip.

Yes, Mary dear, I must say that I like my Carton, and I have a faint idea sometimes that if I had acted him, I could have done something with his life and death.

Believe me, ever your affectionate and faithful.

JOE.

[*To Miss Hogarth.*]

QUEEN'S HEAD, NEWCASTLE, *Friday, Nov. 22nd*, 1861.

I received your letter this morning, and grieve to report that the unlucky Headland has broken down most awfully !

First, as perhaps you remember, this is the place where the bills were " lost " for a week or two. The consequence has been that the agent could not announce all through the " Jenny Lind " time (the most important for announcing), and could but stand still and stare when people came to ask what I was going to read. Last night I read " Copperfield " to the most enthusiastic and appreciative audience imaginable, but in numbers about half what they might have been. To-night we shall have a famous house ; but we might have had it last night too. To-morrow (knowing by this time what can, of a certainty, be done with " Copperfield "), I had, of course, given out " Copperfield " to be read again. Conceive my amazement and dismay when I find the printer to have announced " Little Dombey " ! ! ! This, I declare, I had no more intention of reading than I had of reading an account of the solar system. And this, after a sensation last night, of a really extraordinary nature in its intensity and delight !

Says the unlucky Headland to this first head of misery : " Johnson's mistake " (Johnson being the printer).

Second, I read at Edinburgh for the first time—observe the day—*next Wednesday.* Jenny Lind's concert at Edinburgh is to-night. This morning comes a frantic letter from the Edinburgh agent. " I have no bills, no tickets ; I lose all the announcement I would have made to hundreds upon hundreds of people to-night, all of the most desirable class to be well informed beforehand. I can't announce what Mr. Dickens is going to read ; I can answer no questions ; I have, upon my responsibility, put a dreary advertisement into the papers announcing that he *is* going to read so many times, and that particulars will shortly be ready ; and I stand bound hand and foot." " Johnson's mistake," says the unlucky Headland.

Of course, I know that the man who never made a mistake in poor Arthur's time is not likely to be always making mistakes now. But I have written by this post to Wills, to go to him and investigate. I have also detached Berry from here, and have sent him on by train at a few minutes' notice to Edinburgh, and then to Glasgow (where I have no doubt everything is wrong too). Glasgow we may save ; Edinburgh I hold to be irretrievably damaged. If it can be picked up at all, it can only be at the loss of the two first nights, and by the expenditure of no end of spirits and force. And this is the harder, because it is impossible not to see that the last readings polished and prepared the audiences in general, and that I have not to work them up in any place where I have been before, but that they start with a London intelligence, and with a respect and preparation for what they are going to hear.

I hope by the time you and Mamie come to me, we shall have got into some good method. I must take the thing more into my own hands and look after it from hour to hour. If such a thing as this Edinburgh business could have happened under poor Arthur, I really believe he would have fallen into a fit, or gone distracted. No one can ever know what he was but I who have been with him and without him. Headland is so anxious and so good-tempered that I cannot be very stormy with him; but it is the simple fact that he has no notion of the requirements of such work as this. Without him, and with a larger salary to Berry (though there are objections to the latter as *first* man), I could have done a hundred times better.

As Forster will have a strong interest in knowing all about the proceedings, perhaps you will send him this letter to read. There is no very tremendous harm, indeed, done as yet. At Edinburgh I KNOW what I can do with " Copperfield." I think it is not too much to say that for every one who does come to hear it on the first night, I can get back fifty on the second. And whatever can be worked up there will tell on Glasgow. Berry I shall continue to send on ahead, and I shall take nothing on trust and more as being done.

On Sunday morning at six, I have to start for Berwick.

From Berwick, in the course of that day, I will write again ; to Mamie next time.

With best love to her and Mrs. B.

[*To Miss Dickens.*]

QUEEN'S HEAD, NEWCASTLE-ON-TYNE,
Saturday, Nov. 23rd, 1861.

A most tremendous hall here last night ; something almost terrible in the cram. A fearful thing might have happened. Suddenly, when they were all very still over Smike, my gas batten came down, and it looked as if the room was falling. There were three great galleries crammed to the roof, and a high steep flight of stairs, and a panic must have destroyed numbers of people. A lady in the front row of stalls screamed, and ran out wildly towards me, and for one instant there was a terrible wave in the crowd. I addressed that lady laughing (for I knew she was in sight of everybody there), and called out as if it happened every night, " There's nothing the matter, I assure you ; don't be alarmed ; pray sit down ; " and she sat down directly, and there was a thunder of applause. It took some few minutes to mend, and I looked on with my hands in my pockets ; for I think if I had turned my back for a moment there might still have been a move. My people were dreadfully alarmed, Boylett in particular, who I suppose had some notion that the whole place might have taken fire.

" But there stood the master," he did me the honour to

say afterwards, in addressing the rest, "as cool as ever I see him a-lounging at a railway station."

A telegram from Berry at Edinburgh yesterday evening, to say that he had got the bills, and that they would all be up and dispersed yesterday evening under his own eyes. So no time was lost in setting things as right as they can be set. He has now gone on to Glasgow.

P.S.—Duty to Mrs. Bouncer.

[*To Miss Hogarth.*]

BERWICK-ON-TWEED, *Monday, Nov. 25th,* 1861.

I write (in a gale of wind, with a high sea running), to let you know that we go on to Edinburgh at half-past eight to-morrow morning.

A most ridiculous room was designed for me in this odd out-of-the-way place.   An immense Corn Exchange made of glass and iron, round, dome-topped, lofty, utterly absurd for any such purpose, and full of thundering echoes, with a little lofty crow's-nest of a stone gallery breast high, deep in the wall, into which it was designed to put *me!* I instantly struck, of course, and said I would either read in a room attached to this house (a very snug one, capable of holding five hundred people) or not at all.   Terrified local agents glowered, but fell prostrate.

Berry has this moment come back from Edinburgh and Glasgow with hopeful accounts. He seems to have done the business extremely well, and he says that it was quite curious and cheering to see how the Glasgow people assembled round the bills the instant they were posted, and evidently with a great interest in them.

We left Newcastle yesterday morning in the dark, when it was intensely cold and froze very hard. So it did here. But towards night the wind went round to the S.W., and all night it has been blowing very hard indeed. So it is now.

Tell Mamie that I have the same sitting-room as we had when we came here with poor Arthur, and that my bedroom is the room out of it which she and Katie had. Surely it is the oddest town to read in ! But it is taken on poor Arthur's principle that a place in the way pays the expenses of a through journey ; and the people would seem to be coming up to the scratch gallantly. It was a dull Sunday, though ; O it *was* a dull Sunday, without a book ! For I had forgotten to buy one at Newcastle, until it was too late. So after dark I made a jug of whisky-punch, and drowned the unlucky Headland's remembrance of his failures.

I shall hope to hear very soon that the workmen have " broken through," and that you have been in the state apartments, and that upholstery measurements have come off.

There has been a horrible accident in Edinburgh. One of the seven-storey old houses in the High Street fell when it was full of people. Berry was at the bill-poster's house, a few doors off, waiting for him to come home, when he heard what seemed like thunder, and then the air was darkened with dust, " as if an immense quantity of steam had been blown off," and then all that dismal quarter set up shrieks, which he says were most dreadful.

[*To Miss Dickens.*]

WATERLOO HOTEL, EDINBURGH. *Wednesday, Nov. 27th,* 1861.

Mrs. Bouncer must decidedly come with you to Carlisle. She shall be received with open arms. Apropos of Carlisle, let me know *when* you purpose coming there. We shall be there, please God, on the Saturday in good time, as I finish at Glasgow on the Friday night.

I have very little notion of the state of affairs here, as Headland brought no more decisive information from the agents yesterday (he never *can* get decisive information from any agents), than "the teeckets air joost moving reecht and left." I hope this may be taken as satisfactory. Jenny Lind carried off a world of money from here. Miss Glyn, or Mrs. Dallas, is playing Lady Macbeth at the theatre, and Mr. Shirley Brooks is giving two lectures at the Philosophical Society on the House of Commons and Horace Walpole. Grisi's farewell benefits are (I think) on my last two nights here.

Gordon dined with me yesterday. He is, if anything, rather better, I think, than when we last saw him in town. He was immensely pleased to be with me. I went with him (as his office goes anywhere) right into and among the ruins of the fallen building yesterday. They were still at work trying to find two men (brothers), a young girl, and an old woman, known to be all lying there. On the walls two or three common clocks are still hanging; one of them, judging from the time at which it stopped, would seem to have gone for an hour or so after the fall. Great interest had been taken in a poor linnet in a cage, hanging in the wind and rain high up against the broken wall. A fireman got it down alive, and great exultation had been raised over it. One woman, who was dug out unhurt, staggered into the street, stared all round her, instantly ran away, and has never been heard of since. It is a most extraordinary sight, and of course makes a great sensation.

[*To Miss Dickens.*]

WATERLOO HOTEL, EDINBURGH. *Friday, Nov. 29th,* 1861.

I think it is my turn to write to you, and I therefore send a brief despatch, like a telegram, to let you know that in a gale of wind and a fierce rain, last night, we turned away a thousand people. There was no getting into the hall, no getting near the hall, no stirring among the people, no getting out, no possibility of getting rid of them. And yet, in spite of all that, and of their being steaming wet, they never flagged for an instant, never made a complaint, and took up the trial upon their very shoulders, to the last word, in a triumphant roar.

The talk about "Copperfield" rings through the whole place. It is done again to-morrow night. To-morrow morning I read "Dombey." To-morrow morning is Grisi's "farewell" morning concert, and last night was her "farewell" evening concert. Neither she, nor Jenny Lind, nor

VOL. II.—9

anything, nor anybody seems to make the least effect on the draw of the readings.

I lunch with Blackwood to-day. He was at the reading last night ; a capital audience. Young Blackwood has also called here. A very good young fellow, I think.

[*To Miss Hogarth.*]

CARRICK'S ROYAL HOTEL, GLASGOW, *Tuesday, Dec. 3rd,* 1861.

I send you by this post another *Scotsman.* From a paragraph in it, a letter, and an advertisement, you may be able to form some dim guess of the scene at Edinburgh last night. Such a pouring of hundreds into a place already full to the throat, such indescribable confusion, such a rending and tearing of dresses, and yet such a scene of good humour on the whole. I never saw the faintest approach to it. While I addressed the crowd in the room, Gordon addressed the crowd in the street. Fifty frantic men got up in all parts of the hall and addressed me all at once. Other frantic men made speeches to the walls. The whole Blackwood family were borne in on the top of a wave, and landed with their faces against the front of the platform. I read with the platform crammed with people. I got them to lie down upon it, and it was like some impossible tableau or gigantic picnic ; one pretty girl in full dress lying on her side all night, holding on to one of the legs of my table. It was the most extraordinary sight. And yet from the moment I began to the moment of my leaving off, they never missed a point, and they ended with a burst of cheers.

The confusion was decidedly owing to the local agents. But I think it may have been a little heightened by Headland's way of sending them the tickets to sell in the first instance.

Now, as I must read again in Edinburgh on Saturday night, your travelling arrangements are affected. So observe carefully (you and Mamie) all that I am going to say. It appears to me that the best course will be for you to come to *Edinburgh* on Saturday; taking the fast train from the Great Northern station at nine in the morning. This would bring you to the Waterloo at Edinburgh, at about nine or so at night, and I should be home at ten. We could then have a quiet Sunday in Edinburgh, and go over to Carlisle on the Monday morning.

The expenditure of lungs and spirits was (as you may suppose) rather great last night, and to sleep well was out of the question ; I am therefore rather fagged to-day. And as the hall in which I read to-night is a large one, I must make my letter a short one.

My people were torn to ribbons last night. They have not a hat among them, and scarcely a coat.

Give my love to Mamie. To her question, " Will there be war with America ? " I answer, " Yes ; " I fear the North to be utterly mad, and war to be unavoidable.

[*To Mr. W. H. Wills.*]

VICTORIA HOTEL, PRESTON, *Friday, Dec.* 13*th,* 1861.

MY DEAR WILLS,

The news of the Christmas number is indeed glorious, and nothing can look brighter or better than the prospects of the illustrious publication.

Both Carlisle and Lancaster have come out admirably, though I doubted both, as you did. But, unlike you, I always doubted this place. I do so still. It is a poor place at the best (you remember?), and the mills are working half time, and trade is very bad. The expenses, however, will be a mere nothing. The accounts from Manchester for to-morrow, and from Liverpool for the readings generally, are very cheering indeed.

The young lady who sells the papers at the station is just the same as ever. Has orders for to-night, and is coming "with a person." "*The* person?" said I. "Never *you* mind," said she.

I was so charmed with Robert Chambers's "Traditions of Edinburgh" (which I read *in* Edinburgh), that I was obliged to write to him and say so.

Glasgow finished nobly, and the last night in Edinburgh was signally successful and positively splendid.

Will you give my small Admiral, on his personal application, one sovereign? I have told him to come to you for that recognition of his meritorious services.

Ever faithfully.

[*To Mr. W. H. Wills.*]

ADELPHI HOTEL, LIVERPOOL, *Sunday, Dec.* 15*th*, 1861.

MY DEAR WILLS,

I sent you a telegram to-day, and I write before the answer has come to hand.

I have been very doubtful what to do here. We have a great let for to-morrow night. The Mayor recommends closing to-morrow, and going on on Tuesday and Wednesday, so does the town clerk, so do the agents. But I have a misgiving that they hardly understand what the public general sympathy with the Queen will be. Further, I feel personally that the Queen has always been very considerate and gracious to me, and I would on no account do anything that might seem unfeeling or disrespectful. I shall attach great weight, in this state of indecision, to your telegram.

A capital audience at Preston. Not a capacious room, but full. Great appreciation.

The scene at Manchester last night was really magnificent. I had had the platform carried forward to our " Frozen Deep " point, and my table and screen built in with a proscenium and room scenery. When I went in (there was a very fine hall), they applauded in the most tremendous manner; and the extent to which they were taken aback and taken by storm by " Copperfield " was really a thing to see.

The post closes early here on a Sunday, and I shall close

this also without further reference to "a message from the" W. H. W. being probably on the road.

Radley is ill, and supposed to be fast declining, poor fellow. The house is crammed, the assizes on, and troops perpetually embarking for Canada, and their officers pass-ing through the hotel.

Kindest regards, ever faithfully.

[*To Miss Mary Boyle.*]

GAD'S HILL, HIGHAM BY ROCHESTER, KENT,
Saturday, Dec. 28th, 1861.

MY DEAR MARY,

On Monday (as you know) I am away again, but I am not sorry to see land and a little rest before me ; albeit, these are great experiences of the public heart.

The little Admiral has gone to visit America in the *Orlando,* supposed to be one of the foremost ships in the Service, and the best found, best manned, and best offi-cered that ever sailed from England. He went away much gamer than any giant, attended by a chest in which he could easily have stowed himself and a wife and family of his own proportions.

Ever and always, your affectionate

JOE.

1862.

NARRATIVE.

AT the beginning of this year, Charles Dickens resumed the reading tour which he had commenced at the close of the previous year and continued up to Christmas. The first letter which follows, to Mr. Wills, a New Year's greeting, is written from a railway station between one town and another on this journey. Mr. Macready, who had married for the second time not very long before this, was now settled at Cheltenham. Charles Dickens had arranged to give readings there, chiefly for the pleasure of visiting him, and of having him as one of his audience.

This reading tour went on until the beginning of February. One of the last of the series was in his favourite "beautiful room," the St. George's Hall at Liverpool. In February, he made an exchange of houses with his friends Mr. and Mrs. Hogge, they going to Gad's Hill, and he and his family to Mr. Hogge's house in Hyde Park Gate South. In March he commenced a series of readings at St. James's Hall, which went on until the middle of June, when he, very gladly, returned to his country home.

A letter beginning " My dear Girls," addressed to some American ladies who happened to be at Colchester, in the same inn with him when he was reading there, was published by one of them under the name of " Our Letter," in the "St. Nicholas Magazine," New York, in 1877. We think it best to explain it in the young lady's own words, which are, therefore, appended to the letter.

Mr. Walter Thornbury was one of Charles Dickens's most valuable contributors to "All the Year Round." His letters to him about the subjects of his articles for that journal, are specimens of the minute and careful attention and personal supervision, never neglected or distracted by any other work on which he might be engaged, were it ever so hard or engrossing.

The letter addressed to Mr. Baylis we give chiefly because it has, since Mr. Baylis's death, been added to the collection of MSS. in the British Museum. He was a very intimate and confidential friend of the late Lord Lytton, and accompanied him on a visit to Gad's Hill in that year.

We give an extract from another letter from Charles Dickens to his sister, as a beautiful specimen of a letter of condolence and encouragement to one who was striving, very bravely, but by very slow degrees, to recover from the overwhelming grief of her bereavement. Mr. Wilkie Collins was at this time engaged on his novel of "No Name," which appeared in "All the Year Round," and was threatened with a very serious break-down in health. Charles Dickens wrote the letter which we give, to relieve Mr. Collins's mind as to his work. Happily he recovered sufficiently to make an end to his own story without any help ; but the true friendship and kindness which suggested the offer were none the less appreciated, and may, very likely, by lessening his anxiety, have helped to restore his health. At the end of October in this year, Charles Dickens, accompanied by his daughter and sister-in-law, went to reside for a couple of months in Paris, taking an apartment in the Rue du Faubourg St. Honoré. From thence he writes to M. Charles Fechter. He had been greatly interested in this fine artist from the time of his first appearance in England, and was always one of his warmest friends and supporters during his stay in this country. M. Fechter was, at this time, preparing for the opening of the Lyceum Theatre, under his own management, at the beginning of the following year.

Just before Christmas, Charles Dickens returned to Gad's Hill. The Christmas number for this year was "Somebody's Luggage."

[*To Mr. W. H. Wills.*]

At the Birmingham Station, *Thursday, Jan. 2nd,* 1862.

My dear Wills,

Being stationed here for an hour, on my way from Leamington to Cheltenham, I write to you.

Firstly, to reciprocate all your cordial and affectionate wishes for the New Year, and to express my earnest hope that we may go on through many years to come, as we have gone on through many years that are gone. And I think we can say that we doubt whether any two men can have gone on more happily and smoothly, or with greater trust and confidence in one another.

A little packet will come to you from Hunt and Roskell's, almost at the same time, I think, as this note.

The packet will contain a claret-jug. I hope it is a pretty thing in itself for your table, and I know that you and Mrs. Wills will like it none the worse because it comes from me.

It is not made of a perishable material, and is so far expressive of our friendship. I have had your name and mine set upon it, in token of our many years of mutual reliance and trustfulness. It will never be so full of wine as it is to-day of affectionate regard.

Ever faithfully yours.

[*To Miss Hogarth.*]

Cheltenham, *Friday, Jan. 3rd,* 1862.

My dearest Georgy,

Mrs. Macready in voice is very like poor Mrs. Macready

Vol. II.—9*

dead and gone ; not in the least like her otherwise. She is perfectly satisfactory, and exceedingly winning. Quite perfect in her manner with him and in her ease with his children, sensible, gay, pleasant, sweet-tempered ; not in the faintest degree stiff or pedantic ; accessible instantly. I have very rarely seen a more agreeable woman. The house is (on a smaller scale) any house we have known them in. Furnished with the old furniture, pictures, engravings, mirrors, tables, and chairs. Butty is too tall for strength, I am afraid, but handsome, with a face of great power and character, and a very nice girl. Katie you know all about. Macready, decidedly much older and infirm. Very much changed. His old force has gone out of him strangely. I don't think I left off talking a minute from the time of my entering the house to my going to bed last night, and he was as much amused and interested as ever I saw him ; still he was, and is, unquestionably aged.

And even now I am obliged to cut this letter short by having to go and look after Headland. It would never do to be away from the rest of them. I have no idea what we are doing here ; no notion whether things are right or wrong ; no conception where the room is ; no hold of the business at all. For which reason I cannot rest without going and looking after the worthy man.

[*To Miss Hogarth.*]

TORQUAY, *Wednesday, Jan. 8th,* 1862.

You know, I think, that I was very averse to going to

Plymouth, and would not have gone there again but for poor Arthur. But on the last night I read "Copperfield," and positively enthralled the people. It was a most over-powering effect, and poor Andrew * came behind the screen, after the storm, and cried in the best and manliest manner. Also there were two or three lines of his shipmates and other sailors, and they were extraordinarily affected. But its culminating effect was on Macready at Cheltenham. When I got home after "Copperfield," I found him quite unable to speak, and able to do nothing ·but square his dear old jaw all one side, and roll his eyes (half closed), like Jackson's picture of him. And when I said something light about it, he returned : "No—er—Dickens.! I swear to Heaven that, as a piece of passion and playfulness—er —indescribably mixed up together, it does—er—no, really, Dickens!—amaze me as profoundly as it moves me. But as a piece of art—and you know—er—that I—no, Dickens! By —— ! have seen the best art in a great time—it is in-comprehensible to me. How is it got at—er—how is it done —er—how one man can—well ? It lays me on my—er— back, and it is of no use talking about it!" With which he put his hand upon my breast and pulled out his pocket-handkerchief, and I felt as if I were doing somebody to his Werner. Katie, by-the-bye, is a wonderful audience, and has a great fund of wild feeling in her. Johnny not at all unlike Plorn.

I have not yet seen the room here, but imagine it to be very small. Exeter I know, and that is small also. I am

---

* Lieutenant Andrew Gordon, R.N., son of the Sheriff of Midlothian.

very much used up, on the whole, for I cannot bear this moist warm climate. It would kill me very soon. And I have now got to the point of taking so much out of myself with "Copperfield," that I might as well do Richard Wardour.

You have now, my dearest Georgy, the fullest extent of my tidings. This is a very pretty place—a compound of Hastings, Tunbridge Wells, and little bits of the hills about Naples; but I met four respirators as I came up from the station, and three pale curates without them, who seemed in a bad way.

Frightful intelligence has just been brought in by Boylett, concerning the small size of the room. I have terrified Headland by sending him to look at it, and swearing that if it's too small I will go away to Exeter.

[*To Miss Hogarth.*]

ADELPHI HOTEL, LIVERPOOL, *Tuesday, Jan. 28th,* 1862.

The beautiful room was crammed to excess last night, and numbers were turned away. Its beauty and completeness when it is lighted up are most brilliant to behold, and for a reading it is simply perfect. You remember that a Liverpool audience is usually dull, but they put me on my mettle last night, for I never saw such an audience—no, not even in Edinburgh !

I slept horribly last night, and have been over to Birkenhead for a little change of air to-day. My head is dazed and worn by gas and heat, and I fear that "Copperfield" and "Bob" together to-night won't mend it.

Best love to Mamie and Katie, if still at Gad's. I am going to bring the boys some toffee.

[*To the Misses Armstrong.*]

GAD'S HILL PLACE, HIGHAM BY ROCHESTER, KENT,

Monday, Feb. 10th, 1862.

MY DEAR GIRLS,

For if I were to write "young friends," it would look like a schoolmaster ; and if I were to write "young ladies," it would look like a schoolmistress ; and worse than that, neither form of words would look familiar and natural, or in character with our snowy ride that tooth-chattering morning.

I cannot tell you both how gratified I was by your remembrance, or how often I think of you as I smoke the admirable cigars. But I almost think you must have had some magnetic consciousness across the Atlantic, of my whiffing my love towards you from the garden here.

My daughter says that when you have settled those little public affairs at home, she hopes you will come back to England (possibly in united states) and give a minute or two to this part of Kent. *Her* words are, "a day or two ; " but I remember your Italian flights, and correct the message.

I have only just now finished my country readings, and have had nobody to make breakfast for me since the remote ages of Colchester !

Ever faithfully yours.

OUR LETTER.

By M. F. ARMSTRONG.

"From among all my treasures—to each one of which some pleasant history is bound—I choose this letter, written on coarse blue paper.

The letter was received in answer to cigars sent from America to Mr. Dickens.

The 'little public affairs at home' refers to the war of the Rebellion.

At Colchester, he read 'The Trial' from 'Pickwick,' and selections from 'Nicholas Nickleby.'

The lady, her two sisters, and her brother were Mr. Dickens's guests at the queer old English inn at Colchester.

Through the softly falling snow we came back together to London, and on the railway platform parted, with a hearty hand-shaking, from the man who will for ever be enshrined in our hearts as the kindest and most generous, not to say most brilliant of hosts."

[*To M. de Cerjat.*]

16, HYDE PARK GATE, SOUTH KENSINGTON GORE,
Sunday, March 16th, 1862.

MY DEAR CERJAT,

My daughter naturally liking to be in town at this time of year, I have changed houses with a friend for three months.

My eldest boy is in business as an Eastern merchant in the City, and will do well if he can find continuous energy ; otherwise not. My second boy is with the 42nd Highlanders in India. My third boy, a good steady fellow, is educating expressly for engineers or artillery. My fourth (this sounds like a charade), a born little sailor, is a midshipman in H.M.S. *Orlando*, now at Bermuda, and will make his way anywhere. Remaining two at school, elder of said remaining two very bright and clever. Georgina and Mary keeping house for me ; and Francis Jeffrey (I ought to have counted him as the third boy, so we'll take him in here as number two and a half) in my office at present. Now you have the family bill of fare.

You ask me about Fechter and his Hamlet. It was a performance of extraordinary merit ; by far the most coherent, consistent, and intelligible Hamlet I ever saw. Some of the delicacies with which he rendered his conception clear were extremely subtle ; and in particular he avoided that brutality towards Ophelia which, with a greater or less amount of coarseness, I have seen in all other Hamlets. As a mere *tour de force*, it would have been very remarkable in its disclosure of a perfectly wonderful knowledge of the force of the English language ; but its merit was far beyond and above this. Foreign accent, of course, but not at all a disagreeable one. And he was so obviously safe and at ease, that you were never in pain for him as a foreigner. Add to this a perfectly picturesque and romantic " make up," and a remorseless destruction of all conventionalities, and you have the leading virtues of the impersonation. In Othello he did not succeed. In Iago he is very good. He is an admirable artist, and far beyond anyone on our stage. A real artist and a gentleman.

Last Thursday I began reading again in London—a condensation of " Copperfield," and " Mr. Bob Sawyer's Party," from " Pickwick," to finish merrily. The success of " Copperfield " is astounding. It made an impression that *I* must not describe. I may only remark that I was half dead when I had done ; and that although I had looked forward, all through the summer, when I was carefully getting it up, to its being a London sensation ; and that although Macready, hearing it at Cheltenham, told me to be prepared for a great effect, it even went beyond my hopes. I read again next Thursday, and the rush for places is quite furious. Tell Townshend this with my love, if you see him before I have time to write to him ; and tell him that I thought the people would never let me go away, they became so excited, and showed it so very warmly. I am trying to plan out a new book, but have not got beyond trying.

Yours affectionately.

[*To Mr. Walter Thornbury.*]

OFFICE OF "ALL THE YEAR ROUND,"
Friday, April 18th, 1862.

MY DEAR THORNBURY,

The Bow Street runners ceased out of the land soon after the introduction of the new police. I remember them very well as standing about the door of the office in Bow

Street. They had no other uniform than a blue dress-coat, brass buttons (I am not even now sure that that was necessary), and a bright red cloth waistcoat. The waist-coat was indispensable, and the slang name for them was " redbreasts," in consequence.

They kept company with thieves and the like, much more than the detective police do. I don't know what their pay was, but I have no doubt their principal comple-ments were got under the rose. It was a very slack insti-tution, and its headquarters were The Brown Bear, in Bow Street, a public-house of more than doubtful reputation, opposite the police office ; and either the house which is now the theatrical costume maker's, or the next door to it.

Field, who advertises the Secret Enquiry Office, was a Bow Street runner, and can tell you all about it ; Goddard, who also advertises an enquiry office, was another of the fraternity. They are the only two I know of as yet exist-ing in a " questionable shape."

Faithfully yours always.

[*To Mr. Baylis.*]

GAD'S HILL, ETC., *Wednesday, July 2nd*, 1862.

MY DEAR MR. BAYLIS,

I have been in France, and in London, and in other parts of Kent than this, and everywhere but here, for weeks and weeks. Pray excuse my not having (for this reason specially) answered your kind note sooner.

After carefully cross-examining my daughter, I do NOT believe her to be worthy of the fernery. Last autumn we transplanted into the shrubbery a quantity of evergreens previously clustered close to the front of the house, and trained more ivy about the wall and the like. When I ask her where she would have the fernery and what she would do with it, the witness falters, turns pale, becomes confused, and says: " Perhaps it would be better not to have it at all." I am quite confident that the constancy of the young person is not to be trusted, and that she had better attach her fernery to one of her châteaux in Spain, or one of her English castles in the air. None the less do I thank you for your more than kind proposal.

We have been in great anxiety respecting Miss Hogarth, the sudden decline of whose health and spirits has greatly distressed us. Although she is better than she was, and the doctors are, on the whole, cheerful, she requires great care, and fills us with apprehension. The necessity of providing change for her will probably take us across the water very early in the autumn ; and this again unsettles home schemes here, and withers many kinds of fern. If they knew (by "they" I mean my daughter and Miss Hogarth) that I was writing to you, they would charge me with many messages of regard. But as I am shut up in my room in a ferocious and unapproachable condition, owing to the great accumulation of letters I have to answer, I will tell them at lunch that I have anticipated their wish. As I know they have bills for me to pay, and are at present shy of producing them, I wish to preserve a gloomy and repellent reputation.

My dear Mr. Baylis, faithfully yours always.

[*To Mrs. Henry Austin.*]

GAD'S HILL, *Tuesday, Oct. 7th,* 1862.

*   *   *   *   *   *

I do not preach consolation because I am unwilling to preach at any time, and know my own weakness too well. But in this world there is no stay but the hope of a better, and no reliance but on the mercy and goodness of God. Through those two harbours of a shipwrecked heart, I fully believe that you will, in time, find a peaceful resting-place even on this careworn earth. Heaven speed the time, and do you try hard to help it on ! It is impossible to say but that our prolonged grief for the beloved dead may grieve them in their unknown abiding-place, and give them trouble. The one influencing consideration in all you do as to your disposition of yourself (coupled, of course, with a real earnest strenuous endeavour to recover the lost tone of spirit) is, that you think and feel you *can* do. I do not in the least regard your change of course in going to Havre as any evidence of instability. But I rather hope it is likely that through such restlessness you will come to a far quieter frame of mind. The disturbed mind and affections, like the tossed sea, seldom calm without an intervening time of confusion and trouble.

But nothing is to be attained without striving. In a determined effort to settle the thoughts, to parcel out the day, to find occupation regularly or to make it, to be up and doing something, are chiefly to be found the mere mechanical means which must come to the aid of the best mental efforts.

It is a wilderness of a day, here, in the way of blowing and raining, and as darkly dismal, at four o'clock, as need be. My head is but just now raised from a day's writing, but I will not lose the post without sending you a word.

Katie was here yesterday, just come back from Clara White's (that was), in Scotland. In the midst of her brilliant fortune, it is too clear to me that she is already beckoned away to follow her dead sisters. Macready was here from Saturday evening to yesterday morning, older but looking wonderfully well, and (what is very rare in these times) with the old thick sweep of hair upon his head. Georgina being left alone here the other day, was done no good to by a great consternation among the servants. On going downstairs, she found Marsh (the stableman) seated with great dignity and anguish in an arm-chair, and incessantly crying out : " I am dead." To which the women servants said with great pathos (and with some appearance of reason) : " No, you ain't, Marsh ! " And to which he persisted in replying : " Yes, I am ; I am dead ! " Some neighbouring vagabond was impressed to drive a cart over to Rochester and fetch the doctor, who said (the patient and his consolers being all very anxious that the heart should be the scene of affliction) : " Stomach."

[*To Mr. W. Wilkie Collins.*]

GAD'S HILL PLACE, HIGHAM BY ROCHESTER, KENT,
Tuesday Night, Oct. 14th, 1862.

MY DEAR WILKIE,

Frank Beard has been here this evening, of course since I posted my this day's letter to you, and has told me that you are not at all well, and how he has given you something which he hopes and believes will bring you round. It is not to convey this insignificant piece of intelligence, or to tell you how anxious I am that you should come up with a wet sheet and a flowing sail (as we say at sea when we are not sick), that I write. It is simply to say what follows, which I hope may save you some mental uneasiness. For I was stricken ill when I was doing " Bleak House," and I shall not easily forget what I suffered under the fear of not being able to come up to time.

Dismiss that fear (if you have it) altogether from your mind. Write to me at Paris at any moment, and say you are unequal to your work, and want me, and I will come to London straight and do your work. I am quite confident that, with your notes and a few words of explanation, I could take it up at any time and do it. Absurdly unnecessary to say that it would be a makeshift ! But I could do it at a pinch, so like you as that no one should find out the difference. Don't make much of this offer in your mind ; it is nothing, except to ease it. If you should want help, I am as safe as the bank. The trouble would be nothing to me, and the triumph of overcoming the difficulty great. Think it a Christmas number, an " Idle Apprentice," a " Lighthouse," a " Frozen Deep." I am as ready as in any of these cases to strike in and hammer the hot iron out.

You won't want me. You will be well (and thankless !) in no time. But there I am ; and I hope that the knowledge may be a comfort to you. Call me, and I come.

As Beard always has a sense of medical responsibility, and says anything important about a patient in confidence, I have merely remarked here that " Wilkie " is out of sorts.   Charley (who is here with Katie) has no other cue from me.

Ever affectionately.

[*To M. Charles Fechter.*]

PARIS, RUE DU FAUBOURG ST. HONORÉ, 27,

Tuesday, Nov. 4th, 1862.

MY DEAR FECHTER,

You know, I believe, how our letters crossed, and that I am here until Christmas.   Also, you know with what pleasure and readiness I should have responded to your invitation if I had been in London.

Pray tell Paul Féval that I shall be charmed to know him, and that I shall feel the strongest interest in making his acquaintance.   It almost puts me out of humour with Paris (and it takes a great deal to do that !) to think that I was not at home to prevail upon him to come with you, and be welcomed to Gad's Hill ; but either there or here, I hope to become his friend before this present old year is out.   Pray tell him so.

You say nothing in your note of your Lyceum preparations.   I trust they are all going on well.   There is a fine opening for you, I am sure, with a good beginning ; but the importance of a good beginning is very great.   If you ever have time and inclination to tell me in a short note what you are about, you can scarcely interest me more, as my wishes and strongest sympathies are for and with your success—*mais cela va sans dire.*

I went to the Châtelet (a beautiful theatre !) the other night to see "Rothomago," but was so mortally *gêné* with the poor nature of the piece and of the acting, that I came out again when there was a week or two (I mean an hour or two, but the hours seemed weeks) yet to get through.

My dear Fechter, very faithfully yours always.

[*To Mr. Clarkson Stanfield, R.A.*]

PARIS, RUE DU FAUBOURG ST. HONORÉ, 27,

Friday, Dec. 5th, 1862.

My DEAR STANNY,

We have been here for two months, and I shall probably come back here after Christmas (we go home for Christmas week) and stay on into February. But I shall write and propose a theatre before Christmas is out, so this is to warn you to get yourself into working pantomime order !

I hope Wills has duly sent you our new Christmas number. As you may like to know what I myself wrote of it, understand the Dick contributions to be, *his leaving it till called for,* and *his wonderful end, his boots,* and *his brown paper parcel.*

Since you were at Gad's Hill I have been travelling a good deal, and looking up many odd things for use. I want to know how you are in health and spirits, and it would be the greatest of pleasures to me to have a line under your hand.

God bless you and yours with all the blessings of the time of year, and of all times'!

Ever your affectionate and faithful

DICK.

[*To M. Charles Fechter.*]

PARIS, *Saturday, Dec. 6th,* 1862.

MY DEAR FECHTER,

I have read " The White Rose " attentively, and think it an extremely good play. It is vigorously written with a great knowledge of the stage, and presents many striking situations. I think the close particularly fine, impressive, bold, and new.

But I greatly doubt the expediency of your doing *any* historical play early in your management. By the words " historical play," I mean a play founded on any incident in English history. Our public are accustomed to associate historical plays with Shakespeare. In any other hands, I believe they care very little for crowns and dukedoms. What you want is something with an interest of a more domestic and general nature—an interest as romantic as you please, but having a more general and wider response than a disputed succession to the throne can have for Englishmen at this time of day. Such interest culminated in the last Stuart, and has worn itself out. It would be uphill work to evoke an interest in Perkin Warbeck.

I do not doubt the play's being well received, but my fear is that these people would be looked upon as mere abstractions, and would have but a cold welcome in consequence, and would not lay hold of your audience. Now, when you *have* laid hold of your audience and have accustomed them to your theatre, you may produce " The White Rose," with far greater justice to the author, and to the manager also. Wait. Feel your way. Perkin Warbeck is too far removed from analogy with the sympathies and lives of the people for a beginning.

My dear Fechter, ever faithfully yours.

[*To Miss Mary Boyle.*]

GAD'S HILL PLACE, HIGHAM BY ROCHESTER, KENT,
Saturday, Dec. 27th, 1862.

MY DEAR MARY,

I must send you my Christmas greeting and happy New Year wishes in return for yours; most heartily and fervently reciprocating your interest and affection. You are among the few whom I most care for and best love.

Being in London two evenings in the opening week, I tried to persuade my legs (for whose judgment I have the highest respect) to go to an evening party. But I *could not* induce them to pass Leicester Square. The faltering presentiment under which they laboured so impressed me, that at that point I yielded to their terrors. They immediately ran away to the east, and I accompanied them to the Olympic, where I saw a very good play, "Camilla's Husband," very well played. Real merit in Mr. Neville and Miss Saville.

We came across directly after the gale, with the Channel all bestrewn with floating wreck, and with a hundred and fifty sick schoolboys from Calais on board. I am going back on the morning after Fechter's opening night, and have promised to read " Copperfield " at the Embassy, for a British charity.

Georgy continues wonderfully well, and she and Mary send you their best love. The house is pervaded by boys ; and every boy has (as usual) an unaccountable and awful power of producing himself in every part of the house at every moment, apparently in fourteen pairs of creaking boots.

My dear Mary, ever affectionately your

JOE.

1863.

NARRATIVE.

AT the beginning of this year, Charles Dickens was in Paris for the purpose of giving a reading at the English Embassy.

He remained in Paris until the beginning of February, staying with his servant " John " at the Hôtel du Helder. There was a series of readings in London this season at the Hanover Square Rooms. The Christmas number of " All the Year Round " was entitled " Mrs. Lirriper's Lodgings," to which Charles Dickens contributed the first and last chapter.

The Lyceum Theatre, under the management of M. Fechter, was opened in January with " The Duke's Motto," and the letter given here has reference to this first night.

We regret very much having no letters to Lady Molesworth, who was an old and dear friend of Charles Dickens. But this lady explains to us that she has long ceased to preserve any letters addressed to her.

The "Mr. and Mrs. Humphery" (now Sir William and Lady Humphery) mentioned in the first letter for this year, were dear and intimate friends of his eldest daughter, and were frequent guests in her father's house. Mrs. Humphery and her sister Lady Olliffe were daughters of the late Mr. William Cubitt, M.P.

We have in this year the first letter of Charles Dickens to Mr. Percy Fitzgerald. This gentleman had been a valuable contributor to his journal before he became personally known to Charles Dickens. The acquaintance once made soon ripened into friendship, and for the future Mr. Fitzgerald was a constant and always a welcome visitor to Gad's Hill.

The letter to Mr. Charles Reade alludes to his story, "Hard Cash," which was then appearing in "All the Year Round." As a writer, and as a friend, he was held by Charles Dickens in the highest estimation.

Charles Dickens's correspondence with his solicitor and excellent friend, Mr. Frederic Ouvry (now a vice-president of the Society of Antiquaries), was almost entirely of a business character ; but we are glad to give one or two notes to that gentleman, although of little public interest, in order to have the name in our book of one of the kindest of our own friends.

[*To Miss Dickens.*]

PARIS, HÔTEL DU HELDER, RUE DU HELDER,

Friday, Jan. 16*th*, 1863.

MY DEAREST MAMIE,

As I send a line to your aunt to-day and know that you will not see it, I send another to you to report my safe (and neuralgic) arrival here. My little rooms are perfectly comfortable, and I like the hotel better than any I have ever put up at in Paris. John's amazement at, and appreciation of, Paris are indescribable. He goes about with his mouth open, staring at everything and being tumbled over by everybody.

The state dinner at the Embassy, yesterday, coming off in the room where I am to read, the carpenters did not get in until this morning. But their platforms were ready—or supposed to be—and the preparations are in brisk progress. I think it will be a handsome affair to look at—a very handsome one. There seems to be great artistic curiosity in Paris, to know what kind of thing the reading is.

I know a "rela-shon" (with one weak eye), who is in the gunmaking line, very near here. There is a strong family resemblance—but no muzzle. Lady Molesworth and I have not begun to "toddle" yet, but have exchanged affectionate greetings. I am going round to see her presently, and I dine with her on Sunday. The only remaining news is, that I am beset by mysterious adorers, and smuggle myself in and out of the house in the meanest and basest manner.

With kind regard to Mr. and Mrs. Humphery,

Ever, my dearest Mamey, your affectionate Father.

P.S.—*Hommage à Madame B. !*

[*To Monsieur Regnier.*]

PARIS, *Sunday, Feb. 1st,* 1863.

MY DEAR REGNIER,

I was charmed by the receipt of your cordial and sympathetic letter, and I shall always preserve it carefully as a most noble tribute from a great and real artist.

I wished you had been at the Embassy on Friday evening. The audience was a fine one, and the " Carol " is particularly well adapted to the purpose. It is an uncommon pleasure to me to learn that I am to meet you on Tuesday, for there are not many men whom I meet with greater pleasure than you. Heaven ! how the years roll by ! We are quite old friends now, in counting by years. If we add sympathies, we have been friends at least a thousand years.

Affectionately yours ever.

[*To Miss Dickens.*]

HÔTEL DU HELDER, PARIS, *Sunday, Feb. 1st*, 1863.

MY DEAREST MAMIE,

I cannot give you any idea of the success of the readings here, because no one can imagine the scene of last Friday night at the Embassy. Such audiences and such enthusiasm I have never seen, but the thing culminated on Friday night in a two hours' storm of excitement and pleasure. They actually recommenced and applauded right away into their carriages and down the street.

You know your parent's horror of being lionised, and will not be surprised to hear that I am half dead of it. I cannot leave here until Thursday (though I am every hour in danger of running away) because I have to dine out, to say nothing of breakfasting—think of me break-

fasting !—every intervening day. But my project is to
send John home on Thursday, and then to go on a little
perfectly quiet tour for about ten days, touching the sea
at Boulogne.[1] When I get there, I will write to your aunt
(in case you should not be at home), saying when I shall
arrive at the office. I must go to the office instead of
Gad's, because I have much to do with Forster about
Elliotson.

I enclose a short note for each of the little boys. Give
Harry ten shillings pocket-money, and Plorn six.

The Olliffe girls, very nice. Florence at the readings,
prodigiously excited.

[*To Miss Hogarth.*]

PARIS, *Sunday, Feb. 1st*, 1863.

From my hurried note to Mamie, you will get some
faint general idea of a new star's having arisen in Paris.
But of its brightness you can have no adequate conception.

[John has locked me up and gone out, and the little bell
at the door is ringing demoniacally while I write.]

You have never heard me read yet. I have been twice
goaded and lifted out of myself into a state that astonished *me* almost as much as the audience. I have a cold,
but no neuralgia, and am " as well as can be expected."

I forgot to tell Mamie that I went (with Lady Molesworth) to hear " Faust " last night. It is a splendid work,
in which that noble and sad story is most nobly and sadly

rendered, and perfectly delighted me. But I think it requires too much of the audience to do for a London opera house. The composer must be a very remarkable man indeed. Some management of light throughout the story is also very poetical and fine. We had Carvalho's box. I could hardly bear the thing, it affected me so.

But, as a certain Frenchman said, " No weakness, Danton ! " So I leave off.

[*To M. Charles Fechter.*]

PARIS, *Wednesday, Feb. 4th,* 1863.

MY DEAR FECHTER,

A thousand congratulations on your great success ! Never mind what they say, or do, *pour vous écraser ;* you have the game in your hands. The romantic drama, thoroughly well done (with a touch of Shakespeare now and then), is the speciality of your theatre. Give the public the picturesque, romantic drama, with yourself in it ; and (as I told you in the beginning) you may throw down your gauntlet in defiance of all comers.

It is a most brilliant success indeed, and it thoroughly rejoices my heart !

Unfortunately I cannot now hope to see " Maquet," because I am packing up and going out to dinner (it is late in the afternoon), and I leave to-morrow morning when all sensible people, except myself, are in bed ; and I do not come back to Paris or near it. I had hoped to see him at breakfast last Monday, but he was not there. Paul

Féval was there, and I found him a capital fellow. If I can do anything to help you on with " Maquet " * when I come back I will most gladly do it.

My readings here have had the finest possible reception, and have achieved a most noble success. I never before read to such fine audiences, so very quick of perception, and so enthusiastically responsive.

I shall be heartily pleased to see you again, my dear Fechter, and to share your triumphs with the real earnestness of a real friend. And so go on and prosper, and believe me, as I truly am,

Most cordially yours.

[*To Mr. W. C. Macready.*]

OFFICE OF "ALL THE YEAR ROUND,"

Thursday, Feb. 19th, 1863.

MY DEAREST MACREADY,

I have just come back from Paris, where the readings— " Copperfield," " Dombey " and " Trial," and " Carol " and " Trial "—have made a sensation which modesty (my natural modesty) renders it impossible for me to describe. You know what a noble audience the Paris audience is ! They were at their very noblest with me.

I was very much concerned by hearing hurriedly from Georgy that you were ill. But when I came home at night, she showed me Katie's letter, and that set me up again. Ah, you have the best of companions and nurses,

---

* Alluding to a translation of a play by M. Maquet, which M. Fechter was then preparing for his theatre.

and can afford to be ill now and then for the happiness of being so brought through it. But don't do it again yet awhile for all that.

Legouvé (whom you remember in Paris as writing for the Ristori) was anxious that I should bring you the enclosed. A manly and generous effort, I think? Regnier desired to be warmly remembered to you. He looks just as of yore.

Paris generally is about as wicked and extravagant as in the days of the Regency. Madame Viardot in the "Orphée," most splendid. An opera of "Faust," a very sad and noble rendering of that sad and noble story. Stage management remarkable for some admirable, and really poetical, effects of light. In the more striking situations, Mephistopheles surrounded by an infernal red atmosphere of his own. Marguerite by a pale blue mournful light. The two never blending. After Marguerite has taken the jewels placed in her way in the garden, a weird evening draws on, and the bloom fades from the flowers, and the leaves of the trees droop and lose their fresh green, and mournful shadows overhang her chamber window, which was innocently bright and gay at first. I couldn't bear it, and gave in completely.

Fechter doing wonders over the way here, with a picturesque French drama. Miss Kate Terry, in a small part in it, perfectly charming. You may remember her making a noise, years ago, doing a boy at an inn, in " The Courier of Lyons"? She has a tender love-scene in this piece, which is a really beautiful and artistic thing. I saw her do it at about three in the morning of the day when the theatre opened, surrounded by shavings and carpenters, and (of course) with that inevitable hammer going; and I told Fechter: "That is the very best piece of womanly tenderness I have ever seen on the stage, and you'll find that no audience can miss it." It is a comfort to add that it was instantly seized upon, and is much talked of.

Stanfield was very ill for some months, then suddenly picked up, and is really rosy and jovial again. Going to see him when he was very despondent, I told him the story of Fechter's piece (then in rehearsal) with appropriate action; fighting a duel with the washing-stand, defying the bedstead, and saving the life of the sofa-cushion. This so kindled his old theatrical ardour, that I think he turned the corner on the spot.

With love to Mrs. Macready and Katie, and (be still my heart!) Benvenuta, and the exiled Johnny (not too attentive at school, I hope?), and the personally-unknown young Parr,

Ever, my dearest Macready, your most affectionate.

[*To Miss Power.*]

OFFICE OF "ALL THE YEAR ROUND,"
Thursday, Feb. 26th, 1863.

MY DEAR MARGUERITE,

I think I have found a first-rate title for your book, with an early and a delightful association in most people's minds, and a strong suggestion of Oriental pictures:

"Arabian Days and Nights."

I have sent it to Low's. If they have the wit to see it, do you in your first chapter touch that string, so as to bring a fanciful explanation in aid of the title, and sound it afterwards, now and again, when you come to anything where Haroun al Raschid, and the Grand Vizier, and Mesrour, the chief of the guard, and any of that wonderful *dramatis personæ* are vividly brought to mind.

Ever affectionately.

[*To Mr. Charles Knight.*]

Office of "All the Year Round,"
Wednesday, March 4th, 1863.

My dear Charles Knight,

At a quarter to seven on Monday, the 16th, a stately form will be descried breathing birthday cordialities and affectionate amenities, as it descends the broken and gently dipping ground by which the level country of the Clifton Road is attained. A practised eye will be able to discern two humble figures in attendance, which from their flowing crinolines may, without exposing the prophet to the imputation of rashness, be predicted to be women. Though certes their importance, absorbed and as it were swallowed up in the illustrious bearing and determined purpose of the maturer stranger, will not enthrall the gaze that wanders over the forest of San Giovanni as the night gathers in.

Ever affectionately,
G. P. R. James.

[*To Mrs. Dallas.*]*

EXTRACT.

THE TIME OF THE PRINCESS ALEXANDRA'S ARRIVAL IN LONDON.

It is curious to see London gone mad. Down in the Strand here, the monomaniacal tricks it is playing are grievous to behold, but along Fleet Street and Cheapside it gradually becomes frenzied, dressing itself up in all sorts of odds and ends, and knocking itself about in a most amazing manner. At London Bridge it raves, principally about the Kings of Denmark and their portraits. I have been looking among them for Hamlet's uncle, and have discovered one personage with a high nose, who I think is the man.

Faithfully yours always.

[*To Mrs. Lehmann.*]

OFFICE OF "ALL THE YEAR ROUND," No. 26, WELLINGTON STREET,
STRAND, LONDON, W.C.,
Tuesday, March 10th, 1863.

DEAR MRS. LEHMANN,

Two stalls for to-morrow's reading were sent to you by post before I heard from you this morning. Two will always come to you while you remain a Gummidge, and I hope I need not say that if you want more, none could be better bestowed in my sight.

---

* Now Mrs. Dallas Glyn.

Pray tell Lehmann, when you next write to him, that I find I owe him a mint of money for the delightful Swedish sleigh-bells. They are the wonder, awe, and admiration of the whole country side, and I never go out without them.

Let us make an exchange of child stories. I heard of a little fellow the other day whose mamma had been telling him that a French governess was coming over to him from Paris, and had been expatiating on the blessings and advantages of having foreign tongues. After leaning his plump little cheek against the window glass in a dreary little way for some minutes, he looked round and enquired in a general way, and not as if it had any special application, whether she didn't think "that the Tower of Babel was a great mistake altogether ? "

Ever faithfully yours.

[*To Mrs. Major.*]*

OFFICE OF "ALL THE YEAR ROUND," A WEEKLY JOURNAL, ETC., ETC., 26, WELLINGTON STREET, STRAND,

Thursday, March 12th, 1863.

MY DEAR MARY,

I am quite concerned to hear that you and your party (including your brother Willie) paid for seats at my reading last night. You must promise me never to do so any more. My old affections and attachments are not so lightly cherished or so easily forgotten as that I can bear the thought of you and yours coming to hear me like so many strangers. It will at all times delight me if you will

---

* Formerly Miss Talfourd.

send a little note to me, or to Georgina, or to Mary, saying when you feel inclined to come, and how many stalls you want. You may always be certain, even on the fullest nights, of room being made for you. And I shall always be interested and pleased by knowing that you are present.

Mind! You are to be exceedingly penitent for last night's offence, and to make me a promise that it shall never be repeated. On which condition accept my noble forgiveness.

With kind regard to Mr. Major, my dear Mary,

Affectionately yours.

[*To Mr. W. C. Macready.*]

GAD'S HILL PLACE, HIGHAM BY ROCHESTER, KENT,
Thursday, March 31*st,* 1863.

MY DEAREST MACREADY,

I mean to go on reading into June. For the sake of the finer effects (in " Copperfield " principally), I have changed from St. James's Hall to the Hanover Square Room. The latter is quite a wonderful room for sound, and so easy that the least inflection will tell anywhere in the place exactly as it leaves your lips ; but I miss my dear old shilling galleries—six or eight hundred strong—with a certain roaring sea of response in them, that you have stood upon the beach of many and many a time.

The summer, I hope and trust, will quicken the pace at which you grow stronger again. I am but in dull spirits myself just now, or I should remonstrate with you on your slowness.

Having two little boys sent home from school "to see the illuminations" on the marriage-night, I chartered an enormous van, at a cost of five pounds, and we started in majesty from the office in London, fourteen strong. We crossed Waterloo Bridge with the happy design of beginning the sight at London Bridge, and working our way through the City to Regent Street. In a by-street in the Borough, over against a dead wall and under a railway bridge, we were blocked for four hours. We were obliged to walk home at last, having seen nothing whatever. The wretched van turned up in the course of the next morning; and the best of it was that at Rochester here they illuminated the fine old castle, and really made a very splendid and picturesque thing (so my neighbours tell me).

With love to Mrs. Macready and Katie,

Ever, my dearest Macready, your most affectionate.

[*To Mr. W. Wilkie Collins.*]

GAD'S HILL PLACE, HIGHAM BY ROCHESTER, KENT,
Wednesday, April 22nd, 1863.

ON THE DEATH OF MR. EGG.

EXTRACT.

Ah, poor Egg! I knew what you would think and feel about it. When we saw him in Paris on his way out I was struck by his extreme nervousness, and derived from it an uneasy foreboding of his state. What a large piece of a good many years he seems to have taken with him! How often have I thought, since the news of his death came, of his putting his part in the saucepan (with the cover on) when we rehearsed " The Lighthouse ; " of his falling out of the hammock when we rehearsed " The Frozen Deep ; " of his learning Italian numbers when he ate the garlic in the carriage; of the thousands (I was going to say) of dark mornings when I apostrophised him as " Kernel ; " of his losing my invaluable knife in that beastly stage-coach ; of his posting up that mysterious book* every night !   I hardly know why, but I have always associated that volume most with Venice.   In my memory of the dear gentle little fellow, he will be (as since those days he always has been) eternally posting up that book at the large table in the middle of our Venice sitting-room, incidentally asking the name of an hotel three weeks back !   And his pretty house is to be laid waste and sold.   If there be a sale on the spot I shall try to buy something in loving remembrance of him, good dear little fellow.   Think what a great " Frozen Deep " lay close under those boards we acted on !   My brother Alfred, Luard, Arthur, Albert, Austin, Egg.   Even among the audience, Prince Albert and poor Stone !   " I heard the "—I forget what it was I used to say—" come up from the great deep ; " and it rings in my ears now, like a sort of mad prophecy.

However, this won't do.   We must close up the ranks and march on.

---

* His travelling journal.

[*To Rev. W. Brookfield.*]

GAD'S HILL, *May 17th,* 1863.

MY DEAR BROOKFIELD,

It occurs to me that you may perhaps know, or know of, a kind of man that I want to discover.

One of my boys (the youngest) now is at Wimbledon School. He is a docile, amiable boy of fair abilities, but sensitive and shy. And he writes me so very earnestly that he feels the school to be confusingly large for him, and that he is sure he could do better with some gentleman who gave his own personal attention to the education of half-a-dozen or a dozen boys, as to impress me with the belief that I ought to heed his conviction.

Has any such phenomenon as a good and reliable man in this wise ever come in your way ? Forgive my troubling you, and believe me,

Cordially yours.

[*To Rev. W. Brookfield.*]

GAD'S HILL PLACE, HIGHAM BY ROCHESTER, KENT,

May 24th, 1863.

MY DEAR BROOKFIELD,

I am most truly obliged to you for your kind and ready help.

When I am in town next week, I will call upon the Bishop of Natal, more to thank him than with the hope of profiting by that gentleman of whom he writes, as the limitation to " little boys " seems to stop the way. I want to

find someone with whom this particular boy could remain ;
if there were a mutual interest and liking, that would be a
great point gained.

Why did the kings in the fairy tales want children ?   I
suppose in the weakness of the royal intellect.

Concerning "Nickleby," I am so much of your mind
(comparing it with "Copperfield"), that it was a long time
before I could take a pleasure in reading it.   But I got
better, as I found the audience always taking to it.   I have
been trying, alone by myself, the "Oliver Twist" murder,
but have got something so horrible out of it that I am
afraid to try it in public.

•   Ever faithfully yours.

[To M. de Cerjat.]

GAD'S HILL PLACE, HIGHAM BY ROCHESTER, KENT,
Thursday, May 28th, 1863.

MY DEAR CERJAT,

I don't wonder at your finding it difficult to reconcile
your mind to a French Hamlet ; but I assure you that
Fechter's is a very remarkable performance perfectly
consistent with itself (whether it be my particular Hamlet,
or your particular Hamlet, or no), a coherent and intelligent whole, and done by a true artist.   I have never seen,
I think, an intelligent and clear view of the whole character so well sustained throughout ; and there is a very cap-
tivating air of romance and picturesqueness added, which
is quite new.   Rely upon it, the public were right.   The

thing could not have been sustained by oddity ; it would have perished upon that, very soon. As to the mere accent, there is far less drawback in that than you would suppose. For this reason, he obviously knows English so thoroughly that you feel he is safe. You are never in pain for him. This sense of ease is gained directly, and then you think very little more about it.

The Colenso and Jowett matter is a more difficult question, but here again I don't go with you. The position of the writers of " Essays and Reviews " is, that certain parts of the Old Testament have done their intended function in the education of the world *as it was ;* but that mankind, like the individual man, is designed by the Almighty to have an infancy and a maturity, and that as it advances, the machinery of its education must advance too. For example : inasmuch as ever since there was a sun and there was vapour, there *must have* been a rainbow under certain conditions, so surely it would be better now to recognise that indisputable fact. Similarly, Joshua might command the sun to stand still, under the impression that it moved round the earth ; but he could not possibly have inverted the relations of the earth and the sun, whatever his impressions were. Again, it is contended that the science of geology is quite as much a revelation to man, as books of an immense age and of (at the best) doubtful origin, and that your consideration of the latter must reasonably be influenced by the former. As I understand the importance of timely suggestions such as these, it is, that the Church should not gradually shock and lose the more thoughtful and logical of human minds ; but should be so gently and considerately yielding as to retain them, and, through them, hundreds of thousands. This seems to me, as I understand the temper and tendency of the time, whether for good or evil, to be a very wise and necessary position. And as I understand the danger, it is not chargeable on those who take this ground, but on those who in reply call names and argue nothing. What these bishops and such-like say about revelation, in assuming it to be finished and done with, I can't in the least understand. Nothing is discovered without God's intention and assistance, and I suppose every new knowledge of His works that is conceded to man to be distinctly a revelation by which men are to guide themselves. Lastly, in the mere matter of religious doctrine and dogmas, these men (Protestants—protestors—successors of the men who protested against human judgment being set aside) talk and write as if they were all settled by the direct act of Heaven ; not as if they had been, as we know they were, a matter of temporary accommodation and adjustment among disputing mortals as fallible as you or I.

Coming nearer home, I hope that Georgina is almost quite well. She has no attack of pain or flurry now, and is in all respects immensely better. Mary is neither married nor (that I know of) going to be. She and Katie and a lot of them have been playing croquet outside my window here for these last four days, to a mad and maddening extent. My sailor-boy's ship, the *Orlando*, is fortunately in Chatham Dockyard—so he is pretty constantly at home—while the shipwrights are repairing a leak in her. I am reading in London every Friday just now. Great crams and great enthusiasm. Townshend I suppose to have left Lausanne somewhere about this day. His house in the park is hermetically sealed, ready for him. The Prince and Princess of Wales go about (wisely) very much, and have as fair a chance of popularity as ever prince and princess had. The City ball in their honour is to be a tremendously gorgeous business, and Mary is highly excited by her father's being invited, and she with him. Meantime the unworthy parent is devising all kinds of subterfuges for sending her and getting out of it himself. A very intelligent German friend of mine, just home from America, maintains that the conscription will succeed in the North, and that the war will be indefinitely prolonged. *I* say "No," and that however mad and villainous the North is, the war will finish by reason of its not supplying soldiers. We shall see. The more they brag the more I don't believe in them.

*   *   *   *   *

[*To Mr. Percy Fitzgerald.*]

GAD'S HILL PLACE, *Saturday Night, July 4th*, 1863.

MY DEAR MR. FITZGERALD,

I have been most heartily gratified by the perusal of your article on my dogs. It has given me an amount and a kind of pleasure very unusual, and for which I thank you earnestly. The owner of the renowned dog Cæsar understands me so sympathetically, that I trust with perfect confidence to his feeling what I really mean in these few words. You interest me very much by your kind promise, the redemption of which I hereby claim, to send me your life of Sterne when it comes out. If you should be in England before this, I should be delighted to see you here on the top of Falstaff's own Gad's Hill. It is a very pretty country, not thirty miles from London ; and if you could spare a day or two for its fine walks, I and my two latest dogs, a St. Bernard and a bloodhound, would be charmed with your company as one of ourselves.

Believe me, very faithfully yours.

Friday, July 10th, 1863. *

DEAR MADAM,

I hope you will excuse this tardy reply to your letter. It is often impossible for me, by any means, to keep pace with my correspondents. I must take leave to say, that if there be any general feeling on the part of the intelligent Jewish people, that I have done them what you describe as " a great wrong," they are a far less sensible, a far less just, and a far less good-tempered people than I have always supposed them to be. Fagin, in " Oliver Twist," is a Jew, because it unfortunately was true of the time to which that story refers, that that class of criminal almost invariably was a Jew. But surely no sensible man or wo-

---

* Answer to letter from Jewish lady, remonstrating with him on injustice to the Jews, shown in the character of Fagin, and asking for subscription for the benefit of the Jewish poor.

man of your persuasion can fail to observe—firstly, that all
the rest of the wicked *dramatis personæ* are Christians; and
secondly, that he is called the "Jew," not because of his
religion, but because of his race. If I were to write a
story, in which I described a Frenchman or a Spaniard as
"the Roman Catholic," I should do a very indecent and
unjustifiable thing; but I make mention of Fagin as the
Jew, because he is one of the Jewish people, and because
it conveys that kind of idea of him which I should give my
readers of a Chinaman, by calling him a Chinese.

The enclosed is quite a nominal subscription towards
the good object in which you are interested; but I hope it
may serve to show you that I have no feeling towards the
Jewish people but a friendly one. I always speak well of
them, whether in public or in private, and bear my testimony (as I ought to do) to their perfect good faith in such
transactions as I have ever had with them; and in my
"Child's History of England," I have lost no opportunity
of setting forth their cruel persecution in old times.

Dear Madam, faithfully yours.

In reply to this, the Jewish lady thanks him for his kind
letter and its enclosure, still remonstrating and pointing
out that though, as he observes, "all the other criminal
characters were Christians, they are, at least, contrasted
with characters of good Christians; this wretched Fagin
stands alone as the Jew."

The reply to *this* letter afterwards was the character of
Riah, in "Our Mutual Friend," and some favourable
sketches of Jewish character in the lower class, in some
articles in "All the Year Round."

[*To Mr. Ouvry.*]

GAD'S HILL PLACE, HIGHAM BY ROCHESTER, KENT,
Wednesday Night, July 29th, 1863.

MY DEAR OUVRY,

I have had some undefined idea that you were to let me know if you were coming to the archæologs at Rochester. (I myself am keeping out of their way, as having had enough of crowding and speech-making in London.) Will you tell me where you are, whether you are in this neighbourhood or out of it, whether you will come here on Saturday and stay till Monday or till Tuesday morning? If you will come, I *know* I can give you the heartiest welcome in Kent, and I *think* I can give you the best wine in this part of it. Send me a word in reply. I will fetch you from anywhere, at any indicated time.

We have very pretty places in the neighbourhood, and are not uncomfortable people (I believe) to stay with.

Faithfully yours ever.

[*To Mr. Charles Reade.*]

OFFICE OF " ALL THE YEAR ROUND,"
Wednesday, Sept. 30th, 1863.

MY DEAR READE,

I *must* write you one line to say how interested I am in your story, and to congratulate you upon its admirable art and its surprising grace and vigour.

And to hint my hope, at the same time, that you will be

able to find leisure for a little dash for the Christmas number. It would be a really great and true pleasure to me if you could.   Faithfully yours always.

[*To Miss Hogarth.*]

GAD'S HILL PLACE, HIGHAM BY ROCHESTER, KENT,
Wednesday, Oct. 7th, 1863.

MY DEAREST GEORGY,

You will see by to-day's *Times* that it *was* an earthquake that shook me, and that my watch showed exactly the same time as the man's who writes from Blackheath so near us—twenty minutes past three.

It is a great satisfaction to me to make it out so precisely ; I wish you would enquire whether the servants felt it. I thought it was the voice of the cook that answered me, but that was nearly half an hour later. I am strongly inclined to think that there is a peculiar susceptibility in iron—at all events in our part of the country—to the shock, as though there were something magnetic in it. For, whereas my long iron bedstead was so violently shaken, I certainly heard nothing rattle in the room.

I will write about my return as soon as I get on with the still unbegun " Uncommercial."

Ever affectionately.

[*To Mr. W. H. Wills.*]

GAD'S HILL, *Sunday, Dec. 20th*, 1863.

MY DEAR WILLS,

I am clear that you took my cold. Why didn't you do the thing completely, and take it away from me? for it hangs by me still.

Will you tell Mrs. Linton that in looking over her admirable account (*most* admirable) of Mrs. Gordon's book, I have taken out the references to Lockhart, not because I in the least doubt their justice, but because I knew him and he liked me ; and because one bright day in Rome, I walked about with him for some hours when he was dying fast, and all the old faults had faded out of him, and the now ghost of the handsome man I had first known when Scott's daughter was at the head of his house, had little more to do with this world than she in her grave, or Scott in his, or small Hugh Littlejohn in his. Lockhart had been anxious to see me all the previous day (when I was away on the Campagna), and as we walked about I knew very well that *he* knew very well why. He talked of getting better, but I never saw him again. This makes me stay Mrs. Linton's hand, gentle as it is.

Mrs. Lirriper is indeed a most brilliant old lady. God bless her.

I am glad to hear of your being "haunted," and hope to increase your stock of such ghosts pretty liberally.

Ever faithfully.

1864.

NARRATIVE.

CHARLES DICKENS was, as usual, at Gad's Hill, with a family and friendly party, at the opening of this year, and had been much shocked and distressed by the news of the sudden death of Mr. Thackeray, brought to him by friends arriving from London on the Christmas Eve of 1863, the day on which the sad event happened. He writes of it, in the first letter of the year, to Mr. Wilkie Collins, who was passing the winter in Italy. He tells him, also, of his having got well to work upon a new serial story, the first number of which ("Our Mutual Friend") was published on the 1st of May.

The year began very sadly for Charles Dickens. On the 7th of February (his own birthday) he received the mournful announcement of the death of his second son, Walter Landor (a lieutenant in the 42nd Royal Highlanders), who had died quite suddenly at Calcutta, on the last night of the year of 1863, at the age of twenty-three. His third son, Francis Jeffrey, had started for India at the end of January.

His annual letter to M. de Cerjat contains an allusion to "another generation beginning to peep above the table "— the children of his son Charles, who had been married three years before, to Miss Bessie Evans.

In the middle of February he removed to a house in London (57, Gloucester Place, Hyde Park), where he made a stay of the usual duration, up to the middle of June, all the time being hard at work upon "Our Mutual Friend" and "All the Year Round." Mr. Marcus Stone was the illustrator of the new monthly work, and we give a specimen of one of many letters which he wrote to him about his "subjects."

His old friend, Mr. Charles Knight, with whom for many years Charles Dickens had dined on his birthday, was staying, this spring, in the Isle of Wight. To him he writes of the death of Walter, and of another sad death which happened at this time, and which affected him almost as much. Clara, the last surviving daughter of Mr. and Mrs. White, who had been happily married to Mr. Gordon, of Cluny, not more than two years, had just died at Bonchurch.

Her father, as will be seen by the touching allusion to him in this letter, had died a short time after this daughter's marriage.

A letter to Mr. Edmund Ollier has reference to certain additions which Charles Dickens wished him to make to an article (by Mr. Ollier) on Working Men's Clubs, published in " All the Year Round."

We are glad to have one letter to the Lord Chief Baron, Sir Frederick Pollock, which shows the great friendship and regard Charles Dickens had for him, and his admiration of his qualities in his judicial capacity.

We give a pleasant letter to Mrs. Storrar, for whom, and for her husband, Dr. Storrar, Charles Dickens had affectionate regard, because we are glad to have their names in our book. The letter speaks for itself and needs no explanation.

The latter part of the year was uneventful. Hard at work, he passed the summer and autumn at Gad's Hill, taking holidays by receiving visitors at home (among them, this year, Sir J. Emerson Tennent, his wife and daughter, who were kindly urgent for his paying them a return visit in Ireland) and occasional "runs" into France. The last letters we give are his annual one to M. de Cerjat, and a graceful little New Year's note to his dear old friend " Barry Cornwall."

The Christmas number was "Mrs. Lirriper's Legacy," the first and last part written by himself, as in the case of the previous year's "Mrs. Lirriper."

[*To Mr. W. Wilkie Collins.*]

GAD'S HILL, *Monday, Jan. 24th*, 1864.

EXTRACT.

MY DEAR WILKIE,

I am horribly behindhand in answering your welcome letter; but I have been so busy, and have had the house so full for Christmas and the New Year, and have had so much to see to in getting Frank out to India, that I have not been able to settle down to a regular long letter, which I mean this to be, but which it may not turn out to be, after all.

First, I will answer your enquiries about the Christmas number and the new book. The Christmas number has been the greatest success of all; has shot ahead of last year; has sold about two hundred and twenty thousand; and has made the name of Mrs. Lirriper so swiftly and domestically famous as never was. I had a very strong belief in her when I wrote about her, finding that she made a great effect upon me; but she certainly has gone beyond my hopes. (Probably you know nothing about her? which is a very unpleasant consideration.) Of the new book, I have done the two first numbers, and am now beginning the third. It is a combination of drollery with romance which requires a great deal of pains and a perfect throwing away of points that might be amplified; but I hope it is *very good.* I confess, in short, that I think it is. Strange to say, I felt at first quite dazed in getting back to the large canvas and the big brushes; and even now, I have a sensation as of acting at the San Carlo after Tavistock House, which I could hardly have supposed would have come upon so old a stager.

You will have read about poor Thackeray's death—sudden, and yet not sudden, for he had long been alarmingly ill. At the solicitation of Mr. Smith and some of his friends, I have done what I would most gladly have excused myself from doing, if I felt I could—written a couple of pages about him in what was his own magazine.

Concerning the Italian experiment, De la Rue is more hopeful than you. He and his bank are closely leagued with the powers at Turin, and he has long been devoted to Cavour ; but he gave me the strongest assurances (with illustrations) of the fusion between place and place, and of the blending of small mutually antagonistic characters into one national character, progressing cheeringly and certainly. Of course there must be discouragements and discrepancies in the first struggles of a country previously so degraded and enslaved, and the time, as yet, has been very short.

I should like to have a day with you at the Coliseum, and on the Appian Way, and among the tombs, and with the Orvieto. But Rome and I are wide asunder, physically as well as morally. I wonder whether the dramatic stable, where we saw the marionettes, still receives the Roman public ? And Lord ! when I think of you in that hotel, how I think of poor dear Egg in the long front drawing-room, giving on to the piazza, posting up that wonderful necromantic volume which we never shall see opened !

[*To Mr. Marcus Stone.*]

57, GLOUCESTER PLACE, HYDE PARK,
Tuesday, Feb. 23rd, 1864.

MY DEAR MARCUS,

I think the design for the cover *excellent*, and do not doubt its coming out to perfection. The slight alteration I am going to suggest originates in a business consideration not to be overlooked.

The word "Our" in the title must be out in the open like "Mutual Friend," making the title three distinct large lines—"Our" as big as "Mutual Friend." This would give you too much design at the bottom. I would therefore take out the dustman, and put the Wegg and Boffin composition (which is capital) in its place. I don't want Mr. Inspector or the murder reward bill, because these points are sufficiently indicated in the river at the top. Therefore you can have an indication of the dustman in Mr. Inspector's place. Note, that the dustman's face should be droll, and not horrible. Twemlow's elbow will still go out of the frame as it does now, and the same with Lizzie's skirts on the opposite side. With these changes, work away!

Mrs. Boffin, as I judge of her from the sketch, "very good, indeed." I want Boffin's oddity, without being at all blinked, to be an oddity of a very honest kind, that people will like.

The doll's dressmaker is immensely better than she was.

I think she should now come extremely well. A weird sharpness not without beauty is the thing I want.

Affectionately always.

[*To Mr. Charles Knight.*]

57, GLOUCESTER PLACE, W., *Tuesday, March 1st,* 1864.

MY DEAR KNIGHT,

We knew of your being in the Isle of Wight, and had said that we should have this year to drink your health in your absence. Rely on my being always ready and happy to renew our old friendship in the flesh. In the spirit it needs no renewal, because it has no break.

Ah, poor Mrs. White ! A sad, sad story ! It is better for poor White that that little churchyard by the sea received his ashes a while ago, than that he should have lived to this time.

My poor boy was on his way home from an up-country station, on sick leave. He had been very ill, but was not so at the time. He was talking to some brother-officers in the Calcutta hospital about his preparations for home, when he suddenly became excited, had a rush of blood from the mouth, and was dead. His brother Frank would arrive out at Calcutta, expecting to see him after six years, and he would have been dead a month.

My "working life" is resolving itself at the present into another book, in twenty green leaves. You work like a Trojan at Ventnor, but you do that everywhere ; and that's why you are so young.

Mary and Georgina unite in kindest regard to you, and to Mrs. Knight, and to your daughters. So do I. And I am ever, my dear Knight,

Affectionately yours.

P.S.—Serene View! What a placid address!

[*To Mr. Edmund Ollier.*]

"ALL THE YEAR ROUND" OFFICE, *March*, 1864.

EXTRACT.

I want the article on "Working Men's Clubs" to refer back to "The Poor Man and his Beer" in No. 1, and to maintain the principle involved in that effort.

Also, emphatically, to show that trustfulness is at the bottom of all social institutions, and that to trust a man, as one of a body of men, is to place him under a wholesome restraint of social opinion, and is a very much better thing than to make a baby of him.

Also, to point out that the rejection of beer in this club, tobacco in that club, dancing or what-not in another club, are instances that such clubs are founded on mere whims, and therefore cannot successfully address human nature in the general, and hope to last.

Also, again to urge that patronage is the curse and blight of all such endeavours, and to impress upon the working men that they must originate and manage for themselves. And to ask them the question, can they possibly show their detestation of drunkenness better, or better strive to get rid of it from among them, than to make it a hopeless disqualification in all their clubs, and a reason for expulsion.

Also, to encourage them to declare to themselves and their fellow working men that they want social rest and social recreation for themselves and their families ; and that these clubs are intended for that laudable and necessary purpose, and do not need educational pretences or flourishes.   Do not let them be afraid or ashamed of wanting to be amused and pleased.

[*To the Lord Chief Baron.*]

57, GLOUCESTER PLACE, *Tuesday, March 15th,* 1864.
MY DEAR CHIEF BARON,

Many thanks for your kind letter, which I find on my return from a week's holiday.

Your answer concerning poor Thackeray I will duly make known to the active spirit in that matter, Mr. Shirley Brooks.

Your kind invitation to me to come and see you and yours, and hear the nightingales, I shall not fail to discuss with Forster, and with an eye to spring.   I expect to see him presently ; the rather as I found a note from him when I came back yesterday, describing himself somewhat gloomily as not having been well, and as feeling a little out of heart.

It is not out of order, I hope, to remark that you have been much in my thoughts and on my lips lately ?   For I really have not been able to repress my admiration of the vigorous dignity and sense and spirit, with which one of the best of judges set right one of the dullest of juries in a recent case.

Believe me ever, very faithfully yours.

[*To Mr. John Forster.*]

57, GLOUCESTER PLACE, *Tuesday, March* 29*th*, 1864.

MY DEAR FORSTER,

I meant to write to you last night, but to enable Wills to get away I had to read a book of Fitzgerald's through before I went to bed.

Concerning Eliot, I sat down, as I told you, and read the book through with the strangest interest and the highest admiration. I believe it to be as honest, spirited, patient, reliable, and gallant a piece of biography as ever was written, the care and pains of it astonishing, the completeness of it masterly ; and what I particularly feel about it is that the dignity of the man, and the dignity of the book that tells about the man, always go together, and fit each other. This same quality has always impressed me as the great leading speciality of the Goldsmith, and enjoins sympathy with the subject, knowledge of it, and pursuit of it in its own spirit ; but I think it even more remarkable here. I declare that apart from the interest of having been so put into the time, and enabled to understand it, I personally feel quite as much the credit and honour done to literature by such a book. It quite clears out of the remembrance a thousand pitiful things, and sets one up in heart again. I am not surprised in the least by Bulwer's enthusiasm. I was as confident about the effect of the book when I closed the first volume, as I was when I closed the second with a full heart. No man less in earnest than Eliot himself could have done it, and I make bold to add that it never could have been done by a man who was so distinctly born to do the work as Eliot was to do his.

Saturday at Hastings I must give up. I have wavered and considered, and considered and wavered, but if I take that sort of holiday, I must have a day to spare after it, and at this critical time I have not. If I were to lose a page of the five numbers I have purposed to myself to be ready by the publication day, I should feel that I had fallen short. I have grown hard to satisfy, and write very slowly, and I have so much bad fiction, that *will* be thought of when I don't want to think of it, that I am forced to take more care than I ever took.

Ever affectionately.

[*To Mrs. Storrar.*]

GAD'S HILL PLACE, HIGHAM BY ROCHESTER, KENT,
Sunday Morning, May 15*th*, 1864.

MY DEAR MRS. STORRAR,

Our family dinner must come off at Gad's Hill, where I have improvements to exhibit, and where I shall be truly pleased to see you and the doctor again. I have deferred answering your note, while I have been scheming and scheming for a day between this time and our departure.

But it is all in vain. My engagements have accumulated, and become such a whirl, that no day is left me. Nothing is left me but to get away. I look forward to my release from this dining life with an inexpressible longing after quiet and my own pursuits. What with public speechifying, private eating and drinking, and perpetual simmering in hot rooms, I have made London too hot to hold me and my work together. Mary and Georgina acknowledge the condition of imbecility to which we have become reduced in reference to your kind reminder. They say, when I stare at them in a forlorn way with your note in my hand: " What CAN you do ! " To which I can only reply, implicating them : " See what you have brought me to ! "

With our united kind regard to yourself and Dr. Storrar, I entreat your pity and compassion for an unfortunate wretch whom a too-confiding disposition has brought to this pass. If I had not allowed my " cheeild " to pledge me to all manner of fellow-creatures, I and my digestion might have been in a state of honourable independence this day.

Faithfully and penitently yours.

[*To Mr. Percy Fitzgerald.*]

OFFICE OF " ALL THE YEAR ROUND," ETC. ETC. ETC.
Wednesday, July 27th, 1864.

MY DEAR MR. FITZGERALD,

First, let me assure you that it gave us all real pleasure to see your sister and you at Gad's Hill, and that we all hope you will both come and stay a day or two with us when you are next in England.

Next, let me convey to you the intelligence that I resolve to launch " Miss Manuel," fully confiding in your conviction of the power of the story. On all business points, Wills will communicate with you. I purpose beginning its publication in our first September number, therefore there is no time to be lost.

The only suggestion I have to make as to the MS. in hand and type is, that Captain Fermor wants relief. It is a disagreeable character, as you mean it to be, and I should be afraid to do so much with him, if the case were mine, without taking the taste of him, here and there, out of the reader's mouth. It is remarkable that if you do not administer a disagreeable character carefully, the public have a decided tendency to think that the *story* is disagreeable, and not merely the fictitious person.

What do you think of the title,

NEVER FORGOTTEN ?

It is a good one in itself, would express the eldest sister's pursuit, and glanced at now and then in the text, would hold the reader in suspense. I would propose to add the line,

BY THE AUTHOR OF BELLA DONNA.

Let me know your opinion as to the title. I need not assure you that the greatest care will be taken of you here, and that we shall make you as thoroughly well and widely known as we possibly can.   Very faithfully yours.

[*To Sir James Emerson Tennent.*]

GAD'S HILL PLACE, HIGHAM BY ROCHESTER, KENT,
Friday, Aug. 26th, 1864.

MY DEAR TENNENT,

Believe me, I fully intended to come to you—did not doubt that I should come—and have greatly disappointed Mary and her aunt, as well as myself, by not coming. But I do not feel safe in going out for a visit. The mere knowledge that I had such a thing before me would put me out. It is not the length of time consumed, or the distance traversed, but it is the departure from a settled habit and a continuous sacrifice of pleasures that comes in question. This is an old story with me. I have never divided a book of my writing with anything else, but have always wrought at it to the exclusion of everything else ; and it is now too late to change.

After receiving your kind note I resolved to make another trial. But the hot weather and a few other drawbacks did not mend the matter, for I have dropped astern this month instead of going ahead. So I have seen Forster, and shown him my chains, and am reduced to taking exercise in them, like Baron Trenck.

I am heartily pleased that you set so much store by the dedication. You may be sure that it does not make me the less anxious to take pains, and to work out well what I have in my mind.

Mary and Georgina unite with me in kindest regards to Lady Tennent and Miss Tennent, and wish me to report that while they are seriously disappointed, they still feel there is no help for it. I can testify that they had great pleasure in the anticipation of the visit, and that their faces were very long and blank indeed when I began to hint my doubts. They fought against them valiantly as long as there was a chance, but they see my difficulty as well as anyone not myself can.

Believe me, my dear Tennent, ever faithfully yours.

[*To Mr. Clarkson Stanfield, R.A.*]

THE ATHENÆUM, *Wednesday, Sept. 21st,* 1864.

MY DEAR STANNY,

I met George in the street a few days ago, and he gave me a wonderful account of the effect of your natural element upon you at Ramsgate. I expect you to come back looking about twenty-nine, and feeling about nineteen.

This morning I have looked in here to put down Fechter as a candidate, on the chance of the committee's electing him some day or other. He is a most devoted worshipper of yours, and would take it as a great honour if you would second him. Supposing you to have not the least objection (of course, if you should have any, I can in a moment provide a substitute), will you write your name in the candidates' book as his seconder when you are next in town and passing this way?

Lastly, if you should be in town on his opening night (a Saturday, and in all probability the 22nd of October), will you come and dine at the office and see his new piece? You have not yet "pronounced" in the matter of that new

French stage of his, on which Calcott for the said new piece has built up all manner of villages, camps, Versailles gardens, etc. etc. etc. etc., with no wings, no flies, no looking off in any direction. If you tell me that you are to be in town by that time, I will not fail to refresh your memory as to the precise day.

With kind regard to Mrs. Stanfield,

Believe me, my dear old boy, ever your affectionate

DICK.

[*To M. de Cerjat.*]

GAD'S HILL PLACE, HIGHAM BY ROCHESTER,
Tuesday, Oct. 25th, 1864.

MY DEAR CERJAT,

Here is a limping brute of a reply to your always-welcome Christmas letter ! But, as usual, when I have done my day's work, I jump up from my desk and rush into air and exercise, and find letter-writing the most difficult thing in my daily life.

I hope that your asthmatic tendencies may not be strong just now ; but Townshend's account of the premature winter at Lausanne is not encouraging, and with us here in England all such disorders have been aggravated this autumn. However, a man of your dignity *must* have either asthma or gout, and I hope you have got the better of the two.

In London there is, as you see by the papers, extraordinarily little news. At present the apprehension (rather less than it was thought) of a commercial crisis, and the trial of Müller next Thursday, are the two chief sensations. I hope that gentleman will be hanged, and have hardly a doubt of it, though croakers contrariwise are not wanting. It is difficult to conceive any other line of defence than that the circumstances proved, taken separately, are slight. But a sound judge will immediately charge the jury that the strength of the circumstances lies in their being put together, and will thread them together on a fatal rope.

As to the Church, my friend, I am sick of it. The spectacle presented by the indecent squabbles of priests of most denominations, and the exemplary unfairness and rancour with which they conduct their differences, utterly repel me. And the idea of the Protestant establishment, in the face of its own history, seeking to trample out discussion and private judgment, is an enormity so cool, that I wonder the Right Reverends, Very Reverends, and all other Reverends, who commit it, can look in one another's faces without laughing, as the old soothsayers did. Perhaps they can't and don't. How our sublime and so-different Christian religion is to be administered in the future I cannot pretend to say, but that the Church's hand is at its own throat I am fully convinced. Here, more Popery, there, more Methodism—as many forms of consignment to eternal damnation as there are articles, and all in one forever quarrelling body—the Master of the New Testament put out of sight, and the rage and fury almost always turning on the letter of obscure parts of the Old Testament, which itself has been the subject of accommodation, adaptation, varying interpretation without end—these things cannot last. The Church that is to have its part in the coming time must be a more Christian one, with less arbitrary pretensions and a stronger hold upon the mantle of our Saviour, as He walked and talked upon this earth.

Of family intelligence I have very little. Charles Collins continuing in a very poor way, and showing no signs of amendment. He and my daughter Katie went to Wiesbaden and thence to Nice, where they are now. I have strong apprehensions that he will never recover, and that she will be left a young widow. All the rest are as they were. Mary neither married nor going to be ; Georgina holding them all together and perpetually corresponding with the distant ones ; occasional rallyings coming off here, in which another generation begins to peep above the table. I once used to think what a horrible thing it was to be a grandfather. Finding that the calamity falls upon me without my perceiving any other change in myself, I bear it like a man.

Mrs. Watson has bought a house in town, to which she repairs in the season, for the bringing out of her daughter. She is now at Rockingham. Her eldest son is said to be as good an eldest son as ever was, and to make her position there a perfectly independent and happy one. I have not seen him for some years ; her I often see ; but he ought to be a good fellow, and is very popular in his neighbourhood.

I have altered this place very much since you were here, and have made a pretty (I think an unusually pretty) drawing-room. I wish you would come back and see it. My being on the Dover line, and my being very fond of France, occasion me to cross the Channel perpetually. Whenever I feel that I have worked too much, or am on the eve of overdoing it, and want a change, away I go by the mail-train, and turn up in Paris or anywhere else that suits my humour, next morning. So I come back as fresh as a daisy, and preserve as ruddy a face as though I never leant over a sheet of paper. When I retire from a literary life I think of setting up as a Channel pilot.

Pray give my love to Mrs. Cerjat, and tell her that I should like to go up the Great St. Bernard again, and shall be glad to know if she is open to another ascent. Old days in Switzerland are ever fresh to me, and sometimes I walk with you again, after dark, outside the hotel at Martigny, while Lady Mary Taylour (wasn't it?) sang within very prettily. Lord, how the time goes! How many years ago!   Affectionately yours.

Wednesday, Nov. 16th, 1864. *

DEAR MADAM,

I have received your letter with great pleasure, and hope to be (as I have always been at heart) the best of friends with the Jewish people. The error you point out to me had occurred to me, as most errors do to most people, when it was too late to correct it. But it will do no harm. The peculiarities of dress and manner are fused together for the sake of picturesqueness.

Dear Madam, faithfully yours.

---

* In answer to another letter from the "Jewish lady," in which she gives her reasons for still being dissatisfied with the character of Riah.

[*To Mr. B. W. Procter.*]

GAD'S HILL PLACE, HIGHAM BY ROCHESTER, KENT,
Saturday, Dec. 31st, 1864.

MY DEAR PROCTER,

I have reserved my acknowledgment of your delightful note (the youngest note I have had in all this year) until to-day, in order that I might send, most heartily and affectionately, all seasonable good wishes to you and to Mrs. Procter, and to those who are nearest and dearest to you. Take them from an old friend who loves you.

Mamie returns the tender compliments, and Georgina does what the Americans call "endorse them." Mrs. Lirriper is proud to be so remembered, and says over and over again "that it's worth twenty times the trouble she has taken with the narrative, since Barry Cornwall, Esquire, is pleased to like it."

I got rid of a touch of neuralgia in France (as I always do there), but I found no old friends in my voyages of discovery on that side, such as I have left on this.

My dear Procter, ever your affectionate.

1865.

NARRATIVE.

FOR this spring a furnished house in Somer's Place, Hyde Park, had been taken, which Charles Dickens occupied, with his sister-in-law and daughter, from the beginning of March until June.

During the year he paid two short visits to France.

He was still at work upon "Our Mutual Friend," two numbers of which had been issued in January and February, when the first volume was published, with dedication to Sir James Emerson Tennent. The remaining numbers were issued between March and November, when the complete work was published in two volumes.

The Christmas number, to which Charles Dickens contributed three stories, was called "Doctor Marigold's Prescriptions."

Being out of health, and much overworked, Charles Dickens, at the end of May, took his first short holiday trip into France. And on his way home, and on a day afterwards so fatal to him, the 9th of June, he was in that most terrible railway accident at Staplehurst. Many of our letters for this year have reference to this awful experience—an experience from the effects of which his nerves never wholly recovered. His letters to Mr. Thomas Mitton and to Mrs. Hulkes (an esteemed friend and neighbour) are graphic descriptions of this disaster. But they do NOT tell of the wonderful presence of mind and energy shown by Charles Dickens when most of the terrified passengers were incapable of thought or action, or of his gentleness and goodness to the dead and dying. The Mr. Dickenson* mentioned in the letter to Mrs. Hulkes soon recovered. He always considers that he owes his life to Charles Dickens, the latter having discovered and extricated him from beneath a carriage before it was too late.

Our first letter to Mr. Kent is one of congratulation upon his having become the proprietor of *The Sun* newspaper.

Professor Owen has been so kind as to give us some

---

* Now Captain E. Newton Dickenson.

notes, which we publish for the sake of his great name. Charles Dickens had not much correspondence with Professor Owen, but there was a firm friendship and great mutual admiration between them.

The letter to Mrs. Procter is in answer to one from her, asking Charles Dickens to write a memoir of her daughter Adelaide, as a preface to a collected edition of her poems.

[*To Mr. William Charles Kent.*]

GAD'S HILL PLACE, HIGHAM BY ROCHESTER, KENT,
Tuesday, Jan. 17th, 1865.

MY DEAR KENT,

I meant to have written instantly on the appearance of your paper in its beautiful freshness, to congratulate you on its handsome appearance, and to send you my heartiest good wishes for its thriving and prosperous career. Through a mistake of the postman's that remarkable letter has been tesselated into the Infernal Pavement instead of being delivered in the Strand.

We have been looking and waiting for your being well enough to propose yourself for a mouthful of fresh air. Are you well enough to come on Sunday ? We shall be coming down from Charing Cross on Sunday morning, and I shall be going up again at nine on Monday morning.

It amuses me to find that you don't see your way with a certain "Mutual Friend" of ours. I have a horrible suspicion that you may begin to be fearfully knowing at somewhere about No. 12 or 13. But you shan't if I can help it.

Your note delighted me because it dwelt upon the places in the number that *I* dwell on. Not that that is anything new in your case, but it is always new to me in the pleasure I derive from it, which is truly inexpressible.

Ever cordially yours.

[*To Mrs. Procter.*]

GAD'S HILL PLACE, HIGHAM BY ROCHESTER, KENT,
Wednesday, Feb. 15*th*, 1865.

MY DEAR MRS. PROCTER,

Of course I will do it, and of course I will do it for the love of you and Procter. You can give me my brief, and we can speak about its details. Once again, of course I will do it, and with all my heart.

I have registered a vow (in which there is not the least merit, for I couldn't help it) that when I am, as I am now, very hard at work upon a book, I never will dine out more than one day in a week. Why didn't you ask for the Wednesday, before I stood engaged to Lady Molesworth for the Tuesday ?

It is so delightful to me to sit by your side anywhere and be brightened up, that I lay a handsome sacrifice upon the altar of " Our Mutual Friend " in writing this note, very much against my will. But for as many years as can be made consistent with my present juvenility, I always have given my work the first place in my life, and what can I do now at 35 !—or at least at the two figures, never mind their order.

I send my love to Procter, hoping you may appropriate a little of it by the way.

Affectionately yours.

[*To Mr. W. C. Macready.*]

OFFICE OF "ALL THE YEAR ROUND,"
Wednesday, March 1st, 1865.

MY DEAREST MACREADY,

I have been laid up here with a frost-bitten foot (from hard walking in the snow), or you would have heard from me sooner.

My reply to Professor Agassiz is short, but conclusive. Daily seeing improper uses made of confidential letters in the addressing of them to a public audience that have no business with them, I made not long ago a great fire in my field at Gad's Hill, and burnt every letter I possessed. And now I always destroy every letter I receive not on absolute business, and my mind is so far at ease. Poor dear Felton's letters went up into the air with the rest, or his highly distinguished representative should have had them most willingly.

We never fail to drink old P.'s health on his birthday, or to make him the subject of a thousand loving remembrances. With the best love to Mrs. Macready and Katie,

Ever, my dearest Macready,

Your most affectionate Friend.

[*To Mr. W. C. Macready.*]

16, SOMER'S PLACE, HYDE PARK,
Saturday Night, April 22nd, 1865.

MY DEAREST MACREADY,

A thousand thanks for your kind letter, most heartily welcome.

VOL. II.—12

My frost-bitten foot, after causing me great inconvenience and much pain, has begun to conduct itself amiably. I can now again walk my ten miles in the morning without inconvenience, but am absurdly obliged to sit shoeless all the evening—a very slight penalty, as I detest going out to dinner (which killed the original old Parr by-the-bye).

I am working like a dragon at my book, and am a terror to the household, likewise to all the organs and brass bands in this quarter. Gad's Hill is being gorgeously painted, and we are here until the 1st of June. I wish I might hope you would be there any time this summer; I really *have* made the place comfortable and pretty by this time.

It is delightful to us to hear such good news of Butty. She made so deep an impression on Fechter that he always asks me what Ceylon has done for her, and always beams when I tell him how thoroughly well it has made her. As to *you*, you are the youngest man (worth mentioning as a thorough man) that I know. Oh, let me be as young when I am as——did you think I was going to write "old?" No, sir—withdraw from the wear and tear of busy life is my expression.

Poole still holds out at Kentish Town, and says he is dying of solitude. His memory is astoundingly good. I see him about once in two or three months, and in the meantime he makes notes of questions to ask me when I come. Having fallen in arrear of the time, these generally refer to unknown words he has encountered in the newspapers. His three last (he always reads them with tremendous difficulty through an enormous magnifying-glass) were as follows :

1. What's croquet ?
2. What's an Albert chain ?
3. Let me know the state of mind of the Queen.

When I had delivered a neat exposition on these heads, he turned back to his memoranda, and came to something that the utmost power of the enormous magnifying-glass couldn't render legible. After a quarter of an hour or so, he said : "O yes, I know." And then rose and clasped his hands above his head, and said : "Thank God, I am not a dram-drinker."

. Do think of coming to Gad's in the summer ; and do give my love to Mrs. Macready, and tell her I know she can make you come if she will. Mary and Georgy send best and dearest loves to her, to you, and to Katie, and to baby. Johnny we suppose to be climbing the tree of knowledge elsewhere.

My dearest Macready, ever yours most affectionately.

[*To Mr. W. C. Macready.*]

GAD'S HILL, *Monday, June* 12*th*, 1865.

MY DEAREST MACREADY,

[*So far in his own writing.*]

Many thanks for your kind words of remembrance.* This is not all in my own hand, because I am too much

---

* This was a circular note which he sent in answer to innumerable letters of enquiry, after the accident.

shaken to write many notes. Not by the beating and dragging of the carriage in which I was—it did not go over, but was caught on the turn, among the ruins of the bridge—but by the work afterwards to get out the dying and dead, which was terrible.

[*The rest in his own writing.*]

Ever your affectionate Friend.

P.S.—My love to Mrs. Macready.

[*To Mr. Thomas Mitton.*]

GAD'S HILL PLACE, HIGHAM BY ROCHESTER, KENT,
Tuesday, June 13*th,* 1865.

MY DEAR MITTON,

I should have written to you yesterday or the day be- · fore, if I had been quite up to writing.

I was in the only carriage that did not go over into the stream. It was caught upon the turn by some of the ruin of the bridge, and hung suspended and balanced in an apparently impossible manner. Two ladies were my fellow-passengers, an old one and a young one. This is exactly what passed. You may judge from it the precise length of the suspense : Suddenly we were off the rail, and beating the ground as the car of a half-emptied balloon might. The old lady cried out, "My God !" and the young one screamed. I caught hold of them both (the old lady sat opposite and the young one on my left), and said : "We can't help ourselves, but we can be quiet and composed. Pray don't cry out." The old lady immediately answered: "Thank you. Rely upon me. Upon my soul I will be quiet." We were all tilted down together in a corner of

the carriage, and stopped.' I said to them thereupon :
" You may be sure nothing worse can happen. Our danger *must* be over. Will you remain here without stirring, while I get out of the window ? " They both answered quite collectedly, " Yes," and I got out without
the least notion what had happened. Fortunately I got
out with great caution and stood upon the step. Looking
down I saw the bridge gone, and nothing below me but
the line of rail. Some people in the two other compart-
ments were madly trying to plunge out at window, and
had no idea that there was an open swampy field fifteen
feet down below them, and nothing else ! The two guards
(one with his face cut) were running up and down on the
down side of the bridge (which was not torn up) quite
wildly. I called out to them : " Look at me. Do stop
an instant and look at me, and tell me whether you don't
know me." One of them answered : " We know you very
well, Mr. Dickens." " Then," I said, " my good fellow,
for God's sake give me your key, and send one of those
labourers here, and I'll empty this carriage." We did it
quite safely, by means of a plank or two, and when it was
done I saw all the rest of the train, except the two bag-
gage vans, down in the stream. I got into the carriage
again for my brandy flask, took off my travelling hat for
a basin, climbed down the brickwork, and filled my hat
with water.

Suddenly I came upon a staggering man covered with
blood (I think he must have been flung clean out of his
carriage), with such a frightful cut across the skull that I

couldn't bear to look at him. I poured some water over his face and gave him some to drink, then gave him some brandy, and laid him down on the grass, and he said, " I am gone," and died afterwards. Then I stumbled over a lady lying on her back against a little pollard-tree, with the blood streaming over her face (which was lead colour) in a number of distinct little streams from the head. I asked her if she could swallow a little brandy and she just nodded, and I gave her some and left her for somebody else. The next time I passed her she was dead. Then a man, examined at the inquest yesterday (who evidently had not the least remembrance of what really passed), came running up to me and implored me to help him find his wife, who was afterwards found dead. No imagination can conceive the ruin of the carriages, or the extraordinary weights under which the people were lying, or the complications into which they were twisted up among iron and wood, and mud and water.

I don't want to be examined at the inquest, and I don't want to write about it. I could do no good either way, and I could only seem to speak about myself, which, of course, I would rather not do. I am keeping very quiet here. I have a—I don't know what to call it—constitutional (I suppose) presence of mind, and was not in the least fluttered at the time. I instantly remembered that I had the MS. of a number with me, and clambered back into the carriage for it. But in writing these scanty words of recollection I feel the shake and am obliged to stop.

Ever faithfully.

[*To Mr. Walter Jones.*]

GAD'S HILL PLACE, HIGHAM BY ROCHESTER, KENT,
Saturday, June 17th, 1865.*

SIR,

I beg you to assure the Committee of the News-vendors'
Benevolent and Provident Institution, that I have been
deeply affected by their special remembrance of me in my
late escape from death or mutilation, and that I thank
them with my whole heart.

Faithfully yours and theirs.

[*To Mrs. Hulkes.*]

GAD'S HILL, *Sunday, June 18th,* 1865.

MY DEAR MRS. HULKES,

I return the *Examiner* with many thanks. The account
is true, except that I *had* brandy. By an extraordinary
chance I had a bottle and a half with me. I slung the
half-bottle round my neck, and carried my hat full of
water in my hands. But I can understand the describer
(whoever he is) making the mistake in perfect good faith,
and supposing that I called for brandy, when I really called
to the others who were helping: "I have brandy here."
The Mr. Dickenson mentioned had changed places with a
Frenchman, who did not like the window down, a few
minutes before the accident. The Frenchman was killed,
and a labourer and I got Mr. Dickenson out of a most

---

* This letter was written in reply to the Committee's congratulations upon Mr.
Dickens's escape from the accident to the tidal train from Folkestone, at Staplehurst, just previous to this date.

extraordinary heap of dark ruins, in which he was jammed upside down. He was bleeding at the eyes, ears, nose, and mouth; but he didn't seem to know that afterwards, and of course I didn't tell him. In the moment of going over the viaduct the whole of his pockets were shaken empty! He had no watch, no chain, no money, no pocket-book, no handkerchief, when we got him out. He had been choking a quarter of an hour when I heard him groaning. If I had not had the brandy to give him at the moment, I think he would have been done for. As it was, I brought him up to London in the carriage with me, and couldn't make him believe he was hurt. He was the first person whom the brandy saved. As I ran back to the carriage for the whole full bottle, I saw the first two people I had helped lying dead. A bit of shade from the hot sun, into which we got the unhurt ladies, soon had as many dead in it as living.

Faithfully yours always.

[*To Mr. Arthur Ryland.*]

GAD'S HILL PLACE, HIGHAM BY ROCHESTER, KENT,
Wednesday, June 21st, 1865.

MY DEAR MR. RYLAND,

I need not assure you that I regard the unanimous desire of the Town Council Committee as a great honour, and that I feel the strongest interest in the occasion, and the strongest wish to associate myself with it.

But, after careful consideration, I most unwillingly come to the conclusion that I must decline. At the time in question, I shall, please God, either have just finished, or be just finishing my present book. Country rest and re-flection will then be invaluable to me, before casting about for Christmas. I am a little shaken in my nervous system by the terrible and affecting incidents of the late railway accident, from which I bodily escaped. I am withdrawing myself from engagements of all kinds, in order that I may pursue my story with the comfortable sense of being per-fectly free while it is a-doing, and when it is done. The consciousness of having made this engagement would, if I were to make it, render such sense incomplete, and so open the way to others. This is the real state of the case, and the whole reason for my declining.

Faithfully yours always.

[*To Mrs. Lehmann.*]

GAD'S HILL PLACE, HIGHAM BY ROCHESTER, KENT,
Tuesday, June 29th, 1865.

DEAR MRS. LEHMANN,

Come (with self and partner) on either of the days you name, and you will be heartily welcomed by the humble youth who now addresses you, and will then cast himself at your feet.

I am quite right again, I thank God, and have even got my voice back ; I most unaccountably brought somebody else's out of that terrible scene. The directors have sent me a Resolution of Thanks for assistance to the unhappy passengers.

With kind regards to Lehmann, ever yours.
VOL. II.—12*

[*To Mr. Percy Fitzgerald.*]

OFFICE OF "ALL THE YEAR ROUND,"
·   *Friday, July 7th,* 1865.

MY DEAR FITZGERALD,

I shall be delighted to see you at Gad's Hill on Sunday, and I hope you will bring a bag with you and will not think of returning to London at night.

We are a small party just now, for my daughter Mary has been decoyed to Andover for the election week, in the Conservative interest ; think of my feelings as a Radical parent ! The wrong-headed member and his wife are the friends with whom she hunts, and she helps to receive (and *de*ceive) the voters, which is very awful !

But in the week after next we shall be in great croquet force. I shall hope to persuade you to come back to us then for a few days, and we will try to make you some amends for a dull Sunday. Turn it over in your mind and try to manage it.

Sincerely yours ever.

[*To Professor Owen, F.R.S.*]

GAD'S HILL, *Wednesday, July 12th,* 1865.

MY DEAR OWEN,

Studying the gorilla last night for the twentieth time, it suddenly came into my head that I had never thanked you for that admirable treatise. This is to bear witness to my blushes and repentance. If you knew how much interest it has awakened in me, and how often it has set me a-thinking, you would consider me a more thankless beast than any gorilla that ever lived. But happily you do *not* know, and I am not going to tell you.

Believe me, ever faithfully yours.

[To the Earl Russell.]

GAD'S HILL PLACE, HIGHAM BY ROCHESTER, KENT,

Wednesday, Aug. 16th, 1865.

MY DEAR LORD RUSSELL,

Mr. Dallas, who is a candidate for the Scotch professional chair left vacant by Aytoun's death, has asked me if I would object to introduce to you the first volume of a book he has in the press with my publishers, on " The Gay Science of Art and Criticism." I have replied I would *not* object, as I have read as many of the sheets as I could get, with extreme pleasure, and as I know you will find it a very winning and brilliant piece of writing. Therefore he will send the proofs of the volume to you as soon as he can get them from the printer (at about the end of this week I take it), and if you read them you will not be hard upon me for bearing the responsibility of his doing so, I feel assured.

I suppose Mr. Dallas to have some impression that his pleasing you with his book might advance his Scottish suit. But all I know is, that he is a gentleman of great attainments and erudition, much distinguished as the writer of the best critical literary pieces in *The Times,* and thoroughly versed in the subjects which Professor Aytoun represented officially.

I beg to send my regard to Lady Russell and all the house, and am ever, my dear Lord Russell,

Your faithful and obliged.

P.S.—I am happy to report that my sailor-boy's captain, relinquishing his ship on sick leave, departs from the mere form of certificate given to all the rest, and adds that his obedience to orders is remarkable, and that he is a highly intelligent and promising young officer.

[*To Mr. Marcus Stone.*]

HÔTEL DU HELDER, PARIS, *Wednesday, Sept.* 13*th*, 1865.

MY DEAR MARCUS,

I leave here to-morrow, and propose going to the office by tidal train *next Saturday evening*. Through the whole of next week, on and off, I shall be at the office ; when not there, at Gad's ; but much oftener at the office. The sooner I can know about the subjects you take for illustration the better, as I can then fill the list of illustrations to the second volume for the printer, and enable him to make up his last sheet. Necessarily that list is now left blank, as I cannot give him the titles of the subjects, not knowing them myself.

It has been fearfully hot on this side, but is something cooler.

Ever affectionately yours.

P.S.—On glancing over this note, I find it very like the king's love-letter in " Ruy Blas." " Madam, there is a high wind. I have shot six wolves."

I think the frontispiece to the second volume should be the dustyard with the three mounds, and Mr. Boffin digging up the Dutch .bottle, and Venus restraining Wegg's ardour to get at him. Or Mr. Boffin might be coming down with the bottle, and Venus might be dragging Wegg out of the way as described.

[*To Mr. Percy Fitzgerald.*]

OFFICE OF " ALL THE YEAR ROUND,"

Saturday, Sept. 23rd, 1865.

MY DEAR FITZGERALD,

I cannot thank you too much for Sultan. He is a noble fellow, has fallen into the ways of the family with a grace and dignity that denote the gentleman, and came down to the railway a day or two since to welcome me home (it was our first meeting), with a profound absence of interest in my individual opinion of him which captivated me completely. I am going home to-day to take him about the country, and improve his acquaintance. You will find a perfect understanding between us, I hope, when you next come to Gad's Hill. (He has only swallowed Bouncer once, and temporarily.)

Your hint that you were getting on with your story and liked it was more than golden intelligence to me in foreign parts. The intensity of the heat, both in Paris and the provinces, was such that I found nothing else so refreshing in the course of my rambles.

With many more thanks for the dog than my sheet of paper would hold,

Believe me, ever very faithfully yours.

[*To Mrs. Procter.*]

GAD'S HILL PLACE, HIGHAM BY ROCHESTER, KENT,
Sept. 26th, 1865.

MY DEAR MRS. PROCTER,

I have written the little introduction, and have sent it to my printer, in order that you may read it without trouble. But if you would like to keep the few pages of MS., of course they are yours.

It is brief, and I have aimed at perfect simplicity, and an avoidance of all that your beloved Adelaide would have wished avoided. Do not expect too much from it. If there should be anything wrong in fact, or anything that you would like changed for any reason, *of course you will tell me so*, and of course you will not deem it possible that you can trouble me by making any such request most freely.

You will probably receive the proof either on Friday or Saturday. Don't write to me until you have read it. In the meantime I send you back the two books, with the two letters in the bound one.

With love to Procter,

Ever your affectionate Friend.

[*To Mr. Edmund Yates.*]

HÔTEL DU HELDER, PARIS, *Wednesday, Sept. 30th*, 1865.

MY DEAR EDMUND,

I leave here to-morrow and purpose being at the office on Saturday night ; all next week I shall be there, off and on—" off " meaning Gad's Hill ; the office will be my last address. The heat has been excessive on this side of the Channel, and I got a slight sunstroke last Thursday, and was obliged to be doctored and put to bed for a day ; but, thank God, I am all right again. The man who sells the *tisane* on the Boulevards can't keep the flies out of his glasses, and as he wears them on his red velvet bands, the flies work themselves into the ends of the tumblers, trying to get through and tickle the man. If fly life were long enough, I think they would at last. Three paving blouses came to work at the corner of this street last Monday, pulled up a bit of road, sat down to look at it, and fell asleep. On Tuesday one of the blouses spat on his hands and seemed to be going to begin, but didn't. The other two have shown no sign of life whatever. This morning the industrious one ate a loaf. You may rely upon this as the latest news from the French capital.

Faithfully ever.

[To Mr. William Charles Kent.]

26, WELLINGTON STREET, Monday, Nov. 6th, 1865.

MY DEAR KENT,

No, I *won't* write in this book, because I have sent another to the binder's for you.

I have been unwell with a relaxed throat, or I should have written to you sooner to thank you for your dedication, to assure you that it heartily, most heartily, gratifies me, as the sincere tribute of a true and generous heart, and to tell you that I have been charmed with your book itself.   I am proud of having given a name to anything so picturesque, so sympathetic and spirited.

I hope and believe the " Doctor " is nothing but a good 'un.   He has perfectly astonished Forster, who writes : " Neither good, gooder, nor goodest, but super-excellent ; all through there is such a relish of you at your best, as I could not have believed in, after a long story."

I shall be charmed to see you to-night.

Ever affectionately.

[To M. de Cerjat.]

Gad's Hill Place, Higham by Rochester, Kent,
November 13th, 1865.

EXTRACT.

My dear Cerjat,

Having achieved my book and my Christmas number, and having shaken myself after two years' work, I send you my annual greeting.   How are you?   Asthmatic, I know you will reply ; but as my poor father (who was asthmatic, too, and the jolliest of men) used philosophically to say, "one must have something wrong, I suppose, and I like to know what it is."

In England we are groaning under the brigandage of the butcher, which is being carried to that height that I think I foresee resistance on the part of the middle-class, and some combination in perspective for abolishing the middle-man, whensoever he turns up (which is everywhere) between producer and consumer.   The cattle plague is the butcher's stalking-horse, and it is unquestionably worse than it was ; but seeing that the great majority of creatures lost or destroyed have been cows, and likewise that the rise in butchers' meat bears no reasonable proportion to the market prices of the beasts, one comes to the conclusion that the public is done. The commission has ended very weakly and ineffectually, as such things in England rather frequently do ; and everybody writes to *The Times*, and nobody does anything else.

If the Americans don't embroil us in a war before long it will not be their fault. What with their swagger and bombast, what with their claims for indemnification, what with Ireland and Fenianism, and what with Canada, I have strong apprehensions. With a settled animosity towards the French usurper, I believe him to have always been sound in his desire to divide the States against themselves, and that we were unsound and wrong in "letting I dare not wait upon I would." The Jamaica insurrection is another hopeful piece of business. That platform-sympathy with the black—or the native, or the devil—afar off, and that platform indifference to our own countrymen at enormous odds in the midst of bloodshed and savagery, makes me stark wild. Only the other day, here was a meeting of jawbones of asses at Manchester, to censure the Jamaica Governor for his manner of putting down the insurrection ! So we are badgered about New Zealanders and Hottentots, as if they were identical with men in clean shirts at Camberwell, and were to be bound by pen and ink accordingly. So Exeter Hall holds us in mortal submission to missionaries, who (Livingstone always excepted) are perfect nuisances, and leave every place worse than they found it.

Of all the many evidences that are visible of our being ill-governed, no one is so remarkable to me as our ignorance of what is going on under our Government. What will future generations think of that enormous Indian Mutiny being ripened without suspicion, until whole regiments arose and killed their officers ? A week ago, red tape, half-bouncing and half pooh-poohing what it bounced at, would have scouted the idea of a Dublin jail not being able to hold a political prisoner. But for the blacks in Jamaica being over-impatient and before their time, the whites might have been exterminated, without a previous hint or suspicion that there was anything amiss. *Laissez aller*, and Britons never, never, never !——

Meantime, if your honour were in London, you would see a great embankment rising high and dry out of the Thames on the Middlesex shore, from Westminster Bridge to Blackfriars. A really fine work, and really getting on. Moreover, a great system of drainage. Another really fine work, and likewise really getting on. Lastly, a muddle of railways in all directions possible and impossible, with no general public scheme, no general public supervision, enormous waste of money, no fixable responsibility, no accountability but under Lord Campbell's Act. I think of that accident in which I was preserved. Before the most furious and notable train in the four-and-twenty hours, the head of a gang of workmen takes up the rails. That train changes its time every day as the tide changes, and that head workman is not provided by the railway company with any clock or watch ! Lord Shaftesbury wrote to me to ask me what I thought of an obligation on railway companies to put strong walls to all bridges and viaducts. I told him, of course, that the force of such a shock would carry away anything that any company could set up, and I added : " Ask the minister what *he* thinks about the votes of the railway interest in the House of Commons, and about his being afraid to lay a finger on it with an eye to his majority."

I seem to be grumbling, but I am in the best of humours. All goes well with me and mine, thank God.

Last night my gardener came upon a man in the garden and fired. The man returned the compliment by kicking him in the groin and causing him great pain. I set off, with a great mastiff-bloodhound I have, in pursuit. Couldn't find the evil-doer, but had the greatest difficulty in preventing the dog from tearing two policemen down. They were coming towards us with professional mystery, and he was in the air on his way to the throat of an eminently respectable constable when I caught him.

My daughter Mary and her aunt Georgina send kindest regard and remembrance. Katey and her husband are going to try London this winter, but I rather doubt (for they are both delicate) their being able to weather it out. It has been blowing here tremendously for a fortnight, but to-day is like a spring day, and plenty of roses are growing over the labourers' cottages. The *Great Eastern* lies at her moorings beyond the window where I write these words ; looks very dull and unpromising. A dark column of smoke from Chatham Dockyard, where the iron ship-building is in progress, has a greater significance in it, I fancy.

[*To Miss Dickens.*]

GAD'S HILL PLACE, HIGHAM BY ROCHESTER, KENT,
Tuesday, Nov. 14*th*, 1865.

MY DEAREST MAMIE,

As you want to know my views of the Sphinx, here they are. But I have only seen it once ; and it is so extra-ordinarily well done, that it ought to be observed closely several times.

Anyone who attentively notices the flower trick will see that the two little high tables hung with drapery cover each a trap. Each of those tables, during that trick, hides a confederate, who changes the paper cone twice. When the cone has been changed as often as is required, the trap is closed and the table can be moved.

When the curtain is removed for the performance of the Sphinx trick, there is a covered, that is, draped table on the stage, which is never seen before or afterwards. In front of the middle of it, and between it and the audience, stands one of those little draped tables covering a trap ; this is a third trap in the centre of the stage. The box for the head is then upon IT, and the conjuror takes it off and shows it. The man whose head is afterwards shown in that box is, I conceive, in the table ; that is to say, is lying on his chest in the thickness of the table, in an extremely constrained attitude. To get him into the table and to enable him to use the trap in the table through which his head comes into the box, the two hands of a confederate are necessary. That confederate comes up a trap, and stands in the space afforded by the interval below the stage and the height of the little draped table ! his back is towards the audience. The moment he has assisted the hidden man sufficiently, he closes the trap, and the conjuror then immediately removes the little draped table, and also the drapery of the larger table ; when he places the box on the last-named table *with the slide on* for the head to come into it, he stands with his back to the audience and his face to the box, and masks the box considerably to facilitate the insertion of the head. As soon as he knows the head to be in its place, he undraws the slide. When the verses have been spoken and the trick is done, he loses no time in replacing the slide. The curtain is then immediately dropped, because the man cannot otherwise be got out of the table, and has no doubt had quite enough of it. With kindest regards to all at Penton,

Ever your most affectionate.

1866.

NARRATIVE.

THE furnished house hired by Charles Dickens in the spring of this year was in Southwick Place, Hyde Park.

Having entered into negotiations with the Messrs. Chappell for a series of readings to be given in London, in the English provinces, in Scotland and Ireland, Charles Dickens had no leisure for more than his usual editorial work for "All the Year Round." He contributed four parts to the Christmas number, which was entitled, "Mugby Junction."

For the future all his English readings were given in connection with the Messrs. Chappell, and never in all his career had he more satisfactory or more pleasant business relations than those connected with these gentlemen. Moreover, out of this connection sprang a sincere friendship on both sides.

Mr. Dolby is so constantly mentioned in future letters, that they themselves will tell of the cordial companionship which existed between Charles Dickens and this able and most obliging "manager."

The letter to "Lily" was in answer to a child's letter from Miss Lily Benzon, inviting him to a birthday party.

The play alluded to in the letter to M. Fechter was called "A Long Strike," and was performed at the Lyceum Theatre.

The "Sultan" mentioned in the letter to Mr. Fitzgerald was a noble Irish bloodhound, presented by this gentleman to Charles Dickens. The story of the dog's death is told in a letter to M. de Cerjat, which we give in the following year.

[*To Miss Mary Boyle.*]

OFFICE OF "ALL THE YEAR ROUND,"
Saturday, Jan. 6th, 1866.

MY DEAR MARY,

Feeling pretty certain that I shall never answer your letter unless I answer it at once (I got it this morning), here goes !

I did not dramatise "The Master of Ravenswood," though I did a good deal towards and about the piece, having an earnest desire to put Scott, for once, upon the stage in his own gallant manner. It is *an enormous success*, and increases in attraction nightly. I have never seen the people in all parts of the house so leaning forward, in lines sloping towards the stage, earnestly and intently attractive, as while the story gradually unfolds itself. But the astonishing circumstance of all is, that Miss Leclercq (never thought of for Lucy till all other Lucies had failed), is marvellously good, highly pathetic, and almost unrecognisable in person ! What note it touches in her, always dumb until now, I do not pretend to say, but there is no one on the stage who could play the contract scene better, or more simply and naturally, and I find it impossible to see it without crying ! Almost everyone plays well, the whole is exceedingly picturesque, and there is scarcely a movement throughout, or a look, that is not indicated by Scott. So you get a life romance with beautiful illustrations, and I do not expect ever again to see a book take up its bed and walk in like manner.

I am charmed to learn that you have had a freeze out of my ghost story. It rather did give me a shiver up the back in the writing. " Dr. Marigold " has just now accomplished his two hundred thousand. My only other news about myself is that I am doubtful whether to read or not in London this season. If I decide to do it at all, I shall probably do it on a large scale.

Many happy years to you, my dear Mary. So prays

Your ever affectionate

Jo.

[*To Mr. William Charles Kent.*]

Gad's Hill, *Thursday, Jan. 18th,* 1866.

My dear Kent,

I cannot tell you how grieved we all are here to know that you are suffering again. Your patient tone, however, and the hopefulness and forbearance of Ferguson's course, gives us some reassurance. Apropos of which latter reference I dined with Ferguson at the Lord Mayor's, last Tuesday, and had a grimly distracted impulse upon me to defy the toast-master and rush into a speech about him and his noble art, when I sat pining under the imbecility of constitutional and corporational idiots. I did seize him for a moment by the hair of his head (in proposing the Lady Mayoress), and derived some faint consolation from the company's response to the reference. O ! no man will ever know under what provocation to contradiction and a savage yell of repudiation I suffered at the hands of ——, feebly complacent in the uniform of Madame Tussaud's own military waxers, and almost the worst speaker I ever heard in my life ! Mary and Georgina, sitting on either side of me, urged me to "look pleasant." I replied in expressions not to be repeated. Shea (the judge) was just as good and graceful, as he (the member) was bad and gawky.

Bulwer's " Lost Tales of Miletus " is a most noble book! He is an extraordinary fellow, and fills me with admiration and wonder.

It is of no use writing to you about yourself, my dear Kent, because you are likely to be tired of that constant companion, and so I have gone scratching (with an exceedingly bad pen) about and about you. But I come back to you to let you know that the reputation of this house as a convalescent hospital stands (like the house itself) very high, and that testimonials can be produced from credible persons who have recovered health and spirits here swiftly. Try us, only try us, and we are content to stake the reputation of the establishment on the result.

Ever affectionately yours.

[*To Mr. Percy Fitzgerald.*]

GAD'S HILL, *Friday, Feb. 2nd,* 1866.

MY DEAR FITZGERALD,

I ought to have written to you days and days ago, to thank you for your charming book on Charles Lamb, to tell you with what interest and pleasure I read it as soon as it came here, and to add that I was honestly affected (far more so than your modesty will readily believe) by your intimate knowledge of those touches of mine concerning childhood.

Let me tell you now that I have not in the least cooled, after all, either as to the graceful sympathetic book, or as to the part in it with which I am honoured. It has become a matter of real feeling with me, and I postponed its expression because I couldn't satisfactorily get it out of myself, and at last I came to the conclusion that it must be left in.

My dear Fitzgerald, faithfully yours always.

VOL. II.—13

[*To Miss Hogarth.*]

OFFICE OF " ALL THE YEAR ROUND," *Friday, Feb. 9th*, 1866.

MY DEAREST GEORGY,

I found your letter here when I came back on Wednesday evening, and was extremely glad to get it.

Frank Beard wrote me word that with such a pulse as I described, an examination of the heart was absolutely necessary, and that I had better make an appointment with him alone for the purpose. This I did. I was not at all disconcerted,.for I knew well beforehand that the effect ·could not possibly be without that one cause at the bottom of it. There seems to be degeneration of some functions of the heart. It does not contract as it should. So I have got a prescription of iron, quinine, and digitalis, to set it a-going, and send the blood more quickly through the system. If it should not seem to succeed on a reasonable trial, I will then propose a consultation with someone else. Of course I am not so foolish as to suppose that all my work can have been achieved without *some* penalty, and I have noticed for some time a decided change in my buoyancy and hopefulness—in other words, in my usual " tone."

I shall wait to see Beard again on Monday, and shall most probably come down that day. If I should not, I will telegraph after seeing him. Best love to Mamie.

[*To Mrs. Brookfield.*]

OFFICE OF " ALL THE YEAR ROUND,"
Tuesday, Feb. 2c*th*, 1866.

MY DEAR MRS. BROOKFIELD,

Having gone through your MS. (which I should have done sooner, but that I have not been very well), I write these few following words about it. Firstly, with a limited reference to its unsuitability to these pages. Secondly, with a more enlarged reference to the merits of the story itself.

If you will take any part of it and cut it up (in fancy) into the small portions into which it would have to be divided here for only a month's supply, you will (I think) at once discover the impossibility of publishing it in weekly parts. The scheme of the chapters, the manner of introducing the people, the progress of the interest, the places in which the principal places fall, are all hopelessly against it. It would seem as though the story were never coming, and hardly ever moving. There must be a special design to overcome that specially trying mode of publication, and I cannot better express the difficulty and labour of it than by asking you to turn over any two weekly numbers of " A Tale of Two Cities," or " Great Expectations," or Bulwer's story, or Wilkie Collins's, or Reade's, or " At the Bar," and notice how patiently and expressly the thing has to be planned for presentation in these fragments, and yet for afterwards fusing together as an uninterrupted whole.

Of the story itself I honestly say that I think highly. The style is particularly easy and agreeable, infinitely above ordinary writing, and sometimes reminds me of Mrs. Inchbald at her best. The characters are remarkably well observed, and with a rare mixture of delicacy and truthfulness. I observe this particularly in the brother and sister, and in Mrs. Neville. But it strikes me that you constantly hurry your narrative (and yet without getting on) *by telling it, in a sort of impetuous breathless way, in your own person, when the people should tell it and act it for themselves.* My notion always is, that when I have made the people to play out the play, it is, as it were, their business to do it, and not mine. Then, unless you really have led up to a great situation like Basil's death, you are bound in art to make more of it. Such a scene should form a chapter of itself. Impressed upon the reader's memory, it would go far to make the fortune of the book. Suppose yourself telling that affecting incident in a letter to a friend. Wouldn't you describe how you went through the life and stir of the streets and roads to the sick-room? Wouldn't you say what kind of a room it was, what kind of day it was, whether it was sunlight, starlight, or moonlight? Wouldn't you have a strong impression on your mind of how you were received, when you first met the look of the dying man, what strange contrasts were about you and struck you? I don't want you, in a novel, to present *yourself* to tell such things, but I want the things to be there. You make no more of the situation than the index might, or a descriptive playbill

might in giving a summary of the tragedy under representation.

As a mere piece of mechanical workmanship, I think all
your chapters should be shorter ; that is to say, that they
should be subdivided. Also, when you change from narrative to dialogue, or *vice versâ,* you should make the transition more carefully. Also, taking the pains to sit down
and recall the principal landmarks in your story, you
should then make them far more elaborate and conspicuous
than the rest. Even with these changes I do not believe
that the story would attract the attention due to it, if it
were published even in such monthly portions as the space
of " Fraser " would admit of. Even so brightened, it would
not, to the best of my judgment, express itself piecemeal.
It seems to me to be so constituted as to require to be read
" off the reel." As a book in two volumes I think it would
have good claims to success, and good chances of obtain-
ing success. But I suppose the polishing I have hinted at
(not a meretricious adornment, but positively necessary to
good work and good art) to have been first thoroughly
administered.

Now don't hate me if you can help it. I can afford to
be hated by some people, but I am not rich enough to put
you in possession of that luxury.

Ever faithfully yours.

P.S.—The MS. shall be delivered at your house to-morrow. And your petitioner again prays not to be, etc.

[*To Miss Hogarth.*]

ADELPHI, LIVERPOOL, *Friday, April 13th,* 1866.

MY DEAREST GEORGY,

The reception at Manchester last night was quite a magnificent sight; the whole of the immense audience standing up and cheering. I thought them a little slow with " Marigold," but believe it was only the attention necessary in so vast a place. They gave a splendid burst at the end. And after " Nickleby " (which went to perfection), they set up such a call, that I was obliged to go in again. The unfortunate gasman, a very steady fellow, got a fall off a ladder and sprained his leg. He was put to bed in a public opposite, and was left there, poor man.

This is the first very fine day we have had. I have taken advantage of it by crossing to Birkenhead and getting some air upon the water. It was fresh and beautiful.

I send my best love to Mamie, and hope she is better. I am, of course, tired (the pull of " Marigold " upon one's energy, in the Free Trade Hall, was great) ; but I stick to my tonic, and feel, all things considered, in very good tone. The room here (I mean the hall) being my special favourite and extraordinarily easy, is *almost* a rest !

[*To Miss Dickens.*]

ADELPHI, LIVERPOOL, *Saturday, April 14th,* 1866.

MY DEAREST MAMIE,

The police reported officially that three thousand people were turned away from the hall last night. I doubt if they were so numerous as that, but they carried in the outer doors and pitched into Dolby with great vigour. I need not add that every corner of the place was crammed. They were a very fine audience, and took enthusiastically every point in "Copperfield" and the "Trial." They made the reading a quarter of an hour longer than usual. One man advertised in the morning paper that he would give thirty shillings (double) for three stalls, but nobody would sell, and he didn't get in.

Except that I cannot sleep, I really think myself in much better training than I had anticipated. A dozen oysters and a little champagne between the parts every night, constitute the best restorative I have ever yet tried. John appears low, but I don't know why. A letter comes for him daily; the hand is female; whether Smudger's, or a nearer one still and a dearer one, I don't know. So it may or may not be the cause of his gloom.

"Miss Emily" of Preston is married to a rich cotton lord, rides in open carriages in gorgeous array, and is altogether splendid. With this effective piece of news I close.

[*To Miss Hogarth.*]

GLASGOW, *April 17th*, 1866.

We arrived here at ten yesterday evening. I don't think the journey shook me at all. Dolby provided a superb cold collation and "the best of drinks," and we dined in the carriage, and I made him laugh all the way.

The let here is very large. Every precaution taken to prevent my platform from being captured as it was last time ; but I don't feel at all sure that it will not be stormed at one of the two readings.   Wills is to do the genteel to-night at the stalls, and Dolby is to stem the shilling tide *if* he can.   The poor gasman cannot come on, and we have got a new one here who is to go to Edinburgh with us.   Of Edinburgh we know nothing, but as its first night has always been shady, I suppose it will stick to its ante-cedents.

I like to hear about Harness and his freshness.   The let for the next reading at St. James's is " going," they re-port, " admirably."   Lady Russell asked me to dinner to-morrow, and I have written her a note to-day.   The rest has certainly done me good.   I slept thoroughly well last night, and feel fresh.   What to-night's work, and every night's work this week, may do contrariwise, remains to be seen.

I hope Harry's knee may be in the way of mending, from what you relate of it.

[*To Miss Dickens.*]

WATERLOO HOTEL, EDINBURGH, *Wednesday, April 18th*, 1866.

We had a tremendous house again last night at Glas-gow ; and turned away great numbers.   Not only that, but they were a most brilliant and delicate audience, and took " Marigold " with a fine sense and quickness not to be surpassed.   The shillings pitched into Dolby again, and one man writes a sensible letter in one of the papers this morning, showing to *my* satisfaction (?) that they really had, through the local agent, some cause of complaint.

Nevertheless, the shilling tickets are sold for to-morrow, and it seems to be out of the question to take any money at the doors, the call for all parts is so enormous. The thundering of applause last night was quite staggering, and my people checked off my reception by the minute hand of a watch, and stared at one another, thinking I should never begin. I keep quite well, have happily taken to sleeping these last three nights ; and feel, all things con-sidered, very little conscious of fatigue. I cannot recon-cile my town medicine with the hours and journeys of reading life, and have therefore given it up for the time. But for the moment, I think I am better without it. What we are doing here I have not yet heard. I write at half-past one, and we have been little more than an hour in the house. But I am quite prepared for the inevitable this first Edinburgh night. Endeavours have been made (from Glasgow yesterday) to telegraph the exact facts out of our local agent ; but hydraulic pressure wouldn't have squeezed a straight answer out of him. "Friday and Saturday doing very well, Wednesday not so good." This was all electricity could discover.

I am going to write a line this post to Katie, from whom I have a note. I hope Harry's leg will now step out in the manner of the famous cork leg in the song.

[*To Miss Hogarth.*]

EDINBURGH, *Thursday, April* 19*th,* 1866.

The house was more than twice better than any first night here previously. They were, as usual here, remark-
VOL. II.—13*

ably intelligent, and the reading went *brilliantly*. I have
not sent up any newspapers, as they are generally so poorly
written, that you may know beforehand all the common-
places that they will write. But *The Scotsman* has so pretty
an article this morning, and (so far as I know) so true a
one, that I will try to post it to you, either from here or
Glasgow. John and Dolby went over early, and Wills and
I follow them at half-past eleven. It is cold and wet here.
We have laid half-crown bets with Dolby, that he will be
assaulted to-night at Glasgow. He has a surprising knowledge of what the receipts will be always, and wins half-
crowns every night. Chang is living in this house. John
(not knowing it) was rendered perfectly drivelling last
night, by meeting him on the stairs. The Tartar Dwarf
is always twining himself upstairs sideways, and drinks a
bottle of whisky per day, and is reported to be a surprising little villain.

[*To Miss Dickens.*]

WATERLOO HOTEL, EDINBURGH, *Friday, April 20th*, 1866.

No row at Glasgow last night. Great placards were
posted about the town by the anxious Dolby, announcing
that no money would be taken at the doors. This kept
the crowd off. Two files of policemen and a double staff
everywhere did the rest, and nothing could be better-
tempered or more orderly. Tremendous enthusiasm with
the "Carol" and "Trial." I was dead beat afterwards,

that reading being twenty minutes longer than usual ; but plucked up again, had some supper, slept well, and am quite right to-day.   It is a bright day, and the express ride over from Glasgow was very pleasant.

Everything is gone here for to-night.   But it is difficult to describe what the readings have grown to be.   The let at St. James's Hall is not only immense for next Tuesday, but so large for the next reading afterwards, that Chappell writes : " That will be the greatest house of the three." From Manchester this morning they write : " Send us more tickets instantly, for we are sold out and don't know what to do with the people." Last night the whole of my money under the agreement had been taken.   I notice that a great bank has broken at Liverpool, which may hurt us there, but when last heard of it was going as before.   And the audience, though so enormous, do somehow express a personal affection, which makes them very strange and moving to see.

I have a story to answer you and your aunt with. Before I left Southwick Place for Liverpool, I received a letter from Glasgow, saying, "Your little Emily has been woo'd and married and a'! since you last saw her ; " and describing her house within a mile or two of the city, and asking me to stay there.   I wrote the usual refusal, and supposed Mrs. —— to be some romantic girl whom I had joked with, perhaps at Allison's or where not. On the first night at Glasgow I received a bouquet from ——, and wore one of the flowers. This morning at the Glasgow station, —— appeared, and proved to be the identical Miss Emily, of whose marriage Dolby had told me on our coming through Preston. She was attired in magnificent raiment, and presented the happy ——.

[*To Miss Hogarth.*]

LIVERPOOL, *Thursday, April 26th,* 1866.

We noticed between London and Rugby (the first stoppage) something very odd in our carriage yesterday, not so much in its motion as in its sound. We examined it as well as we could out of both windows, but could make nothing of it. On our arrival at Rugby, it was found to be on fire. And as it was in the middle of the train, the train had to be broken to get it off into a siding by itself and get another carriage on. With this slight exception we came down all right.

My voice is much better, I am glad to report, and I mean to try Beard's remedy after dinner to-day. This is all my present news.

[*To Miss Hogarth.*]

DOWN HOTEL, CLIFTON, *Friday, May 11th,* 1866.

I received your note before I left Birmingham this morning. It has been very heavy work getting up at half-past six each morning after a heavy night, and I am not at all well to-day. We had a tremendous hall at Birmingham last night—two thousand one hundred people. I made a most ridiculous mistake. Had " Nickleby " on my list to finish with, instead of " Trial." Read " Nickleby." with great go, and the people remained. Went back again at ten and explained the accident, and said if they liked, I would give them the "Trial." They *did* like, and I had another half-hour of it in that enormous place.

This stoppage of Overend and Gurney in the City will play the —— with all public gaieties, and with all the arts.

My cold is no better. John fell off a platform about ten feet high yesterday, and fainted. He looks all the colours of the rainbow to-day, but does not seem much hurt beyond being puffed up one hand, arm, and side.

[*To Miss Lily Benzon.*]

GAD'S HILL PLACE, HIGHAM BY ROCHESTER, KENT,
Monday, June 18*th,* 1866.

MY DEAR LILY,

I am sorry that I cannot come to read to you " The Boots at the Holly Tree Inn," as you ask me to do ; but the truth is, that I am tired of reading at this present time, and have come into the country to rest and hear the birds sing. There are a good many birds, I daresay, in Kensington Palace Gardens, and upon my word and honour they are much better worth listening to than I am. So let them sing to you as hard as ever they can, while their sweet voices last (they will be silent when the winter comes) ; and very likely after you and I have eaten our next Christmas pudding and mince-pies, you and I and Uncle Harry may all meet together at St. James's Hall ; Uncle Harry to bring you there, to hear the " Boots ; " I to receive you there, and read the " Boots ; " and you (I

hope) to applaud very much, and tell me that you like the
" Boots." So, God bless you and me, and Uncle Harry,
and the " Boots," and long life and happiness to us all !

Your affectionate Friend.

P.S.—There's a flourish !

[To Mr. B. W. Procter.]

GAD'S HILL PLACE, HIGHAM BY ROCHESTER, KENT,
Monday, Aug. 13th, 1866.

MY DEAR PROCTER,

I have read your biography of Charles Lamb with inexpressible pleasure and interest. I do not think it possible to tell a pathetic story with a more unaffected and
manly tenderness. And as to the force and vigour of the
style, if I did not know you I should have made sure that
there was a printer's error in the opening of your introduction, and that the word " seventy " occupied the place
of " forty."

Let me, my dear friend, most heartily congratulate you
on your achievement. It is not an ordinary triumph to do
such justice to the memory of such a man. And I venture
to add, that the fresh spirit with which you have done it
impresses me as being perfectly wonderful.

Ever affectionately yours.

[To Sir James Emerson Tennent.]

GAD'S HILL, Monday, Aug. 20th, 1866.

MY DEAR TENNENT,

I have been very much interested by your extract, and
am strongly inclined to believe that the founder of the

Refuge for Poor Travellers meant the kind of man to which it refers. Chaucer certainly meant the Pardonere to be a humbug, living on the credulity of the people. After describing the sham reliques he carried, he says :

> But with these relikes whawne that he found
> A poure personne dwelling up on lond
> Upon a day he gat him more monnie
> Than that the personne got in monthes time,
> And thus, with fained flattering and japes
> He made the personne, and the people, his apes.

And the worthy Watts (founder of the charity) may have had these very lines in his mind when he excluded such a man.

When I last heard from my boy he was coming to you, and was full of delight and dignity. My midshipman has just been appointed to the *Bristol*, on the West Coast of Africa, and is on his voyage out to join her. I wish it was another ship and another station. She has been unlucky in losing men.

Kindest regard from all my house to yours.

Faithfully yours ever.

[To M. Charles Fechter.]

GAD'S HILL, Tuesday, Sept. 4th, 1866.

MY DEAR FECHTER,

This morning I received the play to the end of the telegraph scene, and I have since read it twice.

I clearly see the *ground* of Mr. Boucicault's two objections ; but I do not see their *force*.

First, as to the writing. If the characters did not speak

in a terse and homely way, their idea and language would be inconsistent with their dress and station, and they would lose, as characters, before the audience. The dialogue seems to be exactly what is wanted. Its simplicity (particularly in Mr. Boucicault's part) is often very effective ; and throughout there is an honest, straight-to-the-purpose ruggedness in it, like the real life and the real people.

Secondly, as to the absence of the comic element. I really do not see how more of it could be got into the story, and I think Mr. Boucicault underrates the pleasant effect of his own part. The very notion of a sailor, whose life is not among those little courts and streets, and whose business does not lie with the monotonous machinery, but with the four wild winds, is a relief to me in reading the play. I am quite confident of its being an immense relief to the audience when they see the sailor before them, with an entirely different bearing, action, dress, complexion even, from the rest of the men. I would make him the freshest and airiest sailor that ever was seen ; and through him I can distinctly see my way out of the "Black Country" into clearer air. (I speak as one of the audience, mind.) I should like something of this contrast to be expressed in the dialogue between the sailor and Jew, in the second scene of the second act. Again, I feel Widdicomb's part (which is charming, and ought to make the whole house cry) most agreeable and welcome, much better than any amount in such a story, of mere comicality.

It is unnecessary to say that the play is done with a master's hand. Its closeness and movement are quite surprising. Its construction is admirable. I have the strongest belief in its making a great success. But I must add this proviso : I never saw a play so dangerously depending in critical places on strict natural propriety in the manner and perfection in the shaping of the small parts. Those small parts cannot take the play up, but they can let it down. I would not leave a hair on the head of one of them to the chance of the first night, but I would see, to the minutest particular, the make-up of every one of them at a night rehearsal.

Of course you are free to show this note to Mr. Boucicault, and I suppose you will do so ; let me throw out this suggestion to him and you. Might it not ease the way with the Lord Chamberlain's office, and still more with the audience, when there are Manchester champions in it, if instead of "Manchester" you used a fictitious name ? When I did "Hard Times" I called the scene Coketown. Everybody knew what was meant, but every cotton-spinning town said it was the other cotton-spinning town.

I shall be up on Saturday, and will come over about mid-day, unless you name any other time.

Ever heartily.

[To Mr. Walter Thornbury.]

"ALL THE YEAR ROUND" OFFICE, *Saturday, Sept.* 15*th*, 1866.
MY DEAR THORNBURY,

Many thanks for your letter.

In reference to your Shakespeare queries, I am not so much enamoured of the first and third subjects as I am of the Ariosto enquiry, which should be highly interesting.

But if you have so got the matter in your mind, as that its execution would be incomplete and unsatisfactory to you unless you write all the three papers, then by all means write the three, and I will most gladly take them. For some years I have had so much pleasure in reading you, that I can honestly warrant myself as what actors call "a good audience."

The idea of old stories retold is decidedly a good one. I greatly like the notion of that series. Of course you know De Quincey's paper on the Ratcliffe Highway murderer? · Do you know also the illustration (I have it at Gad's Hill), representing the horrible creature as his dead body lay on a cart, with a piece of wood for a pillow, and a stake lying by, ready to be driven through him ?

I don't *quite* like the title, "The Social History of London." I should better like some title to the effect, "The History of London's Social Changes in so many Years." Such a title would promise more, and better express your intention. What do you think of taking for a first title, "London's Changes"? You could then add the second title, "Being a History," etc.

I don't at all desire to fix a limit to the series of old stories retold. I would state the general intention at the beginning of the first paper, and go on like Banquo's line.

Don't let your London title remind people, by so much as the place of the word "civilisation," of Buckle. It seems a ridiculous caution, but the indolent part of the public (a large part !) on such points tumble into extraordinary mistakes.   ·   Faithfully yours always.

[*To Mr. Percy Fitzgerald.*]

GAD'S HILL, *Tuesday, Nov. 6th*, 1866.

MY DEAR FITZGERALD,

It is always pleasant to me to hear from you, and I hope you will believe that this is not a mere fashion of speech.

Concerning the green covers, I find the leaves to be budding—on unquestionable newspaper authority ; but, upon my soul, I have no other knowledge of their being in embryo ! Really, I do not see a chance of my settling myself to such work until after I have accomplished forty-two readings, to which I stand pledged.

I hope to begin this series somewhere about the middle of January, in Dublin. Touching the details of the re-alisation of this hope, will you tell me in a line as soon as you can—*Is the exhibition room a good room for speaking in ?*

Your mention of the late Sultan touches me nearly. He was the finest dog I ever saw, and between him and me there was a perfect understanding. But, to adopt the popular phrase, it was so very confidential that it "went no further." He would fly at anybody else with the greatest enthusiasm for destruction. I saw him, muzzled, pound into the heart of a regiment of the line ; and I have frequently seen him, muzzled, hold a great dog down with his chest and feet. He has broken loose (muzzled) and come home covered with blood, again and again. And yet he never disobeyed me, unless he had first laid hold of a dog.

You heard of his going to execution, evidently supposing the procession to be a party detached in pursuit of something to kill or eat? It was very affecting. And also of his bolting a blue-eyed kitten, and making me acquainted with the circumstance by his agonies of remorse (or indigestion)?

I cannot find out that there is anyone in Rochester (a sleepy old city) who has anything to tell about Garrick, except what is not true. . His brother, the wine merchant, would be more in Rochester way, I think. How on earth do you find time to do all these books?

You make my hair stand on end ; an agreeable sensation, for I am charmed to find that I have any. Why don't you come yourself and look after Garrick? I should be truly delighted to receive you.

My dear Fitzgerald, always faithfully yours.

[*To Mr. W. C. Macready.*]

GAD'S HILL PLACE, HIGHAM BY ROCHESTER, KENT,
Friday, Dec. 28*th*, 1866.
MY DEAREST MACREADY,

I have received your letter with the utmost pleasure and we all send our most affectionate love to you, Mrs. Macready, Katie, Johnny, and the boy of boys. All good Christmas and New Year greetings are to be understood as included.

You will be interested in knowing that, encouraged by

the success of summer cricket-matches, I got up a quantity of foot-races and rustic sports in my field here on the 26th last past: as I have never yet had a case of drunkenness, the landlord of The Falstaff had a drinking-booth on the ground. All the prizes I gave were in money, too. We had two thousand people here. Among the crowd were soldiers, navvies, and labourers of all kinds. Not a stake was pulled up, or a rope slackened, or one farthing's-worth of damage done. To every competitor (only) a printed bill of general rules was given, with the concluding words: " Mr. Dickens puts every man upon his honour to assist in preserving order." There was not a dispute all day, and they went away at sunset rending the air with cheers, and leaving every flag on a six hundred yards' course as neat as they found it when the gates were opened at ten in the morning. Surely this is a bright sign in the neighbourhood of such a place as Chatham !

" Mugby Junction " turned, yesterday afternoon, the extraordinary number of two hundred and fifty thousand !

In the middle of next month I begin a new course of forty-two readings. If any of them bring me within reach of Cheltenham, with an hour to spare, I shall come on to you, even for that hour. More of this when I am afield and have my list, which Dolby (for Chappell) is now preparing.

Forster and Mrs. Forster were to have come to us next Monday, to stay until Saturday. I write " were," because I hear that Forster (who had a touch of bronchitis when he wrote to me on Christmas Eve) is in bed. Katie, who has been ill of low nervous fever, was brought here yesterday from London. She bore the journey much better than I expected, and so I hope will soon recover. This is my little stock of news.

I begin to discover in your riper years, that you have been secretly vain of your handwriting all your life. For I swear I see no change in it ! What it always was since I first knew it (a year or two !) it *is*. This I will maintain against all comers.

Ever affectionately, my dearest Macready.

1867.

NARRATIVE.

As the London and provincial readings were to be resumed early in the year and continued until the end of March, Charles Dickens took no house in London this spring. He came to his office quarters at intervals, for the series in town ; usually starting off again, on his country tour, the day after a London reading. From some passages in his letters to his daughter and sister-in-law during this country course, it will be seen that (though he made very light of the fact) the great exertion of the readings, combined with incessant railway travelling, was beginning to tell upon his health, and he was frequently " heavily beaten" after reading at his best to an enthusiastic audience in a large hall.

During the short intervals between his journeys, he was as constantly and carefully at work upon the business of " All the Year Round " as if he had no other work on hand. A proof of this is given in a letter dated " 5th February." It is written to a young man (the son of a friend), who wrote a long novel when far too juvenile for such a task, and had submitted it to Charles Dickens for his opinion, with a view to publication. In the midst of his own hard and engrossing occupation he read the book, and the letter which he wrote on the subject needs no remark beyond this, that the young writer received the adverse criticism with the best possible sense, and has since, in his literary profession, profited by the advice so kindly given.

At this time the proposals to Charles Dickens for reading in America, which had been perpetually renewed from the time of his first abandoning the idea, became so urgent and so tempting, that he found at last he must, at all events, give the subject his most serious consideration. He took counsel with his two most confidential friends and advisers, Mr. John Forster and Mr. W. H. Wills. They were both, at first, strongly opposed to the undertaking, chiefly on the ground of the trial to his health and strength which it would involve. But they could not deny the counterbalancing advantages. And, after much deliberation, it was resolved that Mr. George Dolby should be sent out by the Messrs. Chappell, to take an impression, on the spot, as to the feeling of the United States about the Readings. His report as to the undoubted enthusiasm and urgency on the other side of the Atlantic it was impossible to resist. Even his friends withdrew their opposition (though still with misgivings as to the effect upon his health, which were but too well founded !), and on the 30th September he telegraphed "Yes" to America.

The "Alfred" alluded to in a letter from Glasgow was Charles Dickens's fourth son, Alfred Tennyson, who had gone to Australia two years previously.

We give, in April, the last letter to one of the friends for whom Charles Dickens had always a most tender love

—Mr. Stanfield. He was then in failing health, and in May he died.

Another death which affected him very deeply happened this summer. Miss Marguerite Power died in July. She had long been very ill, but, until it became impossible for her to travel, she was a frequent and beloved guest at Gad's Hill. The Mrs. Henderson to whom he writes was Miss Power's youngest sister.

Before he started for America it was proposed to wish him God-speed by giving him a public dinner at the Freemasons' Hall. The proposal was most warmly and fully responded to. His zealous friend, Mr. Charles Kent, willingly undertook the whole work of arrangement of this banquet. It took place on the 2nd November, and Lord Lytton presided.

On the 8th he left London for Liverpool, accompanied by his daughters, his sister-in-law, his eldest son, Mr. Arthur Chappell, Mr. Charles Collins, Mr. Wilkie Collins, Mr. Kent, and Mr. Wills. The next morning the whole party took a final leave of Charles Dickens on board the *Cuba*, which sailed that day.

We give a letter which he wrote to Mr. J. L. Toole on the morning of the dinner, thanking him for a parting gift and an earnest letter. That excellent comedian was one of his most appreciative admirers, and, in return, he had for Mr. Toole the greatest admiration and respect.

The Christmas number for this year, " No Thoroughfare," was written by Charles Dickens and Mr. Wilkie Collins. It was dramatised by Mr. Collins chiefly. But, in the midst of all the work of preparation for departure, Charles Dickens gave minute attention to as much of the play as could be completed before he left England. It was produced, after Christmas, at the Adelphi Theatre, where M. Fechter was then acting, under the management of Mr. Benjamin Webster.

[*To M. de Cerjat.*]

GAD'S HILL PLACE, HIGHAM BY ROCHESTER, KENT,
New Year's Day, 1867.

MY DEAR CERJAT,

Thoroughly determined to be beforehand with "the middle of next summer," your penitent friend and remorseful correspondent thus addresses you.

The big dog, on a day last autumn, having seized a little girl (sister to one of the servants) whom he knew, and was bound to respect, was flogged by his master, and then sentenced to be shot at seven next morning. He went out very cheerfully with the half-dozen men told off for the purpose, evidently thinking that they were going to be the death of somebody unknown. But observing in the procession an empty wheelbarrow and a double-barrelled gun, he became meditative, and fixed the bearer of the gun with his eyes. A stone deftly thrown across him by the village blackguard (chief mourner) caused him to look round for an instant, and he then fell dead, shot through the heart. Two posthumous children are at this moment rolling on the lawn ; one will evidently inherit his ferocity, and will probably inherit the gun. The pheasant was a little ailing towards Christmas Day, and was found dead under some ivy in his cage, with his head under his wing, on the morning of the twenty-seventh of December, one thousand eight hundred and sixty-six. I, proprietor of the remains of the two deceased, am working hard, getting up "Barbox" and "The Boy at Mugby," with which I begin a new series of readings in London on the fifteenth. Next morning I believe I start into the country. When I read, I *don't* write. I only edit, and have the proof-sheets sent me for the purpose. Here are your questions an-swered.

As to the Reform question, it should have been, and could have been, perfectly known to any honest man in England that the more intelligent part of the great masses were deeply dissatisfied with the state of representation, but were in a very moderate and patient condition, await-ing the better intellectual cultivation of numbers of their fellows. The old insolent resource of assailing them and making the most audaciously wicked statements that they are politically indifferent, has borne the inevitable fruit. The perpetual taunt, "Where are they?" has called them out with the answer : "Well then, if you *must* know, here we are." The intolerable injustice of vituperating the bribed to an assembly of bribers, has goaded their sense of justice beyond endurance. And now, what they would have taken they won't take, and whatever they are steadily bent upon having they will get. Rely upon it, this is the real state of the case. As to your friend "Punch," you will find him begin to turn at the very selfsame instant when the new game shall manifestly become the losing one. You may notice his shoes pinching him a little already.

My dear fellow, I have no more power to stop that mu-tilation of my books than you have. It is as certain as that every inventor of anything designed for the public good, and offered to the English Government, becomes *ipso facto* a criminal, to have his heart broken on the cir-cumlocutional wheel. It is as certain as that the whole Crimean story will be retold, whenever this country again goes to war. And to tell the truth, I have such a very small opinion of what the great genteel have done for us, that I am very philosophical indeed concerning what the great vulgar may do, having a decided opinion that they can't do worse.

This is the time of year when the theatres do best, there being still numbers of people who make it a sort of reli-gion to see Christmas pantomimes. Having my annual houseful, I have, as yet, seen nothing. Fechter has neither pantomime nor burlesque, but is doing a new version of the old "Trente Ans de la Vie d'un Joueur." I am afraid he will not find his account in it. On the whole, the the-atres, except in the articles of scenery and pictorial effect, are poor enough. But in some of the smaller houses there are actors who, if there were any dramatic head-quarters as a school, might become very good. The most hopeless feature is, that they have the smallest possible idea of an effective and harmonious whole, each " going in " for him-self or herself. The music-halls attract an immense pub-lic, and don't refine the general taste. But such things as they do are well done of their kind, and always briskly and punctually.

The American yacht race is the last sensation. I hope the general interest felt in it on this side will have a wholesome interest on that. It will be a woeful day when John and Jonathan throw their caps into the ring. The

French Emperor is indubitably in a dangerous state. His Parisian popularity wanes, and his army are discontented with him. I hear on high authority that his secret police are always making discoveries that render him desperately uneasy.

You know how we have been swindling in these parts. But perhaps you don't know that Mr. ——, the "eminent" contractor, before he fell into difficulties settled *one million of money* on his wife. Such a good and devoted husband !

My daughter Katie has been very ill of nervous fever. On the 27th of December she was in a condition to be brought down here (old high road and post-horses), and has been steadily getting better ever since. Her husband is here too, and is on the whole as well as he ever is or ever will be, I fear.

We played forfeit-games here, last night, and then pool. For a billiard-room has been added to the house since you were here. Come and play a match with me.

Always affectionately.

[*To Miss Hogarth.*]

ADELPHI HOTEL, LIVERPOOL, *Monday, Jan.* 21*st*, 1867.

MY DEAREST GEORGY,

First I send you my most affectionate wishes for many, many happy returns of your birthday. That done, from my heart of hearts, I go on to my small report of myself.

The readings have produced such an immense effect

here that we are coming back for two more in the middle of February. "Marigold" and the "Trial," on Friday night, and the "Carol," on Saturday afternoon, were a perfect furore; and the surprise about "Barbox" has been amusingly great. It is a most extraordinary thing, after the enormous sale of that Christmas number, that the provincial public seems to have combined to believe that it *won't* make a reading. From Wolverhampton and Leeds we have exactly the same expression of feelings *beforehand*. Exactly as I made "Copperfield"—always to the poorest houses I had with Headland, and against that luminary's entreaty—so I should have to make this, if I hadn't "Marigold" always in demand.

It being next to impossible for people to come out at night with horses, we have felt the weather in the stalls, and expect to do so through this week. The half-crown and shilling publics have crushed to their places most splendidly. The enthusiasm has been unbounded. On Friday night I quite astonished myself; but I was taken so faint afterwards that they laid me on a sofa at the hall for half an hour. I attribute it to my distressing inability to sleep at night, and to nothing worse.

Scott does very well indeed. As a dresser he is perfect. In a quarter of an hour after I go into the retiring-room, where all my clothes are airing and everything is set out neatly in its own allotted space, I am ready; and he then goes softly out, and sits outside the door. In the morning he is equally punctual, quiet, and quick. He has his needles and thread, buttons, and so forth, always at hand;

and in travelling he is very systematic with the luggage. What with Dolby and what with this skilful valet, everything is made as easy to me as it possibly *can* be, and Dolby would do anything to lighten the work, and does everything.

There is great distress here among the poor (four thousand people relieved last Saturday at one workhouse), and there is great anxiety concerning *seven mail-steamers some days overdue.* Such a circumstance as this last has never been known. It is supposed that some great revolving storm has whirled them all out of their course. One of these missing ships is an American mail, another an Australian mail.

Same Afternoon.

We have been out for four hours in the bitter east wind, and walking on the sea-shore, where there is a broad strip of great blocks of ice. My hands are so rigid that I write with great difficulty.

We have been constantly talking of the terrible Regent's Park accident. I hope and believe that nearly the worst of it is now known.

[*To Miss Dickens.*]

CHESTER, *Tuesday, Jan. 22nd,* 1867.

MY DEAREST MAMIE,

We came over here from Liverpool at eleven this forenoon. There was a heavy swell in the Mersey breaking over the boat ; the cold was nipping, and all the roads we saw as we came along were wretched. We find a very moderate let here ; but I am myself rather surprised to know that a hundred and twenty stalls have made up their minds to the undertaking of getting to the hall. This seems to be a very nice hotel, but it is an extraordinarily cold one. Our reading for to-night is "Marigold" and "Trial." With amazing perversity the local agent said to Dolby : "They hoped that Mr. Dickens *might* have given them 'The Boy at Mugby.'"

Barton, the gasman who succeeded the man who sprained his leg, sprained *his* leg yesterday ! ! And that, not at his work, but in running downstairs at the hotel. However, he has hobbled through it so far, and I hope will hobble on, for he knows his work.

I have seldom seen a place look more hopelessly frozen up than this place does. The hall is like a Methodist chapel in low spirits, and with a cold in its head. A few blue people shiver at the corners of the streets. And this house, which is outside the town, looks like an ornament on an immense twelfth cake baked for 1847.

I am now going to the fire to try to warm myself, but have not the least expectation of succeeding. The sitting-room has two large windows in it, down to the ground and facing due east. The adjoining bedroom (mine) has also two large windows in it, down to the ground and facing due east. The very large doors are opposite the large windows, and I feel as if I were something to eat in a pantry.

[*To Miss Hogarth.*]

HEN AND CHICKENS, BIRMINGHAM, *Thursday, Jan. 24th,* 1867.

At Chester we read in a snowstorm and a fall of ice. I think it was the worst weather I ever saw. Nevertheless, the people were enthusiastic. At Wolverhampton last night the thaw had thoroughly set in, and it rained heavily. We had not intended to go back there, but have arranged to do so on the day after Ash Wednesday. Last night I was again heavily beaten. We came on here after the reading (it is only a ride of forty minutes), and it was as much as I could do to hold out the journey. But I was not faint, as at Liverpool ; I was only exhausted. I am all right this morning ; and to-night, as you know, I have a rest. I trust that Charley Collins is better, and that Mamie is strong and well again. Yesterday I had a note from Katie, which seemed hopeful and encouraging.

[*To Miss Dickens.*]

HEN AND CHICKENS, BIRMINGHAM, *Thursday, Jan. 24th,* 1867.

Since I wrote to your aunt just now, I have received your note addressed to Wolverhampton. We left the men there last night, and they brought it on with them at noon to-day.

The maimed gasman's foot is much swollen, but he limps about and does his work. I have doctored him up with arnica. During the "Boy" last night there was an escape of gas from the side of my top batten, which caught the copper-wire and was within a thread of bringing down the heavy reflector into the stalls. It was a very ticklish matter, though the audience knew nothing about it. I saw it, and the gasman and Dolby saw it, and stood at that side of the platform in agonies. We all three calculated that there would be just time to finish and save it; when the gas was turned out the instant I had done, the whole thing was at its very last and utmost extremity. Whom it would have tumbled on, or what might have been set on fire, it is impossible to say.

I hope you rewarded your police escort on Tuesday night. It was the most tremendous night I ever saw at Chester.

[*To Miss Dickens.*]

LEEDS, *Friday, Feb. 1st,* 1867.

We got here prosperously, and had a good (but not great) house for "Barbox" and "Boy" last night. For "Marigold" and "Trial," to-night, everything is gone. And I even have my doubts of the possibility of Dolby's cramming the people in. For "Marigold" and "Trial" at Manchester, to-morrow, we also expect a fine hall.

I shall be at the office for next Wednesday. If Charley Collins should have been got to Gad's, I will come there for that day. If not, I suppose we had best open the official bower again.

This is a beastly place, with a very good hotel. Except Preston, it is one of the nastiest places I know. The room is like a capacious coal cellar, and is incredibly filthy; but for sound it is perfect.

VOL. II.—14*

[*Anonymous.*]

OFFICE OF " ALL THE YEAR ROUND," *Tuesday, Feb. 5th,* 1867.
DEAR SIR,

I have looked at the larger half of the first volume of your novel, and have pursued the more difficult points of the story through the other two volumes.

You will, of course, receive my opinion as that of an individual writer and student of art, who by no means claims to be infallible.

I think you are too ambitious, and that you have not sufficient knowledge of life or character to venture on so comprehensive an attempt. Evidences of inexperience in every way, and of your power being far below the situations that you imagine, present themselves to me in almost every page I have read. It would greatly surprise me if you found a publisher for this story, on trying your fortune in that line, or derived anything from it but weariness and bitterness of spirit.

On the evidence thus put before me, I cannot even entirely satisfy myself that you have the faculty of authorship latent within you. If you have not, and yet pursue a vocation towards which you have no call, you cannot choose but be a wretched man. Let me counsel you to have the patience to form yourself carefully, and the courage to renounce the endeavour if you cannot establish your case on a very much smaller scale. You see around you every day, how many outlets there are for short pieces of fiction in all kinds. Try if you can achieve any success within these modest limits (I have practised in my time what I preach to you), and in the meantime put your three volumes away.

Faithfully yours.

P.S.—Your MS. will be returned separately from this office.

[*To Miss Hogarth.*]

LIVERPOOL, *Friday, Feb.* 15*th*, 1867.

My short report of myself is that we had an enormous turn-away last night, and do not doubt about having a cram to-night. The day has been very fine, and I have turned it to the wholesomest account by walking on the sands at New Brighton all the morning. I am not quite right, but believe it to be an effect of the railway shaking. There is no doubt of the fact that, after the Staplehurst experience, it tells more and more, instead of (as one might have expected) less and less.

The charming room here greatly lessens the fatigue of this fatiguing week. I read last night with no more exertion than if I had been at Gad's, and yet to eleven hundred people, and with astonishing effect. It is "Copperfield" to-night, and Liverpool is the "Copperfield" stronghold.

[*To Miss Dickens.*]

GLASGOW, *Sunday, Feb.* 17*th*, 1867.

We arrived here this morning at our time to the moment, five minutes past ten. We turned away great numbers on both nights at Liverpool; and Manchester last night was a splendid spectacle. They cheered to that extent after it was over, that I was obliged to huddle on my clothes (for I was undressing to prepare for the journey), and go back again.

After so heavy a week, it *was* rather stiff to start on this long journey at a quarter to two in the morning; but I got more sleep than I ever got in a railway-carriage before, and it really was not tedious. The travelling was admirable, and a wonderful contrast to my friend the Midland.

I am not by any means knocked up, though I have, as I had in the last series of readings, a curious feeling of soreness all around the body, which I suppose to arise from the great exertion of voice. It is a mercy that we were not both made really ill at Liverpool. On Friday morning I was taken so faint and sick, that I was obliged to leave the table. On the same afternoon the same thing happened to Dolby. We then found that a part of the hotel close to us was dismantled for painting, and that they were at that moment painting a green passage leading to our rooms, with a most horrible mixture of white lead and arsenic. On pursuing the enquiry, I found that the four lady book-keepers in the bar were all suffering from the poison.

[*To Miss Hogarth.*]

BRIDGE OF ALLAN, *Tuesday, Feb. 19th,* 1867.

I was very glad to get your letter before leaving Glasgow this morning. This is a poor return for it, but the post goes out early, and we come in late.

Yesterday morning I was so unwell that I wrote to Frank Beard, from whom I shall doubtless hear to-morrow. I mention it, only in case you should come in his way, for I know how perversely such things fall out. I felt it a little more exertion to read afterwards, and I passed a sleepless night after that again ; but otherwise I am in good force and spirits to-day. I may say, in the best force.

The quiet of this little place is sure to do me good. The little inn in which we are established seems a capital house of the best country sort.

[*To Miss Dickens.*]

GLASGOW, *Thursday, Feb. 21st*, 1867.

After two days' rest at the Bridge of Allan I am in renewed force, and have nothing to complain of but inability to sleep. I have been in excellent air all day since Tuesday at noon, and made an interesting walk to Stirling yesterday, and saw its lions, and (strange to relate) was not bored by them. Indeed, they left me so fresh that I knocked at the gate of the prison, presented myself to the governor, and took Dolby over the jail, to his unspeakable interest. We then walked back again to our excellent country inn.

Enclosed is a letter from Alfred, which you and your aunt will be interested in reading, and which I meant to send you sooner but forgot it.   Wonderful as it is to mention, the sun shines here to-day !   But to counterbalance that phenomenon I am in close hiding from ——, who has christened his infant son in my name, and, consequently, haunts the building.   He and Dolby have already nearly come into collision, in consequence of the latter being always under the dominion of the one idea that he is bound to knock everybody down who asks for me.

The " Jewish lady," wishing to mark her " appreciation of Mr. Dickens's nobility of character," presented him with a copy of Benisch's Hebrew and English Bible, with this inscription : " Presented to Charles Dickens, in grateful and admiring recognition of his having exercised the noblest quality man can possess—that of atoning for an injury as soon as conscious of having inflicted it."

The acknowledgment of the gift is the following letter :

[*To a Jewish Lady.*]

BRADFORD, YORKSHIRE, *Friday, March 1st,* 1867.

MY DEAR MRS. ——,

I am working through a series of readings, widely dispersed through England, Scotland, and Ireland, and am so constantly occupied that it is very difficult for me to write letters.   I have received your highly esteemed note (forwarded from my home in Kent), and should have replied to it sooner but that I had a hope of being able to get home and see your present first.   As I have not been able to do so, however, and am hardly likely to do so for

two months to come, I delay no longer. It is safely awaiting me on my own desk in my own quiet room. I cannot
thank you for it too cordially, and cannot too earnestly
assure you that I shall always prize it highly. The terms
in which you send me that mark of your remembrance are
more gratifying to me than I can possibly express to you ;
for they assure me that there is nothing but goodwill left
between you and me and a people for whom I have a real
regard, and to whom I would not wilfully have given an
offence or done an injustice for any worldly consideration.

Believe me, very faithfully yours.

[*To Miss Hogarth.*]

NEWCASTLE-ON-TYNE, *Wednesday, March 6th,* 1867.

The readings have made an immense effect in this place,
and it is remarkable that although the people are individu-
ally rough, collectively they are an unusually tender and
sympathetic audience ; while their comic perception is
quite up to the high London standard. The atmosphere
is so very heavy that yesterday we escaped to Tynemouth
for a two hours' sea walk. There was a high north wind
blowing and a magnificent sea running. Large vessels were
being towed in and out over the stormy bar, with prodigious
waves breaking on it ; and spanning the restless uproar
of the waters was a quiet rainbow of transcendent beauty.
The scene was quite wonderful. We were in the full enjoyment of it when a heavy sea caught us, knocked us over,
and in a moment drenched us, and filled even our pockets.

We had nothing for it but to shake ourselves together (like Doctor Marigold) and dry ourselves as well as we could by hard walking in the wind and sunshine! But we were wet through for all that when we came back here to dinner after half an hour's railway ride.

I am wonderfully well, and quite fresh and strong. Have had to doctor Dolby for a bad cold; have not caught it (yet), and have set him on his legs again.

Scott is striking the tents and loading the baggages, so I must deliver up my writing-desk. We meet, please God, on Tuesday.

[*To Miss Hogarth.*]

SHELBOURNE HOTEL, DUBLIN, *Friday, March 15th,* 1867.

We made our journey through an incessant snowstorm on Wednesday night; at last got snowed up among the Welsh mountains in a tremendous storm of wind, came to a stop, and had to dig the engine out. We went to bed at Holyhead at six in the morning of Thursday, and got aboard the packet at two yesterday afternoon. It blew hard, but as the wind was right astern, we only rolled and did not pitch much. As I walked about on the bridge all the four hours, and had cold salt beef and biscuit there and brandy-and-water, you will infer that my Channel training has not worn out.

Our "business" here is *very bad*, though at Belfast it is enormous. There is no doubt that great alarm prevails here. This hotel is constantly filling and emptying as families leave the country, and set in a current to the steamers.

There is apprehension of some disturbance between to-morrow night and Monday night (both inclusive), and I learn this morning that all the drinking-shops are to be closed from to-night until Tuesday. It is rumoured here that the Liverpool people are very uneasy about some apprehended disturbance there at the same time. Very likely you will know more about this than I do, and very likely it may be nothing. There is no doubt whatever that alarm prevails, and the manager of this hotel, an intelligent German, is very gloomy on the subject. On the other hand, there is feasting going on, and I have been asked to dinner-parties by divers civil and military authorities.

Don't *you* be uneasy, I say once again. You may be absolutely certain that there is no cause for it. We are splendidly housed here, and in great comfort.

Love to Charley and Katey.

[*To Miss Dickens.*]

SHELBOURNE HOTEL, DUBLIN, *Saturday, March 16th*, 1867.

I daresay you know already that I held many councils in London about coming to Ireland at all, and was much against it. Everything looked as bad here as need be, but we did very well last night after all.

There is considerable alarm here beyond all question, and great depression in all kinds of trade and commerce. To-morrow being St. Patrick's Day, there are apprehensions of some disturbance, and croakers predict that it will come off between to-night and Monday night. Of course there are preparations on all sides, and large musters of soldiers and police, though they are kept carefully out of sight. One would not suppose, walking about the streets, that any disturbance was impending; and yet there is no doubt that the materials of one lie smouldering up and down the city and all over the country. [I have a letter from Mrs. Bernal Osborne this morning, describing the fortified way in which she is living in her own house in the County Tipperary.]

You may be quite sure that your venerable parent will take good care of himself. If any riot were to break out, I should immediately stop the readings here. Should all remain quiet, I begin to think they will be satisfactorily remunerative after all. At Belfast, we shall have an enormous house. I read "Copperfield" and "Bob" here on Monday; "Marigold" and "Trial" at Belfast, on Wednesday; and "Carol" and "Trial" here, on Friday. This is all my news, except that I am in perfect force.

[*To Miss Hogarth.*]

SHELBOURNE HOTEL, DUBLIN, *Sunday, March 17th*, 1867.

Everything remains in appearance perfectly quiet here. The streets are gay all day, now that the weather is improved, and singularly quiet and deserted at night. But the whole place is secretly girt in with a military force. To-morrow night is supposed to be a critical time; but in view of the enormous preparations, I should say that the chances are at least one hundred to one against any disturbance.

I cannot make sure whether I wrote to you yesterday, and told you that we had done very well at the first reading after all, even in money. The reception was prodigious, and the readings are the town talk. But I rather think I did actually write this to you. My doubt on the subject arises from my having deliberated about writing on a Saturday.

The most curious, and for facilities of mere destruction, such as firing houses in different quarters, the most dangerous piece of intelligence imparted to me on authority is, that the Dublin domestic men-servants as a class are all Fenians.

[*To Miss Hogarth.*]

BELFAST, *Wednesday, March* 20*th*, 1867.

The post goes out at twelve, and I have only time to report myself. The snow not lying between this and Dublin, we got here yesterday to our time, after a cold but pleasant journey. Fitzgerald came on with us. I had a really charming letter from Mrs. Fitzgerald, asking me to stay there. She must be a perfectly unaffected and genuine lady. There are kind messages to you and Mary in it. I have sent it on to Mary, who will probably in her turn show it to you. We had a wonderful crowd at Dublin on Monday, and the greatest appreciation possible. We have a good let, in a large hall, here to-night. But I am perfectly convinced

that the worst part of the Fenian business is to come
yet.

All about the Fitzgeralds and everything else when we
meet.

[*To Miss Dickens.*]

BELFAST, *Thursday, March 21st,* 1867.

In spite of public affairs and dismal weather, we are
doing wonders in Ireland.

That the conspiracy is a far larger and more important
one than would seem from what it has done yet, there is
no doubt. I have had a good deal of talk with a certain
colonel, whose duty it has been to investigate it, day and
night, since last September. That it will give a world of
trouble, and cost a world of money, I take to be (after
what I have thus learned) beyond all question. One regiment has been found to contain five hundred Fenian soldiers every man of whom was sworn in the barrack-yard.
How information is swiftly and secretly conveyed all over
the country, the Government with all its means and money
cannot discover; but every hour it is found that instructions, warnings, and other messages are circulated from
end to end of Ireland. It is a very serious business indeed.

I have just time to send this off, and to report myself
quite well except for a slight cold.

[*To Miss Hogarth.*]

NORWICH, *Friday, March 29th*, 1867.

The reception at Cambridge last night was something to be proud of in such a place. The colleges mustered in full force from the biggest guns to the smallest, and went far beyond even Manchester in the roars of welcome and the rounds of cheers. All through the readings, the whole of the assembly, old men as well as young, and women as well as men, took everything with a heartiness of enjoyment not to be described. The place was crammed, and the success the most brilliant I have ever seen.

What we are doing in this sleepy old place I don't know, but I have no doubt it is mild enough.

[*To Mr. Walter Thornbury.*]

OFFICE OF "ALL THE YEAR ROUND,"
Monday, April 1st, 1867.

MY DEAR THORNBURY,

I am very doubtful indeed about "Vaux," and have kept it out of the number in consequence. The mere details of such a rascal's proceedings, whether recorded by himself or set down by the Reverend Ordinary, are not wholesome for a large audience, and are scarcely justifiable (I think) as claiming to be a piece of literature. I can understand Barrington to be a good subject, as involving the representation of a period, a style of manners, an order of dress, certain habits of street life, assembly-room life, and coffee-room life, etc. ; but there is a very broad distinction between this and mere Newgate Calendar. The latter would assuredly damage your book, and be protested against to me. I have a conviction of it, founded on constant observation and experience here.

Your kind invitation is extremely welcome and acceptable to me, but I am sorry to add that I must not go a-visiting. For this reason : So incessantly have I been "reading," that I have not once been at home at Gad's Hill since last January, and am little likely to get there before the middle of May. Judge how the master's eye must be kept on the place when it does at length get a look at it after so long an absence! I hope you will descry in this a reason for coming to me again, instead of my coming to you.

The extinct prize-fighters, as a body, I take to be a good subject, for much the same reason as George Barrington. Their patrons were a class of men now extinct too, and the whole ring of those days (not to mention Jackson's rooms in Bond Street) is a piece of social history. Now Vaux is not, nor is he even a phenomenon among thieves.

Faithfully yours always.

[*To Mr. Clarkson Stanfield, R.A.*]

GAD'S HILL PLACE, HIGHAM BY ROCHESTER,
Thursday, April 18th, 1867.

MY DEAR STANNY,

The time of year reminds me how the months have gone, since I last heard from you through Mrs. Stanfield.

I hope you have not thought me unmindful of you in the meanwhile. I have been almost constantly travelling and reading. England, Ireland, and Scotland have laid hold of me by turns, and I have had no rest. As soon as I had finished this kind of work last year, I had to fall to work upon "All the Year Round" and the Christmas number. I was no sooner quit of that task, and the Christmas season was but run out to its last day, when I was tempted into another course of fifty readings that are not yet over. I am here now for two days, and have not seen the place since Twelfth Night. When a reading in London has been done, I have been brought up for it from some great distance, and have next morning been carried back again. But the fifty will be "paid out" (as we say at sea) by the middle of May, and then I hope to see you.

Reading at Cheltenham the other day, I saw Macready, who sent his love to you. His face was much more massive and as it used to be, than when I saw him previous to his illness. His wife takes admirable care of him, and is on the happiest terms with his daughter Katie. His boy by the second marriage is a jolly little fellow, and leads a far easier life than the children you and I remember, who used to come in at dessert and have each a biscuit and a glass of water, in which last refreshment I was always convinced that they drank, with the gloomiest malignity, "Destruction to the gormandising grown-up company!"

I hope to look up your latest triumphs on the day of the Academy dinner. Of course as yet I have had no opportunity of even hearing of what anyone has done. I have been (in a general way) snowed up for four months. The locomotive with which I was going to Ireland was dug out of the snow at midnight, in Wales. Both passages across were made in a furious snowstorm. The snow lay ankle-deep in Dublin, and froze hard at Belfast. In Scotland it slanted before a perpetual east wind. In Yorkshire, it derived novelty from thunder and lightning. Whirlwinds everywhere I don't mention.

God bless you and yours. If I look like some weather-beaten pilot when we meet, don't be surprised. Any mahogany-faced stranger who holds out his hand to you will probably turn out, on inspection, to be the old original Dick.

Ever, my dear Stanny, your faithful and affectionate.

P.S.—I wish you could have been with me (of course in a snowstorm) one day on the pier at Tynemouth. There was a very heavy sea running, and a perfect fleet of screw merchantmen were plunging in and out on the turn of the tide at high-water. Suddenly there came a golden horizon, and a most glorious rainbow burst out, arching one large ship, as if she were sailing direct for heaven. I was so enchanted by the scene, that I became oblivious of a few thousand tons of water coming on in an enormous roller, and was knocked down and beaten by its spray when it broke, and so completely wetted through and through, that the very pockets in my pocket-book were full of sea.

[*To Mr. George Stanfield.*]

OFFICE OF "ALL THE YEAR ROUND,"
Sunday, May 19*th*, 1867.

ON THE DEATH OF HIS FATHER.

MY DEAR GEORGE,

When I came up to the house this afternoon and saw what had happened, I had not the courage to ring, though I had thought I was fully prepared by what I heard when I called yesterday. No one of your father's friends can ever have loved him more dearly than I always did, or can have better known the worth of his noble character.

It is idle to suppose that I can do anything for you ; and yet I cannot help saying that I am staying here for some days, and that if I could, it would be a much greater relief to me than it could be a service to you.

Your poor mother has been constantly in my thoughts since I saw the quiet bravery with which she preserved her composure. The beauty of her ministration sank into my heart when I saw him for the last time on earth. May God be with her, and with you all, in your great loss.

Affectionately yours always.

[*To Mr. W. H. Wills.*]

Thursday, June 6*th*, 1867.

MY DEAR WILLS,

I cannot tell you how warmly I feel your letter, or how deeply I appreciate the affection and regard in which it originates. I thank you for it with all my heart.

VOL. II.—15

You will not suppose that I make light of any of your misgivings if I present the other side of the question. Every objection that you make strongly impresses me, and will be revolved in my mind again and again.

When I went to America in '42, I was so much younger, but (I think) very much weaker too. I had had a painful surgical operation performed shortly before going out, and had had the labour from week to week of " Master Humphrey's Clock." My life in the States was a life of continual speech-making (quite as laborious as reading), and I was less patient and more irritable then than I am now. My idea of a course of readings in America is, that it would involve far less travelling than you suppose, that the large first-class rooms would absorb the whole course, and that the receipts would be very much larger than your estimate, unless the demand for the readings is ENORMOUSLY EXAGGERATED ON ALL HANDS. There is considerable reason for this view of the case. And I can hardly think that all the speculators who beset, and all the private correspondents who urge me, are in a conspiracy or under a common delusion.

*   *   *   *   *

I shall never rest much while my faculties last, and (if I know myself) have a certain something in me that would still be active in rusting and corroding me, if I flattered myself that I was in repose. On the other hand, I think that my habit of easy self-abstraction and withdrawal into fancies has always refreshed and strengthened me in short intervals wonderfully. I always seem to myself to have rested far more than I have worked ; and I do really believe that I have some exceptional faculty of accumulating young feelings in short pauses, which obliterates a quantity of wear and tear.

My worldly circumstances (such a large family considered) are very good. I don't want money. All my possessions are free and in the best order. Still, at fifty-five or fifty-six, the likelihood of making a very great addition to one's capital in half a year is an immense consideration. . . . I repeat the phrase, because there should be something large to set against the objections.

I dine with Forster to-day, to talk it over. I have no doubt he will urge most of your objections and particularly the last, though American friends and correspondents he has, have undoubtedly staggered him more than I ever knew him to be staggered on the money question. Be assured that no one can present any argument to me which will weigh more heartily with me than your kind words, and that whatever comes of my present state of abeyance, I shall never forget your letter or cease to be grateful for it.

Ever, my dear Wills, faithfully yours.

[*To Mr. W. H. Wills.*]

GAD'S HILL PLACE, HIGHAM BY ROCHESTER, KENT,

Sunday, June 13th, 1867.

MY DEAR WILLS,

I have read the first three numbers of Wilkie's story this morning, and have gone minutely through the plot of the rest to the last line. It gives a series of " narratives," but it is a very curious story, wild, and yet domestic, with excellent character in it, and great mystery. It is prepared with extraordinary care, and has every chance of being a hit. It is in many respects much better than anything he has done. The question is, how shall we fill up the blank between Mabel's progress and Wilkie? What do you think of proposing to Fitzgerald to do a story three months long? I daresay he has some unfinished or projected something by him.

I have an impression that it was not Silvester who tried Eliza Fenning, but Knowles. One can hardly suppose Thornbury to make such a mistake, but I wish you would look into the Annual Register. I have added a final paragraph about the unfairness of the judge, whoever he was. I distinctly recollect to have read of his "putting down" of Eliza Fenning's father when the old man made some miserable suggestion in his daughter's behalf (this is not noticed by Thornbury), and he also stopped some suggestion that a knife thrust into a loaf adulterated with alum would present the appearance that these knives presented. But I may have got both these points from looking up some pamphlets in Upcott's collection which I once had.

Your account of your journey reminds me of one of the latest American stories, how a traveller by stage-coach said to the driver: "Did you ever see a snail, sir?" "Yes sir." "Where did you meet him, sir?" "I *didn't* meet him, sir!" "Wa'al, sir, I think you did, if you'll excuse me, for I'm damned if you ever overtook him."

Ever faithfully.

[*To Mrs. Henderson.*]

GAD'S HILL, *Thursday, July 4th*, 1867.

MY DEAR MRS. HENDERSON,

I was more shocked than surprised by the receipt of your mother's announcement of our poor dear Marguerite's death. When I heard of the consultation, and recalled what had preceded it and what I have seen here, my hopes were very slight.

Your letter did not reach me until last night, and thus I could not avoid remaining here to-day, to keep an American appointment of unusual importance. You and your mother both know, I think, that I had a great affection for Mârguerite, that we had many dear remembrances together, and that her self-reliance and composed perseverance had awakened my highest admiration in later times. No one could have stood by her grave to-day with a better knowledge of all that was great and good in her than I have, or with a more loving remembrance of her through all her phases since she first came to London a pretty timid girl.

I do not trouble your mother by writing to her separately. It is a sad, sad task to write at all. God help us!

Faithfully yours.

[*To Mr. Percy Fitzgerald.*]

GAD'S HILL, *July 21st*, 1867.

MY DEAR FITZGERALD,

I am heartily glad to get your letter, and shall be thoroughly well pleased to study you again in the pages of A. Y. R.

I have settled nothing yet about America, but am going to send Dolby out on the 3rd of next month to survey the land, and come back with a report on some heads whereon I require accurate information.   Proposals (both from American and English speculators) of a very tempting nature have been repeatedly made to me ; but I cannot endure the thought of binding myself to give so many readings there whether I like it or no ; and if I go at all, am bent on going with Dolby single-handed.

I have been doing two things for America ; one, the little story to which you refer ; the other, four little papers for a child's magazine.   I like them both, and think the latter a queer combination of a child's mind ˑwith a grown-up joke.   I have had them printed to assure correct printing in the United States.   You shall have the proof to read, with the greatest pleasure.   On second thoughts, why shouldn't I send you the children's proof by this same post ?   I will, as I have it here, send it under another cover.   When you return it, you shall have the short story.

Believe me, always heartily yours.

[To Mr. Percy Fitzgerald.]

EXTRACT.

July 28th, 1867.

I am glad you like the children, and particularly glad you like the pirate.   I remember very well when I had a general idea of occupying that place in history at the same age.   But I loved more desperately than Boldheart.

[*To Miss Hogarth.*]

ADELPHI HOTEL, LIVERPOOL, *Friday Night, Aug. 2nd,* 1867.

MY DEAREST GEORGY,

I cannot get a boot on—wear a slipper on my left foot, and consequently am here under difficulties. My foot is occasionally painful, but not very. I don't think it worth while consulting anybody about it as yet. I make out so many reasons against supposing it to be gouty, that I really do not think it is.

Dolby begs me to send all manner of apologetic messages for his going to America. He is very cheerful and hopeful, but evidently feels the separation from his wife and child very much. His sister * was at Euston Square this morning, looking very well. Sainton, too, very light and jovial.

With the view of keeping myself and my foot quiet, I think I will not come to Gad's Hill until Monday. If I don't appear before, send basket to Gravesend to meet me, leaving town by the 12.10 on Monday. This is important, as I couldn't walk a quarter of a mile to-night for five hundred pounds.

Love to all at Gad's.

[*To Mr. W. H. Wills.*]

GAD'S HILL, *Monday, Sept. 2nd,* 1867.

MY DEAR WILLS,

Like you, I was shocked when this new discovery burst upon me on Friday, though, unlike you, I never could be-

---

* Madame Sainton Dolby.

lieve in ——, solely (I think) because, often as I have tried him, I never found him standing by my desk when I was writing a letter without trying to read it.

I fear there is no doubt that since ——'s discharge, he (——) has stolen money at the readings. A case of an abstracted shilling seems to have been clearly brought home to him by Chappell's people, and they know very well what *that* means. I supposed a very clear keeping off from Anne's husband (whom I recommended for employment to Chappell) to have been referable only to —— ; but now I see how hopeless and unjust it would be to expect belief from him with two such cases within his knowledge.

But don't let the thing spoil your holiday. If we try to do our duty by people we employ, by exacting their proper service from them on the one hand, and treating them with all possible consistency, gentleness, and consideration on the other, we know that we do right. Their doing wrong cannot change our doing right, and that should be enough for us.

So I have given *my* feathers a shake, and am all right again. Give *your* feathers a shake, and take a cheery flutter into the air of Hertfordshire.

Great reports from Dolby and also from Fields ! But I keep myself quite calm, and hold my decision in abeyance until I shall have book, chapter, and verse before me. Dolby hoped he could leave Uncle Sam on the 11th of this month.

Sydney has passed as a lieutenant, and appeared at home

yesterday, all of a sudden, with the consequent golden garniture on his sleeve, which I, God forgive me, stared at without the least idea that it meant promotion.

I am glad you see a certain unlikeness to anything in the American story. Upon myself it has made the strangest impression of reality and originality ! ! And I feel as if I had read something (by somebody else), which I should never get out of my mind ! ! ! The main idea of the narrator's position towards the other people was the idea that I *had* for my next novel in A. Y. R. But it is very curious that I did not in the least see how to begin his state of mind until I walked into Hoghton Towers one bright April day with Dolby.

Faithfully ever.

[*To Mr. F. D. Finlay.*]

CONTRADICTING A NEWSPAPER REPORT OF HIS BEING IN
A CRITICAL STATE OF HEALTH.

GAD'S HILL PLACE, HIGHAM BY ROCHESTER, KENT,
Tuesday, Sept. 3rd, 1867.

This is to certify that the undersigned victim of a periodical paragraph-disease, which usually breaks out once in every seven years (proceeding to England by the overland route to India and per Cunard line to America, where it strikes the base of the Rocky Mountains, and, rebounding to Europe, perishes on the steppes of Russia), is *not* in a "critical state of health," and has *not* consulted "eminent surgeons," and never was better in his life, and is *not*

VOL. II.—15*

recommended to proceed to the United States for " cessation from literary labour," and has not had so much as a headache for twenty years.

CHARLES DICKENS.

[*To M. Charles Fechter.*]

" ALL THE YEAR ROUND" OFFICE,
Monday, Sept. 16*th*, 1867.

MY DEAR FECHTER,

Going over the prompt-book carefully, I see one change in your part to which (on Lytton's behalf) I positively object, as I am quite certain he would not consent to it. It is highly injudicious besides, as striking out the best known line in the play.

Turn to your part in Act III., the speech beginning :

Pauline, *by pride*
Angels have fallen ere thy time : by pride——

You have made a passage farther on stand :

Then did I seek to rise
Out of my mean estate.   Thy bright image, etc.

I must stipulate for your restoring it thus :

Then did I seek to rise
Out of the prison of my mean estate ;
And, with such jewels as the exploring mind
Brings from the caves of knowledge, buy my ransom
From those twin jailers of the daring heart—
Low birth and iron fortune.   Thy bright image, etc. etc.

The last figure has been again and again quoted ; is identified with the play ; is fine in itself ; and above all,

I KNOW that Lytton would not let it go. In writing to him to-day, fully explaining the changes in detail, and saying that I disapprove of nothing else, I have told him that I notice this change and that I immediately let you know that it must not be made.

(There will not be a man in the house from any newspaper who would not detect mutilations in that speech, moreover.)

Ever.

[*To Miss Hogarth.*]

Monday, Sept. 30th, 1867.

MY DEAREST GEORGY,

The telegram is despatched to Boston : " Yes. Go ahead." After a very anxious consultation with Forster, and careful heed of what is to be said for and against, I have made up my mind to see it out. I do not expect as much money as the calculators estimate, but I cannot set the hope of a large sum of money aside.

I am so nervous with travelling and anxiety to decide something, that I can hardly write. But I send you these few words as my dearest and best friend.

[*To Miss Dickens.*]

OFFICE OF " ALL THE YEAR ROUND," No. 26, WELLINGTON STREET, STRAND, LONDON, W.C.,

Monday, Sept. 30th, 1867.

MY DEAREST MAMIE,

You will have had my telegram that I go to America. After a long discussion with Forster, and consideration of what is to be said on both sides, I have decided to go through with it. I doubt the profit being as great as the calculation makes it, but the prospect is sufficiently alluring to turn the scale on the American side.

Unless I telegraph to the contrary, I will come to Gravesend (send basket there) by 12 train on Wednesday. Love to all.

We have telegraphed "Yes" to Boston.

I begin to feel myself drawn towards America, as Darnay, in the "Tale of Two Cities," was attracted to the Loadstone Rock, Paris.

[*To Mr. William Charles Kent.*]

26, WELLINGTON STREET, *Saturday, Oct. 19th,* 1867.

MY DEAR KENT,

In the midst of the great trouble you are taking in the cause of your undersigned affectionate friend, I hope the reading of the enclosed may be a sort of small godsend. Of course it is very strictly private. The printers are not yet trusted with the name, but the name will be, "No Thoroughfare." I have done the greater part of it; may you find it interesting!

My solicitor, a man of some mark and well known, is anxious to be on the Committee:

Frederic Ouvry, Esquire,

66, Lincoln's Inn Fields.

Ever affectionately yours.

P.S.—My sailor son!

I forgot him!!

Coming up from Portsmouth for the dinner ! ! !

Der—er—oo not cur—ur—urse me, I implore.

Penitently.

[*To Mrs. Power.*]

GAD'S HILL, *Wednesday, Oct. 23rd*, 1867.

MY DEAR MRS. POWER,

I have a sad pleasure in the knowledge that our dear Marguerite so remembered her old friend, and I shall preserve the token of her remembrance with loving care. The sight of it has brought back many old days.

With kind remembrance to Mrs. Henderson,

Believe me always, very faithfully yours.

[*To Mr. J. L. Toole.*]

GAD'S HILL PLACE, HIGHAM BY ROCHESTER, KENT,
Saturday, Nov. 2nd, 1867.

MY DEAR MR. TOOLE,

I heartily thank you for your elegant token of remembrance, and for your earnest letter. Both have afforded me real pleasure, and the first-named shall go with me on my journey.

Let me take this opportunity of saying that on receipt of your letter concerning to-day's dinner, I immediately forwarded your request to the honorary secretary. I hope you will understand that I could not, in delicacy, otherwise take part in the matter.

Again thanking you most cordially,

Believe me, always faithfully yours.

[*To Mr. W. H. Wills.*]

26, WELLINGTON STREET, *Sunday, Nov. 3rd*, 1867.

MY DEAR WILLS,

If you were to write me many such warm-hearted letters as you send this morning, my heart would fail me ! There is nothing that so breaks down my determination, or shows me what an iron force I put upon myself, and how weak it is, as a touch of true affection from a tried friend.

All that you so earnestly say about the goodwill and devotion of all engaged, I perceived and deeply felt last night. It moved me even more than the demonstration itself, though I do suppose it was the most brilliant ever seen. When I got up to speak, but for taking a desperate hold of myself, I should have lost my sight and voice and sat down again.

God bless you, my dear fellow.   I am, ever and ever,

Your affectionate.

[*To the Hon. Mrs. Watson.*]

OFFICE OF " ALL THE YEAR ROUND,"

Tuesday, Nov. 5th, 1867.

MY DEAR MRS. WATSON,

A thousand thanks for your kind letter, and many congratulations on your having successfully attained a dignity which I never allow to be mentioned in my presence. Charley's children are instructed from their tenderest months only to know me as " Wenerables," which they sincerely believe to be my name, and a kind of title that I have received from a grateful country.

Alas ! I cannot have the pleasure of seeing you before I presently go to Liverpool. Every moment of my time is preoccupied. But I send you my sincere love, and am always truthful to the dear old days, and the memory of one of the dearest friends I ever loved.

Affectionately yours.

[*To Miss Dickens.*]

ABOARD THE "CUBA," QUEENSTOWN HARBOUR,
Sunday, Nov. 10*th*, 1867.

MY DEAREST MAMIE,

We arrived here at seven this morning, and shall probably remain awaiting our mail, until four or five this afternoon. The weather in the passage here was delightful, and we had scarcely any motion beyond that of the screw.

We are nearly but not quite full of passengers. At table I sit next the captain, on his right, on the outside of the table and close to the door. My little cabin is big enough for everything but getting up in and going to bed in. As it has a good window which I can leave open all night, and a door which I can set open too, it suits my chief requirements of it—plenty of air—admirably. On a writing-slab in it, which pulls out when wanted, I now write in a majestic manner.

Many of the passengers are American, and I am already on the best terms with nearly all the ship.

We began our voyage yesterday a very little while after you left us, which was a great relief. The wind is S.E. this morning, and if it would keep so we should go along nobly. My dearest love to your aunt, and also to Katie and all the rest. I am in very good health, thank God, and as well as possible.

[*To Miss Hogarth.*]

ABOARD THE "CUBA," FIVE DAYS OUT,
Wednesday, Nov. 13*th*, 1867.

MY DEAREST GEORGY,

As I wrote to Mamie last, I now write to you, or mean to do it, if the motion of the ship will let me.

We are very nearly halfway to-day. The weather was favourable for us until yesterday morning, when we got a head-wind which still stands by us. We have rolled and pitched, of course ; but on the whole have been wonderfully well off. I have had headache and have felt faint once or twice, *but have not been sick at all.* My spacious cabin is very noisy at night, as the most important working of the ship goes on outside my window and over my head ; but it is very airy, and if the weather be bad and I can't open the window, I can open the door all night. If the weather be fine (as it is now), I can open both door and window, and write between them. Last night, I got a foot-bath under the dignified circumstances of sitting on a camp-stool in my cabin, and having the bath (and my feet) in the passage outside. The officers' quarters are close to me, and, as I know them all, I get reports of the weather and the way we are making when the watch is changed, and I am (as I usually am) lying awake. The motion of the screw is at its slightest vibration in my particular part of the ship. The silent captain, reported gruff, is a very good fellow and an honest fellow. Kelly has been ill all the time, and not of the slightest use, and is ill now. Scott always cheerful, and useful, and ready ; a better servant for the kind of work there never can have been. Young Lowndes has been fearfully sick until midday yesterday. His cabin is pitch dark, and full of blackbeetles. He shares mine until nine o'clock at night, when Scott carries him off to bed. He also dines with me in my magnificent chamber. This passage in winter time cannot be said to be an enjoyable excursion, but I certainly am making it under the best circumstances. (I find Dolby to have been enormously popular on board, and to have known everybody and gone everywhere.)

So much for my news, except that I have been constantly reading, and find that "Pierra" that Mrs. Hogge sent me by Katie to be a very remarkable book, not only for its grim and horrible story, but for its suggestion of wheels within wheels, and sad human mysteries. Baker's second book not nearly so good as his first, but his first anticipated it.

We hope to get to Halifax either on Sunday or Monday, and to Boston either on Tuesday or Wednesday. The glass is rising high to-day, and everybody on board is hopeful of an easterly wind.

[*To Miss Hogarth.*]

Saturday, 16th.

Last Thursday afternoon a heavy gale of wind sprang up and blew hard until dark, when it seemed to lull. But it then came on again with great violence, and blew tremendously all night. The noise, and the rolling and plunging of the ship, were awful. Nobody on board could get any sleep, and numbers of passengers were rolled out of their berths. Having a side-board to mine to keep me in, like a baby, I lay still. But it was a dismal night indeed, and it was curious to see the change it had made in the faces of all the passengers yesterday. It cannot be denied that these winter crossings are very trying and startling ; while the personal discomfort of not being able to wash, and the miseries of getting up and going to bed, with what small means there are all sliding, and sloping, and slopping about, are really in their way distressing.

This forenoon we made Cape Race, and are now running along at full speed with the land beside us. Kelly still useless, and positively declining to show on deck. Scott, with an eight-day-old moustache, more super like than ever. My foot (I hope from walking on the boarded deck) in a very shy condition to-day, and rather painful. I shaved this morning for the first time since Liverpool ; dodging at the glass, very much like Fechter's imitation of ———. The white cat that came off with us in the tender a general favourite. She belongs to the daughter of a Southerner, returning with his wife and family from a two-years' tour in Europe.

Sunday, 17th.

At four o'clock this morning we got into bad weather again, and the state of things at breakfast-time was un-utterably miserable. Nearly all the passengers in their berths—no possibility of standing on deck—sickness and groans—impracticable to pass a cup of tea from one pair of hands to another. It has slightly moderated since (between two and three in the afternoon I write), and the sun is shining, but the rolling of the ship surpasses all imagination or description.

We expect to be at Halifax about an hour after mid-night, and this letter shall be posted there, to make certain of catching the return mail on Wednesday. Boston is only thirty hours from Halifax.

Best love to Mamie, and to Katie and Charley. I know you will report me and my love to Forster and Mrs. For-ster. I write with great difficulty, wedged up in a corner, and having my heels on the paper as often as the pen. Kelly worse than ever, and Scott better than ever.

My desk and I have just arisen from the floor.

[*To Miss Dickens.*]

PARKER HOUSE, BOSTON, *Thursday, Nov. 21st,* 1867.

I arrived here on Tuesday night, after a very slow pass-age from Halifax against head-winds. All the tickets for the first four readings here (all yet announced) were sold immediately on their being issued.

You know that I begin on the 2nd of December with
" Carol" and " Trial " ?   Shall be heartily glad to begin
to count the readings off.

This is an immense hotel, with all manner of white
marble public passages and public rooms.   I live in a
corner high up, and have a hot and cold bath in my bedroom (communicating with the sitting-room), and comforts
not in existence when I was here before.   The cost of living is enormous, but happily we can afford it.   I dine
to-day with Longfellow, Emerson, Holmes, and Agassiz.
Longfellow was here yesterday.   Perfectly white in hair
and beard, but a remarkably handsome and notable-look-
ing man.   The city has increased enormously in five-and-
twenty years.   It has grown more mercantile—is like Leeds
mixed with Preston, and flavoured with New Brighton ;
but for smoke and fog you substitute an exquisitely bright
light air.   I found my rooms beautifully decorated (by
Mrs. Fields) with choice flowers, and set off by a number
of good books.   I am not much persecuted by people in
general, as Dolby has happily made up his mind that the
less I am exhibited for nothing the better.   So our men
sit outside the room door and wrestle with mankind.

We had speech-making and singing in the saloon of the
Cuba after the last dinner of the voyage.   I think I have
acquired a higher reputation from drawing out the captain, and getting him to take the second in " All's Well,"
and likewise in " There's not in the wide world " (your
parent taking first), than from anything previously known
of me on these shores.   I hope the effect of these achieve-

ments may not dim the lustre of the readings. We also sang (with a Chicago lady, and a strong-minded woman from I don't know where) "Auld Lang Syne," with a tender melancholy, expressive of having all four been united from our cradles. The more dismal we were, the more delighted the company were. Once (when we paddled i' the burn) the captain took a little cruise round the compass on his own account, touching at the "Canadian Boat Song," and taking in supplies at "Jubilate," "Seas between us braid ha' roared," and roared like the seas themselves. Finally, I proposed the ladies in a speech that convulsed the stewards, and we closed with a brilliant success. But when you dine with Mr. Forster, ask him to read to you how we got on at church in a heavy sea. Hillard has just been in and sent his love " to those dear girls." He has grown much older. He is now District Attorney of the State of Massachusetts, which is a very good office. Best love to your aunt and Katie, and Charley and all his house, and all friends.

[*To Miss Hogarth.*]

PARKER HOUSE, BOSTON, *Monday, Nov.* 25*th,* 1867.

I cannot remember to whom I wrote last, but it will not much matter if I make a mistake ; this being generally to report myself so well, that I am constantly chafing at not having begun to-night instead of this night week.

The tickets being all sold for next week, and no other announcement being yet made, there is nothing new in that way to tell of. Dolby is over at New York, where we are at our wits' end how to keep tickets out of the hands of speculators.   Morgan is staying with me ; came yesterday to breakfast, and goes home to-morrow.   Fields and Mrs. Fields also dined yesterday.   She is a very nice woman, with a rare relish for humour and a most contagious laugh   The Bostonians having been duly informed that I wish to be quiet, really leave me as much so as I should be in Manchester or Liverpool.   This I cannot expect to last elsewhere ; but it is a most welcome relief here, as I have all the readings to get up.   The people are perfectly kind and perfectly agreeable.   If I stop to look in at a shop-window, a score of passers-by stop ; and after I begin to read, I cannot expect in the natural course of things to get off so easily.   But I every day take from seven to ten miles in peace.

Communications about readings incessantly come in from all parts of the country.   We take no offer whatever, lying by with our plans until after the first series in New York, and designing, if we make a furore there, to travel as little as possible.   I fear I shall have to take Canada at the end of the whole tour.   They make such strong representations from Montreal and Toronto, and from Nova Scotia —represented by St. John's and Halifax—of the slight it would be to them, if I wound up with the States, that I am shaken.

It is sad to see Longfellow's house (the house in which his wife was burnt) with his young daughters in it, and the shadow of that terrible story.   The young undergraduates of Cambridge (he is a professor there) have made a representation to him that they are five hundred strong, and cannot get one ticket. I don't know what is to be done for them ; I suppose I must read there somehow. We are all in the clouds until I shall have broken ground in New York, as to where readings will be possible and where impossible.

Agassiz is one of the most natural and jovial of men. I go out a-visiting as little as I can, but still have to dine, and what is worse, sup pretty often. Socially, I am (as I was here before) wonderfully reminded of Edinburgh when I had many friends in it.

Your account and Mamie's of the return journey to London gave me great pleasure. I was delighted with your report of Wilkie, and not surprised by Chappell's coming out gallantly.

My anxiety to get to work is greater than I can express, because time seems to be making no movement towards home until I shall be reading hard. Then I shall begin to count and count and count the upward steps to May.

If ever you should be in a position to advise a traveller going on a sea voyage, remember that there is some mysterious service done to the bilious system when it is shaken, by baked apples. Noticing that they were produced on board the *Cuba*, every day at lunch and dinner, I thought I would make the experiment of always eating them freely. I am confident that they did wonders, not only at the time, but in stopping the imaginary pitching and rolling after the voyage is over, from which many good amateur sailors suffer. I have hardly had the sensation at all, ex-

cept in washing of a morning.   At that time I still hold on
with one knee to the washing-stand, and could swear that
it rolls from left to right.   The *Cuba* does not return until
Wednesday, the 4th December.   You may suppose that
every officer on board is coming on Monday, and that
Dolby has provided extra stools for them.   His work is
very hard indeed.   Cards are brought to him every minute
in the day ; his correspondence is immense ; and he is
jerked off to New York, and I don't know where else, on the
shortest notice and the most unreasonable times.   Moreover, he has to be at " the bar " every night, and to " liquor
up with all creation " in the small hours.   He does it all
with the greatest good humour, and flies at everybody who
waylays the Chief, furiously.   We have divided our men
into watches, so that one always sits outside the drawing-
room door.   Dolby knows the whole Cunard line, and as
we could not get good English gin, went out in a steamer
yesterday and got two cases (twenty-four bottles) out of
Cunard officers.   Osgood and he were detached together
last evening for New York, whence they telegraph every
other hour about some new point in this precious sale of
tickets.   So distracted a telegram arrived at three that I
have telegraphed back, " Explain yourselves," and am now
waiting for the explanation.   I think you know that Osgood
is a partner in Ticknor and Fields'.

Tuesday morning.—Dolby has come back from New
York, where the prospects seem immense.   We sell tickets
there next Friday and Saturday, and a tremendous rush is
expected.

[*To Mr. Charles Dickens.*]

PARKER HOUSE, BOSTON, U.S., *Saturday, Nov. 30th*, 1867.

MY DEAR CHARLEY,

· You will have heard before now how fortunate I was on my voyage, and how I was not sick for a moment. These screws are tremendous ships for carrying on, and for rolling, and their vibration is rather distressing. But my little cabin, being for'ard of the machinery, was in the best part of the vessel, and I had as much air in it, night and day, as I chose. The saloon being kept absolutely without air, I mostly dined in my own den, in spite of my being allotted the post of honour on the right hand of the captain.

The tickets for the first four readings here (the only readings announced) were all sold immediately, and many are now re-selling at a large premium. The tickets for the first four readings in New York (the only readings announced there also) were on sale yesterday, and were all sold in a few hours. The receipts are very large indeed ; but engagements of any kind and every kind I steadily refuse, being resolved to take what is to be taken myself. Dolby is nearly worked off his legs, is now at New York, and goes backwards and forwards between this place and that (about the distance from London to Liverpool, though they take nine hours to do it) incessantly. Nothing can exceed his energy and good humour, and he is extremely popular everywhere. My great desire is to avoid much travelling, and to try to get the people to come to me, in-

VOL. II.—16

stead of my going to them. If I can effect this to any moderate extent, I shall be saved a great deal of knocking about. My original purpose was not to go to Canada at all ; but Canada is so up in arms on the subject that I think I shall be obliged to take it at last. In that case I should work round to Halifax, Nova Scotia, and then take the packet for home.

As they don't seem (Americans who have heard me on their travels excepted) to have the least idea here of what the readings are like, and as they are accustomed to mere readings out of a book, I am inclined to think the excitement will increase when I shall have begun. Everybody is very kind and considerate, and I have a number of old friends here, at the Bar and connected with the University. I am now negotiating to bring out the dramatic verson of "No Thoroughfare" at New York. It is quite upon the cards that it may turn up trumps.

I was interrupted in that place by a call from my old secretary in the States, Mr. Putnam. It was quite affecting to see his delight in meeting his old master again. And when I told him that Anne was married, and that I had (unacknowledged) grandchildren, he laughed and cried together. I suppose you don't remember Longfellow, though he remembers you in a black velvet frock very well. He is now white-haired and white-bearded, but remarkably handsome. He still lives in his old house, where his beautiful wife was burnt to death. I dined with him the other day, and could not get the terrific scene out of my imagination. She was in a blaze in an instant, rushed into his arms with a wild cry, and never spoke afterwards.

My love to Bessie, and to Mekitty, and all the babbies. I will lay this by until Tuesday morning, and then add a final line to it.

Ever, my dear Charley, your affectionate Father.

Tuesday, Dec. 3rd, 1867.

Success last night beyond description or exaggeration. The whole city is quite frantic about it to-day, and it is impossible that prospects could be more brilliant.

[*To Miss Dickens.*]

PARKER HOUSE, BOSTON, *Sunday, Dec. 1st,* 1867.

I received yours of the 18th November, yesterday. As I left Halifax in the *Cuba* that very day, you probably saw us telegraphed in *The Times* on the 19th.

Dolby came back from another run to New York, this morning. The receipts are very large indeed, far exceeding our careful estimate made at Gad's. I think you had best in future (unless I give you intimation to the contrary) address your letters to me, at the Westminster Hotel, Irving Place, New York City. It is a more central position than this, and we are likely to be much more there than here. I am going to set up a brougham in New York, and keep my rooms at that hotel. The account of Matilda is a very melancholy one, and really distresses me. What she must sink into, it is sad to consider. However, there was nothing for it but to send her away, that is quite clear.

They are said to be a very quiet audience here, appreciative but not demonstrative. I shall try to change their character a little.

I have been going on very well. A horrible custom obtains in these parts of asking you to dinner somewhere at half-past two, and to supper somewhere else about eight. I have run this gauntlet more than once, and its effect is, that there is no day for any useful purpose, and that the length of the evening is multiplied by a hundred. Yesterday I dined with a club at half-past two, and came back here at half-past eight, with a general impression that it was at least two o'clock in the morning. Two days before I dined with Longfellow at half-past two, and came back at eight, supposing it to be midnight. To-day we have a state dinner-party in our rooms at six, Mr. and Mrs. Fields, and Mr. and Mrs. Bigelow. (He is a friend of Forster's, and was American Minister in Paris.) There are no negro waiters here, all the servants are Irish—willing, but not able. The dinners and wines are very good. I keep our own rooms well ventilated by opening the windows, but no window is ever opened in the halls or passages, and they are so overheated by a great furnace, that they make me faint and sick. The air is like that of a pre-Adamite ironing-day in full blast. Your respected parent is immensely popular in Boston society, and its cordiality and unaffected heartiness are charming. I wish I could carry it with me.

The leading New York papers have sent men over for

to-morrow night with instructions to telegraph columns of descriptions. Great excitement and expectation everywhere. Fields says he has looked forward to it so long that he knows he will die at five minutes to eight.

At the New York barriers, where the tickets are on sale and the people ranged as at the Paris theatres, speculators went up and down offering "twenty dollars for anybody's place." The money was in no case accepted. One man sold two tickets for the second, third, and fourth night for "one ticket for the first, fifty dollars" (about seven pounds ten shillings), "and a brandy cocktail," which is an iced bitter drink. The weather has been rather muggy and languid until yesterday, when there was the coldest wind blowing that I ever felt. In the night it froze very hard, and to-day the sky is beautiful.

Tuesday, Dec. 3rd.

Most magnificent reception last night, and most signal and complete success. Nothing could be more triumphant. The people will hear of nothing else and talk of nothing else. Nothing that was ever done here, they all agree, evoked any approach to such enthusiasm. I was quite as cool and quick as if I were reading at Greenwich, and went at it accordingly. Tell your aunt, with my best love, that I have this morning received hers of the 21st, and that I will write to her next. That will be from New York. My love to Mr. and Mrs. Hulkes and the boy, and to Mr. and Mrs. Malleson.*

---

* The nearest neighbours at Higham, and intimate friends.

[*To Miss Hogarth.*]

BOSTON, *Wednesday, Dec. 4th*, 1867.

I find that by going off to the *Cuba* myself this morning I can send you the enclosed for Mary Boyle (I don't know how to address her), whose usual flower for my button-hole was produced in the most extraordinary manner here last Monday night! All well and prosperous. "Copper-field" and "Bob" last night; great success.

[*To Miss Mary Bolye.*]

BOSTON, *December 4th*, 1867.

MY DEAR MEERY,

You can have no idea of the glow of pleasure and amazement with which I saw your remembrance of me lying on my dressing-table here last Monday night. Whosoever undertook that commission accomplished it to a miracle. But you must go away four thousand miles, and have such a token conveyed to *you*, before you can quite appreciate the feeling of receiving it. Ten thousand loving thanks.

Immense success here, and unbounded enthusiasm. My largest expectations far surpassed.

Ever your affectionate

Jo.

[*To Miss Dickens.*]

WESTMINSTER HOTEL, IRVING PLACE, NEW YORK CITY,

Wednesday, Dec. 11th, 1867.

Amazing success here. A very fine audience; *far better than that at Boston.* Great reception. Great, "Carol"

and " Trial," on the first night; still greater, " Copperfield " and " Bob," on the second.   Dolby sends you a few
papers by this post.   You will see from their tone what a
success it is.

I cannot pay this letter, because I give it at the latest
moment to the mail-officer, who is going on board the
Cunard packet in charge of the mails, and who is staying
in this house.   We are now selling (at the hall) the tickets
for the four readings of next week.   At nine o'clock this
morning there were two thousand people in waiting, and
they had begun to assemble in the bitter cold as early as
two o'clock.   All night long Dolby and our man have been
stamping tickets.   (Immediately over my head, by-the-bye,
and keeping me awake.)   This hotel is quite as quiet as
Mivart's, in Brook Street.   It is not very much larger.
There are American hotels close by, with five hundred
bed-rooms, and I don't know how many boarders ; but
this is conducted on what is called " the European principle," and is an admirable mixture of a first-class French
and English house.   I keep a very smart carriage and pair ;
and if you were to behold me driving out, furred up to the
moustache, with furs on the coach-boy and on the driver,
and with an immense white, red, and yellow striped rug
for a covering, you would suppose me to be of Hun-
garian or Polish nationality.

Will you report the success here to Mr. Forster with my
love, and tell him he shall hear from me by next mail ?

Dolby sends his kindest regards.   He is just come in
from our ticket sales, and has put such an immense untidy

heap of paper money on the table that it looks like a family wash. He hardly ever dines, and is always tearing about at unreasonable hours. He works very hard.

My best love to your aunt (to whom I will write next), and to Katie, and to both the Charleys, and all the Christmas circle, not forgetting Chorley, to whom give my special remembrance. You may get this by Christmas Day. *We* shall have to keep it travelling from Boston here ; for I read at Boston on the 23rd and 24th, and here again on the 26th.

[*To Miss Hogarth.*]

WESTMINSTER HOTEL, IRVING PLACE, NEW YORK CITY,
Monday, Dec. 16*th,* 1867.

We have been snowed up here, and the communication with Boston is still very much retarded. Thus we have received no letters by the Cunard steamer that came in last Wednesday, and are in a grim state of mind on that subject.

Last night I was getting into bed just at twelve o'clock, when Dolby came to my door to inform me that the house was on fire (I had previously smelt fire for two hours). I got Scott up directly, told him to pack the books and clothes for the readings first, dressed, and pocketed my jewels and papers, while Dolby stuffed himself out with money. Meanwhile the police and firemen were in the house, endeavouring to find where the fire was. For some time it baffled their endeavours, but at last, bursting out through some stairs, they cut the stairs away, and traced it to its source in a certain fire-grate. By this time the hose was laid all through the house from a great tank on the roof, and everybody turned out to help. It was the oddest sight, and people had put the strangest things on ! After a little chopping and cutting with axes and handing about of water, the fire was confined to a dining-room in which it had originated, and then everybody talked to everybody else, the ladies being particularly loquacious and cheerful. And so we got to bed again at about two.

The excitement of the readings continues unabated, the tickets for readings are sold as soon as they are ready, and the public pay treble prices to the speculators who buy them up. They are a wonderfully fine audience, even better than Edinburgh, and almost, if not quite, as good as Paris.

Dolby continues to be the most unpopular man in America (mainly because he can't get four thousand people into a room that holds two thousand), and is reviled in print daily. Yesterday morning a newspaper proclaims of him : " Surely it is time that the pudding-headed Dolby retired into the native gloom from which he has emerged." He takes it very coolly, and does his best. Mrs. Morgan sent me, the other night, I suppose the finest and costliest basket of flowers ever seen, made of white camellias, yellow roses, pink roses, and I don't know what else. It is a yard and a half round at its smallest part.

I must bring this to a close, as I have to go to the hall to try an enlarged background.

[*To Miss Hogarth.*]

BOSTON, *Sunday, Dec. 22nd*, 1867.

Coming here from New York last night (after a detestable journey), I was delighted to find your letter of the 6th.   I read it at my ten o'clock dinner with the greatest interest and pleasure, and then we talked of home till we went to bed.

Our tour is now being made out, and I hope to be able to send it in my next letter home, which will be to Mamie, from whom I have *not* heard (as you thought I had) by the mail that brought out yours.   After very careful consideration I have reversed Dolby's original plan, and have decided on taking Baltimore, Washington, Cincinnati, *Chicago* (!), St. Louis, and a few other places nearer here, instead of staying in New York.   My reason is that we are doing immensely, both at New York and here, and that I am sure it is in the peculiar character of the people to prize a thing the more the less easily attainable it is made.   Therefore, I want, by absence, to get the greatest rush and pressure upon the five farewell readings in New York in April.   All our announced readings are already crammed.

When we got here last Saturday night, we found that Mrs. Fields had not only garnished the rooms with flowers, but also with holly (with real red berries) and festoons of moss dependent from the looking-glasses and picture frames.   She is one of the dearest little women in the world. The homely Christmas look of the place quite affected us. Yesterday we dined at her house, and there was a plum-pudding brought on blazing, and not to be surpassed in any house in England. There is a certain Captain Dolliver, belonging to the Boston Custom House, who came off in the little steamer that brought me ashore from the *Cuba.* He took it into his head that he would have a piece of English mistletoe brought out in this week's Cunard, which should be laid upon my breakfast-table. And there it was this morning. In such affectionate touches as this, these New England people are especially amiable.

As a general rule, you may lay it down that whatever you see about me in the papers is not true. But although my voyage out was of that highly hilarious description that you first made known to me, you may *generally* lend a more believing ear to the Philadelphia correspondent of *The Times.* I don't know him, but I know the source from which he derives his information, and it is a very respectable one.

Did I tell you in a former letter from here, to tell Anne, with her old master's love, that I had seen Putnam, my old secretary? Grey, and with several front teeth out, but I would have known him anywhere. He is coming to "Copperfield" to-night, accompanied by his wife and daughter, and is in the seventh heaven at having his tickets given him.

Our hotel in New York was on fire *again* the other night. But fires in this country are quite matters of course. There was a large one there at four this morning, and I don't think a single night has passed since I have been under the protection of the Eagle, but I have heard the fire bells dolefully clanging all over the city.

Dolby sends his kindest regard. His hair has become quite white, the effect, I suppose, of the climate. He is so universally hauled over the coals (for no reason on earth), that I fully expect to hear him, one of these nights, assailed with a howl when he precedes me to the platform steps. You may conceive what the low newspapers are here, when one of them yesterday morning had, as an item of news, the intelligence : " Dickens's Readings. The chap calling himself Dolby got drunk last night, and was locked up in a police-station for fighting an Irishman." I don't find that anybody is shocked by this liveliness.

My love to all, and to Mrs. Hulkes and the boy. By-the-bye, when we left New York for this place, Dolby called my amazed attention to the circumstance that Scott was leaning his head against the side of the carriage and weeping bitterly. I asked him what was the matter, and he replied : " The owdacious treatment of the luggage, which was more outrageous than a man could bear." I told him not to make a fool of himself ; but they do knock it about cruelly. I think every trunk we have is already broken.

I must leave off, as I am going out for a walk in a bright sunlight and a complete break-up of the frost and snow. I am much better than I have been during the last week, but have a cold.

[*To Miss Dickens.*]

WESTMINSTER HOTEL, IRVING PLACE, NEW YORK CITY,
Thursday, Dec. 26th, 1867.

I got your aunt's last letter at Boston yesterday, Christmas Day morning, when I was starting at eleven o'clock to come back to this place. I wanted it very much, for I had a frightful cold (English colds are nothing to those of this country), and was exceedingly depressed and miserable. Not that I had any reason but illness for being so, since the Bostonians had been quite astounding in their demonstrations. I never saw anything like them on Christmas Eve. But it is a bad country to be unwell and travelling in ; you are one of say a hundred people in a heated car, with a great stove in it, and all the little windows closed, and the hurrying and banging about are indescribable. The atmosphere is detestable, and the motion often all but intolerable. However, we got our dinner here at eight o'clock, and plucked up a little, and I made some hot gin punch to drink a merry Christmas to all at home in. But it must be confessed that we were both very dull. I have been in bed all day until two o'clock, and here I am now (at three o'clock) a little better. But I am not fit to read, and I must read to-night. After watching the general character pretty closely, I became quite sure that Dolby was wrong on the length of the stay and the number of readings we had proposed in this place. I am quite certain that it is one of the national peculiarities that what they want must be difficult of attainment. I therefore a few days ago made a *coup d'état*, and altered the whole scheme. We shall go to Philadelphia, Baltimore, Washington, also some New England towns between Boston and this place, away to the falls of Niagara, and off far west to Chicago and St.Louis, before coming back for ten farewell readings here, preceded by farewells at Boston, leaving Canada altogether. This will not prolong the list beyond eighty-four readings, the exact original number, and will, please God, work it all out in April. In my next, I daresay, I shall be able to send the exact list, so that you may know every day where we are. There has been a great storm here for a few days, and the streets, though wet, are becoming passable again. Dolby and Osgood are out in it to-day on a variety of business, and left in grave and solemn state. Scott and the gasman are stricken with dumb concern, not having received one single letter from home since they left. What their wives can have done with the letters they take it for granted they have written, is their stormy speculation at the door of my hall dressing-room every night.

If I do not send a letter to Katie by this mail, it will be because I shall probably be obliged to go across the water to Brooklyn to-morrow to see a church, in which it is proposed that I shall read ! ! ! Horrible visions of being put in the pulpit already beset me. And whether the audience will be in pews is another consideration which greatly disturbs my mind. No paper ever comes out without a leader on Dolby, who of course reads them all, and never can understand why I don't, in which he is called all the bad names in (and not in) the language.

We always call him P. H. Dolby now, in consequence of one of these graceful specimens of literature describing him as the "pudding-headed."

I fear that when we travel he will have to be always before me, so that I may not see him six times in as many weeks. However, I shall have done a fourth of the whole this very next week !

Best love to your aunt, and the boys, and Katie, and Charley, and all true friends.

Friday.

I managed to read last night, but it was as much as I could do. To-day I am so very unwell, that I have sent for a doctor ; he has just been, and is in doubt whether I shall not have to stop reading for a while.

[*To Miss Dickens.*]

Westminster Hotel, Irving Place, New York,
Monday, Dec. 30th, 1867.

I am getting all right again. I have not been well, been very low, and have been obliged to have a doctor ; a very agreeable fellow indeed, who soon turned out to be an old friend of Olliffe's.* He has set me on my legs and taken his leave "professionally," though he means to give me a call now and then.

---

* Dr. Fordyce Barker.

In the library at Gad's is a bound book, "Remarkable Criminal Trials," translated by Lady Duff Gordon, from the original by Fauerbach. I want that book, and a copy of Praed's poems, to be sent out to Boston, care of Ticknor and Fields. If you will give the "Criminal Trials" to Wills, and explain my wish, and ask him to buy a copy of Praed's Poems and add it to the parcel, he will know how to send the packet out. I think the "Criminal Trials" book is in the corner book-case, by the window, opposite the door.

No news here. All going on in the regular way. I read in that church I told you of, about the middle of January. It is wonderfully seated for two thousand people, and is as easy to speak in as if there were two hundred. The people are seated in pews, and we let the pews. I stood on a small platform from which the pulpit will be removed for the occasion ! ! I emerge from the vestry ! ! ! Philadelphia, Baltimore, and another two nights in Boston will follow this coming month of January. On Friday next I shall have read a fourth of my whole list, besides having had twelve days' holiday when I first came out. So please God I shall soon get to the half, and so begin to work hopefully round.

I suppose you were at the Adelphi on Thursday night last. They are pirating the bill as well as the play here, everywhere. I have registered the play as the property of an American citizen, but the law is by no means clear that I established a right in it by so doing ; and of course the pirates knew very well that I could not, under existing circumstances, try the question with them in an American court of law. Nothing is being played here scarcely that is not founded on my books—" Cricket," " Oliver Twist," " Our Mutual Friend," and I don't know what else, every night. I can't get down Broadway for my own portrait ; and yet I live almost as quietly in this hotel, as if I were at the office, and go in and out by a side door just as I might there.

I go back to Boston on Saturday to read there on Monday and Tuesday. Then I am back here, and keep within six or seven hours' journey of hereabouts till February. My further movements shall be duly reported as the details are arranged.

I shall be curious to know who were at Gad's Hill on Christmas Day, and how you (as they say in this country) " got along." It is exceedingly cold here again, after two or three quite spring days.

1868.

NARRATIVE.

CHARLES DICKENS remained in America through the winter, returning home from New York in the *Russia*, on the 19th of April. His letters show how entirely he gave himself up to the business of the readings, how severely his health suffered from the climate, and from the perpetual travelling and hard work, and yet how he was able to battle through to the end. These letters are also full of allusions to the many kind and dear friends who contributed so largely to the pleasure of his American visit, and whose love and attention gave a touch of *home* to his private life, and left such affection and gratitude in his heart as he could never forget.   Many of these friends paid visits to Gad's Hill ; the first to come during this summer being Mr. Longfellow, his daughters, and Mr. Appleton, brother-in-law of Mr. Longfellow, and Mr. and Mrs. Charles Eliot Norton, of Cambridge.

For the future, there were to be no more Christmas numbers of " All the Year Round."   Observing the extent to which they were now copied in all directions, Charles Dickens supposed them likely to become tiresome to the public, and so determined that in his journal they should be discontinued.

While still in America, he made an agreement with the Messrs. Chappell to give a series of farewell readings in England, to commence in the autumn of this year.   So, in October, Charles Dickens started off again for a tour in the provinces.   He had for some time been planning, by way of a novelty for this series, a reading from the murder in " Oliver Twist," but finding it so very horrible, he was fearful of trying its effect for the first time on a public audience.   It was therefore resolved, that a trial of it should be made to a limited private audience in St. James's Hall, on the evening of the 18th of November.   This trial proved eminently successful, and " The Murder from Oliver Twist " became one of the most popular of his selections.   But the physical exertion it involved was far greater than that of any of his previous readings, and added immensely to the excitement and exhaustion which they caused him.

One of the first letters of the year from America is addressed to Mr. Samuel Cartwright, of surgical and artistic reputation, and greatly esteemed by Charles Dickens, both in his professional capacity and as a private friend.

The letter written to Mrs. Cattermole, in May, tells of

the illness of Mr. George Cattermole. This dear old friend, so associated with Charles Dickens and his works, died soon afterwards, and the letter to his widow shows that Charles Dickens was exerting himself in her behalf.

The play of " No Thoroughfare " having been translated into French under the title of " L'Abîme," Charles Dickens went over to Paris to be present at the first night of its production.

On the 26th of September, his youngest son, Edward Bulwer Lytton (the " Plorn " so often mentioned), started for Australia, to join his brother Alfred Tennyson, who was already established there. It will be seen by his own words how deeply and how sadly Charles Dickens felt this parting. In October of this year, his son Henry Fielding entered Trinity Hall, Cambridge, as an under-graduate.

The Miss Forster mentioned in the letter to his sister-in-law, and for whom the kind and considerate arrange-ments were suggested, was a sister of Mr. John Forster, and a lady highly esteemed by Charles Dickens. The ill-ness from which she was then suffering was a fatal one. She died in this same year, a few days before Christmas.

Mr. J. C. Parkinson, to whom a letter is addressed, was a gentleman holding a Government appointment, and con-tributing largely to journalism and periodical literature.

As our last letter for this year, we give one which Charles Dickens wrote to his youngest son on his departure for Australia.

[*To Miss Hogarth.*]

WESTMINSTER HOTEL, IRVING PLACE, NEW YORK,
Friday, Jan. 3rd, 1868.

MY DEAREST GEORGY,

I received yours of the 19th from Gad's and the office

this morning. I read here to-night, and go back to Boston to-morrow, to read there Monday and Tuesday.

To-night I read out the first quarter of my list. Our houses have been very fine here, but have never quite recovered the Dolby uproar. It seems impossible to devise any scheme for getting the tickets into the people's hands without the intervention of speculators. The people *will not* help themselves; and, of course, the speculators and all other such prowlers throw as great obstacles in Dolby's way (an Englishman's) as they possibly can. He may be a little injudicious into the bargain. Last night, for instance, he met 'one of the "ushers" (who show people to their seats) coming in with Kelly. It is against orders that anyone employed in front should go out during the readings, and he took this man to task in the British manner. Instantly the free and independent usher put on his hat and walked off. Seeing which, all the other free and independent ushers (some twenty in number) put on *their* hats and walked off, leaving us absolutely devoid and destitute of a staff for to-night. One has since been improvised; but it was a small matter to raise a stir and ill will about, especially as one of our men was equally in fault.

We have a regular clerk, a Bostonian whose name is Wild. He, Osgood, Dolby, Kelly, Scott, George the gasman, and perhaps a boy or two, constitute my body-guard. It seems a large number of people, but the business cannot be done with fewer. The speculators buying the front seats to sell at a premium (and we have found instances of this being done by merchants in good position !), and the public perpetually pitching into Dolby for selling them back seats, the result is that they won't have the back seats, send back their tickets, write and print volumes on the subject, and deter others from coming.

You may get an idea of the staff's work, by what is in hand now. They are preparing, numbering, and stamping six thousand tickets for Philadelphia, and eight thousand tickets for Brooklyn. The moment those are done, another eight thousand tickets will be wanted for Baltimore, and probably another six thousand for Washington. This in addition to the correspondence, advertisements, accounts, travellings, and the mighty business of the reading four times a week.

The Cunard steamers being now removed from Halifax, I have decided *not* to go there, or to St. John's, New Brunswick. And as there would be a perfect uproar if I picked out such a place in Canada as Quebec or Montreal, and excluded those two places (which would guarantee three hundred pounds a night), and further, as I don't want places, having more than enough for my list of eighty-four, I have finally resolved not to go to Canada either. This will enable me embark for home in April instead of May.

Tell Plorn, with my love, that I think he will find himself much interested at that college, * and that it is very likely he may make some acquaintances there that will thereafter be pleasant and useful to him. Sir Sydney Dacres is the best of friends. I have a letter from Mrs.

---

* The Agricultural College, Cirencester.

Hulkes by this post, wherein the boy encloses a violet, now lying on the table before me. Let her know that it arrived safely, and retaining its colour. I took it for granted that Mary would have asked Chorley for Christmas Day, and am very glad she ultimately did so. I am sorry that Harry lost his prize, but believe it was not his fault. Let *him* know *that*, with my love. I would have written to him by this mail in answer to his, but for other occupation. Did I tell you that my landlord made me a drink (brandy, rum, and snow the principal ingredients) called a " Rocky Mountain sneezer " ? Or that the favourite drink before you get up is an "eye-opener"? Or that Roberts (second landlord), no sooner saw me on the night of the first fire, than, with his property blazing, he insisted on taking me down into a roomful of hot smoke to drink brandy and water with him ? We have not been on fire again, by-the-bye, more than once.

There has been another fall of snow, succeeded by a heavy thaw. I have laid down my sledge, and taken up my carriage again, in consequence. I am nearly all right, but cannot get rid of an intolerable cold in the head. No more news.

[*To Miss Hogarth.*]

PARKER HOUSE, BOSTON, U.S., *Jan. 4th*, 1868.

I write to you by this opportunity, though I really have nothing to tell you. The work is hard and the climate is hard. We made a tremendous hit last night with " Nickleby " and " Boots," which the Bostonians certainly on the whole appreciate more than "Copperfield"! Dolby is always going about with an immense bundle that looks like a sofa cushion, but it is in reality paper money ; and always works like a Trojan. His business at night is a mere nothing, for these people are so accustomed to take care of themselves, that one of these immense audiences will fall into their places with an ease amazing to a frequenter of St. James's Hall. And the certainty with which they are all in, before I go on, is a very acceptable mark of respect. I must add, too, that although there is a conventional familiarity in the use of one's name in the newspapers as "Dickens," "Charlie," and what not, I do not in the least see that familiarity in the writers themselves. An inscrutable tone obtains in journalism, which a stranger cannot understand. If I say in common courtesy to one of them, when Dolby introduces, "I am much obliged to you for your interest in me," or so forth, he seems quite shocked, and has a bearing of perfect modesty and propriety. I am rather inclined to think that they suppose their printed tone to be the public's love of smartness, but it is immensely difficult to make out. All I can as yet make out is, that my perfect freedom from bondage, and at any moment to go on or leave off, or otherwise do as I like, is the only safe position to occupy.

Again ; there are two apparently irreconcilable contrasts here. Down below in this hotel every night are the bar loungers, dram drinkers, drunkards, swaggerers, loafers, that one might find in a Boucicault play. Within half an hour is Cambridge, where a delightful domestic life—simple, self-respectful, cordial, and affectionate—is seen in an admirable aspect. All New England is primitive and puritanical. All about and around it is a puddle of mixed human mud, with no such quality in it. Perhaps I may in time sift out some tolerably intelligible whole, but I certainly have not done so yet. It is a good sign, may be, that it all seems immensely more difficult to understand than it was when I was here before.

Felton left two daughters. I have only seen the eldest, a very sensible, frank, pleasant girl of eight-and-twenty, perhaps, rather like him in the face. A striking-looking daughter of Hawthorn's (who is also dead) came into my room last night. The day has slipped on to three o'clock, and I must get up "Dombey" for to-night. Hence this sudden break off. Best love to Mamie, and to Katie and Charley Collins.

[*To Mr. W. Wilkie Collins.*]

Westminster Hotel, New York, *Sunday, Jan. 12th,* 1868.

My Dear Wilkie,

First, of the play.* I am truly delighted to learn that it made so great a success, and I hope I may yet see it on the Adelphi boards. You have had a world of trouble and work with it, but I hope will be repaid in some degree by the pleasure of a triumph. Even for the alteration at the end of the fourth act (of which you tell me in your letter received yesterday), I was fully prepared, for I

---

* "No Thoroughfare."

COULD NOT see the original effect in the reading of the play, and COULD NOT make it go. I agree with Webster in thinking it best that Obenreizer should die on the stage ; but no doubt that point is disposed of. In reading the play before the representation, I felt that it was too long, and that there was a good deal of unnecessary explanation. Those points are, no doubt, disposed of too by this time.

We shall do nothing with it on this side. Pirates are producing their own wretched versions in all directions, thus (as Wills would say) anticipating and glutting " the market." I registered one play as the property of Ticknor and Fields, American citizens. But, besides that the law on the point is extremely doubtful, the manager of the Museum Theatre, Boston, instantly announced his version. (You may suppose what it is and how it is done, when I tell you that it was playing withing ten days of the arrival out of the Christmas number.) Thereupon, Ticknor and Fields gave him notice that he mustn't play it. Unto which he replied, that he meant to play it and would play it. Of course he knew very well that if an injunction were applied for against him, there would be an immediate howl against my persecution of an innocent, and he played it. Then the noble host of pirates rushed in, and it is being done in some mangled form or other, everywhere.

It touches me to read what you write of your poor mother. But, of course, at her age, each winter counts heavily. Do give her my love, and tell her that I asked you about her.

I am going on here at the same great rate, but am always

counting the days that lie between me and home. I got through the first fourth of my readings on Friday, January 3rd. I leave for two readings at Philadelphia this evening.

Being at Boston last Sunday, I took it into my head to go over the medical school, and survey the holes and corners in which that extraordinary murder was done by Webster. There was the furnace—stinking horribly, as if the dismembered pieces were still inside it—and there are all the grim spouts, and sinks, and chemical appliances, and what not. At dinner, afterwards, Longfellow told me a terrific story. He dined with Webster within a year of the murder, one of a party of ten or twelve. As they sat at their wine, Webster suddenly ordered the lights to be turned out, and a bowl of some burning mineral to be placed on the table, that the guests might see how ghostly it made them look. As each man stared at all the rest in the weird light, all were horrified to see Webster *with a rope round his neck*, holding it up, over the bowl, with his head jerked on one side, and his tongue lolled out, representing a man being hanged !

Poking into his life and character, I find (what I would have staked my head upon) that he was always a cruel man.

So no more at present from,

My dear Wilkie, yours ever affectionately.

[*To Miss Hogarth.*]

WESTMINSTER HOTEL, NEW YORK, *Sunday, Jan. 12th,* 1868.

As I am off to Philadelphia this evening, I may as well post my letter here. I have scarcely a word of news.

My cold steadily refuses to leave me ; but otherwise I am as right as one can hope to be under this heavy work. My New York readings are over (except four farewell nights in April), and I look forward to the relief of being out of my hardest hall. Last Friday night, though it was only " Nickleby " and " Boots," I was again dead beat at the end, and was once more laid upon a sofa. But the faintness went off after a little while. We have now cold, bright, frosty weather, without snow—the best weather for me.

Having been in great trepidation about the play, I am correspondingly elated by the belief that it really *is* a success. No doubt the unnecessary explanations will have been taken out, and the flatness of the last act fetched up. At some points I could have done wonders to it, in the way of screwing it up sharply and picturesquely, if I could have rehearsed it. Your account of the first night interested me immensely, but I was afraid to open the letter until Dolby rushed in with the opened *Times.*

On Wednesday I come back here for my four church readings at Brooklyn. Each evening an enormous ferry-boat will convey me and my state carriage (not to mention half-a-dozen waggons, and any number of people, and a few score of horses) across the river, and will bring me back again. The sale of tickets there was an amazing scene. The noble army of speculators are now furnished (this is literally true, and I am quite serious), each man with a straw mattress, a little bag of bread and meat, two blankets, and a bottle of whiskey. With this outfit *they lie down in line on the pavement* the whole night before the tickets are sold, generally taking up their position at about ten. It being severely cold at Brooklyn, they made an immense bonfire in the street—a narrow street of wooden houses !—which the police turned out to extinguish. A general fight then took place, out of which the people farthest off in the line rushed bleeding when they saw a chance of displacing others near the door, and put their mattresses in those places, and then held on by the iron rails. At eight in the morning Dolby appeared with the tickets in a portmanteau. He was immediately saluted with a roar of " Halloa Dolby ! So Charley has let you have the carriage, has he, Dolby ! How is he, Dolby ! Don't drop the tickets, Dolby ! Look alive, Dolby !" etc. etc. etc., in the midst of which he proceeded to business, and concluded (as usual) by giving universal dissatisfaction.

He is now going off upon a little journey " to look over the ground and cut back again." This little journey (to Chicago) is fifteen hundred miles on end, by railway, and back again !

We have an excellent gasman, who is well up to that department. We have enlarged the large staff by another clerk, yet even now the preparation of such an immense number of new tickets constantly, and the keeping and checking of the accounts, keep them hard at it. And they get so oddly divided ! Kelly is at Philadelphia, another man at Baltimore, two others are stamping tickets at the top of this house, another is cruising over New England, and Osgood will come on duty to-morrow (when Dolby starts off) to pick me up after the reading, and take me to the hotel, and mount guard over me, and bring me back here. You see that even such wretched domesticity as Dolby and self by a fireside is broken up under these conditions.

Dolby has been twice poisoned, and Osgood once. Morgan's sharpness has discovered the cause. When the snow is deep upon the ground, and the partridges cannot get their usual food, they eat something (I don't know what, if anybody does) which does not poison *them*, but which poisons the people who eat them. The symptoms, which last some twelve hours, are violent sickness, cold perspiration, and the formation of some detestable mucus in the stomach. You may infer that partridges have been banished from our bill of fare. The appearance of our sufferers was lamentable in the extreme.

Did I tell you that the severity of the weather, and the heat of the intolerable furnaces, dry the hair and break the nails of strangers? There is not a complete nail in the whole British suite, and my hair cracks again when I brush it. (I am losing my hair with great rapidity, and what I don't lose is getting very grey.)

The *Cuba* will bring this. She has a jolly new captain —Moody, of the *Java*—and her people rushed into the reading, the other night, captain-headed, as if I were their peculiar property. Please God I shall come home in her, in my old cabin ; leaving here on the 22nd of April, and finishing my eighty-fourth reading on the previous night! It is likely enough that I shall read and go straight on board.

I think this is all my poor stock of intelligence. By-the-bye, on the last Sunday in the old year, I lost my old year's pocket-book, "which," as Mr. Pepys would add, " do trouble me mightily." Give me Katie's new address; I haven't got it.

[*To Miss Dickens.*]

PHILADELPHIA, *Monday, Jan.* 13*th,* 1868.

I write you this note, a day later than your aunt's, not because I have anything to add to the little I have told her, but because you may like to have it.

We arrived here last night towards twelve o'clock, more than an hour after our time. This is one of the immense American hotels (it is called the Continental) ; but I find myself just as quiet here as elsewhere. Everything is very good indeed, the waiter is German, and the greater part of the house servants seem to be coloured people. The town is very clean, and the day as blue and bright as a fine Italian day. But it freezes very hard. All the tickets being sold here for six nights (three visits of two nights each), the suite complain of want of excitement already, having been here ten hours ! Mr. and Mrs. Barney Williams, with a couple of servants, and a pretty little child-daughter, were in the train each night, and I talked with them a good deal. They are reported to have made an enormous fortune by acting among the Californian gold-diggers. My cold is no better, for the cars are so intoler-ably hot, that I was often obliged to go and stand upon the break outside, and then the frosty air was biting indeed. The great man of this place is one Mr. Childs, a newspaper proprietor, and he is so exactly like Mr. Esse in all conceivable respects except being an inch or so taller, that I was quite confounded when I saw him waiting for me at the station (always called depôt here) with his carriage. During the last two or three days, Dolby and I have been making up accounts, which are excellently kept by Mr. Osgood, and I find them amazing, quite, in their results.

I was very much interested in the home accounts of Christmas Day. I think I have already mentioned that we were in very low spirits on that day. I began to be unwell with my cold that morning, and a long day's travel did not mend the matter. We scarcely spoke (except when we ate our lunch), and sat dolefully staring out of window. I had a few affectionate words from Chorley, dated from my room, on Christmas morning, and will write him, probably by this mail, a brief acknowledgement. I find it necessary (so oppressed am I with this American catarrh, as they call it) to dine at three o'clock instead of four, that I may have more time to get voice, so that the days are cut short, and letter-writing is not easy.

My best love to Katie, and to Charley, and to our Charley, and to all friends. If I could only get to the point of being able to hold my head up and dispense with my pocket-handkerchief for five minutes, I should be all right.

[*To Mr. Charles Dickens.*]

WESTMINSTER HOTEL, IRVING PLACE, NEW YORK,
Wednesday, Jan. 15th, 1868.

MY DEAR CHARLEY,

Finding your letter here this afternoon on my return from Philadelphia (where I have been reading two nights), I take advantage of a spare half-hour in which to answer it at once, though it will not leave here until Saturday. I had previously heard of the play, and had *The Times.* It was a great relief and delight to me, for I had no confidence in its success; being reduced to the confines of despair by its length. If I could have rehearsed it, I should have taken the best part of an hour out of it. Fechter must be very fine, and I should greatly like to see him play the part.

I have not been very well generally, and am oppressed (and I begin to think that I probably shall be until I leave) by a true American cold, which I hope, for the comfort of human nature, may be peculiar to only one of the four quarters of the world. The work, too, is very severe. But I am going on at the same tremendous rate everywhere. The staff, too, has had to be enlarged. Dolby was at Baltimore yesterday, is at Washington to-day, and will come back in the night, and start away again on Friday. We find it absolutely necessary for him to go on ahead. We have not printed or posted a single bill here, and have just sold ninety pounds' worth of paper we had got ready for bills. In such a rush a short newspaper advertisement is all we want. " Doctor Marigold " made a great hit here, and is looked forward to at Boston with especial interest. I go to Boston for another fortnight, on end, the 24th of February. The railway journeys distress me greatly. I get out into the open air (upon the break), and it snows and blows, and the train bumps, and the steam flies at me, until I am driven in again.

I have finished here (except four farewell nights in April), and begin four nights at Brooklyn, on the opposite side of the river, to-night; and thus oscillate between Philadelphia, Baltimore, and Washington, and then cut into New England, and so work my way back to Boston for a fortnight, after which come Chicago, Cincinnati, Detroit and Cleveland, and Buffalo, and then Philadelphia, Boston, and New York farewells. I will not pass my original bound of eighty-four readings in all. My mind was made up as to that long ago. It will be quite enough. Chicago is some fifteen hundred miles from here. What with travelling, and getting ready for reading, and reading, the days are pretty fully occupied. Not the less so because I rest very indifferently at night.

The people are exceedingly kind and considerate, and desire to be most hospitable besides. But I cannot accept hospitality, and never go out, except at Boston, or I should not be fit for the labour. If Dolby holds out well to the last it will be a triumph, for he has to see everybody, drink with everybody, sell all the tickets, take all the blame, and go beforehand to all the places on the list. I shall not see him after to-night for ten days or a fortnight, and he will be perpetually on the road during the interval. When he leaves me, Osgood, a partner in Ticknor and Fields' publishing firm, mounts guard over me, and has to go into the hall from the platform door every night, and see how the public are seating themselves. It is very odd to see how hard he finds it to look a couple of thousand people in the face, on which head, by-the-bye, I notice the papers to take " Mr. Dickens's extraordinary composure " (their great phrase) rather ill, and on the whole to imply that it would be taken as a suitable compliment if I would stagger on to the platform and instantly drop, overpowered by the spectacle before me.

Dinner is announced (by Scott, with a stiff neck and a sore throat), and I must break off with love to Bessie and the incipient Wenerableses. You will be glad to hear of your distinguished parent that Philadelphia has discovered that " he is not like the descriptions we have read of him at the little red desk. He is not at all foppish in appearance. He wears a heavy moustache and a Vandyke beard, and looks like a well-to-do Philadelphian gentleman."

＊ Ever, my dear Charley, your affectionate Father.

P.S.—Your paper is remarkably good. There is not the least doubt that you can write constantly for A. Y. R. I am very pleased with it.

[*To Miss Dickens.*]

WESTMINSTER HOTEL, NEW YORK, *Friday, Jan.* 18*th*, 1868.
This will be but a very short report, as I must get out for a little exercise before dinner.

My "true American catarrh" (the people seem to have a national pride in it) sticks to me, but I am otherwise well. I began my church readings last night, and it was very odd to see the pews crammed full of people, all in a broad roar at the "Carol" and "Trial."

Best love to all. I have written Charley a few lines by this mail, and also Chorley.

[*To Miss Hogarth.*]

WESTMINSTER HOTEL, NEW YORK, *Tuesday*, *Jan.* 21*st*, 1868.

I finished my church to-night. It is Mrs. Stowe's brother's, and a most wonderful place to speak in. We had it enormously full last night ("Marigold" and "Trial"), but it scarcely required an effort. Mr. Ward Beecher (Mrs. Stowe's brother's name) being present in his pew, I sent to invite him to come round before he left; and I found him to be an unostentatious, straightforward, and agreeable fellow.

My cold sticks to me, and I can scarcely exaggerate what I sometimes undergo from sleeplessness. The day before yesterday I could get no rest until morning, and could not get up before twelve. This morning the same. I rarely take any breakfast but an egg and a cup of tea, not even toast or bread-and-butter. My dinner at three, and a little quail or some such light thing when I come home at night, is my daily fare. At the Hall I have established the custom of taking an egg beaten up in sherry before going in, and another between the parts. I think that pulls me up; at all events, I have since had no return of faintness.

As the men work very hard, and always with their hearts cheerfully in the business, I cram them into and outside of the carriage, to bring them back from Brooklyn with me. The other night, Scott (with a portmanteau across his knees and a wideawake hat low down upon his nose) told me that he had presented himself for admission in the circus (as good as Franconi's, by-the-bye), and had been refused. "The only theayter," he said in a melancholy way, "as I was ever in my life turned from the door of." Says Kelly: "There must have been some mistake, Scott, because George and me went, and we said, 'Mr. Dickens's staff,' and they passed us to the best seats in the house. Go again, Scott." "No, I thank you, Kelly," says Scott, more melancholy than before, "I'm not a-going to put myself in the position of being refused again. It's the only theayter as I was ever turned from the door of, and it shan't be done twice. But it's a beastly country!" "Scott," interposed Majesty, "don't you express your opinions about the country." "No, sir," says Scott, "I never do, please, sir, but when you are turned from the door of the only theayter you was ever turned from, sir, and when the beasts in railway cars spits tobacco over your boots, you (privately) find yourself in a beastly country."

I expect shortly to get myself snowed up on some railway or other, for it is snowing hard now, and I begin to move to-morrow. There is so much floating ice in the river that we are obliged to leave a pretty wide margin of time for getting over the ferry to read. The dinner is coming in, and I must leave off.

[*To Miss Dickens.*]

PHILADELPHIA, *Thursday, Jan.* 23rd, 1868.

When I wrote to your aunt by the last mail, I accidentally omitted to touch upon the question of helping Anne. So I will begin in this present writing with reference to her sad position. I think it will be best for you to be guided by an exact knowledge of her *wants*. Try to ascertain from herself what means she has, whether her sick husband gets what he ought to have, whether she is pinched in the articles of necessary clothing, bedding, or the like of that ; add to this intelligence your own observation of the state of things about her, and supply what she most wants, and help her where you find the greatest need. The question, in the case of so old and faithful a servant, is not one of so much or so little money on my side, but how *most efficiently* to ease her mind and help *her*. To do this at once kindly and sensibly is the only consideration by which you have to be guided. Take *carte blanche* from me for all the rest.

My Washington week is the first week in February, beginning on Monday, 3rd. The tickets are sold, and the President is coming, and the chief members of the Cabinet, and the leaders of parties, and so forth, are coming ; and, as the Holly Tree Boots says : " That's where it is, don't you see ! "

In my Washington doubts I recalled Dolby for conference, and he joined me yesterday afternoon, and we have been in great discussion ever since on the possibility of giving up the Far West, and avoiding such immense distances and fatigues as would be involved in travelling to Chicago and Cincinnati. We have sketched another tour for the last half of March, which would be infinitely easier for me, though on the other hand less profitable, the places and the halls being smaller. The worst of it is, that every body one advises with has a monomania respecting Chicago. "Good heaven, sir," the great Philadelphian authority said to me this morning, "if you don't read in Chicago, the people will go into fits." In reference to fatigue, I answered : "Well, I would rather they went into fits than I did." But he didn't seem to see it at all. —— alone constantly writes me : "Don't go to the West ; you can get what you want so much more easily." How we shall finally decide, I don't yet know. My Brooklyn church has been an immense success, and I found its minister was a bachelor, a clever, unparsonic, and straightforward man, and a man with a good knowledge of art into the bargain.

We are not a bit too soon here, for the whole country is beginning to be stirred and shaken by the presidential election, and trade is exceedingly depressed, and will be more so. Fanny Kemble lives near this place, but had gone away a day before my first visit here. *She* is going to read in February or March. Du Chaillu has been lecturing out West about the gorilla, and has been to see me ; I saw the Cunard steamer *Persia* out in the stream, yesterday, beautifully smart, her flags flying, all her steam up, and she only waiting for her mails to slip away. She gave me a horrible touch of home-sickness.

When the 1st of March arrives, and I can say "next month," I shall begin to grow brighter. A fortnight's reading in Boston, too (last week of February and first week of March), will help me on gaily, I hope (the work so far off tells). It is impossible for the people to be more affectionately attached to a third, I really believe, than Fields and his wife are to me ; and they are a landmark in the prospect.

Dolby sends kindest regards, and wishes it to be known that he has not been bullied lately. We do *not* go West at all, but take the easier plan.

[*To Miss Hogarth.*]

BALTIMORE, *Wednesday, Jan. 29th,* 1868.

As I have an hour to spare, before starting to Philadelphia, I begin my letter this morning. It has been snowing hard for four-and-twenty hours, though this place is as far south as Valentia in Spain ; and Dolby, being on his way to New York, has a good chance of being snowed up somewhere.

They are a bright responsive people here, and very pleasant to read to. I have rarely seen so many fine faces in an audience. I read here in a charming little opera-house built by a society of Germans, quite a delightful place for the purpose. I stand on the stage, with a drop curtain down, and my screen before it. The whole scene is very pretty and complete, and the audience have a " ring " in them that sounds in the ear. I go from here to Philadelphia to read to-morrow night and Friday, come through here again on Saturday on my way to Washington, come back here on Saturday week for two finishing nights, then go to Philadelphia for two farewells, and so turn my back on the southern part of the country. Distances and travelling have obliged us to reduce the list of readings by two, leaving eighty-two in all. Of course we afterwards discovered that we had finally settled the list on a Friday ! I shall be half-way through it at Washington, of course, on a Friday also, and my birthday !

Dolby and Osgood, who do the most ridiculous things to keep me in spirits (I am often very heavy, and rarely sleep much), have decided to have a walking-match at Boston, on Saturday, February 29th. Beginning this design in joke, they have become tremendously in earnest, and Dolby has actually sent home (much to his opponent's terror) for a pair of seamless socks to walk in. Our men are hugely excited on the subject, and continually make bets on " the men." Fields and I are to walk out six miles, and " the men " are to turn and walk round us. Neither of them has the least idea what twelve miles at a pace is. Being requested by both to give them " a breather " yesterday, I gave them a stiff one of five miles over a bad road in the snow, half the distance uphill. I took them at a pace of four miles and a half an hour, and you never beheld such objects as they were when we got back ; both smoking like factories, and both obliged to change everything before they could come to dinner. They have the absurdest ideas of what are tests of walking-power, and continually get up in the maddest manner and see *how high they can kick* the wall! The wainscot here, in one place, is scored all over with their pencil-marks. To see them doing this—Dolby, a big man, and Osgood, a very little one, is ridiculous beyond description.

PHILADELPHIA, *Same Night.*

We came on here through a snowstorm all the way, but up to time. Fanny Kemble (who begins to read shortly) is coming to " Marigold " and " Trial " to-morrow night. I have written her a note, telling her that if it will at all assist *her* movements to know *mine*, my list is at her service. Probably I shall see her to-morrow. Tell Mamie (to whom I will write next), with my love, that I found her letter of the 10th of this month awaiting me here. The *Siberia* that brought it is a new Cunarder, and made an unusually slow passage out. Probably because it would be dangerous to work new machinery too fast on the Atlantic.

Thursday, 30*th.*

My cold still sticks to me. The heat of the railway cars and their unventilated condition invariably brings it back when I think it going. This morning my head is as stuffed and heavy as ever! A superb sledge and four horses have been offered me for a ride, but I am afraid to take it, lest I should make the " true American catarrh " worse, and should get hoarse. So I am going to give Osgood another " breather " on foot instead.

The communication with New York is not interrupted, so we consider the zealous Dolby all right. You may imagine what his work is, when you hear that he goes three times to every place we visit. Firstly, to look at the hall, arrange the numberings, and make five hundred acquaintances, whom he immediately calls by their christian-names ; secondly, to sell the tickets—a very nice business, requiring great tact and temper ; thirdly, with me. He will probably turn up at Washington next Sunday, but only for a little while ; for as soon as I am on the platform on Monday night, he will start away again, probably to be seen no more until we pass through New York in the middle of February.

[*To Mr. Samuel Cartwright.*]

BALTIMORE, *Wednesday, Jan. 29th*, 1868.

MY DEAR CARTWRIGHT,

As I promised to report myself to you from this side of the Atlantic, and as I have some leisure this morning, I am going to lighten my conscience by keeping my word.

I am going on at a great pace and with immense success. Next week, at Washington, I shall, please God, have got through half my readings. The remaining half are all arranged, and they will carry me into the third week of April. It is very hard work, but it is brilliantly paid. The changes that I find in the country generally (this place is the least changed of any I have yet seen) exceed my utmost expectations. I had been in New York a couple of days before I began to recognise it at all ; and the handsomest part of Boston was a black swamp when I saw it five-and-twenty years ago. Considerable advances, too, have been made socially. Strange to say, the railways and railway arrangements (both exceedingly defective) seem to have stood still while all other things have been moving.

One of the most comical spectacles I have ever seen in my life was " church," with a heavy sea on, in the saloon of the Cunard steamer coming out. The officiating minister, an extremely modest young man, was brought in between two big stewards, exactly as if he were coming up to the scratch in a prize-fight. The ship was rolling and pitching so, that the two big stewards had to stop and watch their opportunity of making a dart at the reading-desk with their reverend charge, during which pause he held on, now by one steward and now by the other, with the feeblest expression of countenance and no legs whatever. At length they made a dart at the wrong moment, and one steward was immediately beheld alone in the extreme perspective, while the other and the reverend gentleman *held on by the mast* in the middle of the saloon— which the latter embraced with both arms, as if it were his wife. All this time the congregation was breaking up into sects and sliding away ; every sect (as in nature) pounding the other sect. And when at last the reverend gentleman had been tumbled into his place, the desk (a loose one, put upon the dining-table) deserted from the church bodily, and went over to the purser. The scene was so extraordinarily ridiculous, and was made so much more so by the exemplary gravity of all concerned in it, that I was obliged to leave before the service began.

This is one of the places where Butler carried it with so high a hand in the war, and where the ladies used to spit when they passed a Northern soldier. It still wears, I fancy, a look of sullen remembrance. (The ladies are remarkably handsome, with an Eastern look upon them, dress with a strong sense of colour, and make a brilliant audience.) The ghost of slavery haunts the houses ; and the old, untidy, incapable, lounging, shambling black serves you as a free man. Free of course he ought to be ; but the stupendous absurdity of making him a voter glares out of every roll of his eye, stretch of his mouth, and bump of his head. I have a strong impression that the race must fade out of the States very fast. It never can hold its own against a striving, restless, shifty people. In the penitentiary here, the other day, in a room full of all blacks (too dull to be taught any of the work in hand), was one young brooding fellow, very like a black rhinoceros. He sat glowering at life, as if it were just endurable at dinner time, until four of his fellows began to sing, most unmelodiously, a part song. He then set up a dismal howl, and pounded his face on a form. I took him to have been rendered quite desperate by having learnt anything. I send my kind regard to Mrs. Cartwright, and sincerely hope that she and you have no new family distresses or anxieties. My standing address is the Westminster Hotel, Irving Place, New York City. And I am always, my dear Cartwright,

Cordially yours.

[*To Miss Dickens.*]

PHILADELPHIA, *Friday, Jan.* 31*st*, 1868.

Since writing to your aunt I have received yours of the 7th, and am truly glad to have the last news of you confirmed by yourself.

From a letter Wilkie has written to me, it seems there can be no doubt that the " No Thoroughfare " drama is a real, genuine, and great success. It is drawing immensely, and seems to " go " with great effect and applause.

" Doctor Marigold " here last night (for the first time) was an immense success, and all Philadelphia is going to rush at once for tickets for the two Philadelphia farewells the week after next. The tickets are to be sold to-morrow, and great excitement is anticipated in the streets. Dolby not being here, a clerk will sell, and will probably wish himself dead before he has done with it.

It appears to me that Chorley * writes to you on the legacy question because he wishes you to understand that there is no danger of his changing his mind, and at the bottom I descry an honest desire to pledge himself as

---

* The Mr. H. F. Chorley so often mentioned was the well-known musical critic, and a dear and intimate friend of Charles Dickens and his family. We have no letters to him, Mr. Chorley having destroyed all his correspondence before his death.

strongly as possible. You may receive it in that better spirit, or I am much mistaken. Tell your aunt, with my best love, that I wrote to Chauncey weeks ago, in answer to a letter from him. I am now going out in a sleigh (and four) with unconceivable dignity and grandeur; mentioning which reminds me that I am informed by trusty scouts that —— intends to waylay me at Washington, and may even descend upon me in the train to-morrow.

Best love to Katie, the two Charleys, and all.

[*To Miss Dickens.*]

WASHINGTON, *Tuesday, Feb. 4th,* 1868.

I began here last night with great success. The hall being small, the prices were raised to three dollars each ticket. The audience was a superior one, composed of the foremost public men and their families. At the end of the " Carol " they gave a great break out, and applauded, I really believe, for five minutes. You would suppose them to be Manchester shillings instead of Washington half-sovereigns. Immense enthusiasm.

A devoted adherent in this place (an Englishman) had represented to Dolby that if I were taken to an hotel here it would be impossible to secure me a minute's rest, and he undertook to get one Wheleker, a German, who keeps a little Vérey's, to furnish his private dining-rooms for the illustrious traveller's reception. Accordingly here we are, on the first and second floor of a small house, with no one else in it but our people, a French waiter, and a very good

French cuisine. Perfectly private, in the city of all the world (I should say) where the hotels are intolerable, and privacy the least possible, and quite comfortable. "Wheleker's Restaurant" is our rather undignified address for the present week.

I dined (against my rules) with Charles Summer on Sunday, he having been an old friend of mine. Mr. Secretary Staunton (War Minister) was there. He is a man of a very remarkable memory, and famous for his acquaintance with the minutest details of my books. Give him any passage anywhere, and he will instantly cap it and go on with the context. He was commander-in-chief of all the Northern forces concentrated here, and never went to sleep at night without first reading something from my books, which were always with him. I put him through a pretty severe examination, but he was better up than I was.

The gas was very defective indeed last night, and I began with a small speech, to the effect that I must trust to the brightness of their faces for the illumination of mine ; this was taken greatly. In the "Carol," a most ridiculous incident occurred all of a sudden. I saw a dog look out from among the seats into the centre aisle, and look very intently at me. The general attention being fixed on me, I don't think anybody saw the dog ; but I felt so sure of his turning up again and barking, that I kept my eye wandering about in search of him. He was a very comic dog, and it was well for me that I was reading a very comic part of the book. But when he bounced out into the centre aisle again, in an entirely new place (still looking intently at me) and tried the effect of a bark upon my proceedings, I was seized with such a paroxysm of laughter, that it communicated itself to the audience, and we roared at one another loud and long.

The President has sent to me twice, and I am going to see him to-morrow. He has a whole row for his family every night. Dolby rejoined his chief yesterday morning, and will probably remain in the august presence until Sunday night. He and Osgood, "training for the match," are ludicrous beyond belief. I saw them just now coming up a street, each trying to pass the other, and immediately fled. Since I have been writing this, they have burst in at the door and sat down on the floor to blow. Dolby is now writing at a neighbouring table, with his bald head smoking as if he were on fire. Kelly (his great adherent) asked me, when he was last away, whether it was quite fair that I should take Mr. Osgood out for "breathers" when Mr. Dolby had no such advantage. I begin to expect that half Boston will turn out on the 29th to see the match. In which case it will be unspeakably droll.

[*To Miss Hogarth.*]

WASHINGTON, *my Birthday*, 1868.
(*And my cold worse than ever.*)

This will be but a short letter, as I have been to see the President this morning, and have little time before the post goes. He had sent a gentleman to me, most courteously begging me to make my own appointment, and I did so.

A man of very remarkable appearance indeed, of tremendous firmness of purpose. Not to be turned or trifled with.

As I mention my cold's being so bad, I will add that I have never had anything the matter with me since I came here *but* the cold. It is now in my throat, and slightly on my chest. It occasions me great discomfort, and you would suppose, seeing me in the morning, that I could not possibly read at night. But I have always come up to the scratch, have not yet missed one night, and have gradually got used to that. I had got much the better of it ; but the dressing-room at the hall here is singularly cold and draughty, and so I have slid back again.

The papers here having written about this being my birthday, the most exquisite flowers came pouring in at breakfast time from all sorts of people. The room is covered with them, made up into beautiful bouquets, and arranged in all manner of green baskets. Probably I shall find plenty more at the hall to-night. This is considered the dullest and most apathetic place in America. *My* audiences have been superb.

I mentioned the dog on the first night here. Next night I thought I heard (in "Copperfield") a suddenly suppressed bark. It happened in this wise : Osgood, standing just within the door, felt his leg touched, and looking down beheld the dog staring intently at me, and evidently just about to bark. In a transport of presence of mind and fury, he instantly caught him up in both hands and threw him over his own head out into the entry, where the check-takers received him like a game at ball. Last night he came again *with another dog ;* but our people were so sharply on the look-out for him that he didn't get in. He had evidently promised to pass the other dog free.

[*To Miss Dickens.*]

BALTIMORE, U.S., *Tuesday, Feb.* 11*th*, 1868.

The weather has been desperately severe, and my cold quite as bad as ever. I couldn't help laughing at myself on my birthday at Washington. It was observed as much as though I were a little boy. Flowers and garlands (of the most exquisite kind) bloomed all over the room ; letters radiant with good wishes poured in ; a shirt pin, a handsome silver travelling bottle, a set of gold shirt studs, and a set of gold sleeve links were on the dinner-table. After "Boots," at night, the whole audience rose and remained (Secretaries of State, President's family, Judges of Supreme Court, and so forth) standing and cheering until I went back to the table and made them a little speech. On the same august day of the year I was received by the President, a man with a very remarkable and determined face. Each of us looked at each other very hard, and each of us managed the interview (I think) to the satisfaction of the other. In the outer room was sitting a certain sunburnt General Blair, with many evidences of the war upon him. He got up to shake hands with me, and then I found he had been out in the prairie with me, five-and-twenty years ago. That afternoon my " catarrh " was in such a state that Charles Sumner, coming in at five o'clock and finding me covered with mustard poultice, and apparently voiceless, turned to Dolby and said : " Surely, Mr. Dolby, it is impossible that he can read to-night." Says Dolby : " Sir, I have told the dear Chief so four times to-day, and I have been very anxious. But you have no idea how he will change when he gets to the little table." After five minutes of the little table, I was not (for the time) even hoarse. The frequent experience of this return of force when it is wanted saves me a vast amount of anxiety.

I wish you would get from Homan and report to me, as near as he can make, an approximate estimate is the right term in the trade, I believe, of the following work :

1. To re-cover, with red leather, all the dining-room chairs.

2. To ditto, with green leather, all the library chairs and the couch.

3. To provide and lay down new *Brussels* carpets in the front spare and the two top spares. Quality of carpet, quality of yours and mine.

I have some doubts about the state of the hall floor-cloth, and also the floor-cloth in the dining-room. Will you and your aunt carefully examine both (calling in Homan too, if necessary), *and report to me ?*

It would seem that " No Thoroughfare " has really developed as a drama into an amazing success. I begin to think that I shall see it. Dolby is away this morning, to conquer or die in a terrific struggle with the Mayor of Newhaven (where I am to read next week), who has assailed him on a charge of false play in selling tickets.

Osgood, my other keeper, stands at the table to take me out, and have a " breather " for the walking-match, so I must leave off.

Think of my dreaming of Mrs. Bouncer each night ! ! !

[*To Mr. Henry Fielding Dickens.*]

BALTIMORE, U. S., *Tuesday, Feb. 11th,* 1868.

MY DEAR HARRY,

I should have written to you before now, but for constant and arduous occupation.

In reference to the cricket club's not being what it might be, I agree with you in the main. There are some things to be considered, however, which you have hardly taken into account. The first thing to be avoided is, the slightest appearance of patronage (one of the curses of England). The second thing to be avoided is, the deprival of the men of their just right to manage their own affairs. I would rather have no club at all, than have either of these great mistakes made. The way out of them is this : Call the men together, and explain to them that the club might be larger, richer, and better. Say that you think that more of the neighbouring gentlemen could be got to be playing members. That you submit to them that it would be better to have a captain who could correspond with them, and talk to them, and in some sort manage them ; and that, being perfectly acquainted with the game, and having long played it at a great public school, you propose yourself as captain, for the foregoing reasons. That you propose to them to make the subscription of the gentlemen members at least double that of the working men, for no other reason than that the gentlemen can afford it better ; but that both classes of members shall have exactly the same right of voting equally in all that concerns the club. Say that you have consulted me upon the matter, and that I am of these opinions, and am ready to become chairman of the club, and to preside at their meetings, and to overlook its business affairs, and to give it five pounds a year, payable at the commencement of each season. Then, having brought them to this point, draw up the club's rules and regulations, amending them where they want amendment.

Discreetly done, I see no difficulty in this. But it can only be honourably and hopefully done by having the men together. And I would not have them at The Falstaff, but in the hall or dining-room—the servants' hall, an excellent place. Whatever you do, let the men ratify ; and let them feel their little importance, and at once perceive how much better the business begins to be done.

I am very glad to hear of the success of your reading, and still more glad that you went at it in downright earnest. I should never have made my success in life if I had been shy of taking pains, or if I had not bestowed upon the least thing I have ever undertaken exactly the same attention and care that I have bestowed upon the greatest. Do everything at your best. It was but this last year that I set to and learned every word of my readings ; and from ten years ago to last night, I have never read to an audience but I have watched for an opportunity of striking out

something better somewhere.   Look at such of my manu-
scripts as are in the library at Gad's, and think of the
patient hours devoted year after year to single lines.

*   *   *   *   *   *

The weather is very severe here, and the work is very
hard. Dolby, having been violently pitched into by the
Mayor of Newhaven (a town at which I am to read next
week), has gone bodily this morning with defiant written
instructions from me to inform the said mayor that, if he
fail to make out his case, he (Dolby) is to return all the
money taken, and to tell him that I will not set foot in
his jurisdiction; whereupon the Newhaven people will
probably fall upon the mayor in his turn, and lead him a
pleasant life.

Ever, my dear Harry, your affectionate Father.

[*To Miss Hogarth.*]

PHILADELPHIA, *Thursday, Feb. 13th*, 1868.

We have got into an immense difficulty with the people
of Newhaven. I have a strong suspicion that one of our
men (who sold there) has been speculating all this while,
and that he must have put front seats in his pockets, and
sold back ones. He denies what the mayor charges, but
the mayor holds on grimly. Dolby set off from Baltimore
as soon as we found out what was amiss, to examine and
report; but some new feature of difficulty must have come
out, for this morning he telegraphs from New York (where
he had to sleep last night on his way to Newhaven), that

he is coming back for further consultation with the Chief. It will certainly hurt us, and will of course be distorted by the papers into all manner of shapes. My suspicion *may not* be correct, but I have an instinctive belief that it is. We shall probably have the old New York row (and loss) over again, unless I can catch this mayor tripping in an assertion.

In this very place, we are half distressed by the speculators. They have been holding out for such high prices, that the public have held out too ; and now (frightened at what they have done) the speculators are trying to sell their worst seats at half the cost price, so that we are in the ridiculous situation of having sold the room out, and yet not knowing what empty seats there may be. *We* could sell at our box-office to any extent ; but *we* can't buy back of the speculators, because we informed the public that all the tickets were gone. And if we bought *under* our own price and *sold* at our own price, we should at once be in treaty with the speculators, and should be making money by it ! Dolby, the much bullied, will come back here presently, half bereft of his senses ; and I should be half bereft of mine, if the situation were not comically disagreeable.

Nothing will induce the people to believe in the farewells. At Baltimore on Tuesday night (a very brilliant night indeed), they asked as they came out : " When will Mr. Dickens read here again ? " " Never." " Nonsense ! Not come back, after such houses as these ? Come. Say when he'll read again." Just the same here. We could as soon persuade them that I am the President, as that I am going to read here, for the last time, to-morrow night.

There is a child of the Barney Williams's in this house—a little girl—to whom I presented a black doll when I was here last. I have seen her eye at the keyhole since I began writing this, and I think she and the doll are outside still. "When you sent it up to me by the coloured boy," she said after receiving it (coloured boy is the term for black waiter), "I gave such a cream that ma came running in and creamed too, 'cos she fort I'd hurt myself. But I creamed a cream of joy." *She* had a friend to play with her that day, and brought the friend with her, to my infinite confusion. A friend all stockings, and much too tall, who sat on the sofa very far back, with her stockings sticking stiffly out in front of her, and glared at me and never spake word. Dolby found us confronted in a sort of fascination, like serpent and bird.

[*To Miss Hogarth.*]

NEW YORK, *Monday, Feb.* 17*th,* 1868.

I got your letter of the 3rd of February here his morning. As I am off at seven to-morrow morning, I answer it at once, though indeed I have nothing to say.

"True American" still sticking to me. But I am always ready for my work, and therefore don't much mind. Dolby and the Mayor of Newhaven alternately embrace and exchange mortal defiances. In writing out some advertisements towards midnight last night, he made a very good mistake. "The reading will be comprised within two *minutes*, and the audience are earnestly entreated to be seated ten *hours* before its commencement."

The weather has been finer lately, but the streets are in a horrible condition, through half-melted snow, and it is now snowing again. The walking-match (next Saturday week) is already in the Boston papers! I suppose half Boston will turn out on the occasion. As a sure way of not being conspicuous, "the men" are going to walk in flannel! They are in a mingled state of comicality and gravity about it that is highly ridiculous. Yesterday being a bright cool day, I took Dolby for a "buster" of eight miles. As everybody here knows me, the spectacle of our splitting up the fashionable avenue (the only way out of town) excited the greatest amazement. No doubt *that* will be in the papers to-morrow. I give a gorgeous banquet to eighteen (ladies and gentlemen) after the match. Mr. and Mrs. Field, Do. Tichnor, Longfellow and his daughter, Lowell, Holmes and his wife, etc. etc. Sporting speeches to be made, and the stakes (four hats) to be handed over to the winner.

My ship will not be the *Cuba* after all. She is to go into dock, and the *Russia* (a larger ship, and the latest built for the Cunard line) is to take her place.

Very glad to hear of Plorn's success. Best love to Mamie.

[*To M. Charles Fechter.*]

WASHINGTON, *February* 24*th*, 1868.

MY DEAR FECHTER,

Your letter reached me here yesterday. I have sent you a telegram (addressed to the theatre) this morning, and I write this by the earliest return mail.

My dear fellow, consider yourself my representatative. Whatever you do, or desire to do, about the play, I fully authorise beforehand. Tell Webster, with my regard, that I think his proposal honest and fair; that I think it, in a word, like himself; and that I have perfect confidence in his good faith and liberality.

As to making money of the play in the United States here, Boucicault has filled Wilkie's head with golden dreams that have *nothing* in them. He makes no account of the fact that, wherever I go, the theatres (with my name in big letters) instantly begin playing versions of my books, and that the moment the Christmas number came over here they pirated it and played " No Thoroughfare." Now, I have enquired into the law, and am extremely doubtful whether I *could* have prevented this. Why should they pay for the piece as you act it, when they have no actors, and when all they want is my name, and they can get that for nothing ?

Wilkie has uniformly written of you enthusiastically. In a letter I had from him, dated the 10th of January, he described your conception and execution of the part in the most glowing terms. " Here Fechter is magnificent."

" Here his superb playing brings the house down." " I should call even his exit in the last act one of the subtlest and finest things he does in the piece." " You can hardly imagine what he gets out of the part, or what he makes of his passionate love for Marguerite." These expressions, and many others like them, crowded his letter.

I never did so want to see a character played on the stage as I want to see you play Obenreizer. As the play was going when I last heard of it, I have some hopes that I MAY see it yet. Please God, your Adelphi dressing-room will be irradiated with the noble presence of " Never Wrong " (if you are acting), about the evening of Monday, the 4th of May.

I am doing enormous business. It is a wearying life, away from all I love, but I hope that the time will soon begin to spin away. Among the many changes that I find here is the comfortable change that the people are in general extremely considerate, and very observant of my privacy. Even in this place, I am really almost as much my own master as if I were in an English country town. Generally, they are very good audiences indeed. They do not (I think) perceive touches of art to *be* art ; but they are responsive to the broad results of such touches. "Doctor Marigold " is a great favourite, and they laugh so unrestrainedly at " The Trial " from " Pickwick " (which you never heard), that it has grown about half as long again as it used to be.

If I could send you a " brandy cock-tail " by post I would. It is a highly meritorious dram, which I hope to present to you at Gad's. My New York landlord made me a " Rocky Mountain sneezer," which appeared to me to be compounded of all the spirits ever heard of in the world, with bitters, lemons, sugar, and snow. You can only make a true " sneezer " when the snow is lying on the ground.

There, my dear boy, my paper is out, and I am going to read "Copperfield." Count always on my fidelity and true attachment, and look out, as I have already said, for a distinguished visitor about Monday, the 4th of May.

Ever, my dear Fechter,

Your cordial and affectionate Friend.

[*To Miss Dickens.*]

BOSTON, *Tuesday, Feb. 25th,* 1868.

It is so very difficult to know, by any exercise of common sense, what turn or height the political excitement may take next, and it may so easily, and so soon, swallow up all other things, that I think I shall suppress my next week's readings here (by good fortune not yet announced) and watch the course of events. Dolby's sudden desponding under these circumstances is so acute, that it is actually swelling his head as I glance at him in the glass while writing.

The catarrh is no better and no worse. The weather is intensely cold. The walking-match (of which I will send particulars) is to come off on Sunday. Mrs. Fields is more delightful than ever, and Fields more hospitable. **My**

room is always radiant with brilliant flowers of their sending. I don't know whether I told you that the walking-
match is to celebrate the extinction of February, and the
coming of the day when I can say "next month."

[*To Miss Hogarth.*]

BOSTON, *Thursday, Feb. 27th*, 1868.

This morning at breakfast I received yours of the 11th
from Palace Gate House. I have very little news to give
you in return for your budget. The walking-match is to
come off on Saturday, and Fields and I went over the
ground yesterday to measure the miles. We went at a
tremendous pace. The condition of the ground is something indescribable, from half-melted snow, running water,
and sheets and blocks of ice. The two performers have
not the faintest notion of the weight of the task they have
undertaken. I give a dinner afterwards, and have just
now been settling the bill of fare and selecting the wines.

In the first excitement of the presidential impeachment,
our houses instantly went down. After carefully considering the subject, I decided to take advantage of the
fact that next week's four readings here have not yet been
announced, and to abolish them altogether. Nothing in
this country lasts long, and I think the public may be
heartily tired of the President's name by the 9th of March,
when I read at a considerable distance from here. So
behold me with a whole week's holiday in view! The
Boston audiences have come to regard the readings and

the reader as their peculiar property ; and you would be at once amused and pleased if you could see the curious way in which they seem to plume themselves on both. They have taken to applauding too whenever they laugh or cry, and the result is very inspiriting. I shall remain here until Saturday, the 7th, but shall not read here, after to-morrow night, until the 1st of April, when I begin my Boston farewells, six in number.

Friday, 28*th.*

It has been snowing all night, and the city is in a miserable condition. We had a fine house last night for "Carol" and "Trial," and such an enthusiastic one that they persisted in a call after the "Carol," and, while I was out, covered the little table with flowers. The "True American" has taken a fresh start, as if it were quite a novelty, and is on the whole rather worse than ever to-day. The Cunard packet, the *Australasian* (a poor ship), is some days overdue, and Dolby is anxiously looking out for her.   There is a lull in the excitement about the President, but the articles of impeachment are to be produced this afternoon, and then it may set in again.   Osgood came into camp last night from selling in remote places, and reports that at Rochester and Buffalo (both places near the frontier), Canada people bought tickets, who had struggled across the frozen river and clambered over all sorts of obstructions to get them.   Some of those halls turn out to be smaller than represented, but I have no doubt, to use an American expression, that we shall "get along."

To-morrow fortnight we purpose being at the Falls of Niagara, and then we shall turn back and really begin to wind up. I have got to know the "Carol" so well that I can't remember it, and occasionally go dodging about in the wildest manner to pick up lost pieces. They took it so tremendously last night that I was stopped every five minutes. One poor young girl in mourning burst into a passion of grief about Tiny Tim, and was taken out. This is all my news.

Each of the pedestrians is endeavouring to persuade the other to take something unwholesome before starting.

[*To Miss Dickens.*]

BOSTON, *Monday, March 2nd*, 1868.

A heavy gale of wind and a snowstorm oblige me to write suddenly for the Cunard steamer a day earlier than usual. The railroad between this and New York will probably be stopped somewhere. After all the hard weather we have had, this is the worst day we have seen.

The walking-match came off on Saturday, over tremendously difficult ground, against a biting wind, and through deep snow-wreaths. It was so cold, too, that our hair, beards, eyelashes, eyebrows, were frozen hard, and hung with icicles. The course was thirteen miles. They were close together at the turning-point, when Osgood went ahead at a splitting pace and with extraordinary endurance, and won by half a mile. Dolby did very well indeed, and begs that he may not be despised. In the evening I gave a very splendid dinner. Eighteen covers, most magnificent flowers, such table decoration as was never seen in these parts. The whole thing was a great success, and everybody was delighted.

I am holiday-making until Friday, when we start on the round of travel that is to bring us back here for the 1st of April. My holiday-making is simply thorough resting, except on Wednesday, when I dine with Longfellow. There is still great political excitement, but I hope it may not hurt us very much. My fear is that it may damage the farewell. Dolby is not of my mind as to this, and I hope he may be right. We are not quite determined whether Mrs. Fields did not desert our colours, by coming on the ground in a carriage, and having *bread soaked in brandy* put into the winning man's mouth as he steamed along. She pleaded that she would have done as much for Dolby, if *he* had been ahead, so we are inclined to forgive her. As she had done so much for me in the way of flowers, I thought I would show her a sight in that line at the dinner. You never saw anything like it. Two immense crowns; the base, of the choicest exotics; and the loops, oval masses of violets. In the centre of the table an immense basket, overflowing with enormous bell-mouthed lilies; all round the table a bright green border of wreathed creeper, with clustering roses at intervals; a rose for every button-hole, and a bouquet for every lady. They made an exhibition of the table before dinner to numbers of people.

P. H. has just come in with a newspaper, containing a

reference (in good taste !) to the walking-match. He posts it to you by this post.

It is telegraphed that the storm prevails over an immense extent of country, and is just the same at Chicago as here. I hope it may prove a wind-up. We are getting sick of the sound of sleigh-bells even.

Your account of Anne has greatly interested me.

[*To M. Charles Fechter.*]

SYRACUSE, U.S. OF AMERICA,
Sunday Night, March 8th, 1868.

MY DEAR FECHTER,

I am here in a most wonderful out-of-the-world place, which looks as if it had begun to be built yesterday, and were going to be imperfectly knocked together with a nail or two the day after to-morrow. I am in the worst inn that ever was seen, and outside is a thaw that places the whole country under water. I have looked out of window for the people, and I can't find any people. I have tried all the wines in the house, and there are only two wines, for which you pay six shillings a bottle, or fifteen, according as you feel disposed to change the name of the thing you ask for. (The article never changes.) The bill of fare is "in French," and the principal article (the carte is printed) is "Paettie de shay." I asked the Irish waiter what this dish was, and he said : "It was the name the steward giv' to oyster patties—the Frinch name." These are the drinks you are to wash it down with : "Mooseux," "Abasinthe," "Curacco," "Marschine," "Annise," and "Margeaux"!

I am growing very home-sick, and very anxious for the 22nd of April; on which day, please God, I embark for home. I am beginning to be tired, and have been depressed all the time (except when reading), and have lost my appetite. I cannot tell you—but you know, and therefore why should I?—how overjoyed I shall be to see you again, my dear boy, and how sorely I miss a dear friend, and how sorely I miss all art, in these parts. No disparagement to the country, which has a great future in reserve, or to its people, who are very kind to me.

I mean to take my leave of readings in the autumn and winter, in a final series in England with Chappell. This will come into the way of literary work for a time, for, after I have rested—don't laugh—it is a grim reality—I shall have to turn my mind to—ha! ha! ha!—to—ha! ha! ha! (more sepulchrally than before)—the—the CHRISTMAS NUMBER!!! I feel as if I had murdered a Christmas number years ago (perhaps I did!) and its ghost perpetually haunted me. Nevertheless in some blessed rest at Gad's, we will talk over stage matters, and all matters, in an even way, and see what we can make of them, please God. Be sure that I shall not be in London one evening, after disembarking, without coming round to the theatre to embrace you, my dear fellow.

I have had an American cold (the worst in the world) since Christmas Day. I read four times a week, with the

most tremendous energy I can bring to bear upon it. I
travel about pretty heavily. I am very resolute about
calling on people, or receiving people, or dining out, and
so save myself a great deal. I read in all sorts of places—
churches, theatres, concert rooms, lecture halls. Every
night I read I am described (mostly by people who have
not the faintest notion of observing) from the sole of my
boot to where the topmost hair of my head ought to be,
but is not. Sometimes I am described as being "evidently
nervous ; " sometimes it is rather taken ill that "Mr. Dickens is so extraordinarily composed." My eyes are blue,
red, grey, white, green, brown, black, hazel, violet, and
rainbow-coloured. I am like "a well-to-do American
gentleman," and the Emperor of the French, with an occasional touch of the Emperor of China, and a deteriora-
tion from the attributes of our famous townsman, Rufus
W. B. D. Dodge Grumsher Pickville. I say all sorts of
things that I never said, go to all sorts of places that I
never saw or heard of, and have done all manner of things
(in some previous state of existence I suppose) that have
quite escaped my memory. You ask your friend to describe what he is about. This is what he is about, every
day and hour of his American life.

I hope to be back with you before you write to me !

Ever, my dear Fechter,

Your most affectionate and hearty Friend.

P.S.—Don't let Madame Fechter, or Marie, or Paul
forget me !

[*To Miss Hogarth.*]

SYRACUSE, *Sunday, March 8th,* 1868.

As we shall probably be busy all day to-morrow, I write this to-day, though it will not leave New York until Wednesday. This is a very grim place in a heavy thaw, and a most depressing one. The hotel also is surprisingly bad, quite a triumph in that way. We stood out for an hour in the melting snow, and came in again, having to change completely. Then we sat down by the stove (no fireplace), and there we are now. We were so afraid to go to bed last night, the rooms were so close and sour, that we played whist, double dummy, till we couldn't bear each other any longer. We had an old buffalo for supper, and an old pig for breakfast, and we are going to have I don't know what for dinner at six. In the public rooms downstairs, a number of men (speechless) are sitting in rocking-chairs, with their feet against the window-frames, staring out at window and spitting dolefully at intervals. Scott is in tears, and George the gasman is suborning people to go and clean the hall, which is a marvel of dirt. And yet we have taken considerably over three hundred pounds for to-morrow night !

We were at Albany the night before last and yesterday morning ; a very pretty town, where I am to read on the 18th and 19th. This day week we hope to wash out this establishment with the Falls of Niagara. And there is my news, except that your *last letters* to me in America must be posted by the Cunard steamer, which will sail from

Liverpool on *Saturday, the 4th of April.* These I shall be safe to get before embarking.

I send a note to Katie (addressed to Mamie) by this mail. I wrote to Harry some weeks ago, stating to him on what principles he must act in remodelling the cricket club, if he would secure success.

[*To Miss Hogarth.*]

Monday Morning, 9th.

Nothing new. Weather cloudy, and town more dismal than yesterday. It froze again last night, and thaws again this morning. Somebody sent me an Australian newspaper this morning—some citizen of Syracuse I mean—because of a paragraph in it describing the taking of two free-booters, at which taking Alfred was present. Though I do not make out that he had anything in the world to do with it, except having his name pressed into the service of the newspaper.

BUFFALO, *Thursday, March 12th,* 1868.

I hope this may be in time for next Saturday's mail; but this is a long way from New York, and rivers are swollen with melted snow, and travelling is unusually slow.

Just now (two o'clock in the afternoon) I received your sad news of the death of poor dear Chauncey.* It naturally goes to my heart. It is not a light thing to loose such a friend, and I truly loved him. In the first unreasonable

---

* Mr. Chauncey Hare Townshend. He was one of the dearest friends of Charles Dickens and a very constant correspondent; but no letters addressed to him are in existence.

train of feeling, I dwelt more than I should have thought possible on my being unable to attend his funeral. I know how little this really matters ; but I know he would have wished me to be there with real honest tears for his memory, and I feel it very much. I never, never, never was better loved by man than I was by him, I am sure. Poor dear fellow, good affectionate gentle creature.

I have not as yet received any letter from Henri, nor do I think he can have written to New York by your mail. I believe that I am—I know that I *was*—one of the executors. In that case Mr. Jackson, his agent, will either write to me very shortly on Henri's information of my address, or enquiry will be made at Gad's or at the office about it.

It is difficult for me to write more just now. The news is a real shock at such a distance, and I must read to-night, and I must compose my mind. Let Mekitty know that I received her violets with great pleasure, and that I sent her my best love and my best thanks.

On the 25th of February I read "Copperfield" and "Bob" at Boston. Either on that very day, or very close upon it, I was_ describing his (Townshend's) house to Fields, and telling him about the great Danby picture that he should see when he came to London.

[*To Miss Dickens.*]

ROCHESTER, *Sunday, March 16th*, 1868.

I found yours of the 28th February, when I came back here last night. We have had two brilliant sunny days at

Niagara, and have seen that wonderful place under the finest circumstances.

Enclosed I return you Homan's estimate ; let all that work be done, including the curtains.

As to the hall, I have my doubts whether one of the parqueted floors made by Aaron Smith's, of Bond Street, ought not to be better than tiles, for the reason that perhaps the nature of the house's construction might render the " bed " necessary for wooden flooring more easy to be made than the "bed" necessary for tiles. I don't think you can do better than call in the trusty Lillie to advise. Decide with your aunt on which appears to be better, under the circumstances. Have estimate made for *cash*, select patterns and colours, and let the work be done out of hand. (Here's a prompt order ; now I draw breath.) Let it be thoroughly well done—no half measures.

There is a great thaw all over the country here, and I think it has done the catarrh good. I am to read at the famous Newhaven on Tuesday, the 24th. I hope without a row, but cannot say. The readings are running out fast now, and we are growing very restless.

This is a short letter, but we are pressed for time. It is two o'clock, and we dine at three, before reading. To-morrow we rise at six, and have eleven hours' railway or so. We have now come back from our farthest point, and are steadily working towards home.

[*To Mr. W. C. Macready.*]

SPRINGFIELD, MASS., *Saturday, March 21st,* 1868.

MY DEAREST MACREADY,

What with perpetual reading and travelling, what with a " true American catarrh " (on which I am complimented almost boastfully), and what with one of the severest winters ever known, your coals of fire received by the last mail did not burn my head so much as they might have done under less excusatory circumstances. But they scorched it too !

You would find the general aspect of America and Americans decidedly much improved. You would find immeasurably greater consideration and respect for your privacy than of old. You would find a steady change for the better everywhere, except (oddly enough) in the railroads generally, which seem to have stood still, while everything else has moved. But there is an exception westward. There the express trains have now a very delightful carriage called a " drawing-room car," literally a series of little private drawing-rooms, with sofas and a table in each, opening out of a little corridor. In each, too, is a large plate-glass window, with which you can do as you like. As you pay extra for this luxury, it may be regarded as the first move towards two classes of passengers. When the railroad straight away to San Francisco (in six days) shall be opened through, it will not only have these drawing-rooms, but sleeping-rooms too ; a bell in every little apartment communicating with a steward's pantry, a restaurant, a staff of servants, marble washing-stands, and a barber's shop! I looked into one of these cars a day or two ago, and it was very ingeniously arranged and quite complete.

I left Niagara last Sunday, and travelled on to Albany, through three hundred miles of flood, villages deserted, bridges broken, fences drifting away, nothing but tearing water, floating ice, and absolute wreck and ruin. The train gave in altogether at Utica, and the passengers were let loose there for the night. As I was due at Albany, a very active superintendent of works did all he could to "get Mr. Dickens along," and in the morning we resumed our journey through the water, with a hundred men in seven-league boots pushing the ice from before us with long poles. How we got to Albany I can't say, but we got there some-how, just in time for a triumphal "Carol" and "Trial." All the tickets had been sold, and we found the Albanians in a state of great excitement. You may imagine what the flood was when I tell you that we took the passengers out of two trains that had their fires put out by the water four-and-twenty hours before, and cattle from trucks that had been in the water I don't know how long, but so long that the sheep had begun to eat each other! It was a horrible spectacle, and the haggard human misery of their faces was quite a new study. There was a fine breath of spring in the air concurrently with the great thaw; but lo and behold! last night it began to snow again with a strong wind, and to-day a snowdrift covers this place with all the desolation of winter once more. I never was so tired of the sight of snow. As to sleighing, I have been sleighing about to that extent, that I am sick of the sound of a sleigh-bell.

I have seen all our Boston friends, except Curtis. Ticknor is dead. The rest are very little changed, except that Longfellow has a perfectly white flowing beard and long white hair. But he does not otherwise look old, and is infinitely handsomer than he was. I have been constantly with them all, and they have always talked much of you. It is the established joke that Boston is my "native place," and we hold all sorts of hearty foregatherings. They all come to every reading, and are always in a most delightful state of enthusiasm. They give me a parting dinner at the club, on the Thursday before Good Friday. To pass from Boston personal to New York theatrical, I will mention here that one of the proprietors of my New York hotel is one of the proprietors of Niblo's, and the most active. Consequently I have seen the "Black Crook" and the "White Fawn," in majesty, from an armchair in the first entrance, P.S., more than once. Of these astonishing dramas, I beg to report (seriously) that I have found no human creature "behind" who has the slightest idea what they are about (upon my honour, my dearest Macready!), and that having some amiable small talk with a neat little Spanish woman, who is the *première danseuse*, I asked her, in joke, to let me measure her skirt with my dress glove. Holding the glove by the tip of the forefinger, I found the skirt to be just three gloves long, and yet its length was much in excess of the skirts of two hundred other ladies, whom the carpenters were at that moment getting into their places for a transformation scene, on revolving columns, on wires and "travellers" in iron cradles, up in the flies, down in the cellars, on every description of float that Wilmot, gone distracted, could imagine !

I have taken my passage for Liverpool from New York in the Cunarder *Russia*, on the 22nd of April. I had the second officer's cabin on deck coming out, and I have the chief steward's cabin on deck going home, because it will be on the sunny side of the ship. I have experienced nothing here but good humour and cordiality. In the autumn and winter I have arranged with Chappells to take my farewell of reading in the United Kingdom for ever and ever.

I am delighted to hear of Benvenuta's marriage, and I think her husband a very lucky man. Johnnie has my profound sympathy under his examinatorial woes. The noble boy will give me Gavazzi revised and enlarged, I expect, when I next come to Cheltenham. I will give you and Mrs. Macready all my American experiences when you come to London, or, better still, to Gad's. Meanwhile I send my hearty love to all, not forgetting dear Katie.

Niagara is not at all spoiled by a very dizzy-looking suspension bridge. Is to have another still nearer to the Horse-shoe opened in July. My last sight of that scene (last Sunday) was thus : We went up to the rapids above the Horse-shoe—say two miles from it—and through the great cloud of spray.   Everything in the magnificient valley—buildings, forest, high banks, air, water, everything —was *made of rainbow.*   Turner's most imaginative drawing in his finest day has nothing in it so ethereal, so gorgeous in fancy, so celestial.   We said to one another (Dolby and I), "Let it for evermore remain so," and shut our eyes and came away.

God bless you and all dear to you, my dear old Friend !
I am ever your affectionate and loving.

[*To Miss Dickens.*]

PORTLAND, *Sunday, March 29th,* 1868.

I should have written to you by the last mail, but I really was too unwell to do it.   The writing day was last Friday, when I ought to have left Boston for New Bedford (fifty-five miles) before eleven in the morning.   But I was so exhausted that I could not be got up, and had to take my chance of an evening's train producing me in time to read, which it just did.   With the return of snow, nine days ago, the "true American" (which had lulled) came back as bad as ever.   I have coughed from two or three in the morning until five or six, and have been absolutely sleepless.   I have had no appetite besides, and no taste.   Last night here I took some laudanum, and it is the only thing that has done me good.   But the life in this climate is so very hard.   When I did manage to get from Boston to New Bedford, I read with my utmost force and vigour.   Next morning, well or ill, I must turn out at seven to get back to Boston on my way here.

I dine at Boston at three, and at five must come on here (a hundred and thirty miles or so), for to-morrow night ; there being no Sunday train. To-morrow night I read here in a very large place, and Tuesday morning at six I must start again to get back to Boston once more. But after to-morrow night, I have only the Boston and New York farewells, thank God ! I am most grateful to think that when we came to devise the details of the tour, I foresaw that it could never be done, as Dolby and Osgood proposed, by one unassisted man, as if he were a machine. If I had not cut out the work, and cut out Canada, I could never have gone there, I am quite sure. Even as it is, I have just now written to Dolby (who is in New York), to see my doctor there, and ask him to send me some composing medicine that I can take at night, inasmuch as without sleep I cannot get through. However sympathetic and devoted the people are about me, they *can not* be got to comprehend that one's being able to do the two hours with spirit when the time comes round, may be co-existent with the consciousness of great depression and fatigue. I don't mind saying all this, now that the labour is so nearly over. You shall have a brighter account of me, please God, when I close this at Boston.

Monday, March 30th.

Without any artificial aid, I got a splendid night's rest last night, and consequently am very much freshened up to-day. Yesterday I had a fine walk by the sea, and to-day I have had another on the heights overlooking it.

I have safely arrived here, just in time to add a line to that effect, and get this off by to-morrow's English mail from New York. Catarrh rather better. Everything triumphant last night. except no sleep again. I suppose Dolby to be now on his way back to join me here. I am much mistaken if the political crisis do not damage the farewells by almost one half.

I hope that I am certainly better altogether.

My room well decorated with flowers, of course, and Mr. and Mrs. Fields coming to dinner. They are the most devoted of friends, and never in the way and never out of it.

[*To Miss Hogarth.*]

BOSTON, *Wednesday, April 1st*, 1868.

I received your letter of from the 14th to the 17th of March, here, last night. My New York doctor has prescribed for me promptly, and I hope I am better. I am certainly no worse. We shall do (to the best of my belief) *very well* with the farewells here and at New York, but not greatly. Everything is at a standstill, pending the impeachment and the next presidential election. I forgot whether I told you that the New York press are going to give me a public dinner, on Saturday, the 18th.

I hear (but not from himself) that Wills has had a bad fall in hunting, and is, or has been, laid up. I am supposed, I take it, not to know this until I hear it from himself.

Thursday.

My notion of the farewells is pretty certain now to turn out right. It is not at all probable that we shall do anything enormous. Every pulpit in Massachusetts will resound to violent politics to-day and to-night. You remember the Hutchinson family ? * I have had a grateful letter from John Hutchinson. He speaks of " my sister Abby " as living in New York. The immediate object of his note is to invite me to the marriage of his daughter, twenty-one years of age.

You will see by the evidence of this piece of paper that I am using up my stationery. Scott has just been making anxious calculations as to our powers of holding out in the articles of tooth-powder, etc. The calculations encourage him to believe that we shall just hold out, and no more. I think I am still better to-day than I was yesterday ; but I am far from strong, and have no appetite. To see me at my little table at night, you would think me the freshest of the fresh. And this is the marvel of Fields' life.

I don't forget that this is Forster's birthday.

Friday Afternoon, 3rd.

Catarrh worse than ever ! And we don't know (at four) whether I can read to-night or must stop. Otherwise all well.

---

* An American family of brothers and a sister who came to London to give a musical entertainment shortly after Charles Dickens's return from his first visit to America. He had a great interest in, and liking for, these young people.

[To Miss Dickens.]

BOSTON, *Tuesday, April 7th,* 1868.

I not only read last Friday, when I was doubtful of being able to do so, but read as I never did before, and astonished the audience quite as much as myself. You never saw or heard such a scene of excitement.

Longfellow and all the Cambridge men urged me to give in. I have been very near doing so, but feel stronger to-day. I cannot tell whether the catarrh may have done me any lasting injury in the lungs or other breathing organs, until I shall have rested and got home. I hope and believe not. Consider the weather. There have been two snowstorms since I wrote last, and to-day the town is blotted out in a ceaseless whirl of snow and wind.

I cannot eat (to anything like the ordinary extent), and have established this system : At seven in the morning, in bed, a tumbler of new cream and two tablespoonsful of rum. At twelve, a sherry cobbler and a biscuit. At three (dinner time), a pint of champagne. At five minutes to eight, an egg beaten up with a glass of sherry. Between the parts, the strongest beef tea that can be made, drunk hot. At a quarter-past ten, soup, and anything to drink that I can fancy. I don't eat more than half a pound of solid food in the whole four-and-twenty hours, if so much.

If I hold out, as I hope to do, I shall be greatly pressed in leaving here and getting over to New York, before next Saturday's mail from there. Do not, therefore *if all be well*, expect to hear from me by Saturday's mail, but look

for my last letter from America by the mail of the following Wednesday, the 15th. *Be sure* that you shall hear,
however, by Saturday's mail, if I should knock up as to
reading. I am tremendously "beat," but I feel really and
unaffectedly so much stronger to-day, both in my body
and hopes, that I am much encouraged. I have a fancy
that I turned my worst time last night.

Dolby is as tender as a woman and as watchful as a
doctor. He never leaves me during the reading now, but
sits at the side of the platform and keeps his eye upon me
all the time. Ditto George, the gasman, steadiest and
most reliable man I ever employed. I am the more hopeful of my not having to relinquish a reading, because last
night was " Copperfield " and " Bob "—by a quarter of an
hour the longest, and, in consideration of the storm, by
very much the most trying. Yet I was far fresher afterwards than I have been these three weeks.

I have " Dombey " to do to-night, and must go through
it carefully ; so here ends my report. The personal affection of the people in this place is charming to the last.

[*To the Hon. Mrs. Watson.*]

Gad's Hill Place, *Monday, May 11th,* 1868.
My dear Mrs. Watson,

I am delighted to have your letter. It comes to me like
a faithful voice from dear old Rockingham, and awakens
many memories.

The work in America has been so very hard, and the

winter there has been so excessively severe, that I really have been very unwell for some months. But I had not been at sea three days on the passage home when I became myself again.

If you will arrange with Mary Boyle any time for coming here, we shall be charmed to see you, and I will adapt my arrangements accordingly. I make this suggestion because she generally comes here early in the summer season. But if you will propose yourself *anyhow*, giving me a margin of a few days in case of my being pre-engaged for this day or that, we will (as my American friends say) " fix it."

What with travelling, reading night after night, and speech-making day after day, I feel the peace of the country beyond all expression. On board ship coming home, a " deputation " (two in number, of whom only one could get into my cabin, while the other looked in at my window) came to ask me to read to the passengers that evening in the saloon. I respectfully replied that sooner than do it, I would assault the captain, and be put in irons.

Ever affectionately yours.

[*To Mrs. Cattermole.*]

GAD'S HILL PLACE, HIGHAM BY ROCHESTER, KENT,
Saturday, May 16th, 1868.

MY DEAR MRS. CATTERMOLE,

On my return from America just now, I accidentally heard that George had been ill. My sister-in-law had heard it from Forster, but vaguely. Until I received your letter of Wednesday's date, I had no idea that he had been very ill; and should have been greatly shocked by knowing it, were it not for the hopeful and bright assurance you give me that he is greatly better.

My old affection for him has never cooled. The last time he dined with me, I asked him to come again that day ten years, for I was perfectly certain (this was my small joke) that I should not set eyes upon him sooner. The time being fully up, I hope you will remind him, with my love, that he is due. His hand is upon these walls here, so I should like him to see for himself, and *you* to see for *yourself*, and in this hope I shall pursue his complete recovery.

I heartily sympathise with you in your terrible anxiety, and in your vast relief; and, with many thanks for your letter, am ever, my dear Mrs. Cattermole,

Affectionately yours.

[*To Mr. W. C. Macready.*]

GAD'S HILL, *Wednesday, June 10th,* 1868.

MY DEAREST MACREADY,

Since my return from America, I have been so overwhelmed with business that I have not had time even to write to you. You may imagine what six months of arrear are to dispose of; added to this, Wills has received a concussion of the brain (from an accident in the hunting-field), and is sent away by the doctors, and strictly prohibited from even writing a note. Consequently all the business and money details of "All the Year Round" devolve upon me. And I have had to get them up, for I have never had experience of them. Then I am suddenly entreated to go to Paris, to look after the French version of " No Thoroughfare " on the stage. And I go, and come back, leaving it a great success.

I hope Mrs. Macready and you have not abandoned the idea of coming here? The expression of this hope is the principal, if not the only, object of this present note. May the amiable secretary vouchsafe a satisfactory reply !

Katie, Mary, and Georgina send their very best love to your Katie and Mrs. Macready. The undersigned is in his usual brilliant condition, and indeed has greatly disappointed them at home here, by coming back "so brown and looking so well." They expected a wreck, and were, at first, much mortified. But they are getting over it now.

To my particular friends, the noble boy and Johnny, I beg to be warmly remembered.

Ever, my dearest Macready,

Your most affectionate.

[To Mrs. Henry Austin.]

GAD'S HILL PLACE, HIGHAM BY ROCHESTER, KENT,
Tuesday, July 21st, 1868.

ON THE DEATH OF MR. HENRY AUSTIN.*

MY DEAR LETITIA,

You will have had a telegram from me to-day. I received your sad news by this morning's post. They never, without express explanation, mind " Immediate " on a let-

---

* Cousin and adopted child of Mr. and Mrs. Austin.

ter addressed to the office, because half the people who write there on business that does not press, or on no business at all, so mark their letters.

On Thursday I have people to see and matters to attend to, both at the office and at Coutt's, which, in Wills's absence, I cannot forego or depute to another. But, *between ourselves*, I must add something else : I have the greatest objection to attend a funeral in which my affections are not strongly and immediately concerned. I have no notion of a funeral as a matter of form or ceremony. And just as I should expressly prohibit the summoning to my own burial of anybody who was not very near or dear to me, so I revolt from myself appearing at that solemn rite, unless the deceased were very near or dear to me. I cannot endure being dressed up by an undertaker as part of his trade show. I was not in this poor good fellow's house in his lifetime, and I feel that I have no business there when he lies dead in it. My mind is penetrated with sympathy and compassion for the young widow, but that feeling is a real thing, and my attendance as a mourner would not be —to myself. It would be to you, I know, but it would not be to myself. I know full well that you cannot delegate to me your memories of and your associations with the deceased, and the more true and tender they are the more invincible is my objection to become a form in the midst of the most awful realities.

With love and condolence from Georgina, Mary, and Katie,

Believe me, ever your affectionate Brother.

[*To Mrs. George Cattermole.*]

GAD'S HILL, *Wednesday, July 22nd*, 1868.

MY DEAR MRS. CATTERMOLE,

Of course I will sign your memorial to the Academy. If you take either of the Landseers, certainly take Edwin (1, St. John's Wood Road, N.W.) But, if you would be content with Frith, I have already spoken to him, and believe that I can answer for him. I shall be at "All the Year Round " Office, 26, Wellington Street, London, to-morrow, from eleven to three. Frith will be here on Saturday, and I shall be here too. I spoke to him a fortnight ago, and I found him most earnest in the cause. He said he felt absolutely sure that the whole profession in its best and highest representation would do anything for George. I sounded him, having the opportunity of meeting him at dinner at Cartwright's.

Ever yours affectionately.

[*To Mr. W. H. Wills.*]

Friday, July 31st, 1868.

MY DEAR WILLS,

I had such a hard day at the office yesterday, that I had not time to write to you before I left. So I write to-day.

I am very unwilling to abandon the Christmas number, though even in the case of my little Christmas books (which were immensely profitable), I let the idea go when I thought it was wearing out. Ever since I came home, I have hammered at it, more or less, and have been uneasy about it.

I have begun something which is very droll, but it manifestly shapes itself towards a book, and could not in the least admit of even that shadowy approach to a congruous whole on the part of other contributors which they have ever achieved at the best. I have begun something else (aboard the American mail steamer); but I don't like it, because the stories must come limping in after the old fashion, though, of course, what I *have* done will be good for A. Y. R. In short, I have cast about with the greatest pains and patience, and I have been wholly unable to find what I want.

And yet I cannot quite make up my mind to give in without another fight for it. I offered one hundred pounds reward at Gad's to anybody who could suggest a notion to satisfy me. Charles Collins suggested one yesterday morning, in which there is *something*, though not much. I will turn it over and over, and try a few more starts on my own account. Finally, I swear I will not give it up until August is out. Vow registered.

I am clear that a number by " various writers " would not do. If we have not the usual sort of number, we must call the current number for that date the Christmas number, and make it as good as possible.

I sit in the Châlet,* like Mariana in the Moated Grange, and to as much purpose.

I am buying the freehold of the meadow at Gad's, and of an adjoining arable field, so that I shall now have about

---

* A model of a Swiss châlet, and a present from M. Charles Fechter, used by Charles Dickens as a summer writing-room.

eight-and-twenty freehold acres in a ring fence. No more now.

I made up a very good number yesterday. You will see in it a very short article that I have called " Now ! " which is a highly remarkable piece of description. It is done by a new man, from whom I have accepted another article ; but he will never do anything so good again.

Ever affectionately.

[*To M. de Cerjat.*]
—

GAD'S HILL PLACE, HIGHAM BY ROCHESTER, KENT,

Wednesday, Aug. 26*th*, 1868.

MY DEAR CERJAT,

I was happy to receive your esteemed letter a few days ago.

The severity of the winter in America (which was quite exceptional even in that rigorous climate), combined with the hard work I had to do, tried me a good deal. Neuralgia and colds beset me, either by turns or both together, and I had often much to do to get through at night. But the sea voyage home again did wonders in restoring me, and I have been very well indeed, though a little fatigued, ever since. I am now preparing for a final reading campaign in England, Scotland, and Ireland. It will begin on the 6th of October, and will probably last, with short occasional intermissions, until June.

The great subject in England for the moment is the horrible accident to the Irish mail-train. It is now supposed that the petroleum (known to be a powerful anæsthetic) rendered the unfortunate people who were burnt almost instantly insensible to any sensation. My escape in the Staplehurst accident of three years ago is not to be obliterated from my nervous system. To this hour I have sudden vague rushes of terror, even when riding in a hansom cab, which are perfectly unreasonable but quite insurmountable. I used to make nothing of driving a pair of horses habitually through the most crowded parts of London. I cannot now drive, with comfort to myself, on the country roads here ; and I doubt if I could ride at all in the saddle. My reading secretary and companion knows so well when one of these odd momentary seizures comes upon me in a railway carriage, that he instantly produces a dram of brandy, which rallies the blood to the heart and generally prevails. I forget whether I ever told you that my watch (a chronometer) has never gone exactly since the accident ? So the Irish catastrophe naturally revives the dreadful things I saw that day.

The only other news here you know as well as I ; to wit, that the country is going to be ruined, and that the Church is going to be ruined, and that both have become so used to being ruined, that they will go on perfectly well.

* * * * *

[*To Miss Dickens.*]

OFFICE OF " ALL THE YEAR ROUND," No. 26 WELLINGTON STREET, STRAND, LONDON, W.C.,

Saturday, Sept. 26th, 1868.

MY DEAREST MAMIE,

I will add a line to this at the Athenæum, after seeing Plorn off, to tell you how he went away.

ATHENÆUM, *Quarter to Six.*

I can honestly report that he went away, poor dear fellow, as well as could possibly be expected. He was pale, and had been crying, and (Harry said) had broken down in the railway carriage after leaving Higham station ; but only for a short time.

Just before the train started he cried a good deal, but not painfully. (Tell dear Georgy that I bought him his cigars.) These are hard, hard things, but they might have to be done without means or influence, and then they would be far harder. God bless him !

PARLIAMENT. REPLY TO A PROPOSAL MADE THROUGH ALEXANDER RUSSEL, OF THE "SCOTSMAN," THAT HE SHOULD ALLOW HIMSELF TO BE PUT FORWARD AS A CANDIDATE FOR THE REPRESENTATION OF EDINBURGH.

[*To Mr. F. D. Finlay.*]

GAD'S HILL PLACE, HIGHAM BY ROCHESTER, KENT,
Sunday, Oct. 4th, 1868.

MY DEAR FINLAY,

I am much obliged to you in all friendship and sincerity for your letter. I have a great respect for your father-in-law and his paper, and I am much attached to the Edinburgh people. You may suppose, therefore, that if my mind were not fully made up on the parliamentary question, I should waver now.

But my conviction that I am more useful and more happy as I am than I could ever be in Parliament is not to be shaken. I considered it some weeks ago, when I had a stirring proposal from the Birmingham people, and I then set it up on a rock for ever and a day.

Do tell Mr. Russel that I truly feel this mark of confidence, and that I hope to acknowledge it in person in Edinburgh before Christmas. There is no man in Scotland from whom I should consider his suggestion a greater honour.

Ever yours.

[To M. Charles Fechter.]

* * * * *

Poor Plorn is gone to Australia. It was a hard parting at the last. He seemed to me to become once more my youngest and favourite little child as the day drew near, and I did not think I could have been so shaken. You were his idol to the hour of his departure, and he asked me to tell you how much he wanted to bid you good-bye.

Kindest love from all.

Ever heartily.

[To M. Charles Fechter.]

OFFICE OF "ALL THE YEAR ROUND,"
Wednesday, Oct. 7th, 1868.

MY DEAR FECHTER,

I got your letter sent to Gad's Hill this morning. Until I received it, I supposed the piece to have been put into English from your French by young Ben. If I understand that the English is yours, then I say that it is extraordinarily good, written by one in another country.

I do not read again in London until the 20th ; and then " Copperfield." But by that time you will be at work yourself.

Let us dine at six to-day, in order that we may not have to hurry for the comic dog.

Ever faithfully.

[*To Miss Hogarth.*]

QUEEN'S HOTEL, MANCHESTER, *Sunday, Oct.* 11*th*, 1868.
MY DEAREST GEORGY,

We had a fine audience last night in the Free Trade Hall, though not what we consider a large money-house. The let in Liverpool is extremely good, and we are going over there at half-past one. We got down here pleasantly enough and in good time ; so all has gone well you see.

Titiens, Santley, and an opera company of that class are at the theatre here. They have been doing very poorly in Manchester.

There is the whole of my scanty news. I was in wonderful voice last night, but croak a little this morning, after so much speaking in so very large a place. Otherwise I am all right. I find myself constantly thinking of Plorn.

[*To Miss Dickens.*]

ADELPHI HOTEL, LIVERPOOL, *Monday, Oct.* 12*th*, 1868.
MY DEAREST MAMIE,

Our lets here are excellent, and we shall have a great house to-night. We had a very fine and enthusiastic audience in the Free Trade Hall, at Manchester, on Saturday ;

but our first nights there never count up in money, as the rest do. Yesterday, "Charlotte," Sainton, and Piatti stayed with us here ; and they went on to Hull this morning. It was pleasant to be alone again, though they were all very agreeable.

The exertion of going on for two hours in that immense place at Manchester being very great, I was hoarse all day yesterday, though I was not much distressed on Saturday night. I am becoming melodious again (at three in the afternoon) rapidly, and count on being quite restored by a basin of turtle at dinner.

I am glad to hear about Armitage, and hope that a service begun in a personal attachment to Plorn may go on well. I shall never be over-confident in such matters, I think, any more.

The day is delicious here. We have had a blow on the Mersey this morning, and exulted over the American steamers. With kind regard to Sir William and Lady Humphery.

[*To Miss Hogarth.*]

ADELPHI HOTEL, LIVERPOOL, *Tuesday, Oct. 13th*, 1868.

As I sent a line to Mary yesterday, I enclose you Alfred's letter. Please send it on to her when you next write to Penton.

I have just now written to Mrs. Forster, asking her to explain to Miss Forster how she could have an easy-chair or a sofa behind my side screen on Tuesday, without occasioning the smallest inconvenience to anybody. Also, how she would have a door close at hand, leading at once to cool passages and a quiet room, etc., etc., etc. It is a sad story.

We had a fine house here last night, and a large turn-away. "Marigold" and "Trial" went immensely. I doubt if "Marigold" were ever more enthusiastically received. "Copperfield" and "Bob" to-night, and a large let. This notwithstanding election meetings and all sorts of things.

My favourite room brought my voice round last night, and I am in considerable force.

Dolby sends kindest regard, and the message: "Everton toffee shall not be forgotten."

[*To Mr. Henry Fielding Dickens.*]

ADELPHI HOTEL, LIVERPOOL, *Thursday, Oct.* 15*th*, 1868.

MY DEAR HARRY,

I have your letter here this morning. I enclose you another cheque for twenty-five pounds, and I write to London by this post, ordering three dozen sherry, two dozen port, and three dozen light claret, to be sent down to you.

Now, observe attentively. We must have no shadow of debt. Square up everything whatsoever that it has been necessary to buy. Let not a farthing be outstanding on any account, when we begin together with your allowance. Be particular in the minutest detail.

I wish to have no secret from you in the relations we

are to establish together, and I therefore send you Joe Chitty's letter bodily. Reading it, you will know exactly what I know, and will understand that I treat you with perfect confidence. It appears to me that an allowance of two hundred and fifty pounds a year will be handsome for all your wants, if I send you your wines. I mean this to include your tailor's bills as well as every other expense; and I strongly recommend you to buy nothing in Cambridge, and to take credit for nothing but the clothes with which your tailor provides you. As soon as you have got your furniture accounts in, let us wipe all those preliminary expenses clean out, and I will then send you your first quarter. We will count in it October, November, and December; and your second quarter will begin with the New Year. If you dislike, at first, taking charge of so large a sum as sixty-two pounds ten shillings, you can have your money from me half-quarterly.

You know how hard I work for what I get, and I think you know that I never had money help from any human creature after I was a child. You know that you are one of many heavy charges on me, and that I trust to your so exercising your abilities and improving the advantages of your past expensive education, as soon to diminish *this* charge. I say no more on that head.

Whatever you do, above all other things keep out of debt and confide in me. If you ever find yourself on the verge of any perplexity or difficulty, come to me. You will never find me hard with you while you are manly and truthful.

As your brothers have gone away one by one, I have written to each of them what I am now going to write to you. You know that you have never been hampered with religious forms of restraint, and that with mere unmeaning forms I have no sympathy. But I most strongly and affectionately impress upou you the priceless value of the New Testament, and the study of that book as the one unfailing guide in life. Deeply respecting it, and bowing down before the character of our Saviour, as separated from the vain constructions and inventions of men, you cannot go very wrong, and will always preserve at heart a true spirit of veneration and humility. Similarly I impress upon you the habit of saying a Christian prayer every night and morning. These things have stood by me all through my life, and remember that I tried to render the New Testament intelligible to you and lovable by you when you were a mere baby.

And so God bless you.

Ever your affectionate Father.

[*To Mr. William Charles Kent.*]

OFFICE OF " ALL THE YEAR ROUND,"
Monday, Nov. 16*th,* 1868.

MY DEAR KENT,

· I was on the eve of writing to you.

We thought of keeping the trial private ; but Oxenford has suggested to Chappell that he would like to take the opportunity of to-morrow night's reading, of saying something about "Oliver" in *Wednesday's paper.* Chappell has told Levy of this, and also Mr. Tompkin, of *The Post,* who was there. Consequently, on Wednesday evening your charming article can come out to the best advantage.

You have no idea of the difficulty of getting in the end of Sikes. As to the man with the invaluable composition! my dear fellow, believe me, no audience on earth could be held for ten minutes after the girl's death. Give them time, and they would be revengeful for having had such a strain put upon them. Trust me to be right. I stand there, and I know.

Concerning Harry, I like to guide the boys to a distinct choice, rather than to press it on them. That will be my course as to the Middle Temple, of which I think as you do.

With cordial thanks for every word in your letter,

Affectionately yours always.

[*To Mrs. F. Lehmann.*]

KENNEDY'S HOTEL, EDINBURGH, *Sunday, Dec. 6th,* 1868.

MY DEAR MRS. LEHMANN,

I hope you will see Nancy with the light of a great audience upon her some time between this and May; always supposing that she should not prove too weird and woeful for the general public.

You know the aspect of this city on a Sunday, and how gay and bright it is. The merry music of the blithe bells, the waving flags, the prettily decorated houses with their draperies of various colours, and the radiant countenances at the windows and in the streets, how charming they are ! The usual preparations are making for the band in the open air, in the afternoon ; and the usual pretty children (selected for that purpose) are at this moment hanging garlands round the Scott monument, preparatory to the innocent Sunday dance round that edifice, with which the diversions invariably close. It is pleasant to think that these customs were themselves of the early Christians, those early birds who *didn't* catch the worm—and nothing else—and choke their young with it.

Faithfully yours always.

[*To Miss Hogarth.*]

KENNEDY'S HOTEL, EDINBURGH, *Sunday, Dec. 6th,* 1868.

We got down here to our time to the moment ; and, considering the length of the journey, very easily. I made a calculation on the road, that the railway travelling over such a distance involves something more than thirty thousand shocks to the nerves. Dolby didn't like it at all.

The signals for a gale were up at Berwick, and along the road between there and here. It came on just as we arrived, and blew tremendously hard all night. The wind is still very high, though the sky is bright and the sun shining. We couldn't sleep for the noise.

We are very comfortably quartered. I fancy that the " business " will be on the whole better here than in Glasgow, where trade is said to be very bad. But I think I shall be pretty correct in both places as to the run being on the final readings.

We are going up Arthur's Seat presently, which will be a pull for our fat friend.

Scott, in a new Mephistopheles hat, baffles imagination and description.

[*To Mr. W. Wilkie Collins.*]

KENNEDY'S HOTEL, EDINBURGH, *Tuesday, Dec. 8th,* 1868.

MY DEAR WILKIE,

I am hard at it here as usual, though with an audience so finely perceptive that the labour is much diminished. I have got together in a very short space the conclusion of "Oliver Twist" that you suggested, and am trying it daily with the object of rising from that blank state of horror into a fierce and passionate rush for the end. As yet I cannot make a certain effect of it ; but when I shall have gone over it as many score of times as over the rest of that reading, perhaps I may strike one out.

I shall be very glad to hear when you have done your play, and I *am* glad to hear that you like the steamer. I agree with you about the reading perfectly. In No. 3 you will see an exact account of some places I visited at Ratcliffe. There are two little instances in it of something comic rising up in the midst of the direst misery, that struck me very humorously at the time.

As I have determined not to do the "Oliver Murder" until after the fifth of January, when I shall ascertain its effect on a great audience, it is curious to notice how the shadow of its coming affects the Scotch mind. There was such a disposition to hold back for it here (until I return to finish in February) that we had next to no "let" when we arrived. It all came with a rush yesterday. They gave me a most magnificent welcome back from America last night.

I am perpetually counting the weeks before me to be "read" through, and am perpetually longing for the end of them; and yet I sometimes wonder whether I shall miss something when they are over.

It is a very, very bad day here, very dark and very wet. Dolby is over at Glasgow, and I am sitting at a side window looking up the length of Prince's Street, watching the mist change over the Castle and murdering Nancy by turns.

Ever affectionately.

P.S.—I have read the whole of Fitzgerald's "Zero," and the idea is exceedingly well wrought out.

[To Miss Hogarth.]

KENNEDY'S HOTEL, EDINBURGH, Saturday, Dec. 12th, 1868.

I send another *Scotsman* by this post, because it is really a good newspaper, well written, and well managed. We had an immense house here last night, and a very large turn-away.

We have four guests to dinner to-day : Peter Fraser, Ballantine, John Blackwood, and Mr. Russell. Immense preparations are making in the establishment, "on account," Mr. Kennedy says, "of a' four yon chiels being chiels wha' ken a guid dinner." I enquired after poor Doctor Burt, not having the least idea that he was dead.

My voice holds out splendidly so far, and 1 have had no return of the American. But I sleep very indifferently indeed.

It blew appallingly here the night before last, but the wind has since shifted northward, and it is now bright and cold. The *Star of Hope*, that picked up those shipwrecked people in the boat, came into Leith yesterday, and was received with tremendous cheers. Her captain must be a good man and a noble fellow.

[*To Miss Hogarth.*]

KENNEDY'S HOTEL, EDINBURGH, *Monday, Dec.* 14th, 1868.

The dinner-party of Saturday last was an immense success. Russell swore on the occasion that he would go over to Belfast expressly to dine with me at the Finlays'. Ballantine informed me that he was going to send you some Scotch remembrance (I don't know what) at Christmas !

The Edinburgh houses are very fine. The Glasgow room is a big wandering place, with five prices in it, which makes it the more aggravating, as the people get into knots which they can't break, as if they were afraid of one another.

Forgery of my name is becoming popular. You sent

me, this morning, a letter from Russell Sturgis, answering a supposed letter of mine (presented by " Miss Jefferies "), and assuring me of his readiness to give not only the ten pounds I asked for, but any contribution I wanted, towards sending that lady and her family back to Boston.

I wish you would take an opportunity of forewarning Lady Tennent that the first night's reading she will attend is an experiment quite out of the way, and that she may find it rather horrible.

The keeper of the Edinburgh Hall, a fine old soldier, presented me, on Friday night, with the finest red camellia for my button-hole that ever was seen. Nobody can imagine how he came by it, as the florists had had a considerable demand for that colour from ladies in the stalls, and could get no such thing.

The day is dark, wet, and windy. The weather is likely to be vile indeed at Glasgow, where it always rains, and where the sun is never seen through the smoke. We go over there to-morrow at ten.

[*To Miss Dickens.*]

CARRICK'S ROYAL HOTEL, GLASGOW,
Tuesday, Dec. 15*th*, 1868.

It occurs to me that my táble at St. James's Hall might be appropriately ornamented with a little holly next Tuesday. If the two front legs were entwined with it, for instance, and a border of it ran round the top of the fringe in front, with a little sprig by way of bouquet at each corner, it would present a seasonable appearance.

If you will think of this, and will have the materials ready in a little basket, I will call for you at the office at half-past twelve on Tuesday, and take you up to the hall, where the table will be ready for you.

No news, except that we had a great crush and a wonderful audience in Edinburgh last night.

[*To Miss Hogarth.*]

CARRICK'S ROYAL HOTEL, GLASGOW,
Wednesday, Dec. 16th, 1868.

This is to report all well, except that I have wretched nights. The weather is diabolical here, and times are very bad. I cut "Copperfield" with a bold dexterity that amazed myself and utterly confounded George at the wing ; knocking off that and " Bob " by ten minutes to ten.

I don't know anything about the Liverpool banquet, except from *The Times*. As I don't finish there in February (as they seem to have supposed), but in April, it may, perhaps, stand over or blow over altogether. Such a thing would be a serious addition to the work, and yet refusal on my part would be too ungracious.

The density and darkness of this atmosphere are fearful. I shall be heartily glad to start for Edinburgh again on Friday morning.

[*To Miss Hogarth.*]

KENNEDY'S HOTEL, EDINBURGH, *Friday, Dec. 18th,* 1868.

I am heartily glad to get back here this afternoon. The day is bright and cheerful, and the relief from Glasgow inexpressible. The affectionate regard of the people exceeds all bounds, and is shown in every way. The manager of the railway being at the reading the other night, wrote to me next morning, saying that a large saloon should be prepared for my journey up, if I would let him know when I purposed making the journey. On my accepting the offer he wrote again, saying that he had inspected " our Northern saloons," and not finding them so convenient for sleeping in as the best English, had sent up to King's Cross for the best of the latter ; which I would please consider my own carriage as long as I wanted it. The audiences do everything but embrace me, and take as much pains with the readings as I do.

I find your Christmas present (just arrived) to be a haggis and shortbread !

[*To Mr. J. C. Parkinson.*]

GAD'S HILL PLACE, HIGHAM BY ROCHESTER, KENT,
Christmas Day, 1868.

MY DEAR PARKINSON,

When you letter was delivered at " All the Year Round " Office yesterday, I was attending a funeral. It comes to hand here consequently to-day.

I am diffident of addressing Mr. Gladstone on the subject of your desire to be appointed to the vacant Commissionership of Inland Revenue, because, although my respect for him and confidence in him are second to those of no man in England (a bold word at this time, but a truthful one), my personal acquaintance with him is very slight.

But you may make, through any of your friends, any use you please of this letter, towards the end of bringing its contents under Mr. Gladstone's notice.

In expressing my conviction that you deserve the place, and are in every way qualified for it, I found my testimony upon as accurate a knowledge of your character and abilities as anyone can possibly have acquired. In my editorship both of "Household Words" and "All the Year Round," you know very well that I have invariably offered you those subjects of political and social interest to write upon, in which integrity, exactness, a remarkable power of generalising evidence and balancing facts, and a special clearness in stating the case, were indispensable on the part of the writer. My confidence in your powers has never been misplaced, and through all our literary intercourse you have never been hasty or wrong. Whatever trust you have undertaken has been so completely discharged, that it has become my habit to read your proofs rather for my own edification than (as in other cases) for the detection of some slip here or there, or the more pithy presentation of the subject.

That your literary work has never interfered with the discharge of your official duties, I may assume to be at least as well known to your colleagues as it is to me. It is idle to say that if the post were in my gift you should have it, because you have had, for some years, most of the posts of high trust that have been at my disposal. An excellent public servant in your literary sphere of action, I should be heartily glad if you could have this new opportunity of distinguishing yourself in the same character. And this is at least unselfish in me, for I suppose I should then lose you ?

Always faithfully yours.

[*To Mr. Edward Bulwer Lytton Dickens.*]

LETTER TO HIS YOUNGEST SON ON HIS DEPARTURE FOR AUSTRALIA IN 1868.*

MY DEAREST PLORN,

I write this note to-day because your going away is much upon my mind, and because I want you to have a few parting words from me to think of now and then at quiet times. I need not tell you that I love you dearly, and am very, very sorry in my heart to part with you. But this life is half made up of partings, and these pains must be borne. It is my comfort and my sincere conviction that you are going to try the life for which you are best fitted. I think its freedom and wildness more suited to you than any experiment in a study or office would ever have been ; and without that training, you could have followed no other suitable occupation.

What you have already wanted until now has been a set, steady, constant purpose. I therefore exhort you to persevere in a thorough determination to do whatever you have to do as well as you can do it. I was not so old as you are now when I first had to win my food, and do this out of this determination, and I have never slackened in it since.

---

* This letter has been already published by Mr. Forster in his "Life."

Never take a mean advantage of anyone in any trans-
action, and never be hard upon people who are in your
power. Try to do to others, as you would have them do to
you, and do not be discouraged if they fail sometimes. It
is much better for you that they should fail in obeying the
greatest rule laid down by our Saviour, than that you
should.

I put a New Testament among your books, for the very
same reasons, and with the very same hopes that made me
write an easy account of it for you, when you were a little
child. Because it is the best book that ever was or will be
known in the world, and because it teaches you the best
lessons by which any human creature who tries to be truthful and faithful to duty can possibly be guided. As your
brothers have gone away, one by one, I have written to
each such words as I am now writing to you, and have
entreated them all to guide themselves by this book, putting aside the interpretations and inventions of men.

You will remember that you have never at home been
wearied about religious observances or mere formalities. I
have always been anxious not to weary my children with
such things before they are old enough to form opinions
respecting them. You will therefore understand the better
that I now most solemnly impress upon you the truth and
beauty of the Christian religion, as it came from Christ
Himself, and the impossibility of your going far wrong if
you humbly but heartily respect it.

Only one thing more on this head. The more we are in
earnest as to feeling it, the less we are disposed to hold

forth about it.   Never abandon the wholesome practice of
saying your own private prayers, night and morning.   I
have never abandoned it myself, and I know the comfort
of it.

I hope you will always be able to say in after life that you
had a kind father.   You cannot show your affection for
him so well, or make him so happy, as by doing your duty.

Your affectionate Father.

1869.

NARRATIVE.

THE "Farewell Readings" in town and country were resumed immediately after the beginning of this year, and
were to have been continued until the end of May.   The
work was even harder than it had ever been.   Charles
Dickens began his country tour in Ireland early in January,
and read continuously in all parts of England and Scotland until the end of April.   A public dinner (in commem-
oration of his last readings in the town) was given to him
in Liverpool the 10th April.   Besides all this severe country work, he was giving a series of readings at St. James's
Hall, and reading the "Murder" from "Oliver Twist," in
London and in the country, frequently four times a week.
In the second week of February, a sudden and unusually
violent attack of the old trouble in his foot made it impera-
tively necessary to postpone a reading at St. James's Hall,
and to delay for a day or two his departure for Scotland.
The foot continued to cause him pain and inconvenience,
but, as will be seen from his letters, he generally spoke of
himself as otherwise well, until he arrived at Preston,
where he was to read on the 22nd of April.   The day be-

fore this appointed reading, he writes home of some grave symptoms which he had observed in himself, and had reported to his doctor, Mr. F. Carr Beard. That gentleman, taking alarm at what he considered "indisputable evidences of overwork," wisely resolved not to content himself with written consultations, but went down to Preston on the day appointed for the reading there, and, after seeing his patient, peremptorily stopped it, carried him off to Liverpool, and the next day to London. There he consulted Sir Thomas Watson, who entirely corroborated Mr. Beard's opinion. And the two doctors agreed that the course of readings must be stopped for this year, and that reading, *combined with travelling*, must be stopped *for ever.* Charles Dickens had no alternative but to acquiesce in this verdict; but he felt it keenly, not only for himself but for the sake of the Messrs. Chappell, who showed the most disinterested kindness and solicitude on the occasion. He at once returned home to Gad's Hill, and the rest and quiet of the country restored him, for the time, to almost his usual condition of health and spirits. But it was observed, by all who loved him, that from this time forth he never regained his old vigour and elasticity. The attack at Preston was the "beginning of the end!"

During the spring and summer of this year, he received visits from many dearly valued American friends. In May, he stayed with his daughter and sister-in-law for two or three weeks at the St. James's Hotel, Piccadily, having promised to be in London at the time of the arrival of Mr. and Mrs. Fields, of Boston, who visited Europe, accompanied by Miss Mabel Lowell (the daughter of the famous American poet) this year. Besides these friends, Mr. and Mrs. Childs, of Philadelphia—from whom he had received the greatest kindness and hospitality, and for whom he had a hearty regard—Dr. Fordyce Barker and his son, Mr.

Eytinge (an illustrator of an American edition of Charles Dickens's works), and Mr. Bayard Taylor paid visits to Gad's Hill, which were thoroughly enjoyed by Charles Dickens and his family. This last summer was a very happy one. He had the annual summer visitors and parties of his friends in the neighbourhood. He was, as usual, projecting improvements in his beloved country home ; one, which he called the "crowning improvement of all," was a large conservatory, which was to be added during the absence of the family in London in the following spring.

The state of Mr. Wills's health made it necessary for him now to retire altogether from the editorship of "All the Year Round." Charles Dickens's own letters express the regret which he felt at the dissolution of this long and always pleasant association. Mr. Wills's place at the office was filled by Charles Dickens's eldest son, now sole editor and proprietor of the journal.

In September Charles Dickens went to Birmingham, accompanied by his son Harry, and presided at the opening of the session of (what he calls in his letter to Mr. Arthur Ryland, "*our* Institution ") the Midland Institute. He made a speech on education to the young students, and promised to go back early in the following year and distribute the prizes. In one of the letters which we give to Mr. Ryland, he speaks of himself as "being in full force again," and "going to finish his farewell readings soon after Christmas." He had obtained the sanction of Sir Thomas Watson to giving twelve readings, *in London only,* which he had fixed for the beginning of the following year.

The letter to his friend Mr. Finlay, which opens the year, was in reply to a proposal for a public banquet at Belfast, projected by the Mayor of that town, and conveyed through Mr. Finlay. This gentleman was at that time proprietor of *The Northern Whig* newspaper at Belfast, and he was son-in-law to Mr. Alexander Russel, editor of *The Scotsman.*

Charles Dickens's letter this New Year to M. de Cerjat was his last. That faithful and affectionate friend died very shortly afterwards.

To Miss Mary Boyle he writes to acknowledge a New Year's gift, which he had been much touched by receiving from her, at a time when he knew she was deeply afflicted by the sudden death of her brother, Captain Cavendish Boyle, for whom Charles Dickens had a true regard and friendship.

While he was giving his series of London readings in the spring, he received a numerously signed circular letter from actors and actresses of the various London theatres. They were very curious about his new reading of the "Oliver Twist" murder, and representing to him the impossibility of their attending an evening, requested him to give a morning reading, for their especial benefit. We give his answer, complying with the request. And the occasion was, to him, a most gratifying and deeply interesting one.

The letter to Mr. Edmund Ollier was in answer to an invitation to be present at the inauguration of a bust of Mr. Leigh Hunt, which was to be placed over his grave at Kensal Green.

The letter to Mr. Shirley Brooks, the well-known writer, who succeeded Mr. Mark Lemon as editor of "Punch," and for whom Charles Dickens had a cordial regard, was on the subject of a memorial on behalf of Mrs. Peter Cunningham, whose husband had recently died.

The "remarkable story," of which he writes to his daughter in August, was called "An Experience." It was written by a lady (who prefers to be anonymous) who had been a contributor to "Household Words" from its first starting, and was always highly valued in this capacity by Charles Dickens.

Our latest letters for this year are in October. One to Mr. Charles Kent, sympathising with him on a disappointment which he had experienced in a business undertaking, and one to Mr. Macready, in which he tells him of his being in the "preliminary agonies" of a new book. The first number of "Edwin Drood" was to appear before the end of his course of readings in March; and he was at work so long beforehand with a view to sparing himself, and having some numbers ready before the publication of the first one.

[*To Mr. F. D. Finlay.*]

THE ATHENÆUM (CLUB), *New Year's Day*, 1869.

MY DEAR FINLAY,

First, my heartfelt wishes for many prosperous and happy years. Next, as to the mayor's kind intentions. I feel really grateful to him and gratified by the whole idea, but acceptance of the distinction on my part would be impracticable. My time in Ireland is all anticipated, and I could not possibly prolong my stay, because I *must* be back in London to read on Tuesday fortnight, and then must immediately set forth for the West of England. It is not likely, besides, that I shall get through these farewells before the end of May. And the work is so hard, and my voice is so precious, that I fear to add an ounce to the fatigue, or I might be overweighted. The avoidance of gas and crowds when I am not in the act of being cooked before those lights of mine, is an essential part of the training to which (as I think, you know) I strictly adhere, and although I have accepted the Liverpool invitation, I have done so as an exception ; the Liverpool people having always treated me in our public relations with a kind of personal affection.

I am sincerely anxious that the Mayor of Belfast should know how the case stands with me. If you will kindly set me straight and right, I shall be truly obliged to you.

My sister-in-law has been very unwell (though she is now much better), and is recommended a brisk change. As she is a good sailor, I mean to bring her to Ireland with me ; at which she is highly delighted.

Faithfully yours ever.

[*To M. de Cerjat.*]

GAD'S HILL PLACE, HIGHAM BY ROCHESTER, KENT,
Monday, Jan. 4th, 1869.

MY DEAR CERJAT,

I will answer your question first. Have I done with my farewell readings ? Lord bless you, no ; and I shall think myself well out of it if I get done by the end of May. I have undertaken one hundred and six, and have as yet only vanquished twenty-eight. To-morrow night I read in London for the first time the "Murder" from "Oliver Twist," which I have re-arranged for the purpose. Next day I start for Dublin and Belfast. I am just back from Scotland for a few Christmas holidays. I go back there next month ; and in the meantime and afterwards go everywhere else.

Take my guarantee for it, you may be quite comfortable on the subject of papal aspirations and encroachments. The English people are in unconquerable opposition to that church. They have the animosity in the blood, derived from the history of the past, though perhaps unconsciously. But they do sincerely want to win Ireland over if they can. They know that since the Union she has been hardly used. They know that Scotland has *her* religion, and a very uncomfortable one. They know that Scotland, though intensely anti-papal, perceives it to be unjust that Ireland has not *her* religion too, and has very emphatically declared her opinion in the late elections. They know that a richly-endowed church, forced upon a people who don't belong to it, is a grievance with these people. They know that many things, but especially an artfully and schemingly managed institution like the Romish Church, thrive upon a grievance, and that Rome has thriven exceedingly upon this, and made the most of it. Lastly, the best among them know that there is a gathering cloud in the West, considerably bigger than a man's hand, under which a powerful Irish-American body, rich and active, is always drawing Ireland in that direction. And that these are not times in which other powers would back our holding Ireland by force, unless we could make our claim good in proving fair and equal government.

Poor Townshend charged me in his will "to publish without alteration his religious opinions, which he sincerely believed would tend to the happiness of mankind." To publish them without alteration is absolutely impossible, for they are distributed in the strangest fragments through the strangest note-books, pocket-books, slips of paper and what not, and produce a most incoherent and tautological result. I infer that he must have held some always-postponed idea of fitting them together. For these reasons I would certainly publish nothing about them, if I had any discretion in the matter. Having none, I suppose a book must be made. His pictures and rings are gone to the South Kensington Museum, and are now exhibiting there.

Charley Collins is no better and no worse. Katie looks very young and very pretty. Her sister and Miss Hogarth (my joint housekeepers) have been on duty this Christmas, and have had enough to do. My boys are now all dispersed in South America, India, and Australia, except Charley, whom I have taken on at "All the Year Round" Office, and Henry, who is an undergraduate at Trinity Hall, and I hope will make his mark there. All well.

The Thames Embankment is (faults of ugliness in detail apart) the finest public work yet done. From Westminster Bridge to near Waterloo it is now lighted up at night, and has a fine effect. They have begun to plant it with trees, and the footway (not the road) is already open to the Temple. Besides its beauty, and its usefulness in relieving the crowded streets, it will greatly quicken and deepen what is learnedly called the "scour" of the river. But the Corporation of London and some other nuisances have brought the weirs above Twickenham into a very bare and unsound condition, and they already begin to give and vanish, as the stream runs faster and stronger.

Your undersigned friend has had a few occasional re-minders of his "true American catarrh." Although I have exerted my voice very much, it has not yet been once touched. In America I was obliged to patch it up constantly.

I like to read your patriarchal account of yourself among your Swiss vines and fig-trees. You wouldn't recognise Gad's Hill now ; I have so changed it, and bought land about it. And yet I often think that if Mary were to marry (which she won't) I should sell it and go genteelly vagabondising over the face of the earth. Then indeed I might see Lausanne again. But I don't seem in the way of it at present, for the older I get, the more I do and the harder I work.

Yours ever affectionately.

[*To Miss Mary Boyle.*]

OFFICE OF " ALL THE YEAR ROUND,"
Wednesday, Jan. 6th, 1869.

MY DEAR MARY,

I was more affected than you can easily believe, by the sight of your gift lying on my dressing-table on the morning of the new year. To be remembered in a friend's heart when it is sore is a touching thing ; and that and the remembrance of the dead quite overpowered me, the one being inseparable from the other.

You may be sure that I shall attach a special interest and value to the beautiful present, and shall wear it as a kind of charm. God bless you, and may we carry the friendship through many coming years !

My preparations for a certain murder that I had to do last night have rendered me unfit for letter-writing these last few days, or you would have heard from me sooner. The crime being completely off my mind and the blood spilled, I am (like many of my fellow-criminals) in a highly edifying state to-day.

Ever believe me, your affectionate Friend.

[*To Miss Dickens.*]

TORQUAY, *Wednesday, Jan. 27th*, 1869.

MY DEAREST MAMIE,

We have been doing immensely.

This place is most beautiful, though colder now than one would expect. This hotel, an immense place, built among picturesque broken rocks out in. the blue sea, is quite delicious. There are bright green trees in the garden, and new peas a foot high. Our rooms are *en suite*, all commanding the sea, and each with two very large plate-glass windows. Everything good and well served.

A *pantomime* was being done last night, in the place where I am to read to-night. It is something between a theatre, a circus, a riding-school, a Methodist chapel, and a cow-house. I was so disgusted with its acoustic properties on going in to look at it, that the whole unfortunate staff have been all day, and now are, sticking up baize and carpets in it to prevent echoes.

I have rarely seen a more uncomfortable edifice than I thought it last night.

At Clifton, on Monday night, we had a contagion of fainting. And yet the place was not hot. I should think we had from a dozen to twenty ladies borne out, stiff and rigid, at various times. It became quite ridiculous.

[*To Miss Hogarth.*]

BATH, *Friday, Jan. 29th,* 1869.

MY DEAREST GEORGY,

You must not trust blank places in my list, because many have been, and will be, gradually filled up. After the Tuesday's reading in London, I have TWO for that same week in the country—Nottingham and Leicester. In the following week I have none; but my arrangements are all at sea as yet, for I must somehow and somewhere do an "Uncommercial" in that week, and I also want to get poor Chauncey's "opinions" to the printer.

This mouldy old roosting-place comes out mouldily as to let of course. I hate the sight of the bygone assembly rooms, and the Bath chairs trundling the dowagers about the streets. As to to-morrow morning in the daylight !——

I have no cold to speak of. Dolby sends kindest regard.

[*To Mrs. Lehmann.*]

OFFICE, *Wednesday, Feb. 3rd,* 1869.

DEAR MRS. LEHMANN,

Before getting your kind note, I had written to Lehmann, explaining why I cannot allow myself any social pleasure while my farewell task is yet unfinished. The work is so very hard, that every little scrap of rest *and silence* I can pick up is precious. And even those morsels are so flavoured with " All the Year Round," that they are not quite the genuine article.

Joachim * came round to see me at the hall last night, and I told him how sorry I was to forego the pleasure of meeting him (he is a noble fellow !) at your pleasant table.

I am glad you are coming to the " Murder " on the 2nd of March. (The house will be prodigious.) Such little changes as I have made shall be carefully presented to your critical notice, and I hope will be crowned with your approval. But you are always such a fine audience that I have no fear on that head. I saw Chorley yesterday in his own room. A sad and solitary sight. The widowed Drake with a certain *gin*coherence of manner, presented a blooming countenance and buxom form in the passage ; so buxom indeed that she was obliged to retire before me like a modest stopper, before I could get into the dining decanter where poor Chorley reposed.

Faithfully yours always.

P.S.—My love to Rudie.

[*To Miss Hogarth.*]

GLASGOW, *Thursday, Feb. 25th,* 1869.

I received your letter at Edinburgh this morning. I did not write to you yesterday, as there had been no reading on the previous night.

---

* Herr Joseph Joachim, the renowned violinist.

The foot bears the fatigue wonderfully well, and really occasions me no inconvenience beyond the necessity of wearing the big work of art. Syme saw me again this morning, and utterly scouted the gout notion altogether. I think the Edinburgh audience understood the "Murder" better last night than any audience that has heard it yet. "Business" is enormous, and Dolby jubilant.

It is a most deplorable afternoon here, deplorable even for Glasgow. A great wind blowing, and sleet driving before it in a storm of heavy blobs. We had to drive our train dead in the teeth of the wind, and got in here late, and are pressed for time.

Strange that in the North we have had absolutely no snow. There was a very thin scattering on the Pentlands for an hour or two, but no more.

[*To Miss Hogarth.*]

EDINBURGH, *Friday, Feb.* 26*th*, 1869.

Writing to-morrow morning would be all but impracticable for me ; would be quite so for Dolby, who has to go to the agents and "settle up" in the midst of his breakfast. So I write to-day, in reply to your note received at Glasgow this morning.

The foot conducts itself splendidly. We had a most enormous cram at Glasgow. Syme saw me again yesterday (before I left here for Glasgow) and repeated "Gout!" with the greatest indignation and contempt, several times. The aching is going off as the day goes on, if it be worth mentioning again. The ride from Glasgow was charming this morning ; the sun shining brilliantly, and the country looking beautiful.

I told you what the Nortons were. Mabel Lowell is a charming little thing, and very retiring in manner and expression.

We shall have a scene here to-night, no doubt. The night before last, Ballantyne, unable to get in, had a seat behind the screen, and was nearly frightened off it by the "Murder." Every vestige of colour had left his face when I came off, and he sat staring over a glass of champagne in the wildest way. I have utterly left off *my* champagne, and, I think, with good results. Nothing during the readings but a very little weak iced brandy-and-water.

I hope you will find me greatly improved on Tuesday.

[*To Miss Dickens.*]

BIRMINGHAM, *Friday, March 5th,* 1869.

This is to send you my best love, and to wish you many and many happy returns of morrow, which I miraculously remember to be your birthday.

I saw this morning a very pretty fan here. I was going to buy it as a remembrance of the occasion, when I was checked by a dim misgiving that you had a fan not long ago from Chorley. Tell me what you would like better, and consider me your debtor in that article, whatever it may be.

VOL. II.—21

I have had my usual left boot on this morning, and have had an hour's walk. It was in a gale of wind and a simoom of dust, but I greatly enjoyed it. Immense enthusiasm at Wolverhampton last night over " Marigold." Scott made a most amazing ass of himself yesterday. He.reported that he had left behind somewhere three books—" Boots," " Murder," and " Gamp." We immediately telegraphed to the office. Answer, no books there. As my impression was that he must have left them at St. James's Hall, we then arranged to send him up to London at seven this morning. Meanwhile (though not reproached), he wept copiously and audibly. I had asked him over and over again, was he sure he had not put them in my large black trunk ? Too sure, too sure. Hadn't opened that trunk after Tuesday night's reading. He opened it to get some clothes out when I went to bed, and there the books were ! He produced them with an air of injured surprise, as if we had put them there.

[*To Miss Hogarth.*]

QUEEN'S HOTEL, MANCHESTER, *Sunday, March 7th,* 1869.

We have had our sitting-room chimney afire this morning, and have had to turn out elsewhere to breakfast ; but the chamber has since been cleaned up, and we are reinstated. Manchester is (*for* Manchester) bright and fresh.

Tell Russell that a crop of hay is to be got off the meadow this year, before the club use it. They did not make such use of it last year as reconciles me to losing another hay-crop. So they must wait until the hay is in, before they commence active operations.

Poor Olliffe ! I am truly sorry to read those sad words about his suffering, and fear that the end is not far off.

We are very comfortably housed here, and certainly that immense hall is a wonderful place for its size. Without much greater expenditure of voice than usual, I a little enlarged the action last night, and Dolby (who went to all the distant points of view) reported that he could detect no difference between it and any other place. As always happens now—and did not at first—they were unanimously taken by Noah Claypole's laugh. But the go, throughout, was enormous. Sims Reeves was doing Henry Bertram at the theatre, and of course took some of our shillings. It was a night of excitement for Cottonopolis.

I received from Mrs. Keeley this morning a very good photograph of poor old Bob. Yesterday I had a letter from Harry, reminding me that our intended Cambridge day is the day next after that of the boat-race. Clearly it must be changed.

[*To Miss Hogarth.*]

QUEEN'S HOTEL, MANCHESTER, *Saturday, March 20th,* 1869.

Getting yours and its enclosure, Mary's note, at two this afternoon, I write a line at once in order that you may have it on Monday morning.

The Theatre Royal, Liverpool, will be a charming place

to read in. Ladies are to dine at the dinner, and we hear it is to be a very grand affair. Dolby is doubtful whether it may not "hurt the business," by drawing a great deal of money in another direction, which I think possible enough. Trade is very bad *here*, and the gloom of the Preston strike seems to brood over the place. The Titiens Company have been doing wretchedly. I should have a greater sympathy with them if they were not practising in the next room now.

My love to Letitia and Harriette,* wherein Dolby (highly gratified by being held in remembrance) joins with the same to you.

[*To Miss Hogarth.*]

MANCHESTER, *Sunday, March 21st,* 1869.

Will you tell Mary that I have had a letter from Frith, in which he says that he will be happy to show her his pictures "any day in the first week of April"? I have replied that she will be proud to receive his invitation. His object in writing was to relieve his mind about the "Murder," of which he cannot say enough.

Tremendous enthusiasm here last night, calling in the most thunderous manner after "Marigold," and again after "The Trial," shaking the great hall, and cheering furiously.

Love to all.

---

* His sister-in-law, Mrs. Augustus Dickens, always a welcome visitor at Gad's Hill.

[*To Mr. John Clarke.*]

GAD'S HILL PLACE, HIGHAM BY ROCHESTER, KENT,
Wednesday, March 24th, 1869.

LADIES AND GENTLEMEN,

I beg to assure you that I am much gratified by the desire you do me the honor to express in your letter handed to me by Mr. John Clarke.

Before that letter reached me, I had heard of your wish, and had mentioned to Messrs. Chappell that it would be highly agreeable to me to anticipate it, if possible. They readily responded, and we agreed upon having three morning readings in London. As they are not yet publicly announced, I add a note of the days and subjects :

Saturday, May 1st. "Boots at the Holly-Tree Inn," and "Sikes and Nancy" from "Oliver Twist."

Saturday, May 8th. "The Christmas Carol."

Saturday, May 22nd. "Sikes and Nancy" from "Oliver Twist," and "The Trial" from "Pickwick."

With the warmest interest in your art, and in its claims upon the general gratitude and respect,

Believe me, always faithfully your friend.

[*To Miss Hogarth.*]

ADELPHI HOTEL. LIVERPOOL, *Sunday, April 4th,* 1869.

By this post I send to Mary the truly affecting account of poor dear Katie Macready's death. It is as sorrowful as anything so peaceful and trustful can be !

Both my feet are very tender, and often feel as though

they were in hot water. But I was wonderfully well and strong, thank God ! and had no end of voice for the two nights running in that great Birmingham Hall. We had enormous houses.

So far as I understand the dinner arrangements here, they are much too long. As to the acoustics of that hall, and the position of the tables (both as bad as bad can be), my only consolation is that, if anybody can be heard, *I* probably can be. The honorary secretary tells me that six hundred people are to dine. The mayor, being no speaker and out of health besides, hands over the toast of the evening to Lord Dufferin. The town is full·of the festival. The Theatre Royal, touched up for the occasion, will look remarkably bright and well for the readings, and our lets are large. It is remarkable that our largest let as yet is for Thursday, not Friday. I infer that the dinner damages Friday, but Dolby does not think so. There appears to be great curiosity to hear the " Murder," (On Friday night last I read to two thousand people, and odd hundreds.)

I hear that Anthony Trollope, Dixon, Lord Houghton, Lemon, Esquiros (of the *Revue des Deux Mondes*), and Sala are to be called upon to speak ; the last, for the newspaper press. All the Liverpool notabilities are to muster. And Manchester is to be represented by its mayor with due formality.

I had been this morning to look at St. George's Hall, and suggest what can be done to improve its acoustics. As usually happens in such cases, their most important arrangements are already made and unchangeable. I should not have placed the tables in the committee's way at all, and could certainly have placed the daïs to much greater advantage. So all the good I could do was to show where banners could be hung with some hope of stopping echoes. Such is my small news, soon exhausted. We arrived here at three yesterday afternoon; it is now midday; Chorley has not yet appeared, but he had called at the local agent's while I was at Birmingham.

It is a curious little instance of the way in which things fit together that there is a ship-of-war in the Mersey, whose flags and so forth are to be brought up to St. George's Hall for the dinner. She is the *Donegal*, of which Paynter told me he had just been captain, when he told me all about Sydney at Bath.

One of the pleasantest things I have experienced here this time, is the manner in which I am stopped in the streets by working men, who want to shake hands with me, and tell me they know my books. I never go out but this happens. Down at the docks just now, a cooper with a fearful stutter presented himself in this way. His modesty, combined with a conviction that if he were in earnest I would see it and wouldn't repel him, made up as true a piece of natural politeness as I ever saw.

[*To Miss Hogarth.*]

IMPERIAL HOTEL, BLACKPOOL, *Wednesday, April 21st,* 1869.

I send you this hasty line to let you know that I have come to this sea-beach hotel (charming) for a day's rest.

I am much better than I was on Sunday, but shall want careful looking to, to get through the readings. My weakness and deadness are all *on the left side,* and if I don't look at anything I try to touch with my left hand, I don't know where it is. I am in (secret) consultation with Frank Beard; he recognises, in the exact description I have given him, indisputable evidences of overwork, which he would wish to treat immediately. So I have said : " Go in and win."

I have had a delicious walk by the sea to-day, and I sleep soundly, and have picked up amazingly in appetite. My foot is greatly better too, and I wear my own boot.

[*To Miss Dickens.*]

PRESTON, *Thursday Evening, April 22nd,* 1869.

Don't be in the least alarmed. Beard has come down, and instantly echoes my impression (perfectly unknown to him), that the readings must be *stopped.* I have had symptoms that must not be disregarded. I go to Liverpool to-night with him (to get away from here) and proceed to the office to-morrow.

[*To the Lord John Russell.*]

GAD'S HILL PLACE, HIGHAM BY ROCHESTER, KENT,
Wednesday, May 26th, 1869.

MY DEAR LORD RUSSELL,

I have delayed in answering your kind letter, in order that you might get home before I wrote. I am happy to report myself quite well again, and I shall be charmed to come to Pembroke Lodge on any day that may be most convenient to Lady Russell and yourself after the middle of June.

You gratify me beyond expression by your reference to the Liverpool dinner. I made the allusion to you with all my heart at least, and it was most magnificently received.

I beg to send my kind regard to Lady Russell, with many thanks for her remembrance, and am ever,

My dear Lord Russell, faithfully yours.

[*To Mr. W. H. Wills.*]

OFFICE OF "ALL THE YEAR ROUND,"
Thursday, June 24th, 1869.

MY DEAR WILLS,

At a great meeting* compounded of your late "Chief," Charley, Morley, Grieve, and Telbin, your letter was read to-day, and a very sincere record of regret and thanks was placed on the books of the great institution.

Many thanks for the suggestion about the condition of churches. I am so aweary of church questions of all sorts that I am not quite clear as to tackling this. But I am turning it in my mind. I am afraid of two things: firstly, that the thing would not be picturesquely done ; secondly, that a general cucumber-coolness would pervade the mind of our circulation.

---

* Of the Guild of Literature and Art.

Nothing new here but a speaking-pipe, a post-box, and a mouldy smell from some forgotten crypt—an extra mouldy smell, mouldier than of yore. Lillie sniffs, projects one eye into nineteen hundred and ninety-nine, and does no more.

I have been to Chadwick's, to look at a new kind of cottage he has built (very ingenious and cheap).

We were all much disappointed last Saturday afternoon by a neighbouring fire being only at a carpenter's, and not at Drury Lane Theatre. Ellen's * child having an eye nearly poked out by a young friend, and being asked whether the young friend was not very sorry afterwards, replied : " No. *She* wasn't. *I* was."

London execrable.

Ever affectionately yours.

P.S.—Love to Mrs. Wills.

[*To Mr. Shirley Brooks.*]

GAD'S HILL PLACE, HIGHAM BY ROCHESTER, KENT,
Tuesday, July 12th, 1869.

MY DEAR BROOKS,

I have appended my sign manual to the memorial, which I think is very discreetly drawn up. I have a strong feeling of sympathy with poor Mrs. Cunningham, for I remember the pretty house she managed charmingly. She has always done her duty well, and has had hard trials.

---

* The housekeeper at the office.

But I greatly doubt the success of the memorial, I am sorry to add.

It was hotter here yesterday on this Kentish chalk than I have felt it anywhere for many a day. Now it is overcast and raining hard, much to the satisfaction of great farmers like myself.

I am glad to infer from your companionship with the Cocked Hats, that there is no such thing as gout within several miles of you. May it keep its distance.

Ever, my dear Brooks, faithfully yours.

[*To Mr. W. C. Macready.*]

GAD'S HILL, *Tuesday, July 20th,* 1869.

MY DEAREST MACREADY,

I have received your letter here to-day, and deeply feel with you and for you the affliction of poor dear Katie's loss. I was not unprepared for the sad news, but it comes in such a rush of old remembrances and withered joys that strikes to the heart.

God bless you! Love and youth are still beside you, and in that thought I take comfort for my dear old friend.

I am happy to report myself perfectly well and flourishing. We are just now announcing the resumption and conclusion of the broken series of farewell readings in a London course of twelve, beginning early in the new year.

Scarcely a day has gone by this summer in which we

have not talked of you and yours. Georgina, Mary, and I continually speak of you. In the spirit we certainly are even more together than we used to be in the body in the old times. I don't know whether you have heard that Harry has taken the second scholarship (fifty pounds a year) at Trinity Hall, Cambridge. The bigwigs expect him to do a good deal there.

Wills having given up in consequence of broken health (he has been my sub-editor for twenty years), I have taken Charley into "All the Year Round." He is a very good man of business, and evinces considerable aptitude in sub-editing work.

This place is immensely improved since you were here, and really is now very pretty indeed. We are sorry that there is no present prospect of your coming to see it ; but I like to know of your being at the sea, and having to do —*from the beach*, as Mrs. Keeley used to say in "The Prisoner of War "—with the winds and the waves and all their freshening influences.

I dined at Greenwich a few days ago with Delane. He asked me about you with much interest. He looks as if he had never seen a printing-office, and had never been out of bed after midnight.

Great excitement caused here by your capital news of Butty. I suppose Willy has at least a dozen children by this time.

Our loves to the noble boy and to dear Mrs. Macready.

> Ever, my dearest Macready,
>> Your attached and affectionate.

[*To Mr. Edmund Ollier.*]

GAD'S HILL PLACE, HIGHAM BY ROCHESTER, KENT,
Tuesday, Aug. 3rd, 1869.

MY DEAR MR. OLLIER,

I am very sensible of the feeling of the Committee towards me ; and I receive their invitation (conveyed through you) as a most acceptable mark of their consideration.

But I have a very strong objection to speech-making beside graves. I do not expect or wish my feeling in this wise to guide other men ; still, it is so serious with me, and the idea of ever being the subject of such a ceremony myself is so repugnant to my soul, that I must decline to officiate.

Faithfully yours always.

[*To Miss Dickens.*]

OFFICE OF "ALL THE YEAR ROUND," No. 26, WELLINGTON STREET,
STRAND, LONDON, W.C.,
Tuesday, Aug. 3rd, 1869.

MY DEAREST MAMIE,

I send you the second chapter of the remarkable story. The printer is late with it, and I have not had time to read it, and as I altered it considerably here and there, I have no doubt there are some verbal mistakes in it. However, they will probably express themselves.

But I offer a prize of six pairs of gloves—between you, and your aunt, and Ellen Stone, as competitors—to whomsoever will tell me what idea in this second part is mine. I don't mean an idea in language, in the turning of a sentence, in any little description of an action, or a gesture, or what not in a small way, but an idea, distinctly affecting the whole story *as I found it.* You are all to assume that I found it in the main as you read it, with one· exception. If I had written it, I should have made the woman love the man at last. And I should have shadowed that possibility out, by the child's bringing them a little more together on that holiday Sunday.

But I didn't write it. So, finding that it wanted something, I put that something in. What was it ?

Love to Ellen Stone.

[*To Mr. Arthur Ryland.*]

GAD'S HILL PLACE, HIGHAM BY ROCHESTER, KENT,
Friday, Aug. 13th, 1869.

MY DEAR MR. RYLAND,

Many thanks for your letter.

I have very strong opinions on the subject of speechification, and hold that there is, everywhere, a vast amount too much of it. A sense of absurdity would be so strong upon me, if I got up at Birmingham to make a flourish on the advantages of education in the abstract for all sorts and conditions of men, that I should inevitably check myself and present a surprising incarnation of the soul of wit. But if I could interest myself in the practical usefulness of the particular institution ; in the ways of life of the students ; in their examples of perseverance and determination to get on ; in their numbers, their favourite studies, the number of hours they must daily give to the work that must be done for a livelihood, before they can devote themselves to the acquisition of new knowledge, and so forth, then I could interest others. This is the kind of information I want. Mere holding forth " I utterly detest, abominate, and abjure."

I fear I shall not be in London next week. But if you will kindly send me here, at your leisure, the roughest notes of such points as I have indicated, I shall be heartily obliged to you, and will take care of their falling into shape and order in my mind. Meantime I " make a note of " Monday, 27th September, and of writing to you touching your kind offer of hospitality, three weeks before that date.

I beg to send my kind regard to Mrs. and Miss Ryland, and am always,

Very faithfully yours.

[*To Mr. Frederic Ouvry.*]

GAD'S HILL PLACE, HIGHAM BY ROCHESTER, KENT,
Sunday, Aug. 22nd, 1869.

MY DEAR OUVRY,

I will expect a call from you at the office, on Thursday, at your own most convenient hour. I admit the soft impeachment concerning Mrs. Gamp : I likes my payments to be made reg'lar, and I likewise likes my publisher to draw it mild.

Ever yours.

[*To Mr. Arthur Ryland.*]

GAD'S HILL PLACE, HIGHAM BY ROCHESTER, KENT,
Monday, Sept. 6th, 1869.

MY DEAR MR. RYLAND,

I am sorry to find—I had a foreshadowing of it some
weeks ago—that I shall not be able to profit by your kind
offer of hospitality when I come to Birmingham for *our*
Institution. I must come down in time for a quiet dinner
at the hotel wth my "Readings" secretary, Mr. Dolby,
and must away next morning. Besides having a great
deal in hand just now (the title of a new book among
other things), I shall have visitors from abroad here at the
time, and am severely claimed by my daughter, who indeed is disloyal to Birmingham in the matter of my going
away at all. Pray represent me to Mrs. Ryland as the
innocent victim of circumstances, and as sacrificing pleasure to the work I have to do, and to the training under
which alone I can do it without feeling it.

You will see from the enclosed that I am in full force,
and going to finish my readings, please God, after Christmas. I am in the hope of receiving your promised notes
in due course, and continue in the irreverent condition in
which I last reported myself on the subject of speech-
making. Now that men not only make the nights of the
session hideous by what the Americans call "orating" in
Parliament, but trouble the peace of the vacation by saying over again what they said there (with the addition of

what they *didn't* say there, and never will have the courage to say there), I feel indeed that silence, like gold across the Atlantic, is a rarity at a premium.

Faithfully yours always.

[*To Mr. William Charles Kent.*]

OFFICE OF "ALL THE YEAR ROUND,"

Thursday, Oct. 7th, 1869.

MY DEAR KENT, •

I felt that you would be deeply disappointed. I thought it better not to make the first sign while you were depressed, but my mind has been constantly with you. And not mine alone. You cannot think with what affection and sympathy you have been made the subject of our family dinner talk at Gad's Hill these last three days. Nothing could exceed the interest of my daughters and my sister-in-law, or the earnestness of their feeling about it. I have been really touched by its warm and genuine expression.

Cheer up, my dear fellow; cheer up, for God's sake. That is, for the sake of all that is good in you and around you.

Ever your affectionate Friend.

[*To Mr. W. C. Macready.*]

GAD'S HILL, *Monday, Oct. 18th,* 1869.

MY DEAREST MACREADY,

I duly received your letter nearly a fortnight ago, with the greatest interest and pleasure. Above all things I am delighted with the prospect of seeing you here next summer ; a prospect which has been received with nine times nine and one more by the whole house. You will hardly know the place again, it is so changed. You are not expected to admire, but there *is* a conservatory building at this moment—be still, my soul !

This leaves me in the preliminary agonies of a new book, which I hope to begin publishing (in twelve numbers, not twenty) next March. The coming readings being all in London, and being, after the first fortnight, only once a week, will divert my attention very little, I hope.

Harry has just gone up to Cambridge again, and I hope will get a fellowship in good time.

Wills is much gratified by your remembrance, and sends you his warm regard. He wishes me to represent that he is very little to be pitied. That he suffers no pain, scarcely inconvenience, even, so long as he is idle. That he likes idleness exceedingly. He has bought a country place by Welwyn in Hertfordshire, near Lytton's, and takes possession presently.

My boy Sydney is now a second lieutenant, the youngest in the Service, I believe. He has the highest testimonials as an officer.

You may be quite sure there will be no international racing in American waters. Oxford knows better, or I am mistaken. The Harvard crew were a very good set of fellows, and very modest.

Ryland of Birmingham doesn't look a day older, and was full of interest in you, and asked me to remind you of him. By-the-bye, at Elkington's I saw a pair of immense tea-urns from a railway station (Stafford), sent there to be repaired. They were honeycombed within in all directions, and had been supplying the passengers, under the active agency of hot water, with decomposed lead, copper, and a few other deadly poisons, for heaven knows how many years !

I must leave off in a hurry to catch the post, after a hard day's work.

Ever, my dearest Macready,

Your most affectionate and attached.

1870.

NARRATIVE.

CHARLES DICKENS passed his last Christmas and New Year's Day at Gad's Hill, with a party of family and friends, in the usual way, except that he was suffering again from an attack of the foot trouble, particularly on Christmas Day, when he was quite disabled by it and unable to walk at all—able only to join the party in the evening by keeping his room all day. However, he was better in a day or two, and early in January he went to London, where he had taken the house of his friends, Mr. and Mrs. Milner Gibson, for the séason.

His series of " Farewell Readings " at St. James's Hall, began in January, and ended on the 16th March. He was writing " Edwin Drood " also, and was, of course, constantly occupied with " All the Year Round " work. In the beginning of January, he fulfilled his promise of paying a second visit to Birmingham and making a speech, of which he writes in his last letter to Mr. Macready.

For his last reading he gave "Christmas Carol" and " The Trial " from " Pickwick," and at the end of the evening he addressed a few farewell words to his audience. It was a memorable and splendid occasion. He was very deeply affected by the loving enthusiasm of his greeting, and it was a real sorrow to him to give up for ever the personal associations with thousands of the readers of his books. But when the pain, mingled with pleasure, of this last reading was over, he felt greatly the relief of having undisturbed time for his own quieter pursuits, and looked forward to writing the last numbers of " Edwin Drood " at Gad's Hill, where he was to return in June.

The last public appearance of any kind that he made was at the Royal Academy dinner in May. He was at the time far from well, but he made a great effort to be present and to speak, from his strong desire to pay a tribute to the memory of his dear old friend Mr. Maclise, who died in April.

Her Majesty having expressed a wish, conveyed through Mr. Helps (afterwards Sir Arthur Helps), to have a personal interview with Charles Dickens, he accompanied Mr. Helps to Buckingham Palace one afternoon in March. He was most graciously and kindly received by her Majesty, and came away with a hope that the visit had been mutually agreeable. The Queen presented him with a copy of her " Journal in the Highlands," with an autograph inscription. And he had afterwards the pleasure of requesting her acceptance of a set of his books. He attended a levee held by the Prince of Wales in April, and the last time he dined out in London was at a party given by Lord Houghton for the King of the Belgians and the Prince of Wales, who had both expressed a desire to meet Charles Dickens. All through the season he had been suffering, at intervals, from the swollen foot, and on this occasion it was so bad, that up to the last moment it was very doubtful whether he could fulfill his engagement.

We have very few letters for this year, and none of any very particular interest, but we give them all as they are *the last.*

Mr. S. L. Fildes was his "new illustrator," to whom he alludes in a note to Mr. Frith ; we also give a short note to Mr. Fildes himself.

The correspondence of Charles Dickens with Mrs. Dallas Glyn, the celebrated actress, for whom he had a great friendship, is so much on the subject of her own business, that we have only been able to select two notes of any public interest.

In explanation of *the last letter,* we give an extract from a letter addressed to *The Daily News* by Mr. J. M. Makeham, soon after the death of Charles Dickens, as follows: "That the public may exactly understand the circumstances under which Charles Dickens's letter to me was written, I am bound to explain that it is in reply to a letter which I addressed to him in reference to a passage in the tenth chapter of "Edwin Drood," respecting which I ventured to suggest that he had, perhaps, forgotten that the figure of speech alluded to by him, in a way which, to my certain knowledge, was distasteful to some of his admirers, was drawn from a passage of Holy Writ which is greatly reverenced by a large number of his countrymen as a prophetic description of the sufferings of our Saviour."

The MS. of the little "History of the New Testament" is now in the possession of his eldest daughter. She has (together with her aunt) received many earnest entreaties, both from friends and strangers, that this history might be allowed to be published, for the benefit of other children.

These many petitions have his daughter's fullest sympathy. But she knows that her father wrote this history ONLY for his own children, that it was his particular wish that it never should be published, and she therefore holds this wish as sacred and irrevocable.

[*To Mr. W. H. Wills.*]

5, HYDE PARK PLACE, LONDON, W., *Sunday, Jan. 23rd*, 1870.
MY DEAR WILLS,

In the note I had from you about Nancy and Sikes, you seem to refer to some other note you had written me. Therefore I think it well merely to mention that I have received no other note.

I do not wonder at your not being up to the undertaking (even if you had had no cough) under the wearing circumstances. It was a very curious scene. The actors and actresses (most of the latter looking very pretty) mustered in extraordinary force, and were a fine audience. I set myself to carrying out of themselves and their observation, those who were bent on watching how the effects were got ; and I believe I succeeded. Coming back to it again, however, I feel it was madness ever to do it so continuously. My ordinary pulse is seventy-two, and it runs up under this effort to one hundred and twelve. Besides which, it takes me ten or twelve minutes to get my wind back at all ; I being, in the meantime, like the man who lost the fight—in fact, his express image. Frank Beard was in attendance to make divers experiments to report to Watson ; and although, as you know, he stopped it instantly when he found me at Preston, he was very much astonished by the effects of the reading on the reader.

So I hope you may be able to come and hear it before it is silent for ever. It is done again on the evenings of the 1st February, 15th February, and 8th March. I hope, now I have got over the mornings, that I may be able to work on my book. But up to this time the great preparation required in getting the subjects up again, and the twice a week besides, have almost exclusively occupied me.

I have something the matter with my right thumb, and can't (as you see) write plainly. I sent a word to poor Robert Chambers,* and I send my love to Mrs. Wills.

Ever, my dear Wills, affectionately yours.

[To Mrs. Dallas.]

Office of " All the Year Round,"
Wednesday, Jan. 16th, 1870.

My dear Mrs. Dallas,

It is perfectly delightful to me to get your fervent and sympathetic note this morning. A thousand thanks for it. I will take care that two places on the front row, by my daughter, are reserved for your occasion next time. I cannot see you in too good a seat, or too often.

Believe me, ever very faithfully yours.

---

* On the death of his second wife.

[*To Mr. S. L. Fildes.*]

OFFICE OF " ALL THE YEAR ROUND,

Wednesday, Jan. 16*th*, 1870.

DEAR SIR,

I beg to thank you for the highly meritorious and interesting specimens of your art that you have had the
kindness to send me.   I return them herewith, after having examined them with the greatest pleasure.

I am naturally curious to see your drawing from " David
Copperfield," in order that I may compare it with my own
idea.   In the meanwhile, I can honestly assure you that I
entertain the greatest admiration for your remarkable
powers.

Faithfully yours.

[*To Mr. Henry Fielding Dickens.*]

5, HYDE PARK PLACE, W., *Thursday, Feb.* 17*th*, 1870.

MY DEAR HARRY,

I am extremely glad to hear that you have made a good
start at the Union.   Take any amount of pains about it ;
open your mouth well and roundly, speak to the last person visible, and give yourself time.

Loves from all, ever affectionately.

[*To Mr. W. C. Macready.*]

Wednesday, March 2*nd*, 1870.

MY DEAREST MACREADY,

This is to wish you and yours all happiness and pros-
perity at the well-remembered anniversary to-morrow.

You may be sure that loves and happy returns will not be forgotten at *our* table.

I have been getting on very well with my book, and we are having immense audiences at St. James's Hall. Mary has been celebrating the first glimpses of spring by having the measles. She got over the disorder very easily, but a weakness remains behind. Katie is blooming. Georgina is in perfect order, and all send you their very best loves. It gave me true pleasure to have your sympathy with me in the second little speech at Birmingham. I was determined that my Radicalism should not be called in question. The electric wires are not very exact in their reporting, but at all events the sense was there. Ryland, as usual, made all sorts of enquiries about you.

With love to dear Mrs. Macready and the noble boy my particular friend, and a hearty embrace to you,

I am ever, my dearest Macready,

Your most affectionate.

[*To Mr. Percy Fitzgerald.*]

OFFICE OF " ALL THE YEAR ROUND,"
Wednesday, March 9th, 1870.

MY DEAR FITZGERALD,

You make me very uneasy on the subject of your new long story here, by sowing your name broadcast in so many fields at once, and undertaking such an impossible amount of fiction at one time. Just as you are coming on with us, you have another story in progress in " The Gentleman's Magazine," and another announced in " Once a Week." And so far as I know the art we both profess, it cannot be reasonably pursued in this way. I think the short story you are now finishing in these pages obviously marked by traces of great haste and small consideration ; and a long story similarly blemished would really do the publication irreparable harm.

These considerations are so much upon my mind that I cannot forbear representing them to you, in the hope that they may induce you to take a little more into account the necessity of care and preparation, and some self-denial in the quantity done. I am quite sure that I write fully as much in your interest as in that of " All the Year Round."

Believe me, always faithfully yours.

[*To Mr. Percy Fitzgerald.*]

5, HYDE PARK PLACE, *Friday, March 11th*, 1870.
MY DEAR FITZGERALD,

Of course the engagement between us is to continue, and I am sure you know me too well to suppose that I have ever had a thought to the contrary. Your explanation is (as it naturally would be, being yours) manly and honest, and I am both satisfied and hopeful.

Ever yours.

[*To Mr. William Charles Kent.*]

5, HYDE PARK PLACE, W., *Saturday, March 26th*, 1870.
MY DEAR KENT,

I received both copies of *The Sun*, with the tenderest pleasure and gratification.

Everything that I can let you have in aid of the proposed record* (which, *of course*, would be far more agreeable to me if done by you than by any other hand), shall be at your service. Dolby has all the figures relating to America, and you shall have for reference the books from which I read. They are afterwards going into Forster's collection.†

> Ever affectionately.

[*To Mr. Henry Fielding Dickens.*]

5, HYDE PARK PLACE, W., *Tuesday, March 29th*, 1870.
MY DEAR HARRY,

Your next Tuesday's subject is a very good one. I would not lose the point that narrow-minded fanatics, who decry the theatre and defame its artists, are absolutely the advocates of depraved and barbarous amusements. For wherever a good drama and a well-regulated theatre decline, some distorted form of theatrical entertainment will infallibly arise in their place. In one of the last chapters of "Hard Times," Mr. Sleary says something to the effect: "People will be entertained thomehow, thquire. Make the betht of uth, and not the wortht."

> Ever affectionately.

---

* Of the Readings. The intention was carried out. Mr. Kent's book, "Charles Dickens as a Reader," was published in 1872.

† No doubt Charles Dickens intended to add the Reading Books to the legacy of his MSS. to Mr. Forster. But he did not do so, therefore the "Readings" are *not* a part of the "Forster Collection" at the South Kensington Museum.

[*To Mr. Shirley Brooks.*]

4, HYDE PARK PLACE, W., *Friday, April 1st,* 1870.

MY DEAR SHIRLEY BROOKS,

I have written to Mr. Low, expressing my regret that I cannot comply with his request, backed as it is by my friend S. B. But I have told him what is perfectly true—that I leave town for the peaceful following of my own pursuits, at the end of next month ; that I have excused myself from filling all manner of claims, on the ground that the public engagements I could make for the season were very few and were all made ; and that I cannot bear hot rooms when I am at work. I have smoothed this as you would have me smooth it.

With your longing for fresh air I can thoroughly sympathise. May you get it soon, and may you enjoy it, and profit by it half as much as I wish !

Ever faithfully yours.

[*To Mr. W. P. Frith, R.A.*]

5, HYDE PARK PLACE, W., *Saturday, April 16th,* 1870.

MY DEAR FRITH,

I shall be happy to go on Wednesday evening, if convenient.

You please me with what you say of my new illustrator, of whom I have great hopes.

Faithfully yours ever.

[*To Mr. William Charles Kent.*]

Monday Morning, April 25th, 1870.

MY DEAR KENT,

I received your book* with the greatest pleasure, and heartily thank you for it. It is a volume of a highly pre-possessing appearance, and a most friendly look. I felt as if I should have taken to it at sight ; even (a very large even) though I had known nothing of its contents, or of its author !

For the last week I have been most perseveringly and ding-dong-doggedly at work, making headway but slowly. The spring always has a restless influence over me ; and I weary, at any season, of this London dining-out beyond expression ; and I yearn for the country again. This is my excuse for not having written to you sooner. Besides which, I had a baseless conviction that I should see you at the office last Thursday. Not having done so, I fear you must be worse, or no better ? If you *can* let me have a report of yourself, pray do.

[*To Mrs. Frederick Pollock.*]

5, HYDE PARK PLACE, W., *Monday, May 2nd,* 1870.

MY DEAR MRS. POLLOCK,

Pray tell the illustrious Philip van Artevelde, that I will deal with the nefarious case in question if I can. I am a

---

* A new collective edition of " Kent's Poems," dedicated to his cousin, Colonel Kent, of the 77th Regiment.

little doubtful of the practicability of doing so, and frisking outside the bounds of the law of libel. I have that high opinion of the law of England generally, which one is likely to derive from the impression that it puts all the honest men under the diabolical hoofs of all the scoundrels. It makes me cautious of doing right; an admirable instance of its wisdom!

I was very sorry to have gone astray from you that Sunday; but as the earlier disciples entertained angels unawares, so the later often missed them haphazard.

Your description of La Font's acting is the complete truth in one short sentence. Nature's triumph over art; reversing the copy-book axiom! But the Lord deliver us from Plessy's mechanical ingenuousness!!

And your petitioner will ever pray.

And ever be,

Faithfully yours.

[*To Mrs. E. M. Ward.*]

5, HYDE PARK PLACE, W., *Wednesday, May 11th*, 1870.

MY DEAR MRS. WARD,

I grieve to say that I am literally laid by the heels, and incapable of dining with you to-morrow. A neuralgic affection of the foot, which usually seizes me about twice a year, and which will yield to nothing but days of fomentation and horizontal rest, set in last night, and has caused me very great pain ever since, and will too clearly be no better until it has had its usual time in which to wear itself out. I send my kindest regard to Ward, and beg to be pitied.

> Believe me, faithfully yours always.

[*To Mr. William Charles Kent.*]

5, HYDE PARK PLACE, W., *Tuesday, May 17th,* 1870.

MY DEAR KENT,

Many, many thanks! It is only my neuralgic foot. It has given me such a sharp twist this time that I have not been able, in its extreme sensitiveness, to put any covering upon it except scalding fomentations. Having viciously bubbled and blistered it in all directions, I hope it now begins to see the folly of its ways.

> Affectionately ever.

P.S.—I hope the Sun shines.

[*To Mrs. Bancroft.*]

GAD'S HILL PLACE, HIGHAM BY ROCHESTER, KENT,

> *Thursday, May 31st,* 1870.

MY DEAR MRS. BANCROFT,*

I am most heartily obliged to you for your kind note, which I received here only last night, having come here from town circuitously to get a little change of air on the road. My sense of your interest cannot be better proved than by my trying the remedy you recommend, and that I will do immediately. As I shall be in town on Thursday,

---

* Miss Marie Wilton.

my troubling you to order it would be quite unjustifiable. I will use your name in applying for it, and will report the result after a fair trial. Whether this remedy succeeds or fails as to the neuralgia, I shall always consider myself under an obligation to it for having indirectly procured me the great pleasure of receiving a communication from you. For I hope I may lay claim to being one of the most earnest and delighted of your many artistic admirers.

Believe me, faithfully yours.

[*To Mr. William Charles Kent.*]

Gad's Hill Place,
Higham by Rochester, Kent.*

Wednesday Eighth June 1870

My dear Kent

Tomorrow is a very bad day
for me to make a call, as, in
addition to my usual office business, I
have a mass of accounts to settle
with Wills. But I hope I may be
ready for you at 3 o'clock. If I
can't be ready, then I shant be.

You must really get rid of
those Opal enjoyments. They are too
overpowering:

"These violent delights have violent ends."

I think it was a father of your church
who made the wise remark to a young
gentleman who got up early (or
stayed out late) at Verona?

Ever affectionately

CD

* This letter has lately been presented by Mr. Charles Kent to the British Mu-

[*To Mr. John M. Makeham.*]

Gad's Hill Place,
Higham by Rochester, Kent.

Wednesday Eighth June 1870

My Dear Sir

It would be quite inconceivable that — but for your letter — that any reasonable reader could possibly attach a scriptural reference to a passage in a book of mine, reproducing a much abused social figure of speech, impressed into all sorts of service, on all sorts of inappropriate occasions, without the faintest connexion of it with its original source. I am truly shocked to find that any reader can make the mistake

I have always striven in my
writings to express veneration for
the life and lessons of Our Saviour;
because I feel it; and because I
re-wrote that history for my
children — every one of whom
knew it from having it repeated
to them — long before they could

read, and almost as soon as they could speak.

But I have never made
proclamation of this from the house tops

Faithfully Yours

Charles Dickens

John M. Makeham Esqr.

All through this spring in London, Charles Dickens had been ailing in health, and it was remarked by many friends that he had a weary look, and was "aged" and altered. But he was generally in good spirits, and his family had no uneasiness about him, relying upon the country quiet and comparative rest at Gad's Hill to have their usual influence in restoring his health and strength.   On the 2nd June he attended a private play at the house of Mr. and Mrs. Freake, where his two daughters were among the actresses.   The next day he went back to Gad's Hill.   His daughter Kate (whose home was here at all times when she chose, and almost always through the summer months) went down on Sunday, the 5th June, for a day's visit, to see the "great improvement of the conservatory."   Her father laughingly assured her she had now seen "the last" improvement at Gad's Hill.   At this time he was tolerably well, but she remarked to her sister and aunt how strangely he was tired, and what a curious grey colour he had in his face after a very short walk on that Sunday afternoon. However, he seemed quite himself again in the evening. The next day his daughter Kate went back, accompanied by her sister, who was to pay her a short visit, to London.

Charles Dickens was very hard at work on the sixth number of "Edwin Drood."   On the Monday and Tuesday he was well, but he was unequal to much exercise. His last walk was one of his greatest favourites—through Cobham Park and Wood—on the afternoon of Tuesday.

On the morning of Wednesday, the 8th (one of the loveliest days of a lovely summer), he was very well ; in excellent spirits about his book, of which he said he *must* finish his number that day—the next (Thursday) being the day of his weekly visit to "All the Year Round," office. Therefore, he would write all day in the Châlet, and take no walk or drive until the evening.   In the middle of the day he came to the house for an hour's rest, and smoked a cigar in the conservatory—out of which new addition to the house he was taking the greatest personal enjoyment —and seemed perfectly well, and exceedingly cheerful and hopeful. When he came again to the house, about an hour before the time fixed for the early dinner, he seemed very tired, silent, and absorbed. But this was so usual with him after a day of engrossing work, that it caused no alarm or surprise to his sister-in-law—the only member of his household who happened to be at home. He wrote some letters—among them, these last letters which we give—in the library of the house, and also arranged many trifling business matters, with a view to his departure for London the next morning. He was to be accompanied, on his return at the end of the week, by Mr. Fildes, to introduce the "new illustrator" to the neighbourhood in which many of the scenes of this last book of Charles Dickens, as of his first, were laid.

It was not until they were seated at the dinner-table that a striking change in the colour and expression of his face startled his sister-in-law, and on her asking him if he was ill, he said, "Yes, very ill; I have been very ill for the last hour." But on her expressing an intention of sending instantly for a doctor, he stopped her, and said : "No, he would go on with dinner, and go afterwards to London." And then he made an effort to struggle against the fit that was fast coming on him, and talked, but incoherently, and soon very indistinctly. It being now evident that he *was* ill, and very seriously ill, his sister-in-law begged him to come to his own room before she sent off for medical help. "Come and lie down," she entreated. "Yes, on the ground," he said, very distinctly—these were the last words he spoke —and he slid from her arm, and fell upon the floor.

The servants brought a couch into the dining-room,

where he was laid. A messenger was despatched for Mr. Steele, the Rochester doctor, and with a telegram to his doctor in London, and to his daughters. This was a few minutes after six o'clock.

His daughters arrived, with Mr. Frank Beard, this same evening. His eldest son the next morning, and his son Henry and his sister Letitia in the evening of the 9th—too late, alas !

All through the night, Charles Dickens never opened his eyes, or showed a sign of consciousness. In the afternoon of the 9th, Dr. Russell Reynolds arrived at Gad's Hill, having been summoned by Mr. Frank Beard to meet himself and Mr. Steele. But he could only confirm their hopeless verdict, and made his opinion known with much kind sympathy, to the family, before returning to London.

Charles Dickens remained in the same unconscious state until the evening of this day, when, at ten minutes past six, the watchers saw a shudder pass over him, heard him give a deep sigh, saw one tear roll down his cheek, and he was gone from them. And as they saw the dark shadow steal across his calm, beautiful face, not one among them —could they have been given such a power—would have recalled his sweet spirit back to earth.

As his family were aware that Charles Dickens had a wish to be buried near Gad's Hill, arrangements were made for his burial in the pretty churchyard of Shorne, a neighbouring village, of which he was very fond. But this intention was abandoned in consequence of a pressing request from the Dean and Chapter of Rochester Cathedral that his remains might be placed there. A grave was prepared and everything arranged, when it was made known to the family, through Dean Stanley, that there was a general and very earnest desire that Charles Dickens should find his resting-place in Westminster Abbey. To such a fitting tribute to his memory they could make no possible objection, although it was with great regret that they relinquished the idea of laying him in a place so closely identified with his life and his works. His name, notwithstanding, is associated with Rochester, a tablet to his memory having been placed by his executors on the wall of Rochester Cathedral.

With regard to Westminster Abbey, his family only stipulated that the funeral might be made as private as possible, and that the words of his will, " I emphatically direct that I be buried in an inexpensive, unostentatious, and strictly private manner," should be religiously adhered to. And so they were. The solemn service in the vast cathedral being as private as the most thoughtful consideration could make it.

The family of Charles Dickens were deeply grateful to all in authority who so carried out his wishes. And more especially to Dean Stanley and to the (late) Lady Augusta Stanley,.for the tender sympathy shown by them to the mourners on this day, and also on Sunday, the 19th, when the Dean preached his beautiful funeral sermon.

As during his life Charles Dickens's fondness for air, light, and gay colours amounted almost to a passion, so when he lay dead in the home he had so dearly loved, these things were not forgotten.

The pretty room opening into the conservatory (from which he had never been removed since his seizure) was kept bright with the most beautiful of all kinds of flowers, and flooded with the summer sun :

" And nothing stirred in the room. The old, old fashion. The fashion that came in with our first garments, and will last unchanged until our race has run its course, and the wide firmament is rolled up like a scroll. The old, old fashion—death !

" Oh, thank God, all who see it, for that older fashion yet, of immortality ! "

INDEX.

THE END.

CPSIA information can be obtained at www.ICGtesting.com
Printed in the USA
BVOW06*1921250516

449564BV00004B/9/P